Praise for the first edition:

'A provocative and timely publication, this book will stimulate public debate about national accounting issues and deserves thorough study by managers, regulators, accountants, investors and politicians.'
J.G. Service, Chairman of the Advance Bank

'This book makes a valuable contribution to the history of accounting practice and of corporate regulation in Australia. Many of the lessons from corporate failures have not previously been identified, let alone learned.'
Professor Robert Walker, University of New South Wales

'A very dismal story ... one of the most important studies in corporate accounting behaviour undertaken in many years ... required reading for all academic accountants, senior students, professional accountants and regulators.'
Emeritus Professor Alan Barton, Australian National University

D1339253

uuu20314 2

Corporate Collapse

ACCOUNTING, REGULATORY AND ETHICAL FAILURE

This revised edition of Clarke, Dean and Oliver's provocative book tells why accounting has failed to deliver the truth about a company's state of affairs or to give warning of its drift towards failure. By studying a number of well-known cases of corporate collapse from the 1960s to the present day, the authors observe that little has changed. They balance broad interpretations and recommendations for reform with fine detail of particular cases, insightful analysis of contemporary practices and dissection of the pervading commercial rhetoric. This revised edition includes a detailed examination of HIH and other case vignettes, Patrick/MUA, Ansett, One.Tel and Enron and shows that the cult of the individual in media coverage has masked serious endemic problems in the system of reporting financial information. *Corporate Collapse* is essential reading for professional accountants and auditors, company directors and managers, regulators, corporate lawyers, investors and everyone aspiring to join their ranks.

Frank Clarke is Emeritus Professor of Accounting at the University of Newcastle.

Graeme Dean is Professor and Head of Accounting at The University of Sydney.

Kyle Oliver is a Lecturer at the School of Law, University of Western Sydney.

Corporate Collapse

Accounting, Regulatory and Ethical Failure

Second Edition

FRANK CLARKE

University of Newcastle

GRAEME DEAN

University of Sydney

KYLE OLIVER

University of Western Sydney

CAMBRIDGE
UNIVERSITY PRESS

PUBLISHED BY THE PRESS SYNDICATE OF THE UNIVERSITY OF CAMBRIDGE
The Pitt Building, Trumpington Street, Cambridge, United Kingdom

CAMBRIDGE UNIVERSITY PRESS
The Edinburgh Building, Cambridge CB2 2RU, UK
40 West 20th Street, New York, NY 10011–4211, USA
477 Williamstown Road, Port Melbourne, VIC 3207, Australia
Ruiz de Alarcón 13, 28014 Madrid, Spain
Dock House, The Waterfront, Cape Town 8001, South Africa

http://www.cambridge.org

First published 1997
Second edition first published 2003

Printed in Australia by BPA Print Group

Typeface Times New Roman 10/13 pt.   *System* QuarkXPress®   [PH]

A catalogue record for this book is available from the British Library

National Library of Australia Cataloguing in Publication data
Clarke, Frank L.
Corporate collapse: accounting, regulatory and ethical failure.
2nd ed.
Bibliography.
Includes index.
ISBN 0 521 82684 5.
ISBN 0 521 53426 7 (pbk.).
1. Business failures. 2. Corporations – Accounting.
3. Business ethics. I. Dean, G.W. II. Oliver, Kyle Gaius, 1965– .
III. Title.
174.9657

ISBN 0 521 82684 5 hardback
ISBN 0 521 53426 7 paperback

Waiver
The publisher has used its best endeavours to ensure that the URLs for external
websites referred to in this book are correct and active at the time of going to
press. However, the publisher has no responsibility for the websites and can
make no guarantee that a site will remain live or that the content is or will
remain appropriate.

Contents

Illustrations

Figures

Tables

Dramatis personae

Adler, Rodney   Chairman of FAI and non-executive Director of HIH.

Adsteam   Adsteam conglomerate with the flagship company, The
                Adelaide Steamship Co. Limited. John Spalvins was at its
                helm from 1977 to 1990. It was perceived as a 1980s
                corporate 'high-flier'.

Ansett   Ansett Transport Industries Ltd, a major transport company
                and 49 per cent shareholder in ASL, was headed by Sir
                Reginald Ansett. In 1978, Ansett declined to finance further
                ASL's operations, thereby precipitating its ultimate collapse.

ASL   Associated Securities Limited (ASL group).

BCH   Bond Corp (or Bond Corporation Holdings Limited),
                renamed in 1993 Southern Equities Corporation Limited,
                was one of Australia's largest and most internationally
                known entrepreneurial companies of the 1980s. Alan Bond
                was its founder and chairman from 1967 to 1991.

Bosch, Henry   Chairman of the NCSC (1985–1990) and major
                spokesperson on corporate governance in the 1990s. He was
                extremely critical of the accounting practices of Westmex
                and Bond Corporation.

Brierley,   Founder of Industrial Equity Limited and a major
  Sir Ron   antipodean investor from the 1970s to the 1990s.
  A takeover   Brierley proved to be a major factor in the downfall of
  'whiz kid'   Adsteam, especially his fatal 'consolidated' account of the
                conglomerate's state of affairs.

Cambridge   Cambridge Credit Corporation Limited (Cambridge group),
                run by R.E.M. (Mort) Hutcheson.

Chambers, Ray   Foundation Professor of Accounting at The University of Sydney.
                His iconclastic reforms included the development of the
                method of Continuously Contemporary Accounting (CoCoA);
                entailing a completely integrated mark-to-market system.

Dallhold   Dallhold Investments Proprietary Limited (Alan Bond's
                family company).

Enron	Once the seventh largest publicly-listed entity in the USA, it suddenly crashed to become one of the USA's largest bankruptcies. Its Chairman, Kennett Lay, presided over a period of intense scrutiny of its accounting practices culminating in the demise of Enron's audit firm, Andersen (one of the then 'Big Five' accounting firms), due to its alleged document shredding at Enron.
H.G. Palmer	H.G. Palmer (Consolidated) Limited, named after its founder Herbie Palmer. Palmer refers to H.G. Palmer (Consolidated) Limited (Palmer group).
HIH	HIH was one of Australia's largest insurance companies, one of its largest liquidations and now the catalyst for the first mooted litigation against the federal government and its prudential regulator, APRA. Its founder and Chairman was Ray Williams, a leading Sydney philanthropist before HIH's collapse early in 2001.
HIHRC	HIH Royal Commission was appointed in May 2001 with Justice Neville Owen as its Royal Commissioner. Hearings were held throughout 2001 and 2002 generating nearly 2000 pages of transcript and several million pages of submissions and images. A report is expected in April, 2003.
Insull, Samuel	Insull Utility Investments Inc., a major 1920s US utility conglomerate which took its name from its founder, Samuel Insull.
Kreuger, Ivar	Kreuger and Toll Inc., a major 1920s multinational match company headed by Ivar Kreuger.
Monet, Claude	Impressionist painter of *La Promenade*, the acquisition and sale of which by Bond Corporation was central to the gaoling of Alan Bond in 1996 on conspiracy to defraud charges.
Maxwell, Robert	British newspaper and communications baron throughout the 1970s and 1980s, who was found drowned in 1991 thereby sparking a series of investigations, a mountain of corporate debt and many unanswered questions about his financial empire. Maxwell's mysterious death is now creating speculation that his death was not related to his financial dealings, but was more likely related to political and espionage intrigue.
Minsec	Mineral Securities of Australia Limited, or MSAL, refers to a loose collection of companies known as the Minsec group managed by Ken McMahon and Tom Nestel in the late 1960s and early 1970s.
Murphy, Peter (QC)	Investigator appointed by the Victorian government to inquire into the affairs of Stanhill Development Finance Limited and related companies.

Murray, B.L. & B.J. Shaw (QCs)	Investigators appointed by the Victorian government to inquire into the affairs of the Reid Murray Holdings group.
Reid Murray	RMH, or Reid Murray Holdings Limited (Reid Murray group), headed by Ossie O'Grady.
One.Tel	One of Australia's most notorious telcos. It had a meteoric rise and fall in the late 1990s and early 2000s. Its founders, Jodee Rich and Brad Keeling, and some of its 'financiers', Lachlan Murdoch and James Packer, were described by journalist Paul Barry as the 'Rich Kids'.
RMA	Reid Murray Acceptance Limited, formed to act as a corporate 'banker' for RMH.
Rothwells	Western Australia-based merchant bank headed by the colourful financier Laurie Connell. Rothwells was pejoratively described as a 'lender of last resort' for high-risk ventures. Rothwells' and Connell's activities were scrutinised during the WA Royal Commission into WA Inc.
Rowland, Roland (*Tiny*)	Founder of the multinational Lonrho and a crucial player in the final downfall of Bond Corporation, especially the world-wide distribution in late 1988 of the notorious 'Financial Analysis' document detailing Bond Corporation's 'insolvent' state of affairs.
Royal Mail	Royal Mail group, headed by the Royal Mail Steam Packet Company Ltd – the world's largest 1920s UK ocean liner group run by the former Governor of the City of London, Lord Kylsant.
Stanhill	Stanhill Proprietary Ltd, family company of Stanley Korman, founder of the SDF group including SCL (Stanhill Consolidated Limited), SDF (Stanhill Development Finance Limited), Chevron (Chevron Limited) and SD Pty Ltd (Stanhill Development Proprietary Limited).
Van Gogh, Vincent	Impressionist painter of *Irises*, which was acquired in the mid-1980s by the Bond Corporation group.
Westmex	Westmex Limited was a 1980s conglomerate 'high-flier' headed by Russell Goward during its brief rise and fall from 1986 to 1990.
Whiz kids	Phrase coined to describe those takeover wizards of the securities market who engaged in conglomerate takeovers in the mid-1960s and more conventional acquisitions in the early 1970s. They included Sir Ronald Brierley and Alexander Barton in Australia, Harold Geneen of ITT fame and Sir James Goldsmith (Britain). Subsequently applied to some Australian 1980s 'high-fliers', including Russell Goward.
Williams, Ray	One time Deputy Chairman and Chief Executive Officer of HIH.

Abbreviations

AARF	Australian Accounting Research Foundation, formed in 1966 as part of the profession's response to the spate of 1960s' corporate collapses.
AAS	Australian Accounting Standards, which have had the force of law under Australia's Corporations Law since 1992.
AASB	Australian Accounting Standards Board, the major standards-setting body since 1992.
AFC	Australian Finance Conference.
AICPA	American Institute of Certified Public Accountants.
APB	Accounting Principles Board (United States Accounting Principles-setting body, 1959–1971).
APRA	Australian prudential regulator since 1998. It regulates activities of the banks and other financial intermediaries.
ASA	Australian Society of Accountants (predecessor body of the ASCPA).
ASC	Australian Securities Commission, the successor to the NCSC as Australia's national corporate regulator (1991–1998). Replaced by ASIC.
ASIC	Australian Securities and Investments Commission, the successor to the ASC as Australia's national corporate regulator (1998–).
ASCPA	Australian Society of Certified Practising Accountants; was replaced in the late 1990s by CPA Australia. Together with the ICAA, this body represents the public face of Australia's accounting profession.
ASX	Australian Stock Exchange Ltd, formed in 1990 from an amalgamation of Australia's state Stock Exchanges.
CEO	Chief Executive Officer.
CFO	Chief Financial Officer.
CLERP 9	Company Law and Economic Reform Programme No 9.
FASB	Financial Accounting Standards Board (United States Accounting Standards-setting body, 1972–).
Financial Review	*Australian Financial Review.*
FITB	Future income tax benefit.
FRCLSE	Financial Reporting Council of the London Stock Exchange (1990–).

FRC Australia's Financial Reporting Council. Formed in 2001, it has general Government oversight responsibility for the governance of corporate financial reporting practices under the Corporations Act.

GAAP Generally Accepted Accounting Principles.

IASC International Accounting Standards Committee (International Accounting Standards-setting body, 1973–2001).

ISC Insurance Supervisory Commission (–1998). It was replaced by APRA in 1998.

IASB International Accounting Standards Board. Formed in 2001, it has carriage for the setting of International Financial Reporting Standards.

ICAA The Institute of Chartered Accountants in Australia (1928–).

ICAEW The Institute of Chartered Accountants in England and Wales (1880–).

IFRS International Financial Reporting Standards set by the IASB. Previously IAS.

ISOYD Inverse sum of the years' digits depreciation method.

JCPAA Joint Committee on Public Accounts and Audit – a joint committee of Australia's federal parliament.

Mark-to-market accounting The process of stating all non-monetary assets at their current market prices.

Mark-to-Model A method of mark-to-market accounting used by Enron. The model was used by Enron, drawing on discounting procedures, to arrive at a 'synthetic' market price for Enron's asset holdings of energy (and other) derivatives.

NCSC National Companies and Securities Commission – national corporate regulatory body (1981–1990). Replaced by the ASC.

NPV Net present value.

POB Public Oversight Board (part of the SEC Practice Section of the AICPA).

Ramsay Report An Australian federal government initiated report finalised in late 2001 by Harold Ford, Professor of Law at The University of Melbourne, Ian Ramsay, about issues related to auditor independence.

Rule of 78 A recognised arbitrary method of apportioning interest on term contracts, such as hire purchase finance.

SEC Securities Exchange Commission, formed in the United States in 1933 during the Depression as part of America's 'New Deal'. It took many functions previously held by the Federal Trade Commission.

Tax Effect Accounting A method of accounting for income taxes.

UIG Urgent Issues Group, formed at the end of 1994 with the aim of 'providing timely guidance on urgent financial reporting issues'.

Foreword

The second edition of this book appears six years after the first. The context is the end of an 18-year bull market – one of the longest during the twentieth century, with the emergence and passing of the dot.com hype, and significant turbulence and loss of confidence on corporate financial markets generally, and with corporate governance in particular. The Long Term Capital Market rise and demise in 1998, the crash of many dot.coms in early 2000, as well as the more recent collapses of several large, 'old' and 'new' economy companies, like HIH, Harris Scarfe, One.Tel, Pasminco and Centaur in Australia, Enron and WorldCom and Adelphia Communications in the US, characterise the setting.

This revised edition is going to print in circumstances that contradict what many had imagined might flow from the insights and developments in purported efficient markets and rational pricing theories, and the hype associated with the Internet's ability to create an information superhighway. Some commentators are claiming that the major financial markets are experiencing unprecedented turbulence of an enduring nature. Certainly the actions of those charged with mutual fund and pension investments have resulted in a major retreat from investing in the stock market, and moving into cash and other perceived 'defensive investments'. This has caused substantial declines in, and increased volatility of, stock market indices worldwide. The resulting reduced collateral has placed pressure on those who had borrowed to sustain their share investments. Concerns exist that the declines in the stock market could spill over into the real economy and that the oft-disputed US 'speculative bubble' had burst. This would inevitably affect other stock markets, like Australia's. Such 'effects' rebuke the myth that those market declines produce only 'paper losses'.

World capital markets' participants, academics and regulators alike, eulogised the benefits of the newly-coined 'new economy', and associated new methods of valuing companies as P/E multiples reached peaks seen ominously only during the previous twentieth century 'market bubbles' of 1929, 1969 and 1987. As with those previous booms, an 'irrational exuberance', remarked upon in 1996 by Federal Reserve Chair Alan Greenspan, appeared to have been partly responsible for what, in respect of the 1920s boom period, John Kenneth Galbraith described as an 'inventory of undiscovered embezzlement'.

Those 'in the know' had declared that the end of the second millennium would prove to be different, that this was no financial 'bubble'. It was suggested that technological developments, the impact of the baby boomers and the information revolution had created new ways of creating and measuring sustainable shareholder value. Recurrent, tell-tale symptoms of macro financial problems linked to excessive merger and acquisition activity, often heavily debt financed, have been ignored; remarkably, just as they had been in episodes like the 1600s Tulipmania, the 1700s South Sea Bubble, the 19th century Railway manias and the 1920s investment trust boom presaging the 1929 Great Depression.

But for many, events on capital markets in April/May 2000 portending the demise of the dot.com phenomenon were to change that way of thinking. Share price indices for technology stocks tumbled 40–60% across various capital markets, as billions of dollars were wiped off corporate market capitalisations, especially off those eulogised new economy companies. Dot.coms became part of the tech-wreck flotsam as they either went into liquidation or were taken over by the surviving 'old economy' companies. Within a year or two the financial meltdown in the main stock markets would affect many old economy, merger-driven conglomerates, like Enron, Vivendi, WorldCom, AOL Time Warner, Waste Management, Global Crossing, and others.

As before, few see the similarities between the latest crises and those of preceding generations.

The latest boom/bust era has generated new labels – rather than conglomerates and creative accounting, we had 'new economy companies', 'pro forma' or 'aggressive' earnings, 'earnings management' as the new mantras. But, from an accounting and financial management perspective, it was merely more of the same. More creative accounting and an inadequately informed capital market combined to produce a lack of investor confidence in the market and, predictably, the bears took over from the bulls.

The 'old' cries for better quality, more transparent accounting re-emerged. Clearly these events demonstrated that there is 'nothing new under the sun'. Disputed claims that some countries had better accounting standards, a *principles-based* rather than a *Standards-based* system, have enjoyed popular currency. Much of this was without foundation and ill-informed.

Our first edition provided evidence that perceived poor quality financial reporting was a major factor in the continued criticism of accounting and

auditing practices following *large*, often *unexpected* corporate collapses. Responses to our first edition and to what is occurring at present indicate that our
emphasis on the *unexpected* nature of the collapses and the implications for
accounting have not been sufficiently heeded. Company failures *per se* are not
on our radar as much as how accounting data mask any trends that would
indicate impending failure.

Against that background we advocate a complete mark-to-market system of
accounting and a return to the professional ethos that published accounts
should satisfy the 'true and fair view' criterion as a 'first order' requirement. We
take heart that six years on some of the larger accounting firms, individual
members of the profession, lawyers, journalists and others are also advocating
this. In contrast neither regulators nor governments seem to be convinced –
seemingly more determined to invoke a regime of International Financial
Reporting Standards. Unless the move to full mark-to-market occurs we predict
that auditors will continue to be on a 'mission impossible' and that regulators,
directors and auditors will continue to be exposed to the 'time-bomb' in verified
published accounts that are based on a primarily capitalisation-of-expenditure
model. Further, that, by failing as professionals to get their house in order,
accountants face losing that respect associated with a mature profession. They
risk losing their professional status. At a macro level, the impact will be disastrous as trust in the disclosure regime, characterised by (*inter alia*) Federal
Reserve Chair Alan Greenspan's observations in a 2002 US Senate Committee address as 'essential' for an effective market system, will continue to be
undermined.

New millennium crises such as those at HIH in Australia and Enron in
the United States have seen those first edition prophecies fulfilled. As with the
demise of the large accounting firm Lowenthal in the early 1990s, the Andersen
firm did not survive the brouhaha and litigation emerging from those recent collapses and the revealed irregularities in and inherent ineptitude of accounting
and auditing practices. The profession suffers the ignominy of the almost un-
believable daily national and international media headlines lamenting the
corporate 'earnings malaise' and 'accounting irregularities' in the reported
audited results of major corporations, prompting massive write downs and
other adjustments later. Almost daily, press headlines repeat phrases similar to
those reported in the first edition with respect to previous *unexpected* collapses:
'Accounting in crisis', 'Hey presto! The magical world of creative accounting',
'Articles of faith. How investors got taken by the false profits', 'Lies, damn lies
and annual reports', 'Hocus pocus accounting', 'Pick a number, any number,'
'Abracadabra accounting', 'Nasdaq firms' pro-forma alchemy', 'Off-balance-
sheet land is where the death spirals lurk', 'Auditors called to account',
'"System is broken": world needs tougher rules for accounting'.

Governments' proposed reactions are misguided. Current events reinforce our claims in the first edition that the prevailing accounting practices permit social injustices through the existence of an ill-informed capital market. The trust that arises from a properly informed market continues to be undermined by poor quality accounting. A prius is that the previous call for a mark-to-market accounting system be heeded.

Our aim from this account is to improve the public perception of members of the profession and to restore public confidence generally through the provision of a well-informed capital market.

While our first edition's 'hope that the observations which follow will jolt accountants and company regulators into long overdue action' was not realised, we remain forever optimistic.

Preface

In the first edition we observed that, over more than three decades of corporate collapse, continued criticism of accounting was the result of inaction by regulators in general and the accounting profession in particular. Complaints regarding the unserviceability of accounting and published financial data continue to pervade commercial discourse, notwithstanding changes from accounting self-regulation in the 1950s to the present regime of mixed government and professional intervention. Over the years a miscellany of Accounting Standards has been issued and legislatively endorsed. Diversity in the outcomes of accounting for similar commercial events remains, misleading data prevail – creative accounting reigns supreme. Our *leitmotif* is that corporate consumers, i.e. the users of corporate accounts, have not been served well. That observation remains apt as another round of turbulent economic activities has resulted in many, often *unexpected*, corporate collapses. Again market confidence is shaken as the trust in the reported information – the glue of the capitalist system – is proved to be unreliable.

Standardisation of the inputs to the accounting process has been based on an incorrect premise that controlling the input necessarily enhances the quality of the output. Uniformity of process has been substituted for the serviceability of output. Unless there is a shift from the present thinking and the practice it nurtures, the current criticisms of the products of accounting and auditing filling the financial press are destined to continue. The increased litigation in the 1990s is bound to be repeated during the next round in the cycle of economic boom and subsequent corporate failures.

Corporate collapses uniquely provide the raw material for a post-mortem of the *system* of accounting and auditing currently endorsed. Liquidators' accounts, and the official reports of Inspectors into failures, give an unusually candid insight into the administration of companies and provide a contrast between the financial truth of their positions at various times during their lives and what they reported them to be. While perhaps not the primary cause of corporate collapse and financial shenanigans, accounting has systematically failed to inform its consumers adequately, and in a timely fashion, of the drift of the financial affairs of businesses towards impending failure, leading to involuntary wealth redistributions along the way and, in some cases, exacerbating the extent of the financial losses.

The new millennium has revealed that the buck-passing feature of the accountancy profession's response to company failures is a repeated theme. Nine major Australian corporate collapses from the 1960s, '70s and '80s were examined in detail in the first edition, while others were referred to briefly. These were purposely selected for the specific instances they illustrate, the universality of the organisational and accounting practices they entailed, and the defects in the financial data that resulted. They flesh out the role played by accounting in the financing, investing and other managerial moves prior to a corporate collapse. This revised edition provides additional Australian case analyses – one in depth – HIH, and other case vignettes – Patrick/MUA, Ansett, One.Tel, and Enron in the US. Some of the 1960s case analyses have been truncated. Accounting is shown to have been a willing traveller, revealing in many instances surprisingly very little along the corporate path to failure. Many of the companies examined collapsed unexpectedly, just after reporting healthy audited profit figures. Ineffective regulatory action also is shown to have played a role.

While not highlighted in the collapses covered here, we do not wish to downplay the possibility of managers' intent to deceive, using, amongst other things in the 1980s, new financial instruments, such as derivatives, and put and call options, sometimes off-balance sheet, as evident in the special purpose vehicles used at Enron.

Chapter 2 precedes those analyses by inquiring into the notion and significance of *creative accounting*. This contrasts with what we have coined *feral accounting*, the use of a specific accounting practice with the intention to mislead. But the effects of creative accounting are equally insidious. While there is equivocation within accounting and regulatory circles regarding the precise meaning of creative accounting, there are sound reasons why it has arisen repeatedly as a matter of importance in corporate post-mortems.

The utterances of the accountancy profession over the last 40-odd years in response to complaint and criticism of the product of conventional accounting are an old refrain. Arguably, the profession has remained reactive in responding to the need to have accounting produce financial data serviceable for assessing the wealth and progress of corporations. Professional attention has been directed to important, but mainly peripheral, issues. Overall, the generic defects that have beset conventional accounting practice for decades have survived virtually intact into the new millennium. Particular practices have been outlawed, but the generic organisational and accounting defects to which they contributed remain. Official standards-setting bodies have been established and modified over time. They continue to receive increased resourcing. Due process for forging Accounting Standards has been devised and revised, but the quality of the end products has not improved. Events at HIH, Enron and other recent collapses confirm that it has deteriorated. A miscellany of often inconsistent processing and valuation rules continues to form the basis of the compulsory conventional accounting procedures and policies. Diversity in accounting practice persists. The practices it endorses imply that the profession has retained its long-stated position that the balance sheet (or, in today's idiom, statement of financial position) is not a statement of net worth and that all that is required is that the public be educated as to the limitation of accounts. When there is an inquiry invariably the public is fed the notion that the financial data are misleading and creative, by virtue of practitioners deviating from, or deliberately misinterpreting, the prescribed Accounting Standards. Those analyses have lacked the Jesuitical verve so necessary to get to the truth. The reality from our perspective is that compliance with Accounting Standards is as likely a major cause of accounting creativity. The equivocal data underpinning the dispute in the HIH Royal Commission regarding assessments of HIH's solvency, and the use by Enron of special purpose off-balance sheet entities to quarantine group liabilities are apt new millennial examples. Unquestionably, there remains chaos in the counting-house.

A siege mentality has prevailed when analysing various accounting anomalies, including those associated with corporate failures. Repeatedly, blame has been sheeted home in the financial press and the professional literature to the nebulous 'bad management', inadequate compliance with Accounting Standards and ineffective regulatory monitoring of that compliance, contiguous with criticisms of declining business ethics and even poor accounting education. Everything, it would seem, has been at fault, except the patchwork bases of accounting and its unserviceable products. Chapters 16, 17, 18 and 19 examine those matters in some detail. Buck-passing is endemic to an immature profession – the current system of accounting deserves to be put on trial; hence our sub-title, *Accounting, regulatory and ethical failure*.

Anecdote supports the view that a virulent form of social injustice has emerged within the commercial and business community by virtue of the compulsory production of financial data unfit for the purposes for which they are commonly used. Radical restructuring of conventional accounting practice is needed, a matter pursued in Chapters 17, 18 and 19.

Effective reconstruction of accounting is impossible without reform of the legal and social structure in which it operates. Some of the current legal structures demonstrably need to be abandoned. Others need remodelling if they are to fulfil their traditional objectives. In this context Chapters 16 and 17 contest the role of, and the continued need for, subsidiaries and labyrinthine corporate group structures. Some of the pervading practices of accounting require a closer look by a more critical eye than the regulators appear to have given them. Regulators continue to examine and monitor accounting practices but fail to consider proposals outside of the conventional. In Chapter 19 it is demonstrated that some approved practices are without commercial foundation, others are without a coherent structure and many have neither foundation nor structure, in the social setting of property rights and a financial system in which money, prices, price levels, price structures and markets have a dominant place.

This case for reform emphasises various aspects of corporate failure, especially the commingling of accounting, financing and investing in the managerial process. In that process the market worth of physical assets is an essential element in assessing a firm's solvency, its capacity to borrow, whether to liquidate specific assets and redirect resources and otherwise adapt to changing circumstances, as well as to any calculation of its wealth and financial progress. The HIH Royal Commission is examining the issue of solvency in respect of HIH and related companies as part of its brief. Neither internal nor external *informed* financial decisions can be taken without that information mix. This commingling provides the context for analysing the role of accounting. The reform proposal proceeds with the firm conviction that the public at large are consumers of financial information regarding the companies they deal with, are employed by, invest in, and otherwise are related to in the wider economy. That information product is currently of poor quality. A leading standards setting authority, Sir Bryan Carsberg, and eminent practitioners and regulators like former Chief Accountant of the SEC Walter Schuetze rate the current quality of reported financial information lower now than it was decades ago.

What follows may cause offence to those who hold dear the conventional practices and conventions of accounting. There are mental blinkers or a shutter on an open debate when it comes to being critical of accounting practice *from within*. Over the years, leading accounting authorities Leonard Spacek, Ray Chambers, Robert Sterling and Abe Briloff, *inter alios*, have been witness to that. Questioning the *status quo* is often denigrated, false motives often attributed, the character of those who question often impugned. Yet, the reality is that practitioners, the professional accountancy bodies, and the legislative and quasi-legislative agencies regulating corporate activity have not scored too highly in developing and monitoring a system that meets consumers' needs. Accountants *per se* are not under attack here. It is our profession too and we are less than happy with the way it is regressing. Accountants have to practise with a system that places them at great risk – damned by the consumers of accounting in many cases if they comply with approved Standards and damned by their governing bodies in all cases if they don't. Mostly, none of that is their fault – it is the *system* we put on trial here.

It is reasonable for the wider community to wonder why this situation has arisen. Why, given accountants' specialised knowledge of their craft – its *differentia specifica*, an inside view of the difficulties they face and the litigation danger they confront – practitioners have not forced corrective action before now.

Likely as not, many believe the current Standards-setting exercise is corrective action. Our thesis is that the proliferation of official Standards and their mandatory compliance has not addressed the problem. Perhaps accountants have not mastered the intricacies of their own inventions – the accounting artifacts. Perhaps they are too close to the action, not sufficiently detached or independently placed, to see it for what it is – warts and all. Oscar Wilde captured that quirk of human behaviour in his *An Ideal Husband* – perhaps they have had all the experience but not had the privilege of 'making' the 'observations'.

Our hope is that the observations that follow will jolt accountants and company regulators into long overdue action.

Acknowledgements

This book would not be, except for the assistance received from numerous sources. In particular, we owe a debt to many colleagues for their critiques of our interpretations of observations and ideas for reform; known and unknown reviewers of the first and second editions; Ron Ringer for his continued technical help and advice; Amanda Threlfo, Kim Johnstsone, Sofia Lemaitre and Christian Balanza who were successive research assistants on the project; those too numerous to name who alerted us to various aspects of the events we address; and to those whose valuable work we cite – some we agree with and much which we do not, but all of which provided a test of our interpretations and conclusions. In particular, we are deeply grateful for the guidance of the editorial and production team at Cambridge University Press. Regarding the substantially revised second edition Cambridge's Peter Debus is singled out for providing us with another opportunity to disseminate the controversial reforms that had been outlined in the first edition and which we believe so clearly are needed following the latest spate of Australian financial sagas at HIH, Ansett, One.Tel, Harris Scarfe, and (say) Enron, WorldCom, Adelphia Communications, and Xerox in the USA. Those financial crises evoke a *déjà vu* cry. The first edition's proposed accounting and corporate structural reforms are even more necessary now. There is an almost universal demand that accounting 'clean up' its act – much as we had pleaded for in the first edition. But the fact that accounting data are misleading without any intent to deceive appears still to elude those pursuing reform in the wake of HIH and Enron-type collapses and associated revelations from official inquiries – the ASIC, JCPAA and the Royal Commission inquiries into HIH in Australia, and the SEC and US Congressional reviews into Enron and other similar cases in the United States. Perhaps the mooted novel litigation by the HIH administrator against Australia's federal government and its prudential regulator, APRA, may be the catalyst for change.

Finally, we publicly acknowledge our gratitude to Angelika and Nicole Dean, and to Jeanette Clarke, for their continued encouragement and forbearance over the many years it took to bring our examination of corporate collapse and accounting to this point, and to the accounting iconoclast Ray Chambers, without whose mentorship and inspiration (even in death) it would never have commenced nor have continued into a second edition. It is with much sadness that we note that Ray Chambers died in September 1999 after suffering a fall. Through this revised edition his ideas remain, in his words, 'an irritant to the accounting profession to ensure that it continues to seek ways of continually improving its practices' and concomitantly to improve the products on which users of accounting information so desperately rely. Only then will the market system be able to restore the public trust that has been so shaken over the years by events like those at, say, HIH and Enron.

PART I

Accounting in Crisis – a Farce to be Reckoned With

CHAPTER 1

Chaos in the Counting-house

Corporate accounting does not do violence to the truth occasionally
and trivially, but comprehensively, systematically, and universally,
annually and perennially.

R.J. Chambers, 1991, p. 19.

When Bond Corp first announced its loss of almost $1 billion in October 1989
it surprised most of those who felt that they had their finger on the pulse of
Australian corporate life.[1]

Perhaps it shouldn't have been such a surprise, for it had all happened
before, many times, over many decades, all around the world. Different characters, different settings, different companies in different industries – but in similar
circumstances – a common pervading regulatory philosophy – procedural input
processing rules within a capitalisation-of-expenditure model coupled to
sanctions for non-compliance, even when non-compliance made more sense in
reporting an entity's financial state of affairs. And it would happen again.

Happen again, indeed! In mid-2001 it hit with added force as the media
grappled with Australia's contribution to the *tech-wreck* – the dot.com collapses
of telcos such as One.Tel. But it was not only the new economy companies that
were falling over. HIH, one of Australia's old economy companies and largest
insurers, had collapsed *unexpectedly* in circumstances rivalling the collapse
of Bond Corp. HIH's collapse was claimed to be Australia's largest corporate collapse. Typically it embroiled the affairs of many of the big names in
commerce and the accounting profession. It would produce Australia's first
accounting-related negligence litigation against the federal government and
its prudential regulator, APRA. Several months later in the United States the
'reported' superstar Enron would become its largest bankruptcy up to that time,
with asset book values in excess of US$60 billion and an estimated deficiency
in shareholder value of over US$63 billion. No sooner was Enron's enormity
grasped than it was eclipsed by WorldCom's US$103 billion bankruptcy,[2]
the demise of several technology companies, including Adelphia Communications, Global Crossing, and by the alleged massive 'accounting irregularities'
at several large US companies in 2002, such as Disney, WorldCom, Xerox,
Merck and Qwest Communications, forcing 'earnings restatements'.

Again, the stellar performers at the sharp end of town were in disgrace.

Back in 1989 it had been the turn of Alan Bond, one-time Australian 'Businessman of the Year', then 'Father of the Year', and local folk hero for bankrolling the 1983 America's Cup challenge that had seen the famed cup unscrewed from its Rhode Island mantelpiece and sent to Australia. Bond Corporation's assets (it seemed) were not as gold-plated as they had been represented to be. Indeed, it was being said that they were mostly *water*. One top-value asset, the accounting-created Future Income Tax Benefits had a massive $453.4 million written off it. Unbelievable! Well, at least it was to those who had an inadequate understanding of the annals of corporate history. And that included, it seemed, almost everyone.

In 2001–02 some of the contemporary corporate high-fliers were under a similar cloud: in Australia, Williams, the doyen of the insurance industry; Rich, the entrepreneur extraordinaire; and other 'big' names such as Keeling and Cooper. Household names such as Murdoch and Packer were hitting the headlines by virtue of their association with One.Tel. In the United States 'Chainsaw' Dunlap of Sunbeam, Lay, Fastow and Skilling from Enron, Ebbers from WorldCom, Tyco's Kozlowski, the Rigas family from Adelphia, were all making the news; President Bush's time with Harken and Vice-President Cheney's stint at Halliburton also enjoyed considerable print space. It had become a familiar story.

In its time, the 1990s aftermath of Bond Corp's announced 'record reported loss' had a lot in common with its antecedents too. Media commentators would zoom in on the personalities, intrude into their private lives, pick up and highlight the gossip regarding their peccadillos. A *regulatory theatre* provided old refrains of indignation and outrage, promises of retribution to offenders, justice to the aggrieved. The *cult of the individual* would be revived. Connell, Yuill, Goldberg, Bond, Skase, Goward and other major players in the 1980s failures would be labelled 'corporate cowboys' and their life in the saddle exposed. Huge sums would be spent attempting to bring the high-fliers to ground, extract them from their hideaways. Skase was chased to Majorca, where he eventually died in 2001. Following his death the attention continued – witness the 'Spurned Skase heirs dob in Pixie' headline.[3] A decade after his time as leader of the Liberal Party, John Elliott was being questioned over his role as non-executive director of the insolvent Water Wheel Ltd.[4]

Of course, the search for scapegoats has been time-consuming. But again, attention has been on individuals – individual auditors, individual accountants, or the firms of which they were partners; individual directors, or the Boards of which they were members; individual bankers and financial intermediaries, or the financial institutions which they headed. Their business morality, their ethics, would be raked over and called into question. Ethics would be equated with corporate governance. It is an exemplar of what Neil Postman described as *Amusing Ourselves to Death* – entertainment! But it is entertainment that is reduced to the point where the seriousness of the affairs is lost from sight in the short term and completely forgotten in the longer term.

Whilst resources were increased in the early 1990s to assist regulatory bodies, virtually nowhere would there be concerted attention paid to rectifying the system that permitted it all to occur, even facilitated it – the generic imperfections in the mechanisms supposedly regulating corporate activities, their financial reporting, permissive corporate structures under Australian law, or the pervading ideas on corporate governance.

A decade on and the refrain continues. The major collapses of HIH, One.Tel, Ansett, Harris Scarfe, Centaur and the financial difficulties at Pasminco in Australia, and similar headline grabbers – Enron, WorldCom, Xerox, Adelphia and Qwest Communications (especially) in the United States – have rekindled interest in the arcane world of accounting and auditing. Size is obviously a drawcard. Just prior to their collapses or financial dilemmas, HIH was one of Australia's largest insurance companies; Enron was the world's largest buyer and seller of natural gas and the seventh-largest listed US company; WorldCom was once the sixth-biggest corporate borrower in the United States and Xerox was synonymous with business copiers.

Déjà vu is pervasive. Consistent with our descriptions of the 'cult of the individual' during earlier periods, the media inquiries quickly honed in on the lives of HIH's Ray Williams, Rodney Adler and Brad Cooper; One.Tel's 'Rich Kids' – Jodee Rich and Brad Keeling – and heirs to the business dynasties, James Packer and Lachlan Murdoch. A scapegoat had to be found for HIH, One.Tel and other collapses through the HIH Royal Commission's deliberations, Liquidators' hearings and regulatory court actions. Initial cries of 'Where were the auditors?', 'How could such entities collapse so suddenly?', 'Accounting in crisis', 'How crooked is Wall Street?', 'Who can you trust?' 'Accounting in chaos', emerged right on cue. Calls for changes to auditing practices thundered – quarantine audit and non-audit services, compulsorily rotate auditors and impose a mandatory audit committee regime! A new Audit Independence Supervisory Board was proposed. Other regulatory layers have been proposed, including: 'independence boards' within audit firms to monitor potential conflicts of interest, criminal sanctions for company employees and officers who provide misleading information to auditors and to the public respectively. All of this in the guise of seeking to make auditors more independent, and presumably, to avoid future *unexpected* corporate collapses. And while the profession has pursued the limitations of auditors' liabilities individual audit firms like PricewaterhouseCoopers have changed the wording of their audit opinion to achieve that result.[5]

In the United States the SEC and Congress have head-hunted too. Few have been spared. The Enron fallout blanketed the corporate vista from CEO Kenneth Lay, President Skilling and CFO Fastow to the US President's mother.

US president George W. Bush and Vice-President Cheney have had to weather alleged questionable conduct of their involvement as executives in Harken and Halliburton respectively. *Champion* CEO 'Chainsaw' Al Dunlap has been cut down for his shenanigans at Sunbeam. Enron's CEO Kenneth Lay and President Jeffrey Skilling, WorldCom's Bernard Ebbers and Tyco's Dennis Kozlowski have each incurred a hefty 'going over'. But most of the reactions have been off-target. Scalps have been collected by the regulators, but virtually nothing done that is likely to rectify the corporate financial system. Rather than more serviceable accounting practices, accounting rules regulating the expensing of share options have been proposed. Inadequate attention is being given to rethinking the nature of the accountability checks in the financial reporting system. This, notwithstanding that many commentators are lamenting the poor quality of the existing information system generally.[6]

As the securities market grapples with the current spate of collapses, corporate mayhem continues across the board. Huge write-downs by AOL Time-Warner (US$100 billion), News Corp (US$7.4 billion) and NAB ($4 billion) have substantially reduced shareholders' value, and the AMP is poised at the end of 2002 to delete $1.2 billion from its net assets. The Andersen accounting firm, which was found guilty of obstructing the course of justice in the United States by allegedly shredding Enron documents, provided an immediate scapegoat, even though the remaining Big Four accounting firms are also under inquiry by the SEC (see Table 19.1). These include Deloitte & Touche on account of its alleged failure to tell its client Adelphia Communications that the company's founding family had used Adelphia credit lines to purchase stock in the company; Ernst & Young for its alleged involvement in agreements to sell software with its client Peoplesoft; KPMG for alleged failure to detect revenue-inflating capers by its Xerox client. While PricewaterhouseCoopers has settled (without prejudice) the SEC charge of revenue overstatement by MicroStrategy, there remains unfinished business. Further, there is a shadow over its self-examination of its involvement with the Russian energy company Gaz Prom; and the accounting practices at Global Crossing, Lucent Technologies, Qwest Communications, Adelphia Communications and WorldCom are under the scrutiny of the SEC and numerous prosecutors.

There are further allegations that Lucent boosted revenue by US$679 million by booking further sales before they had actually occurred; Waste Management officers inflated profits by US$1.7 billion by extending the depreciable life of its truck fleet; K-mart under-reported losses in 2001 to the tune of US$1.8 billion; Adelphia Communications inadequately reported US$5.6 billion of loan guarantees. WorldCom's goodwill and US$408 million of loans treatment have the SEC upset. Alleged conflicts of interest between Merrill Lynch's investment advisors and its merchant banking arms resulted in a reported US$100 million settlement, as allegedly did CSFB for a similar amount of allocation of IPOs to customers for excessive commissions. Some analysts have been held to have had conflicts of interest. Regulators too are under siege. SEC Chief Harvey Pitt resigned under a cloud for his alleged 'soft action' on the accounting profession for which he once had been counsel. Those alleged conflicts of interest have led to calls for major reforms on the 'street'.

Regarding financial reporting, a recent US survey suggested that more than 150 of the 450 SEC-registered companies had to restate their financial filings after queries from the SEC.[7] And the CEOs of nearly 1000 of the largest US corporates had to review financial statements in their latest SEC filings, and by the middle of August 2002 swear that there were no 'untrue' figures disclosed. Interestingly, *truth* was invoked as the benchmark. A similar request was made by Australia's regulator, the Australian Securities and Investments Commission (ASIC), for listed companies filing their 2002 annual financial statements.[8]

By mid-2002 not only did the corporate failures bear witness to the crisis in corporate regulation, but the cloud over the major accounting firms, accountants, company officers, securities advisors, auditors and regulators gave weight to the inevitable conclusion of 'accounting, regulatory and ethical failure' – that the system was fractured.

A window on corporate failure

A necessity for regulatory and quasi-regulatory reform of accounting and auditing practices has been prominent for several decades in Australia and overseas. Unanswered calls for reform have been the norm. Yet, despite flurries of action there has been little progress. If the initial responses to collapses like HIH and Enron are any guide, little is likely to change.

Bankruptcies and liquidations in the early years of the 1990s evoked the familiar rhetoric, but little effective action to prevent *unexpected* failures. Financial and social fallout from the larger unexpected Australian company failures in the latter part of the 1980s – the failures of Ariadne, Hooker, Qintex, Westmex, Parry Corporation, Judge Corporation, Adsteam, Budget Corporation, Tricontinental, Pyramid Building Society, Rothwells, National Safety Council of Australia, the State Bank of Victoria and the State Bank of South Australia, Spedley Securities, the Battery, Duke, Girvan and Linter Groups, Estate Mortgage and Aust-Wide Trusts, the liquidation of Southern Equities Corporation (formerly Bond Corporation), and the dilemmas at Harlin/Fosters Brewing, Westpac and Coles Myer – were well documented in the financial press. However, that focus runs contrary to the frequent commentaries on how to achieve business admiration and invites the question: 'Why undertake inquiry into failure, rather than success?'

'Success' is pursued in countless 'how to get rich' books. Few seem to heed the *message* of the one-time adulation and the interest in Dunlap's genius compared with the disgrace he now endures.[9] Enron's way of doing business was applauded – a *Fortune* magazine survey rated Enron as the 'most innovative' American company five years running; HIH's insurance dominance was once lauded! Indeed, virtually all of the prominent companies which failed over the past few decades (and their leaders) could earlier have been written up as paragons of how to be successful, like Bob Ansett in Australia and Donald Trump and Tyco's Dennis Kozlowski (one of *BusinessWeek*'s 'top 25 managers in 2001') in the United States. Alan Bond was 'Businessman of the Year' in 1978; Asil Nadir rode high when Polly Peck was in its prime in the United Kingdom. Everyone wanted to be Michael Milken's mate when junk bonds were the flavour of the month in the 1980s. Many courted Robert Maxwell's friendship. Few shied away from involvement with Qintex, Equiticorp, or the Hooker Corporation during their good times. More often than not, those who failed had been heralded and lauded earlier as a major success. Adsteam was a model for many before it ran aground. So, in a sense, examining the process of failure is merely the other end of examining success, though for a number of reasons – primarily related to access to more objective data – failure is likely to be more capable of objective dissection and evaluation.[10]

The increase in corporate failures in Australia (many unexpected) during the late 1980s, 1990s and in the early 2000s is evident in Table 1.1. In 1991 the AMP Society estimated that 'the collapse of our corporate high-fliers has cost shareholders more than $8 billion'.[11] Others have claimed the figure to be closer to $20 billion.[12] One collapse alone in 2001, HIH, is expected to result in over $5.3 billion of losses! In the United States, five large companies – including

Table 1.1   Corporate insolvencies, selected years, 1976–2001

Year end 30/6	Number	Year end 30/6	Number
1976	1,178	1993	8,859
–	–	1994	7,772
1981	1,565	1995	7,240
1987	5,816	1996	8,964
1988	4,836	1997	8,666
1989	6,189	1998	7,920
1990	7,394	1999	7,617
1991	8,366	2000	8,650
1992	10,361	2001	10,015

Source: 1976 and 1981 Corporate Affairs Commission *Annual Reports*; 1987–98 data compiled from NCSC and ASC releases; 1998–2002 ASIC releases.

Enron, WorldCom and Tyco – account for a loss of over US$450 billion in shareholder value.

What's a billion or two between corporate friends? The 1980s high priests of corporate finance, now the disgraced entrepreneurs, certainly had no qualms in lending hundreds of millions of dollars to each other. Revelations in the HIH Royal Commission indicate that little may have changed over the subsequent two decades – they refer to alleged corporate largesse with 'other people's money', in the form of a 'river of money' flowing from HIH just prior to its liquidation. It was reported in the press that Counsel for the HIH Royal Commission alleged that CEO Ray Williams dished out millions of dollars on executive rewards, bonuses and funding to associates and charities prior to HIH's collapse.[13]

Some specific results of Australia's largest companies, revealed in Table 1.2, further highlight the extent of the battering Australia's corporate profile took during the early 1990s. Little wonder that the *corporate cowboys* tag was ascribed to the investment and financing behaviour of some of the more publicised entrepreneurs of the 1980s. As our story unfolds here, it will reveal that the corporate cowboys were able to do their thing only because they had the open ranges on which to run wild. We show that those commercial ranges have been, in many respects, untouched for decades. The tag seems equally apposite today. And the ranges remain *open*.

While Table 1.1 reveals that Australian corporate failures in the 1980s increased relative to the Australian company population, the number of failures remains small. For the years 1962–81, annual liquidations of companies in New South Wales, for example, averaged 77.1 companies per 10,000 companies registered. The highest rate of failure in a single year was 104 liquidations per 10,000 companies in 1977.[14] Figures from the late 1880s through to 1960 reveal a similar incidence of failure.[15] In the depression following the October 1987 stock market crash, Australian Securities Commission (ASC) annual reports disclosed national business failure rates at levels of 0.77 per cent (1989), 0.88 per cent (1990), 0.95 per cent (1991), 1 per cent in 1992, just over 1 per cent in 1993 and declining to less than 1 per cent in the mid-1990s. This relatively low failure rate is in line with US data over the last 60 years produced by Dun and Bradstreet Corporation's Business Failure Record.[16] It continued until the end of the millennium, then rose slightly with the tech-wreck and GST impacts in early 2000.[17]

Despite the inevitable hysteria, Australian experience with corporate failures is far from unique. Similar corporate crises also occurred in the United Kingdom and the United States in the 1980s and 1990s, and during previous decades. Moreover, official responses to the latest Australian corporate failures fit the pattern elsewhere.

Table 1.2 Selected corporate losses 1990–92* (Consolidated operating and extraordinary figures, after tax, attributable to members of the holding (parent) company for the 1990, '91 and '92 financial years.)

Institution	1990 $bn	1991 $bn	1992 $bn
Bond Corporation	2.250	1.066	0.310
State Bank of South Australia	–	2.180	–
State Bank of Victoria	1.978	–	–
Westpac Banking Corporation	–	–	1.670
Adelaide Steamship	–	1.358	0.049
David Jones	–	1.381	0.061
Fosters Brewing Group	1.264	0.043	0.949
Tooth and Co.	–	0.720	0.038
Bell Resources (Aust. Cons. Invest.)	0.829	0.108	0.034
National Consolidated	–	0.390	0.044
Industrial Equity	–	0.341	–
Petersville Sleigh	–	0.309	–
News Corp	–	0.296	–
TNT	–	0.275	0.024
Barrack Mines	0.169	0.130	–
FAI Insurances Group	–	0.144	0.049
Ariadne Australia	0.067	0.019	0.103

Note: * A '–' in a loss column indicates the company reported a profit for that period.
Source: Annual Reports of companies for the 1990, 1991 and 1992 financial years.

The relatively low frequency of corporate failure is likely to mask its historical significance and commercial impact. Real resource allocation has social consequences. One large failure, or a large number of small failures, are events of historic, rather than merely historical, dimensions, causing considerable hardship and outrage amongst shareholders, creditors and the general public.[18] Damage done before and after the excesses of the 1980s and the new millennium has also had far reaching direct consequences; undermining confidence in Australia's securities markets, inciting public outrage and creating a perception by some that Australia's self-regulatory Accounting Standards-setting process is deficient, much more so than in the United Kingdom or the United States.[19]

Thus, following Lonrho's well-publicised 1972 liquidity crisis and allegations of corrupt business practices, UK Prime Minister Edward Heath labelled Tiny Rowland's actions at Lohnro 'the unpleasant and unacceptable face of capitalism'. Apt too are the comments of a group of British Labour Party members, that those actions were 'the inevitable logic of capitalism'.[20]

Note their symmetry with the comment made nearly 50 years earlier in the United Kingdom in the wake of the Royal Mail failure, that it was 'an offence [by Lord Kylsant, Chairman of the Royal Mail Steam Packet Co.], which however innocently committed, struck deep at the roots of investment confidence and menaced the whole stability of commercial financial practice'.[21] Similar Australian sentiments were evident in the aftermath of 1960s corporate collapses, for example, this editorial comment following the H.G. Palmer failure: 'the questions raised ... are so serious and affect so seriously the confidence felt in the conduct of our business affairs that only the most thorough inquiry can now satisfy the public',[22] and following the 1970s Minsec collapse: '[It] was the biggest borrower on the Australian unofficial money markets. Its fall sparked one of the biggest money panics in Australian history ... whiteanting the whole Australian money market.'[23]

Today there are similar events, similar refrains. Table 1.3 confirms the extent of reported corporate 'losses'.

It is easy to find near identical comments to those in the 1960s and 1970s following the belatedly revealed 1980s excesses of Australia's failed entrepreneurs:

> ... thanks to Spedley ... the security blanket of audited accounts is an illusion ...[24]
>
> The failure of the accounting profession to establish and adhere to decent standards has ... proved that many of their figures cannot be trusted ... Billions of dollars of investors' funds vanished ... Accounts ... in many cases cannot be trusted.[25]
>
> ... arguably the September 1991 accounts [of Westpac] are now shown to have been grossly misleading ... something like two billion dollars of assets claimed in those accounts did not exist ... Westpac ... reported assets and profits that

Table 1.3 Selected reported deficiencies and investment writedowns for specified years

Institution	2000 $bn	2001 $bn	2002 $bn
HIH	5.3	–	–
Ansett	–	1.50	–
One.Tel	–	0.07	1.5
Pasminco	–	2.48	–
NAB	–	–	4.0
News Corp	–	0.75	12.8

Note: A '–' in a column indicates the company failed to report a deficiency or writedown for that period.
Source: Annual reports of companies for the 2000–02 financial years; as well as liquidators' or administrators' reports.

were grossly inflated and untrue, and that those untruths were then ticked
[by the auditors].[26]

[P]roprietors are entitled to ask why they were misled by their directors. The
property market has not deteriorated to anywhere near the extent recorded in the
Westpac figures over the last three months; it's been on a deep slide for two years.[27]

And so it is today, *post*-HIH and Enron:

[Under the caption – 'Costello: Audit crisis of confidence'] The Federal
Government signalled yesterday that it would make the overhaul of the besieged
auditing profession a priority ... Most of the public believes auditors are sort of
there to detect fraud ... Treasurer Peter Costello launched a blistering attack on
industry standards.[28]

Corporate Australia is worried about its 'Enron potential' ... In the post-Enron
environment audit committees need to get more involved in determining what
accounting policies the company is following.[29]

The Chief Executive Officer of CPA Australia, Greg Larsen said yesterday that
his [CPA reform] blueprint had been triggered by recent corporate collapses which
had dramatically affected public confidence in financial reporting standards.[30]

The collapse of Enron has disclosed [companies'] accounts were misleading ...
faith in corporate America hasn't been so strained since the early 1900s.[31]

The profits were an illusion. The multi-million dollar rewards for executives
were real. Over the last few years, executives at some companies have released
inaccurate earnings statements and, before correcting them, sold large parcels of
stock at inflated prices. Martha Stewart did not invent the tactic. Indeed, Bush and
Cheney are alleged to have been practitioners of the art, too.[32]

Not since the 1930s has the quality of corporate earnings ... [been] so difficult
for investors to determine ... US financial markets have a reputation for integrity
that took decades to build. It has made the US the gold standard for financial
reporting and the preeminent place to invest ... That a company like Enron ... one
of the largest companies on the New York Stock Exchange, could fall so far so fast
shows how badly that gold standard has been tarnished. 'The profession of
auditing and accounting is, in fact, in crisis,' says Paul Volcker, former chairman of
the Federal Reserve and now one of the leaders of the International Accounting
Standards Board.[33]

Indeed the Enron scandal and the swift bankruptcy of upstart telecom Global
Crossing Ltd have cast a long shadow of suspicion about possible accounting
improprieties at company after company ... The usual investor watchdogs – the
board, auditors and regulators – all seem to have been asleep or deeply conflicted
about their roles ...[34]

As shocking as Enron is, it's only the latest in a dizzying succession of
accounting meltdowns, from Waste Management to Cendant ... [I]n the past half

dozen years investors have lost close to US$200 billion in earnings restatements and lost market capitalization following audit failures ... Between 1997–2000 the number of restatements doubled from 116 to 233.[35]

One might imagine the anguish on the part of representatives of the accounting profession faced with such comments, for each is incontestable. Occasionally members have expressed horror. With members facing massive litigation claims the official professional bodies (as well as some of the commentators above) have described the profession as being 'in crisis'.[36] Mostly, however, the comments have evoked a flurry of attention by the professional accountancy bodies to search out something, or more commonly 'someone', they might blame – bad management, declining business ethics and inadequate resources for education and regulatory agencies have each had their turn.[37] Similar responses in the United States followed criticisms by the SEC Chief Accountant Scheutze regarding what constitutes an asset.[38]

Indicative of the search for causes is the 1994 Australian study by Greatorex et al., *Corporate Collapses: Lessons for the future*, surveying 162 Australian liquidators[39] – lack of CEO management skills, over-reliance on debt and the failure to have sufficient capital for ongoing development or survival – emerged. Post-2000 the cause seems to have been sheeted home to bad ethical behaviour – a time-honoured scapegoat. Ethics and corporate governance have been equated. Equally pertinent might have been to ask why the accounts of those who failed had shortly before shown the companies to be profitable, sometimes 'highly successful'.

With this departure from the inept CEO syndrome of earlier decades came a much greater emphasis placed on the possibility of unprofessional behaviour by auditors and the unethical behaviour (the pursuit of short-term gains possibly to maximise bonus arrangements) of some directors. Allegations have been made that auditors have not acted independently, that there have been soft audits to protect revenues from non-audit services to their clients. 'Audit failure' (not accounting failure) rather than 'management failure' is now portrayed as the culprit in the 2000s for corporate collapses, or, more importantly, the exacerbation of their losses. There has been a pervasive lament that instances of inadequate information flows and accountability checks threaten the trust that is so essential to the capitalist market-based system. Yet, after all the huff and puff in Australia and the United States, where the defaults were the most talked of, where regulators have declared they will get tough, and where government-sponsored inquiries have taken place, there seems little attempt to change fundamentally the system of accounting – tinkerings and fine tunings have been preferred. The main aim seems to be to retain the primarily self-regulated expenditure capitalisation system at all costs.[40]

Cult of the individual

Many of the participants in corporate collapses are household names. Ensuing publicity has emphasised the *fallen* in the entrepreneurial 'cult' – the individuals involved. How their families cope with their anxieties and other personal matters have become fodder for the media.[41] Exploiting inquisitiveness, the media has diverted attention to the 'cult of the individual'. This has facilitated the general ineffectiveness of the regulatory mechanisms, allowing the parts played by accounting and auditing in exacerbating failure to survive more or less untouched.

Descriptions of the financial difficulties experienced by particular companies (Chapter 3–15) are as diverse in style and substance as they are with respect to the extent to which fraud or other illegalities influenced the events to which they refer. Some have been the subject of official investigations (Royal Commissions, inspectors' investigations or liquidators' analyses), others simply the subject of secular commentary. However, they are far less diverse insofar as accounting and other financial reports, subsequently found to be false, passed the scrutiny of auditors. Some also had passed the so-described informed and efficient securities market in general, and (many) analysts in particular. Accounting and audit failure has continued to slip through the regulatory net, evoking the issues to be addressed here. Of particular interest is whether the incidence of failure suggests that the securities market is uninformed?; whether a more centralised and greater-resourced APRA and ASIC regulatory mechanism would prove more effective than its regulatory predecessors?; in what practical sense is the market supposed to be efficient?; whether the commercial society is getting value for money from audits of publicly listed companies?; whether the role of an auditor is currently feasible or are auditors engaged in a mission impossible?; whether the professionally-endorsed responses of auditor or audit firm rotation, the separation of audit and non-audit services, an auditor disciplinary board guaranteeing swift and open hearings, the mandatory introduction of audit committees, audit firm incorporation or putting a cap on auditor liability are likely to be effective regulatory responses? Or is it, as we will propose, that a fundamental reconstruction of accounting is necessary?

Underlying our analysis and speculations are the pertinent wider issues relating to the education of 'professional' accountants and auditors, and indeed the education of the regulators, their motivating philosophy and the structure of their *modus operandi*. Professional accountancy bodies and the regulatory bodies have justifiably come under greater scrutiny and, now for APRA, proposed litigation. They have had ample opportunity to influence the status quo, but generally have not. Accounting's professional bodies suggest, *inter alia*, that the remedy is more education – educate the public about the limited utility of traditional accounting information. Another post-2000 move has been a greater drive to cap auditors' statutory liability for negligence and the push that following the professional standards will be a sufficient defence. This approach remains a curious example of *caveat emptor*.

Clearly, the paradox is that success and failure are closely linked – 'success itself and the things that cause success seem very much to contribute to decline. In order for firms to remain competitive they must learn to master these "perils of excellence".'[42] Nearly all of the collapsed companies featured here, at times in their corporate history, were lauded as being successful, sometimes exceedingly so. Most were household names. In some cases this praise occurred just prior to collapse. For some, that timely praise was warranted. For others it was wishful thinking. For others still, it was thoughtless!

There is no dispute, for example, that Reid Murray was a successfully aggressive retailer in 1960s Australia. In three years the company had grown, albeit by takeover, to be the fourth-largest publicly listed company in Australia. H.G. Palmer was Australia's largest electrical retailer by the early 1960s with 140 branches, and Cox Brothers was Australia's fastest growing retailer in the late 1950s. They were eminently successful. Similarly, Minsec, formed in 1965, had within four years undeniable claims to the position of leading money market operator in Australia. By contrast, it is doubtful, notwithstanding their sales growth, whether Reid Murray or H.G. Palmer were ever *truly* profitable, or whether Rothwells was ever one of the leading finance companies of the 1980s. With hindsight, it is also debatable whether Bond Corporation or West-mex *actually* operated successfully from the mid-1980s. It has been suggested that Bond Corporation possibly was in financial distress as long ago as 1984![43] But before their declines became public both Westmex and Bond Corporation were lauded in the financial press as corporate high-fliers. Their chief executives were referred to with great deference as leading business people. Indeed, as mentioned earlier, in 1978 Alan Bond was 'Businessman of the Year', in 1985 he was fêted for his Castlemaine Tooheys 'Takeover of the Year' and in 1987 awarded 'Australian of the Year'. By the end of 1989 Bond's shine had worn off. Russell Goward was described as a financial whiz kid and awarded the 1987 'Acorn Business Award'. His Westmex was perceived to be a successful conglomerate, as was John Spalvins' Adsteam.

Likewise, in the 1990s and beyond. HIH's Ray Williams and FAI's (and ultimately also HIH's) Rodney Adler were lauded as leading players in the Australian insurance industry. Both were members of the Insurance Council of Australia. Ansett Australia was undoubtedly an Australian airline icon, though by the time of its collapse the Ansett family had long departed its management. Harris Scarfe was the epitome of a successful, conservative, established retailer. And in both the good times and bad, One.Tel was the archetype dot.com and

telco! Its founder Jodee Rich, despite having setbacks, enjoyed a high reputation. In the financial press, adulation of those chief executives continued
until just prior to each company's respective fall. And when collapse came
it dissolved in the same authoritative haze, with the same speed that had
characterised its rise.

Enron's place in the US corporate hierarchy, especially its innovatory drive,
cannot be disputed, nor can its groundbreaking innovation in energy marketing,
Sunbeam's place in electrical appliance manufacture, or WorldCom's status as
an Internet provider. At various times their leaders were properly lauded.

Indisputably, these leading companies had another common factor. They all
collapsed or reported financial difficulties *suddenly*, *unexpectedly*. For many,
those difficulties followed news releases of reportedly successful operations;
certainly after the issue of successive financials inviting the expectation of good
things to come. Only occasionally in advance of collapse were those companies
identified to be ailing over a period of years.

Certainly according to many in the press and those in the market claiming
to be in the know, they were not facing financial difficulties. Understandably so,
for their financial reports had failed to indicate those financial troubles. Despite
claims by the 'punters' (the uninformed investors) that they are denied information apparently available to others in the market, the published financial
statements are the primary source of financial information to virtually all in-
the-know punters (e.g. the institutional investors) too. History demonstrates
that corporate failure does not appear to have had a lengthy public incubation
period. While symptoms are there and some ferret them out, the financial
reporting system masks them. Therein lies a major problem – financial matters
of unquestionable public interest can be kept private.

Public complaint, criticism and questioning of the role of accountants
and auditors in highly publicised bankruptcies or financial dilemmas are
international phenomena.[44] Comments on the crumbled empires of Asil Nadir,
Aghan Abedi and Robert Maxwell in the United Kingdom indicate that 'the
crumbling of firms like Polly Peck, BCCI, and Maxwell Communication all
[occurred] within months of getting a clean bill of health from their auditors,
[and] has raised serious questions about the usefulness of company accounts'.[45]
Likewise in this assessment on the US Savings and Loans affair:

> [Democratic Congressman] Wyden and others lay a large part of the blame for
> the S&L crisis at the door of the accounting profession. 'Accountants didn't
> cause the S&L crisis', says Wyden. 'But they could have saved taxpayers a lot
> of money if they did their jobs properly and set off enough warning alarms
> for regulators.'[46]

And the similar lament in a 1993 United States Public Oversight Board Report:

> The accounting profession has suffered a serious erosion of confidence ... *in its standards, in the relevance of its work and the financial reporting process* ... [because] in some cases, not long before an entity failed, it received an auditor's report giving no indication that the entity was in its latter days.[47]

But, the 'crisis', 'system is broken' tags were to reappear following the *unexpected* collapses of Enron, WorldCom and other major corporates, as well as alleged 'accounting irregularities' at Enron, WorldCom, Xerox, Qwest Communications, Disney, Merck and others. The demise of Andersen, one of the (then) Big Five auditing firms, was presented as a kind of confirmation that the system was in good shape, but allegedly manipulated by unscrupulous accountants, auditors and executives. Newspapers and other media were replete with references to the market suffering form 'Enronitis'– the plight of the *crooked-E* coined a new commercial label – attaching to profit figures allegedly being manipulated (see footnotes 24–35 for instances).

Public criticism was legion following the October 1987 crash: 'Auditors are being called to account', 'The accounts are a joke', 'Audit served no useful purpose', 'What makes an audit "true and fair"?', 'Uproar on accounting proposals', 'Auditors in danger from $2.5 bn claims' and 'Accountants want to stop the carnage'.[48] In the aftermath of the tech-wreck crashes in May 2000 and the financial troubles of HIH, Ansett, One.Tel, Harris Scarfe and Centaur, newspaper headlines appeared such as: 'Accounting and auditing practices are in crisis', 'Auditors called to account', 'Taking stock of auditors', 'Lies, damn lies and annual reports', 'System is broken: world looks for tougher rules for accounting', 'Nasdaq firms pro forma accounting alchemy', 'Who can you believe?'. Those comments were indicative of sentiment in the financial press regarding the current state of Australian (and US) accounting and auditing practices. Unquestionably, they recall the past, for similar headlines had adorned the 1960s and 1970s business pages in Australia and elsewhere following company crashes.[49]

Again, virtually none of the commentaries have attacked the organisational and accounting fundamentals – nearly all imply devious manipulation of the current Accounting and Auditing Standards, arguing that they have not been applied adequately. None observe that even if they had been, it would not have solved the problem. Generally, the responses entail a push for more rules, more sanctions of the kind already in place. The focus continues to be on clobbering someone for not following the rules – for scalps – all with an implied perception that if the rules had been complied with, the behaviour complained of would not have occurred. Nothing is further from the truth!

Current attitudes and the perceived remedies are almost identical to those trundled out in the past. More of the same – more Accounting and Auditing Standards, more committees, oversight boards and the like. That strategy did not work in the past and there is no compelling reason to expect it to work in the future. Indeed, a theme to be pursued here is that existing regulations – in particular, the current accounting prescriptions – possibly contribute to the collapse of many companies being so *unexpected*. They certainly exacerbate the ultimate losses incurred by the companies as they continue to lose shareholder value long after their actual financial position would have justified their being wound up, had it been communicated through the public channels for financial information – the companies' published financial statements. The adverse drift in these companies' financial affairs is not publicly disclosed, accounting is not geared to reflect it, and the evidence suggests that more of the same type of accounting prescriptions will not facilitate the provision of useful, predictive data.

For, whereas there has been a surge in Accounting and Auditing Standards, the generic defects in conventional accounting remain. Notwithstanding more Standards with which companies' accounts must conform, resulting data continue to be unserviceable in determining a company's financial position, its solvency, its past financial performance and associated trends in its wealth and progress. Certainly, particular Standards have addressed and eliminated individual accounting infelicities, but therein is the problem. Remedial action has been cosmetic and episodic. It has attacked the symptoms but done little to eradicate the cause.

Anxiety spawned by the corporate collapses following the October 1987 stock market crash produced increasing pressures on regulators to implement reforms. Predictably, the fall of HIH, Harris Scarfe and One.Tel in reasonably quick succession prompted the same response. There was a new Australian Corporations Law after 1987 with additional sections including those relating to loans to directors and related party transactions, directors' duties regarding insolvent trading, aspects of liquidations and winding-ups, new prospectus provisions; and centralisation of the monitoring body the ASC (predecessor of the ASIC) – resourced with nearly one billion dollars over five years. In conjunction with the Australian Stock Exchange (ASX), a continuous disclosure reporting system was introduced. But it has done little other than speed up the communication of misleading data – a pyrrhic victory for the ASX at best. On cue in 2002, the demands for increased resourcing of regulatory bodies like ASIC and APRA recur. *CLERP 9* made recommendations of the same genre. Overall, the impact is likely to be more dramatic on Australia's forests than on the serviceability of accounting reports.

Not surprisingly in this climate, the accounting profession has also perceived a need to react. Suggestions proffered have included: auditor rotation; a greater justification for mandatory audit committees; various proposals to limit auditor liability; initially quickening, but then stalling, the development of a *mandatory* conceptual framework underlying accounting practice and method; renewed (albeit failed) attempts to merge the two major professional accountancy bodies; revised quality assurance procedures and a push for professional ethics components to be given greater emphasis in university educational programmes. Post-2000, additional reforms in the United States environment have included an additional supervisory board of accounting and audit practices (presumably to augment the SEC's existing oversight role) and audit firms voluntarily adding a new in-house monitoring committee to ensure ethically-based best practices are being undertaken by all auditing staff. This is commendable action, but somewhat belated, and it merely increases the tempo of an old, familiar and overplayed tune. The assurers in 2002 are the same as those in the 1990s.

A move away from general 'fuzzy law' to a more 'black-letter' (adherence to the rules) approach underpinned the combined self- and government regulatory developments. This was criticised by the Business Council of Australia and others. Yet leading members of the accounting profession continue to call for more of the same type of Accounting Standards.

One objective seems to have been to eliminate *totally* the qualitative *true and fair* view override criterion by seeking to remove it from the then Corporations Law (and now Corporations Act).[50] Yet the true and fair view override is a succinct, general quality criterion, which captures the essence of what consumer laws struggle to enshrine; it has virtual worldwide currency and is unique to accounting. In the mid-1990s it had been proposed that in view of global competition and bundling of capital in ever increasingly complex financial packaging, 'these imprecise adjectives ["true and fair"] had become increasingly meaningless' and the clause had become patently 'an anachronism'.[51]

We argued in the first edition of this book that that this is a peculiar analysis indeed, for historical and contemporary evidence from the autopsies of corporate failures illustrate the continuing, even increasing, need for enforcement of a qualitative, 'fuzzy' criterion, and less (even a decreasing) need of a formula-driven, prescriptive, rules-based accounting system. Interestingly, following the disillusionment arising from many current events, some leading commentators are now proposing that the true and fair view override be retained to ensure an informed capital market exists.[52] These include Sir Bryan Carsberg, former Chair of the UK Accounting Standards Committee and a foundation member of the IASB, and spokespersons for several of the largest accounting firms (including from KPMG, Michael Coleman, National Managing Partner, Risk and Regulation; and Lindsay Maxsted, Chief Executive Officer and a former partner of one of the then 'Big Five', Wayne Lonergan), Melbourne solicitor and Coles Myer director, Mark Leibler, and several academics. The latest interest in the need for the return to such a criterion supports our first edition push – something that some reviewers of that edition felt was unnecessary.

The need for systemic rather than cosmetic changes in the mechanics and function of accounting is clear. But, inexplicably, it is still not on the agendas of the professional accountancy bodies or other regulatory agencies. The evidence adduced in the first edition, and iterated in this revised edition, of *Corporate Collapse* is not new. Nor are the problems to which it relates. Lawyers appointed as inspectors in 1965 into the affairs of Reid Murray collapse appositely remarked:

> [N]either of us is skilled in accountancy and ... much ... we have said will not be acceptable by the accounting profession generally. [We use] ... commonsense, and commonsense has compelled us to reject a number of practices used in the group and apparently regarded as acceptable by accountants.[53]

The financial press concurred with this lament: 'Accountants and directors also have a duty in a public company and the Reid Murray story has again brought home the realisation of the position of trust they hold for investors.'[54] Need for a 'commonsense' approach and recognition of a 'public duty' would seem to be grist to the mill for every professional. Yet, in accounting debates over the last four decades suggestions for such a 'professional' response generally have gone unheeded.

Regulatory theatre

'Corporate governance' and 'ethics' became two of the buzz phrases of the 1990s, and a crescendo by the 2000s. They provided fertile ground for producing reports and codes of practice.

Following the 1960s failures, the Australian accountancy profession sheeted most of the blame to poor management in its white paper, *Accounting Principles and Practices Discussed in Reports on Company Failures*.[55] Analysis of the 1980s' collapses contained more of the same, blaming bad management and declining ethics. It was the same the world over. Pratten's 1991 inquiry into UK failures commissioned by The Institute of Chartered Accountants in England and Wales (ICAEW) trots out the same rhetoric, despite evidence in the affairs of Polly Peck, Maxwell and BCCI of more fundamental problems in corporate governance.[56] Since then there has been little effective introspection by the accounting profession despite a disturbing repetition of past behaviour.

One might have expected increased promulgation of Accounting and Auditing Standards to be accompanied by decreased complaint and criticism. But just the opposite is the case – increased specification of accounting and auditing practices by the profession is positively correlated with increased litigation. One account in the United States suggests that there have been significant increases in litigation in the late 1990s and early 2000s.[57] This development is understandable, for compliance with Standards then in vogue was just as likely to have contributed to creative accounting as deviation from them. Perversely, corporate regulators and the accounting profession are calling for more Accounting and Auditing Standards.

One pervading problem in seeking to reform corporate conduct is the populace's soft attitude with respect to corporate crime – at least until it affects them. White-collar crime occurs in a world remote to many. It appears to be so different from a mugging in the park. To many Australians, corporate offenders possibly fit neatly into the Ned Kelly syndrome; for Americans, they conjure up the inexplicable fascination with the exploits of Bonnie and Clyde or of Butch Cassidy and the Sundance Kid; for the British they possibly rekindle the best of the fantasies regarding Robin Hood – their boldness almost always evoking curiosity, their acts more admired for their daring than deplored for their offence against the rights of others. They are perceived as reluctantly fleecing their victims rather than being callously indifferent to their welfare.

That delusion is endemic of the way financial finagling is perceived. It always has been. Accounts of the seventeenth century Tulipmania, John Blunt's eighteenth century deception underlying the collapse of the South Sea Company and of John Law's fraudulent Mississippi Scheme fit the romantic image. Lord Kylsant is misrepresented as a *victim* rather than a manipulator of the 1905 *Companies Act* (UK), as it affected his misreporting of the Royal Mail's affairs; Samuel Insull presents as a rather kindly, lonely entrepreneur, despite the financial misery caused by the collapse of his utilities' empire at the commencement of the Great Depression; Swedish 'match king', Ivar Kreuger emerges as the financial genius of the 1920s and 1930s, duping governments and investors over a 30-year rampage; Philip Musica's masquerade, underpinning the 1930s McKesson and Robbins fraud, becomes an impish pre-war escapade; Tino de Angelis' swindles in vegetable oils appear more the actions of a lovable eccentric dabbling in the post-war aid schemes than of a corporate criminal indifferent to any hardship his actions may have imposed on others.[58] That also is the general style of the populist coverage of the failure of the US thrifts in the 1980s.[59]

Coverage given to Michael Milken's junk bond exploits in the gutsy 1980s captures more of his daring than exposing the glaring regulatory gaps that facilitated the investors' losses. Asil Nadir, fleeing to Turkish Cyprus to avoid answering for dubious gains with his Polly Peck empire, is labelled romantically as a modern Ronnie Biggs, *as if* that were a virtue. The financial subterfuge of BCCI's Aghan Abedi is relegated to the bottom line in favour of description of his life at the top. Germany's Jurgen Schneider's demise early in 1994 is described in *Time* magazine as 'The King Absconds'.

Nearly a decade on in Germany, the Munich media baron Leo Kirch's fall from grace was described in one account as an exemplar of business political intrigue.[60] As was the contemporary demise of France's media mogul Jean-Marie Messier of Vivendi fame. And, seemingly, everyone gets more joy from the Catholic Church's embarrassment from Robert Calvi's Banco Ambrosiano and Vatican Bank foreign currency affair than from contemplating the defects of the national and international monetary systems that facilitated it. The delusion continues – the release in 2002 of the movie *I Banchieri di Dio* on the Banco-Ambrosiano affair and the revelations that Robert Calvi had not committed suicide but had been strangled (he was found hanging under London's Blackfriars Bridge in the early 1980s) ensure that that saga is not dead. Who said business *heroes* were boring?

Australia's media has had a field day pursuing Ray Williams' private affairs and the comings and goings of (what financial journalist Barry described as) the 'Rich Kids' – Jodee Rich, Rodney Adler, Lachlan Murdoch and James Packer – as well as Brad Keeling and Brad Cooper. The commercial paparazzi have worked overtime. In the United States, Kenneth Lay and Jeffrey Skilling have been given top billing in coverage of the Enron affair. WorldCom's Bernie Ebbers and Tyco's Dennis Kozlowski have been in the press's sights, too, whilst the Andersen audit firm's involvement in both the Enron and HIH collapses has been the 'bonus of all bonuses' for the media.

Generally sidelined by the media throughout all of those episodes was that the failure of the publicly available financial information to disclose a true and fair view of companies' financial positions facilitated deception and in some cases exacerbated the losses.

There is perhaps a glimmer of hope for our proposals. Addressing, then redressing, generic defects in *the system* are the hallmarks of one of Australia's best-known (albeit under-resourced and much maligned) regulators of the 1980s, Henry Bosch. He addressed matters pertaining to the system. He has been very active in promoting his assessment of the existing corporate regulatory mechanisms in Australia and his remedies for its ills. We challenge his understanding of the effectiveness of Accounting Standards and especially his call for more of them.[61] His general advocacy for changing the regulatory mechanism to a more legislative-bound setting is appealing. As is his plea for regulatory mechanisms with teeth. Few should object to that. It *is* an acknowledgment that human nature cannot be changed, whereas the system can. We can gaol the individuals and they can die off but there will always be another team to replace them next season. Likewise, the current ASIC Chairman David Knott's implementation of the ASIC (June 2002) surveillance project aimed at identifying non-compliance with Accounting Standards, hits at the system (see fn. 10 above). But notwithstanding these exceptions there is an institutional blind spot regarding the generic defects of accounting and auditing practices.

To this point, no other professional activities have enjoyed such levels of continued support in the wake of a prolonged public record of default. With the recent brouhaha and outrage following events at HIH, One.Tel, Enron, WorldCom and the like, one wonders whether a point of departure might be on the horizon.

The HIH Administrator's proposed suit against the federal government, its prudential regulator and 205 partners of the now defunct Andersen may represent a point of departure – we are told the audit profession is being 'cleaned up', 'at last'. Some aspects of the workings of the profession, yes! – insofar as close ties between 'audit' and 'non-audit services' functions are being examined. But audit as a 'process' remains virtually untouched, for neither the process of audit nor the professionalism of auditors has been lifted to a higher plane by this limited examination. Arguably, assuming prevention of *unexpected* failures is the goal, the investing public is no better protected now, than it was prior to the HIH, Ansett, Harris Scarfe, One.Tel, Centaur or Enron and the other contemporary US crises. And of particular concern is whether additional Standards and layers of oversight as part of the revised governance mechanisms being introduced will produce any better protection in the future – namely, more timely warnings of impending corporate collapses.

What follows catalogues events leading to several notorious *unexpected* collapses, reveals repeated accounting anomalies and exposes the accounting profession's inadequate responses. It is a sorry tale, one inimical to a profession but needing to be told. It is not a story about the personal defects of people, *per se*; it does not set out to draw up who might be placed on a swindlers' list. It is about the posturing of the regulatory theatre, its rhetoric and its inaction, about the defects in critical accountability elements of the regulatory environment – the inherent defects in rules and conventional practices – in which those who have made the headlines operated. Indeed, it is doubtful in respect of some matters whether some of those headline-grabbers deserve to be on a *list* of bad guys any more than those well-intentioned individuals who made the rules and drafted the Accounting and Auditing Standards that have proved so unfit for informing and protecting commercial society. In many ways those on whom the media has focused are victims of the system too. Without the regulatory system being as it is, many of the events of which the corporate watchdogs and the financial media have cried 'foul' might not have occurred.

Auditors were described in the first edition as being on a 'mission impossible' and that, combined with the defects in the conventional system of accounting, amounted to a potential commercial 'time bomb'. The recent fall of the Andersen firm – indictment and conviction in the United States, cessation of its US auditing operations, and the sale of its activities in Australia to Ernst & Young; WorldCom (now the largest US bankruptcy) being sued by the biggest US pension fund and three others over their US$423 million in bond losses following WorldCom's revelations that it had capitalised US$3.9 billion in operating costs; the reported Bond Corp A$110 million out-of-court settlement in mid-2002 and the filleting of the accounting profession to separate auditing and non-audit services almost worldwide, justify both assessments of the inherent perils of the audit task and the time-bomb prediction. Regarding the essence of accounting and audit practices, only minor titivation at the edges has occurred – auditors are no better placed now and the arsenal of time bombs is not diminished. Regulators' increased anxiety is testimony to that.

Those defects and their contribution to the financial impact of *unexpected* corporate collapse are the subject of what follows. We stated in the first edition that no doubt what was to follow would please few, enrage many and enlighten some. Clearly, too few were enlightened!

CHAPTER 2

Creative Accounting –
Mind the GAAP

The proper object of standards is to reduce this permissiveness. It has
long been said by the leaders of the profession that the diversity of
accounting rules should be reduced.
Accounting Standards Review Committee (1978), p. 62.

That would be a laudable sentiment were it to result in more truthful financial
statements. Generally on the national fronts the stated aim has been to strive
for less diversity. Perversely, to the extent that this has been achieved, it has
been at the expense of creating increased opportunities for deception. Conventional accounting produces institutionalised window-dressing. Arguably,
the overall 'quality of GAAP-based' accounting is poorer than before the
advent of mandatory 'compliance Standards regime'. The current accounting
and auditing storms swirling around the commercial world are testament
to that.

Vehement complaint and criticism regarding the serviceability of the end
products of conventional accounting and auditing processes have accompanied
corporate failures over many decades. Disbelief has followed the collapse of
companies soon after they have reported profits and received clean audit
reports. Whereas the 'what-the-hell-has-happened?' type of cry has been common, the fact that conventional accounting is unlikely to produce data serviceable for determining the wealth and progress of companies, by and large, has
attracted little comment.

This continues. In the first years of the new millennium in the aftermath
of the tech-wreck of April/May 2000 the bears expelled the bulls from the
securities markets around the world. The anguish over the collapses and revealed accounting malpractices at, say, HIH and Enron have highlighted to the
regulators and the accounting profession the need to reform. But the extant
capitalisation of expenditures-based accounting system seems to have escaped
unscathed again!

Habitually, financial indicators such as profitability, earnings per share,
solvency, liquidity, rate of return, asset backing, the ratio of debt to equity, and
the like, are calculated in the financial press and by financial analysts from the
data in the published accounts. Calculated from the annual financial statements
conforming to the Accounting Standards endorsed by the accounting profession, those derived data are reasonably expected to expose and help explain

the salient financial characteristics of firms. The problem is, generally they do not; indeed they cannot.

Existing Accounting Standards have failed to match the admirable objectives and claims of the leaders of the profession – namely that compliance with them would reduce the diversity of accounting practices and thereby provide data relevant to the making of informed financial assessments. Debris from unexpected failures exposes little progress on either front. Whatever progress there has been gives cold comfort to everybody wanting to draw inferences from published financial statements.

Compulsory use of 'tax effect accounting' has meant that the resulting accounting fictions (provisions for deferred income tax debits and future income tax credits) have to come into the calculation of profit and loss and into the balance sheet. Those tax effect data are delusory.[1] 'Tax effect accounting' refers to a method mandated by the profession of reporting the financial effects owing to differences between actual taxation payable and tax that would be payable were it to be based on the professional accounting treatments of transactions. Resulting deferred tax assets and liabilities do not have any real-world referent. They are fictions. One leading radio personality described these items as akin to the mythical Australian 'Bunyip' character. Those fictions are legitimately the product of applying the Standard. Fictions arise too through the artifacts of consolidated financial statements – goodwill and discounts emerging entirely from the mechanics of consolidation, the elimination of the effects of transactions between related companies without regard for the actual financial outcomes, the exacerbated, consolidated impact of injecting tax effect accounting. In respect of *groups*, it relates to a concentration on whether an entity is controlled, or has facilitated some inter-corporate investments not being accounted for.

Consider the particulars of the Enron episode (see pp. 259–62). At the root of the problem lie sets of puerile rules evoking tailored practices for specified relationships between business entities, incorporated and unincorporated alike, rather than a general rule requiring the financial consequences of each and every transaction to be reported – as it is – notwithstanding the relationship between vendor and purchaser, lessor and lessee, borrower and lender. Too many rules, too many assessments to be made as to which rule to apply – too many opportunities for genuine error and deliberate manipulations.

Another dilemma arises under foreign currency accounting – whether to record the financial effects of beneficial foreign exchange movements as part of operating profits or as an increment to reserves. This hinges perversely on whether the foreign operations are 'sustaining' or 'temporary'. Consider also having to inject charges for depreciation irrespective of whether there has been a decline in the market worth of physical assets; compulsory valuation (in most circumstances) of saleable inventories at a variety of costs, rather than always at market selling price; and the implied requirement to value some physical assets by reference to hypothetical calculations of the net present (discounted) value of the income streams expected from their future use. This can do nothing but mislead the users (the consumers) of the resulting data which do not relate in any sensible way to financial realities. Other dilemmas are created by capitalising expenses as assets (as WorldCom did), and recourse to the abnormal/extraordinary items classifications.[2] These and many other examples emerge below.

Paradoxically, the best-case scenario from the Standards-setters' point of view – that there is *less* diversity in accounting practices now than in the past – possibly has done more to reduce the usefulness of accounting data than enhancing accountants' capacity to exercise their professional judgment on how to account for, and report on, the outcome of financial matters would have done.

According to the corporate regulators, deviation from the prescribed practices or the deceitful misinterpretation of the Standards produces *creative* (misleading) accounting. Defying financial commonsense, producing the 'standard' nonsensical, fictional, financial outcomes are not regarded by either the regulators or (so it seems) the accounting profession to be a wilful indulgence in creative accounting. Inexplicably, the most common financial nonsense arising from compliance with an endorsed accounting practice is implied to be acceptable, whereas the commonsense arising from deviation from many of the endorsed practices is not.

It is no wonder that the public at large is nonplussed. Over several decades companies with strings of reported good performances and a succession of clean audit reports, some even eulogised in the financial press as the jewels in the nation's corporate crown, have *suddenly* gone belly up – H.G. Palmer, Reid Murray, Neon Signs in the 1960s; Minsec, Gollins and Cambridge Credit in the 1970s; Ariadne, Qintex, Bond, Hooker, Westmex, Adsteam in the 1980s; and HIH, One.Tel, Ansett, Harris Scarfe and a plethora of dot.coms in the new century. This has been against a background of the international ramifications for both company regulation, accounting and audit, particularly in relation to the Enron and WorldCom collapses and myriad 'accounting scandals' in the United States.

Creative Standards

A little history is informative. In 1978 the NSW Government Accounting Standards Review Committee concluded that, despite the Standards then in force, diversity in accounting practice was to the fore.[3] Earlier in the 1960s, the Chairman of the 1978 Review Committee, Professor Ray Chambers, had demonstrated that there were: 'A million sets of mutually exclusive rules each giving a true and fair view of a company's state of affairs and its profits! This is absurd'.[4]

Absurd, yes! But evidently not so absurd as to ensure change. Notwithstanding the addition for nearly 25 years of numerous legislatively endorsed professional Accounting Standards to the accountants' armoury, that variety persists, indeed it probably grows. Today's jargon refers to this as 'earnings management'. There are still more than a million possible reported sets of accounting data for one company in any one period.[5] Little of substance has changed over the past 50-odd years. Thus the quality, the serviceability, of financial reporting continues to be exceedingly problematic and the subject of public questioning.

Similar 'absurd' comments have been made for decades; for example, 'BHP's annual statement of profitability is an accountant's dream – you can produce almost any trend you want depending on which adjustments you make',[6] and under the headline, 'Take your pick of accounting methods, all of them are confusing': 'Accounts and statements released in the last 48 hours by five leading companies – BHP, APM, Actrol, Clark Rubber and CRA – reveal an amazing variation in accounting practices which must be confusing all but the most qualified of analysts'.[7]

A decade later, then National Companies and Securities Commission (NCSC) chairman Henry Bosch expressed similar sentiments – that accounts of some companies were being distorted by what the NCSC perceived to be unjustifiable accounting, producing unfairly favourable results.[8] Bosch was perceived as a guardian of 1980s accounts and he contemplated making a test case of one of the high-fliers' accounts. Allegedly this was aborted on advice that there would be difficulty getting expert accounting opinion to support the Commission's view. This may be even more difficult now that the Big Five has been reduced to the Big Four.

We demonstrate later that much the same had been said in the fallout from the 1960s and new millennium company failures. One is tempted to muse that little has changed in accounting's serviceability in the interregnum. Whatever changes there have been in the form of due process in Standards-setting, tighter Standard prescriptions, greater-resourced regulatory bodies and limited recourse to market price information do not appear to have improved matters substantially. The *unexpected* failures continue.

Invariably, unexpected corporate collapses have been associated worldwide with a crisis in confidence in the accounting profession,[9] manifested primarily in calls for accountants and auditors to clean up their act. To this end, long-standing critic of the US accounting profession, Abe Briloff, persistently criticised accounting and auditing practices in the US Savings and Loans and other 1980s financial scandals, with little visible success.[10]

Corporate collapses, instances of takeover and other asset plays in the 1980s through to the present were the catalyst for calls for change to eliminate creative accounting practices in Anglo-American countries.[11] But *creative accounting* takes on many meanings. To management analyst John Argenti (in the 1970s), it was a deliberate policy pursued by managers to deceive shareholders, creditors and themselves (or all three) regarding a company's wealth and progress in general and its financial difficulties in particular.

That possibly captures the prevailing perception of creative accounting – practices deviating from accounting principles (Standards) underlying the preparation of financial statements. Others have drawn a more explicit bead on specific accounting practices, sometimes delineating a distinction between window-dressing, earnings management, creative accounting and cooking the books.[12] Generally it is left unstated whether these accounting practices are intentionally or unintentionally used. But such a distinction is important in

A CORRECTION FOR CREATIVE ACCOUNTANTS

Henry Bosch, NCSC Chairman (1985–89), depicted here as the guardian of corporate accounts in the 1980s in a caption to an article, by H. Killen, 'A correction for creative accountants', *Australian Financial Review*, 15 May 1987, p. 10.
Courtesy of Pascal Locanto.

differentiating the deceitful (the *feral*) from the accidental, the blameworthy from the blameless. Our use of the term *feral accounting* in the first edition to describe accounting creativity with the intent to deceive appears to have been received favourably by financial commentators.

Argenti listed 'creative' techniques under the heading of accounting and business practices.[13] This schema was developed following extensive world-wide conglomerate takeover activity by financial 'whiz kids' – including Slater Walker and James Goldsmith in the UK, James Ling and Harold Geneen in the United States, while in Australia, amongst others, Alexander Barton and Ronald Brierley plied their trade.

However defined, 'creative accounting' generally conjures up financial per-missiveness, a feature with a long history. It has been used by many observers – including: in the United States Ripley and Berle and Means in the 1920s; Twentieth Century Fund (1937) and Briloff (1972, 1976 and 1981); in the UK, Stamp and Marley (1970); and in Australia, Chambers (1965, 1973).[14] None of those observers was popular with the accountancy profession for 'telling it how they saw it'.

The practices to which those critical commentaries refer preceded the speculative frenzy of the so-called greedy '80s, the '90s and beyond. Under-standably, further catalogues of creative accounting techniques have appeared.[15]

While 'creative accounting' provides continuing fertile ground for debate, despite the criticisms, to date little has been produced in terms of effective reforms to the general system of accounting. There has been an ever-growing list of professional Accounting and Auditing Standards in Australia. Undoubtedly they have thwarted particular misleading accounting mechanisms. But they have done little to nothing in respect of removing the primary generic problems of which those practices were merely contemporary *modus operandi*. Thus, reported results over many years for 1960s failures at Reid Murray, Latec, Stanhill, H.G. Palmer, and 1970s failures at Minsec, Cambridge, Gollins and ASL, arguably were as misleading in a generic sense as those at Adsteam, Westmex, Qintex, Bond, and the like, in the 1980s, the 1990s, and beyond. Justifiably, criticism of the serviceability of accounting data remains both within and outside the accountancy profession.

Subsequent analyses of creative accounting have produced a mixed assessment. Jameson advocates a theme with which we have sympathy – that creative accounting (bordering on our descriptor *feral*) refers to a practice entirely within the framework of the law and Accounting Standards, but with intention to defeat the spirit of both. It is 'essentially a process of using the rules ... to make financial statements look somewhat different from what was intended by the rule ... rule bending and loophole-seeking'.[16] Implied is the idea that such a practice is against the public good. Jameson described two insidious consequences of creative accounting: (i) Standards avoidance designed to thwart the objectives of the lawmakers, and (ii) opinion-shopping, the practice of asking a number of firms of auditors about their attitude to a particular accounting treatment or practice.[17]

In contrast, Griffiths sees some merit in creative accounting, arguing that creative accounting (if used *appropriately*) can result in the presentation of substance over form, 'merely *reflecting the underlying trends* in the value of the business which would not always be apparent *if the accounts were prepared and presented in accordance with a strict interpretation of the appropriate accounting rules and regulations*'.[18] Griffiths' statement, however, begs consideration of the potential danger of creative accounting being used to *support* the results of a company experiencing ongoing trading difficulties. Creative accounting can be used to offset otherwise bad news. While this cannot continue in perpetuity without resort by managers to a 'foozle' – dubious, misleading actions bordering on the illegal – or a definite fraud,[19] our cases reveal that sometimes the delusion can last for one or two decades.

In Australia, Professor Bob Walker, another critic of conventional accounting, identified at least ten legal, creative accounting practices: creating 'assets' by mere bookkeeping entries; reporting gains and losses 'above or below the line' to achieve desired results; adjustments after balance date; capitalisation of expenses; sales with options to reverse the outcome after balance date; manipulating compliance with Standards by inventive interpretations; changing accounting methods and the like.[20]

On the regulatory front, Henry Bosch was particularly concerned about the use of creative accounting (or as he preferred 'cosmetic accounting' – and in the '2002' idiom, 'earnings management') to present company results in the most favourable light. His primary theme was that accounting creativity arose from deliberate manipulation of, and non-compliance with, the profession's approved Accounting Standards – that complying with the black-letter of the Standards would produce serviceable data. True to his theme, Bosch described departures from the Standards as unethical behaviour, 'which, if they became known, would damage the reputation of the profession or the market or which would be considered unfair by the great majority of market participants'.[21] His two-tier catalogue of creative practices was similar to Walker's: first tier – moving capital gains and losses in and out of the same statement, accruing profits of related companies, off-balance sheet financing, and the transfer of assets between related companies;[22] and the second tier – arrangements to reverse transactions after balance date, pyramiding asset values through related-party transactions,[23] and general consolidation foozles.[24]

Interestingly, the practices in Walker's list and (many) in Bosch's list were and remain legally permissible over a decade on. Moreover, while some may not be intended explicitly by the profession, many are permissible (and some required) under the existing Standards. On pages 26–27 we referred to other professionally endorsed devices not mentioned by Bosch or Walker, which were used by entrepreneurs of the 1980s and beyond to mask the true performance of their entities. All that suggests that the way Argenti was using the label *creative accounting*, while broader in its purview, was not far removed from its earlier 1960s usage, and its usage subsequently in the 1980s and the 1990s. Overall, the dominant theme has been to lump creative accounting in with wilful deceit and intention to mislead. Our feral accounting differentiates the two.

Creative accounting – compliant, rather than deviant

There is not much on the mechanics of creative accounting from Griffiths, Jameson, Bosch or Walker with which to disagree, other than a pervading overtone that it always is with the intent to deceive, mislead, cajole or trick. No doubt much of it does have that intent. There is incontestable evidence in support of that judgment from the analyses of many of the practices of companies to be described here. Events surrounding the revelations at Enron, WorldCom, Waste Management, Xerox and the like have led to allegations of fraud. There will always be cheats and tricksters. The obverse is true too. There will always be those who are scrupulously honest, trying to tell it how it is by complying with the rules. Our view is that, perversely, conventional accounting practices frequently frustrate those attempts to tell the financial truth. Whether this results in increased or decreased earnings volatility is not our main concern. The facts should be disclosed to all those operating in the market.

Contrary to the popular view, we hold that compliance with the so-called *spirit* of many conventional practices and endorsed Standards produces grossly misleading data, without necessarily any intention to deceive on anybody's part. This is notwithstanding that in respect of physical assets, the Corporations Act requires directors to 'take reasonable steps to find out whether the value of any non-current asset [does not exceed an] amount that would be reasonable for the company to spend to acquire the asset as at the end of the financial year'. Also, Accounting Standard AASB 1010, *Accounting for the Revaluation of Non-Current Assets*, prohibits directors from reporting non-current assets that have been revalued at an amount more than their recoverable amount – i.e. no more than the amounts expected to be recovered from continued use and disposal.[25] Interestingly, neither the law nor the profession's Standards prohibit either accidental or deliberate understatement of the worth of assets. Yet understatements are equally misleading as overstatements.

Over the decades of boom and bust during which the corporate crises discussed here occurred, misleading data in published financial statements has been a pervading characteristic. In the boom period of the late 1990s *earnings management* – the manipulation or favourable interpretations of the Accounting Standards to achieve desired performance targets – became a dominant feature of corporate activity. In keying executive remunerations to often short-term performance targets, usually profit targets likely as not increasing shareholder wealth, conventional accounting has been a convenient ally. Accounting alchemy that turns losses and bad news into good news has reached new heights.[26] Averting and diverting bad news (albeit for a short period) through *pro forma earnings statements* that rename catch-up adjustments relating to asset write-downs as *one-off* losses have become an art form.

The underlying idea has been to convince shareholders, analysts and the public at large that the only financial outcome they should be concerned with is that relating to the company's *core* business. They are being encouraged by the rhetoric and metaphors used to ignore the big hits on the bottom line to take into account shortfalls in previous charges for depreciation, the un-capitalising of expenses previously capitalised and carried as assets, writing off the costs of investments in failed or failing projects and the like. *Earnings before the bad stuff* is being promoted as the datum of significance. Thus, when in accord with current accounting rules, News Corp initially wrote US$7.4 billion off its assets (mainly its Gemstar Investment) in 2002, after an otherwise acceptable 'core' result, its share price rose. NAB's $4 billion 2002 write-down of its US Homeside investment, in accord with the rules, likewise was soon expunged from the memory of the financial press – *mea culpa* in respect of accounting adjustments has the appearance of virtue for its exponents, rather than injecting an awareness of the inherent defects in the conventional system.

In that respect, little is different now from the outcomes in the earlier periods in the annals of finance. A peculiarity of the brouhaha surrounding corporate failures is that many of the companies in the early 1990s that reported losses appeared to have fared reasonably well during the post-October 1987 reporting periods, at least so according to conventional accounting. However, in the early 1990s these good performances were reversed through subsequent extraordinary and abnormal asset value write-offs.[27] Write-offs are warmly received – as 'one-offs'. It seems nobody should be overly concerned.

The impact of abnormals and extraordinaries continued in 1992–93; in respect of companies reporting in the half year to December 1992:

> The profit performance of the *Top 500* was buoyed by a second successive half year of lower abnormal and extraordinary losses … from $1.4 billion to $879 million … abnormal losses two years ago was $2.96 billion.[28]

Many over this period had their conventionally calculated *operating* results pruned by asset write-offs. In the 18-month period ending March 1991, for example, 'a total of nearly $6.2 billion was written off the net assets of the companies concerned'.[29] Bond Corporation was a case in point. Its reported 1988–89 loss of $980 million included a $453.4 million write-off of a 'future income tax benefit' (FITB). The accounts had been injected with this item in compliance with the prescribed professional Accounting Standard on tax accounting AAS 3. Tooth & Co's 1990–91 $95 million operating loss was increased by a $625 million abnormal loss, including a $46.6 million deferred tax benefit write-off.

Tax effect adjustments featured prominently. Write-downs have been common. Adsteam had built up substantial FITBs by the early 1990s which were the subject of litigation (details in Chapter 11). In another instance, TNT wrote off $76 million as part of a reported 1992–93 loss of $133.7 million. As with the Bond Corporation's 1989 FITB write-down, it was not so much that the benefits in question had been lost as that they never existed in the first place.

Westpac's 1992 first-half-year results reveal that directors had decided to revise the provisioning policy on its portfolio of commercial property and property-related loans. The $2.6 billion write-off produced a $2.3 billion before-tax and $1.67 billion after-tax loss – at that time, in absolute terms, the fourth largest reported corporate 'loss' in the annals of corporate Australia. Westpac's rationale, according to the managing director, was to make public what was already 'well known'.[30]

A decade later the reported comments of Rupert Murdoch following the investment write-offs of US$7.4 billion from News Corp and AOL Time Warner's almost US$100 billion in 2002 suggest that accounting history repeats itself. Understandably so, for despite the rhetoric of change, nothing really has changed. While News Corp's share price had declined considerably in the period prior to the announcement, whether the full extent of the loss was known is arguable and, if it was 'well known', why were the write-offs not made earlier? Expressions of surprise and bewilderment following the announcement of the size of those write-downs invites the inference that the positions of Westpac, AOL and News Corp were not as generally well known by the financial press as suggested. In respect of Westpac, it could be seen in reactions of market participants evident in the post-announcement stock price declines (albeit relatively minor) in the United Kingdom and Australia, and the decision by rating agencies to reassess Westpac. Recall that, in contrast, AOL's and News Corp's share prices rose. That reinforces the view that the all-wise market, influenced by the financial cognoscenti, was long on rhetoric but caught rather short on performance.

Most 'depreciation' accounting mechanisms attempt to simulate what is easily observed from the market. Simulation is unnecessary. It is inexplicable why simulations are prescribed, why there should not first be recourse to the potentially more objective selling price indicators. Underpinning those mechanisms is the conventional accounting dictum that depreciation is the 'allocation of the cost of an asset over its useful life'. But outside the accounting sophistry, for most depreciation is no such thing.

Depreciation (*de pretium*) is the decrease in the asset's price, not the allocation of a cost, as the conventional accounting rationale would have it. Amounts injected into the accounts for depreciation are more than often wide of the mark. Long after the event that fact becomes obvious. Consider the gains and losses on the sale of fixed assets habitually reported previously as extra-ordinary items.[31] At that time extraordinary and abnormal items respectively were a major adjusting mechanism in the accounts.[32]

Adjustments such as those occur on much the same scale year after year. They are questionable enough to indicate the unreliability of the results of the previous years and the annual representations of the companies' financial positions. True to form, the disastrous outcomes of the write-downs and the publicity they received (Westpac's 1992 humiliation, and NAB's and News Corp's 2002 debacle are good examples) initiate mainly *ad hoc*, knee-jerk reactions from the accountancy profession's Standards-setters. Under the revised prescription in AASB 1018, extraordinary and abnormal items must be included above the line. What good that is likely to do is far from clear. It certainly will not change the critical character of the incorrect data being adjustments to whatever had been reported in previous years. In any event, those adjustments were all too late to influence the decisions taken in the meantime and nothing has really changed under AASB 1018. At least by being below the line, as they were prior to AASB 1018, they were automatically highlighted.

Whereas their positioning might have encouraged readers not to treat them as part of the ordinary scheme of things, the *one-off, significant, non-recurring, special* labels and the advent of 'pro-forma earnings statements' and the subterfuge in which they are engaged positively direct that they be ignored. Whereas some analysts have raised doubts about the new practice in AASB 1018,[33] for the most part the trend to avoid the bad stuff gains ground.

All that stands in stark contrast with the new nomenclature introduced in 2000 and 2001 respectively, through AASB 1018 and AASB 1040. *Profit and Loss Account* and *Balance Sheet* have been replaced by a *Statement of Financial Performance* and *Statement of Financial Position*. This has been a move almost devoid of any changes in the contents of the statements that will make either the former more indicative of the change in the wealth and progress of the company, or the latter any more indicative of the nature, composition and current money's worth of its assets or the amount of its liabilities.

The new labels create the illusion that the compulsory statements have greater financial credibility than the previous profit and loss accounts and balance sheets, are more relevant to assessing a company's wealth and progress than before the rebadging, contain greater reliability, are more comparable on both a static and temporal basis than before, and are consequently more understandable. Curiously, though consistent with the past performance of the Standards-setters, neither *financial performance* nor *financial position* is defined, other than to indicate that while the label has changed, the content has not.

No doubt the objective is to restrict flexibility in the manner in which catch-up adjustments are dealt with in calculating profits and losses. However, para-doxically, such fiddling with the previously reported results may be even less obvious now than it was under the old regime. Consider the position prior to the introduction of the new regime. Abnormal adjustments in the 1995 reporting season illustrate the state of play leading up to the change. Under the caption 'The great profit recovery', the *Australian Financial Review* (*AFR*) reported that a huge turnaround in 1995 corporate profits – five times 1994 results – 'was obscured in bottom-line earnings, which were hit by a big rise in abnormal losses … more than a billion dollars in abnormal write-offs' in the com-panies surveyed by the *AFR* and the ASX.[34] Big, abnormal write-offs at that time included BHP ($318 million), MIM ($224.4 million), Gold Mines of Kalgoorlie ($334.9 million), Adelaide Brighton ($455.8 million), and Good-man Fielder's net $150 million abnormal loss caused by writing down goodwill on its European and Australian poultry operations. AWA Ltd reported abnormal losses amounting to $26.2 million, half of which related to Research and Development.[35] Also noted were the consequential distortions in respect of pre-vious years' accounts.

Perhaps ironically, as in 1977, BHP's 1996 profit report would again grab the financial headlines: 'BHP slumps 20 pc to $1.29 bn'. The commentary continued, citing a $222 abnormal million write-off from its Newcastle blast furnace, probably leaving a balance around zero.[36] The hoary valuation issue and its relation to earnings management had surfaced again.

The only way to fix the problem is to remove the cause (in many cases, the delayed reporting of movements in the market selling prices of companies' physical assets) by bringing to account universally changes in selling prices as they arise. This is a theme pursued throughout this book and discussed in detail in Chapter 17 within a group accounting context. Of primary concern are the obvious defects in the asset valuation mechanism in the current package of Standard practices.

Valuation problems in Australia with AASB 1010 were well aired.[37] Now the AASB 1041 prescription provides the option – value non-current (physical long-lived) assets at their 'fair value' (what amounts to their current selling price) or at cost (subject to the 'recoverable amount' limitation). Central to the physical asset valuation problem is the muddled reasoning underlying AASB 1010's prescription that long-lived physical assets be 'valued' at amounts not exceeding their 'recoverable amount' – the amount expected to be recovered through the net cash inflows arising from their continued use and subsequent disposal (AASB 1010, para. 13). Ordinarily the prevailing situation would have to be that an asset's 'recoverable amount' calculated in that fashion would have to exceed its current selling price. If it did not, management would sell it to optimise the return. And it would have to exceed the asset's current replacement price too, for if it did not, management would sell the asset and replace it at a lower cost. Everything we know of price theory tells us that an excess of the selling prices of such assets over their current replacement prices cannot prevail in existing imperfect markets. So whereas current assets are to be valued at the 'lower of cost and net realisable value', non-current assets are to be valued at either the 'lower of cost and recoverable amount' or at 'net realisable value'. The upper basis for current assets is potentially lower than that for non-current assets.

Two things flow from that. First, cash inflows and outflows are anticipatory, imaginary. And if AASB 1010 is to be taken to imply that they are to be discounted (a point still in dispute), they must be considered even more problematic. Second, the anticipated cash inflows and outflows or the net present (discounted?) value thereof (for which current replacement price is commonly regarded a surrogate) must ordinarily be greater than the asset's immediate cash value. So, compliance with AASB 1010 almost certainly will result in long-lived physical assets being stated at amounts which are not serviceable for determining a company's current capacity to meet its debts. Yet recent Australian inquiries at HIH and Water Wheel, inter alia, show that solvency is a critical and legislatively prescribed financial indicator that one might imagine every investor would want to have access to. Curiously, the central issue in the recent debate on AASB 1010 (that led to AASB 1041) appears to be whether the calculation of 'recoverable amount' entails discounting anticipated future income streams. Some experts tell us that surely it does, and the debate has proceeded as if net present values (NPVs) actually exist, as if they are hard data. But no company *has* the NPV of its expected future income streams. Companies (or their managements) have hopes, expectations to be sure, some of them very well founded and many equally not, but they never have the NPV *per se*. NPVs are pure fiction, mere calculations based upon what is *thought*, not what *is*, no matter how well intended, no matter how much integrity is possessed by those who do the thinking. In a true financial accountability sense, they are *non-data*. This is illustrated aptly by Enron's experience with the valuation of its energy contracts using the derivative 'mark-to-model' basis.[38] Notwithstanding, discounting has become a feature of recent Australian Standards – for example, in lease accounting (AASB 1008), debt defeasance (AASB 1014), general insurers (AASB 1023), superannuation funds (AAS 25) and life insurers (AASB 1038).

Those examples are typical. They disclose how the Standards work quite contrary to the fundamental purpose they are intended to serve, almost certainly producing misleading data even where there are best of intentions on the part of the preparers. If the data are reliable, and serviceable in calculating the usual financial indicators, it is more by accident than design. Consider the impossibility of calculating periodic profits and losses with the injection of such data. Consider too the nature of solvency assessments, calculations of debt to equity, asset backing, and the like. How can such subjectively based data, and non-data, lead to a reasonably reliable indication of the financial position of the enterprise – data integral to all the above financial indicators – at any particular time? It cannot, never could and never will.

It is sobering to reflect that many data of the net present value genre arise *not* from the manipulation of the prescribed Accounting Standards, but from compliance with them. Yet, as noted in the 1978 Accounting Standards Review Committee's Report, departure from the prescribed Accounting Standards has been targeted as the root *modus operandi* of creative accounting (see also fn. 10, ch 1). Much of the rhetoric about creative accounting has been misplaced. Departure from the Standards is, as often as not, the only way to produce data likely to accord with the financial facts.

Directors of an Australian company are between a 'sword and the wall' – 'a rock and a hard place'. Under the Corporations Act they are required to ensure that the published profit and loss account and balance sheet comply with the AAS and AASB Accounting Standards *and* portray a true and fair view of their company's results for the period and its state of affairs. They also have to give a 'solvency statement' – whether the company is (in their opinion) able to pay its debts as they fall due. Even so, this is a confusing setting, for under the Corporations Act a company has to keep such accounts and records as will 'explain its transactions ... and financial position'. Nowhere is it explained what the difference is between the 'state of affairs' on which the directors have to report and the 'financial position' which has to be explicable by the accounting records. All this is to be achieved against a background of the profession's dictum that complying with the Accounting Standards will achieve those ends and the empirical evidence revealed in chs 3–15, for example, that arguably it will not. Directors are further required to declare if their assessment is that the accounts do not disclose the true position of the company. There are few such declarations. But when one does occur, usually the recalcitrant company is persuaded in future to conform to the Standards. Auditors are in an invidious situation as well. They also are to report whether the accounts conform to the Accounting Standards and show a true and fair view of the same matters on which the directors are to report and the accounting records are required to explain. It is a curious arrangement. For, arguably the pre-1992 override that the accounts had to conform to the Standards, subject to them showing a true and fair view, has been removed from the law as a first order imperative. At least many have thought this to be so. Company directors are on a hiding to nothing when it comes to trusting their reputations to the accounting statements for which they are responsible. Recently several leading accountants and lawyers have questioned this downgrading of the override.[39] It is in this curious context that auditors are on a mission impossible!

The actions of directors in the early 1990s were instructive. In 1992 the actions of directors of QBE and NRMA in publishing two sets of statements, one complying with the Standards and the other not complying but declaring to show a true and fair view, were on the right track, though we would argue for the wrong reasons. Their objections were against the outcome of reporting the adjustments from the mark-to-market mechanisms prescribed in AASB 1023. Those deviations from the Standards are rare instances.

Advocacy of marking-to-market is one instance where we would argue the Standards-setters are on the right track. But the motives of the directors of QBE and NRMA are to be applauded. Despite our disagreement with their reasoning, the directors had followed the historically valid pursuit of informing the public at large of what they perceived to be the true and fair view of their companies' wealth and progress. As a matter of professional judgment they rejected the Standard prescriptions, which they believed failed to disclose it.

Compliance, for instance, with AASBs 1018–1021 cannot (except by accident) produce data which are serviceable for the purposes stated above, for none is directed towards producing data indicative of the measurement of actual amounts of money or its equivalent. Compliance with AASB 1008, AASB 1009, AASB 1010, AASB 1011, AASB 1013, AASB 1015, AASB 1018, AASB 1022 and AASB 1041 facilitate money *spent* being treated as if it were still in possession – the ultimate in the counterfactual.

For a 'self-sustaining' foreign operation, AASB 1003 prescribes converting (translating) past prices, money spent and no longer in possession, by applying the current price of the domestic currency for a foreign currency, as if everything in the foreign operation's accounts represented actual money or its equivalent. For 'integrated' foreign entities, exchange rates applicable at the time of the transactions are to be applied. Net outcomes from the former do not hit the calculation of income; they are to be excluded, whereas outcomes from the latter are to be included. AASB 1003 thereby promotes the absurdity that the prices for foreign currency can be applied to convert any number in accounts, but some of the gains and losses thereby calculated are to be accounted for as real gains and losses and others not – the ultimate in asymmetry.

How a convincing defence could be mounted that the financial data from using those Accounting Standards are generally serviceable to assess the vital financial characteristics of companies is beyond comprehension. Equally perplexing is the current push for more Accounting Standards of the kind already failing to measure up. Instead of producing a perceived improvement in the quality of accounting data, the increase in the number of Standards is correlated positively with increased complaint, criticism, bewilderment, frustration, disbelief and, ultimately, increased litigation.

Large adjustments to asset balances to approximate their current worths divorced annual income calculation and the inferences to be drawn from the related balance sheet data from meaningful representations of a company's financial progress and its wealth. Consider the write-offs from the recorded amounts of physical assets. Consider too the extraordinary and abnormal adjustments to which we have referred. Two matters are sobering. It is most unlikely, virtually impossible, that the entire changes in the worth of those assets occurred only over the year immediately prior to the write-offs. Failure to mark assets to market progressively has meant that successive financial positions are distorted, profits of earlier years are overstated (or losses understated), and balance sheets could not possibly have been reliable indicators of the company's periodic progress and wealth. Second, many of the write-downs appear to be approximations of current selling prices and most of the extraordinary items are adjustments to selling prices. One must wonder why accountants, and regulators seemingly, have no qualms in accepting selling prices as the relevant valuation bases for determining those companies' financial positions when they are in trouble, but not so enthusiastically in the ordinary course of events when they are perceived to be travelling well.[40]

Scope for manipulating results legally is indicated by the response to the Australian government's changes to the tax rates (for example, the public company rate from 33 to 36 per cent, to the current 30 per cent). As tax effect balances increased and decreased in accord with the rate changes, counterintuitively, balance sheets could appear 'better' with a tax rate hike and 'worse' with a tax rate reduction. Immediately there is talk of increasing or decreasing stock valuations, delaying or advancing asset write-offs, increasing or reducing the depreciation rate to shift profits into the new tax regime currently in force, and delaying or advancing inducing the losses until the new rate regime commences – each apparently legal, each within the Standards mechanisms and each virtually impossible to forbid. They exploit the rubbery rules of thumb and speculations built into the Standards.

Possibly the limited and non-systematic recourse to selling price data by regulators and others can be explained through a crisis theory scenario. Some Australian instances are instructive. In 1979 anguish was expressed that Ansett Ltd was withdrawing support for its 49 per cent associated company Associated Securities Limited, which was in financial difficulty due to its overexposure to property and property-related loans. Immediately regulatory changes required the provision of market price data for land contained in prospectuses. Early in 1988, following the October 1987 stock market crash, NCSC Release 135 urged fuller disclosure of the basis of current valuations of assets in prospectuses, annual reports and expert reports. Similarly, the NCSC acted to require all listed companies to provide market price information on listed investments. A spate of asset write-downs and explanations resulted. Yet, it was suggested that 'in the midst of the [early 1990s] recession many listed companies are carrying properties on their balance sheets at figures far in excess of their current resale value'.[41] Also it is clear some were then and still are carrying properties at well below their current resale price. This is equally misleading, understates asset-backing, borrowing capacity, the denominator in the rate of return calculation, and the like. We might spare a thought for those who buy and sell shares under those conditions. Secret reserves, the *sine qua non* of the UK's Royal Mail saga (see Chapter 16) 70-odd years ago, are almost certainly alive and well, albeit under a new guise. Continuing the international scope in the 1990s, the tale of Sumitomo Corporation's 1996 copper losses is apposite. In announcing those losses, Sumitomo was able to disclose that they would be offset by the equivalent of over $4 billion in secret reserves. Generally, for banks around the world inadequate bad loan provisioning policies in the late 1990s and beyond, facilitated secret reserves – creativity at its professionally endorsed best.

Accounting's role in analyses of corporate collapse has in the main been brushed aside. Those failures and the accounting relied upon prior to each collapse deserve closer attention to illustrate the points raised to date. Importantly, what need noting are the myriad earnings possibilities seemingly available, a feature which has led commentators to calculate that there are millions of potential income (earnings, numbers) possible under GAAP – and these are dictated by management without any external corroboration. The possibility of unravelling the earnings permutations is nigh impossible – confirming that the efficient marketers' claim of being able to unbundle accounting numbers has been found wanting – again!

Everyone needs to *mind-the-GAAP*!

Happier times. Stanley Korman (left) and Conrad Hilton at Hawaiian Village Hotel to mark the signing of the momentous agreement between the Australian and US tourist industries, through Conrad Hilton representing the world organisation Hilton International and Stanley Korman, head of Stanhill-Chevron Group of Tourism Industry in Australia. Courtesy of News Ltd.

Stanley Korman outside Melbourne City Court. Courtesy of News Ltd.

H.G. Palmer on big
game fishing boat.
14 April 1963.
Courtesy of John
Fairfax Holdings Ltd.

Headline and photos of
Reid Murray directors,
upon release of the
*Inspector's Interim
Report into the Affairs
of the Reid Murray
Group. Sydney
Morning Herald*,
4 December 1963.
Courtesy of John
Fairfax Holding Ltd.

GROUP FIGURES

MR O. J. O'GRADY   K. N. WILKINSON   MR R. REID   MR M. E. BATES

PART II

The 1960s

CHAPTER 3

The Corporate 1960s: Dubious Credit and Tangled Webs

A true and fair view of the financial state of affairs of an entity?
An impossible dream or commercial imperative?

Conventionally prepared Statements of Financial Performance and Financial Position do not 'tell it as it is'. Nor will they until the professionally endorsed accounting practices *comprehensively* and *continuously* incorporate current market prices and periodic changes in them to report companies' financial positions and calculate their profits and losses.[1] Nearly 40 years ago the fundamental error of not doing that, irrespective of deliberate deceit, was aptly illustrated (Table 3.1) in the affairs of New Investments, Latec Investments, Cox Brothers, Stanhill Development Finance, Reid Murray Holdings and H.G. Palmer (Consolidated) Ltd.

Conventional practice of the time was exposed for ignoring the movements in the market worth of investments, resting upon the contractual amount of debts despite the decrease in the worth of the related hire-purchase assets and, indeed, concerns about the collectability of the debts *per se*. In many instances these were hidden behind the fictional artifacts of consolidation accounting, aggregating the moneys spent to acquire land and develop it to invent its value, in contradiction of the evidence of its contemporary market price, and the general overall failure to match up and reconcile the derived outcome of accounting procedures with evidence of the market worth of physical assets. The outcomes were exacerbated losses for investors, prosecution and, in a few instances, gaol for company officers. In retrospect it is fair to suggest that perhaps a very fine line existed between deceit on the part of many corporate officers and their being bamboozled, misled or seduced by the accounting data.

In respect of the veracity of information in published financial statements, virtually nothing has changed. The proliferation of endorsed Accounting Standards since has created a false climate of security. The current Standards have done no more than plug holes and eject idiosyncratic practices from the scene. They have not eliminated the generic problems. Nor have they created a system providing financial data that will disclose the wealth and progress of firms with any greater certainty than in the past.

Table 3.1 Major company failures in Australia, 1961–65

Year of failure – date administrator appointed	Name of company	Basis of criticism	Actions against auditors/ officials
November 1961	New Investments *et al.*	Failure to write off investments in associates which had been trading at a loss.	n.a.
September 1962	Latec Investments	(i) Inadequate debtors provisioning; and (ii) Unearned income on debts.	n.a.
December 1962	Stanhill Development Finance	(i) Consolidation practices; (ii) Intermingling of private and public companies; and (iii) Valuation of land and shares.	Stanley Korman gaoled for six months.
April 1963	Reid Murray Holdings/ Reid Murray Acceptance	(i) Consolidation practices; (ii) Valuation of debtors; (iii) Treatment of unearned income – judicious use of Rule of 78; and (iv) Intermingling of private and public company interests.	Directors O'Grady, Wilkinson and Wolstenholme were fined £400 each; L.A. Borg, director of Paynes Properties, gaoled for nine years.
October 1965	H.G. Palmer (Consolidated) Ltd	(i) Omitting material particulars in the profit statement in a prospectus; (ii) Valuation of debtors; and (iii) Treatment of unearned income.	$1 million civil action settlement. Herbert Palmer gaoled for four years, auditor J. McBlane for three years.

Source: Expanded version of Table 7.1 From A.T. Craswell, *Auditing* (New York: Garland Publishing Inc., 1984).

Following the 1960s, the professional bodies and regulators claimed to have tightened the rules governing accounting practices, supported by an impression of frenetic activity within due process to develop useful Standards. Inquiries into the failure of accounting data to disclose the financial positions and financial performances of the likes of HIH, One.Tel, Enron, WorldCom, for example, and the frequency of actual or implied earnings restatements expose the survival of those generic defects in the system. Accounting 'reform' emerges as little more than a seductive window-dressing.

Table 3.1 lists some of the criticisms of inspectors and the actions against auditors and company officers in respect of those major 1960s failures. An ineffective response by the accounting profession in respect of the issues of measurement and asset valuation exposed by the 1960s' accounting practices is instructive for our analysis of the pattern of events to unfold in the 1970s, 1980s and post-2000.

Professional response – *sotto voce!*

There was some response, yes, but more *sotto* than *voce*!

Fallout from those 1960s collapses was far-reaching. The Australian accounting profession was struggling to attain a professional image. Professional rule-making by accountants was in its infancy. Birkett and Walker captured the extensive 1950s debate on whether the existing role of the profession needed strengthening, its general 'confusion' and the concentration on 'form rather than substance'. They noted:

> The response of *The Accountant* to dicta of Mr Justice Vaisey in the [UK] *Press Caps* case received considerable notice and approval. The judge had said:
> ... the market value of a share quoted on the stock exchange is seriously
> affected by the balance sheets, which are available for inspection. If you find
> such an undervaluation of a most important asset, of no less than £60,000,
> I should have thought that threw a great deal of doubt on the sufficiency of
> the balance sheet as an estimate of value, and also threw doubt on the market
> price of the shares...[2]

By 1959 the Australian accounting profession had firmed up its position. Recommendations on accounting practices had increased, and clearly more directives were on the way. Whether to enforce those practices had been left unresolved. Then the company failures in the early 1960s redirected attention to the role of the professional accountancy bodies. Birkett and Walker recount a public perception of the inadequacy of the existing position that emerged in the financial press:

Yesterday ['Black Thursday', 12 December 1963] was one of the darkest days in Australia's financial history. Six public companies, including three in the [Stanley Korman] Australian Factors group, revealed losses totalling more than [$7.2 million]. (*AFR*, 13 December 1963)

Latec revealed further losses of $4.6 million. Chevron Sydney Ltd reported further losses of $1 million. The Australian Factors group losses were $1 million. Neon Signs (Australasia) Ltd disclosed a loss of $0.5 million – six weeks after the company's chairman had indicated that he expected a small profit. (*AFR*, 30 October 1963)

[Thus] ... public criticism began to be directed at the accounting profession. Some criticisms were cautiously expressed:

One point that does emerge clearly from these results is that several companies concerned have very misleading statements of profits in the previous year's accounts and in interim statements last year. (*AFR*, 22 January 1963)

Others were more extravagant:

... there must have been collusion between directors, accountants and auditors to what amounts to fraud.

An academic was reported as describing all investment as 'gambling' in 'state of affairs'. 'No accountant or skilled investment dealer (and therefore investor) could tell from present balance sheets whether they represented the facts *per se* or the method of presentation'. (*AFR*, 19 March 1963)

Stock exchange officials claimed that 'poor accounting ... brought about these situations'. (*AFR*, 22 January 1963)

A financial journalist stated that '"a ready acceptance of responsibility to the community" has been lacking in too many accounting places in the recent period of company distresses.' (J.C. Horsfall, *The Bulletin*, 27 July 1963)[3]

Disturbingly, each of those comments is apt in respect of post-2000 events. Following protracted debate, the profession commissioned an official inquiry. A portent of all subsequent professional inquiries followed. 'Bad management' and 'non-compliance with recommended and approved accounting practices' attracted considerable blame for the 1960s corporate failures in the resulting report, *Accounting Principles and Practices Discussed in Reports on Company Failures* (1966). More official prescription of accounting procedures formulated under due process and compulsory compliance with them was the proposed remedy. While the report recommended some incremental change, with few exceptions the fundamental structure and tenets of conventional accounting were left untouched – the remedy was to educate the public on the limitations of accounts as an information source. It was an old response.

In the United States in the 1930s, George O. May, a spokesperson for the profession, had first used the 'limitation of accounts' defence. It would be recycled in the responses to unexpected failures of the 1980s and beyond, but then other scapegoats would be sought.

Comments in the financial press in the aftermath of the 1960s boom–bust cycle suggested a widespread malaise in business practice in general and in accounting in particular. It is debatable whether the post-1980s public criticisms of accounting exceeded those in the 1960s and 1970s.[4] Many well-known companies unexpectedly collapsed in those earlier decades with drama, trauma, individual hardship for investors and creditors, and immense legal problems for their directors and auditors. Forty years on, the comments are identical, the perceived problems identical, and sadly the proposed remedies also identical. Virtually nothing of substance has changed.

While losses to the 1960s investors may initially appear small, they were substantial in context and are actually very large in today's dollars. One million dollars in 1960 equates to approximately $11 million in 2002 general purchasing power terms and much more in relative Gross Domestic Product terms. Understandably, then, the level of outrage, the cry for someone's blood, was as strong following those earlier episodes as it is now. Then, also as now, scapegoats had to be found. Blame had to be sheeted home. Although the causes of corporate collapse are varied, there is general agreement that internal rather than external factors are the more significant. Hence, it is not surprising to hear the suggestion repeatedly that 'bad management' is the *primary cause* of the majority of company failures.[5] But this is a limp explanation. The concept is nebulous, capable of such wide a definition as encompasses any and all the defects of failed companies, as are some other more recent alleged causes such as low corporate morality (see Chapter 19).

Surprisingly, the role of accounting has often been ignored and its significance generally denied.[6] Modern exceptions were a 1990 report by the Australian Bankers Association and Chambers' 1991 questioning of that role and the ethics of the profession refusing to acknowledge it.[7] This error applied equally in the 1960s as in the 1980s. When the opportunity came for the profession to examine accounting's role, the 1966 *Report of the General Council of the Australian Society of Accountants* virtually exonerated accounting – characteristically, management (or the lack of it) was identified as the main culprit:

Criticism of Accounting Principles Generally

General Council is aware that some members of the profession have expressed the view that accounting reports prepared on the basis of 'generally accepted accounting principles' do not provide the data which company management, shareholders, investors and creditors need if they are to make informed decisions.

... it therefore proposes that a research group and the new Accounting Research Foundation be asked to investigate and report on these wider issues.

Criticism of Financial and Management Policies

Much of the criticism levelled at the companies under investigation appears to be related not to accounting principles, but to financial policies and apparent deficiencies in management.[8]

The General Council proposed several remedial actions:

- formulation, promulgation and regular review of accounting principles by the professional bodies;
- continued adherence to generally accepted accounting principles on the part of members of the profession;
- audit of accounts required review in the areas of: (i) the responsibilities of auditors, (ii) the independence of the auditor, and (iii) the audit of the accounts of subsidiary or related companies;
- the need for reconsideration of the relationship between the management and the accountant; and
- general questioning of the adequacy, form and content of published financial statements.

The General Council concluded there was little evidence that accounting played any fundamental role in company collapses. Hence, there was no need for any fundamental change to the conventional cost-based accounting practices. Inevitably the General Council's reforms mainly comprised more accounting prescriptions, administrative changes to the manner in which they were determined, and only an *ad hoc* tinkering with the historical cost-based system of accounting. Substantive changes aimed at shifting the attention from cost to market-price information, although recognised by some members of the profession as being needed, were not considered by the General Council as worthy of immediate action: 'Unless and until a sound basis is established which has the force of law, it can be expected that some companies will use the present somewhat unsatisfactory system in doubtful ways – and still remain technically within the law.'[9] It is here that there is room for debate. In this and later chapters we explore this aspect in the light of the profession's ineffectual response to company failures over the past four decades and the fact that since the early 1990s in Australia, Accounting Standards have had the force of law.

Those crashes highlighted the need for fundamental changes to the way accounting is practised: 'Piece-meal patching will not make a worm-eaten craft seaworthy; neither will the piece-meal tinkering of individuals, boards and committees make cost-based valuations trustworthy.'[10] Nevertheless, the substance of that has fallen on deaf ears, for whereas the promulgated Standards that have emerged *may* have reduced diversity through compulsory compliance rules, arguably the 'permissiveness' has increased!

Despite the 1966 ASA Committee Report having noted that the 'present system is somewhat unsatisfactory', inertia has reigned supreme. Some members of the profession had argued that accounting reports could only become meaningful to users were they to be based on current market values or their equivalent, but to little effect. For nearly 40 years, virtually nothing *systematic* has been done by the profession to require its members to provide for the general disclosure of contemporary market prices of assets.

Despite all the evidence of its defects, the accounting profession remains wedded to variants of historical cost accounting, in essence, taking into account the prices encountered in transactions when they occurred in the past and ignoring changes in the selling prices until assets are disposed of. In the interregnum there have been limited modifications incorporating market prices in Australia and elsewhere – the introduction of the mark-to-market approach in some Australian Accounting Standards (for example, on a voluntary basis in AASB 1041) and recourse to valuing fixed assets at recoverable amounts (if the cost basis is retrained under AASB 1041), as well as comparable national and international Accounting Standards.

Window-dressing remains the pervading philosophy of Accounting Standards-setting. Re-badging the profit and loss account and the balance sheet as the Statement of Financial Performance and Statement of Financial Position (in AASB 1018 and AASB 1040, respectively) are salient examples. The profession has never revoked its utterance in UK Recommendation XV that *a balance sheet is not a statement of current worth*, but now announces that a Statement of Financial Position is what previously was 'in a balance sheet'. Thus, according to AASB 1040, a Statement of Financial Position is not an indication of the nature, composition and money's worth of a company's assets or necessarily indicative of its liabilities, or of the components of its shareholders' equity. On that score, clearly a Statement of Financial Performance cannot disclose financial performance in any meaningful monetary manner either. It is inconceivable that anyone outside of accounting could possibly hold an understanding of financial position or financial performance, consistent with how the Accounting Standards are representing them.

Professional intransigence on the general issue of marking-to-market is clearly evident in our explanations of selected corporate crashes in the 1960s, 1970s, 1980s, 1990s and post-2000. First, we consider the *causes célèbres* of the 1960s: the rise and fall of the large retail chain Reid Murray, augmented by a summary of some aspects of the financial effects of Stanley Korman's spinning of public and private corporate webs over Sydney Guarantee and Stanhill Consolidated; and, finally, the sorry saga of electrical and whitegoods supplier, the House of Palmer.

Those events of the 1960s (and the succeeding decades) are instructive for a considered assessment of professional ethics and business techniques, transactions, structures and accounting employed by entrepreneurs of the 1990s and beyond. Fallout covered all sectors of the community, from the financial *cognoscenti* (including the major financial institutions) to the smallest of investors. The government-imposed credit squeeze in 1960 had an impact on all industries, the greatest impact possibly being on the finance and property sectors. It was a new corporate setting for the post-war baby boomers.

CHAPTER 4

Reid Murray:
The Archetypal Failure*

The rearrangement of Reid Murray Holdings ... allowed Mr R.C. Borg,
a director of Payne's and later a director of Reid Murray Holdings, so
as to entangle his and his family business affairs with those of the Reid
Murray Group that they became withal partners, and in some cases
competitors, so far as profits are concerned with at any rate.
B.L. Murray and B.J. Shaw (1963)

Reid Murray Holdings Ltd was one of the largest retailers in Australia in the
early 1960s. It was placed in receivership most *unexpectedly* in May 1963.

Its financial *fundamentals* had been either masked by the prevailing accounting practices or otherwise ignored by an investing public whose expectations
had been inflated to unrealistic levels by unusually buoyant economic conditions. The Reid Murray affair is indicative of the potential dilemmas created
when private and public investments and financial interests become entangled.
With over 220 subsidiaries, it illustrates how complex structures and consolidated accounting practices coalesced to cloak the wealth and progress of
the Reid Murray group. In this respect it is an exemplar of many of the other
collapses examined in this volume – a model failure. The number of subsidiaries approximates that employed at HIH and One.Tel, for example.

Karmel and Brunt's *The Structure of the Australian Economy*[1] listed Reid
Murray Holdings (RMH) as the fourth-largest Australian-owned company in
1961, in terms of *consolidated assets*. Only BHP, CSR and ICI were ahead.
It was in the very best of company indeed. However, little separates success
from failure, even for the largest companies and the most fêted of entrepreneurs. Less than three years later, in May 1963, a court order directed the
winding up of the RMH group. Total losses amounted to £23.727 million, a
shortfall of approximately $450 million in equivalent 2002-dollar terms.[2]

RMH had been formed in 1957 by the merger of Robert Reid & Co. Ltd
(RR) with David Murray Holdings Ltd (DMH). The former was a long-
established warehousing and retailing company, with branches in all capital
cities and a chain of cash-order retailers in the southeastern states. Conservatively financed and managed, DMH was the outgrowth of a series of ventures
of Oswald (Ossie) O'Grady. An accountant, O'Grady had entered the cash
order business in South Australia in 1931, extended into retail merchandising
on credit, set up a company listed on the Stock Exchange (to increase potential
sources of funds), acquired other companies and in the mid-1950s sought
to step up its credit-retailing business in other states. DMH was much less

conservatively financed than RR; in October 1957 their debt to equity ratios were 4.2 and 1.7 respectively. Combining RR and DMH consolidated the finances of the group (provided a larger equity base) and enabled debt-financed expansion of the DMH style of trading.

Early in 1958 RMH raised about £1.6 million by issues of registered unsecured notes. Under the Stock Exchange listing rules at the time, these could not be listed. Reid Murray wanted its securities 'in the market', so, in true group enterprise spirit, a related company and ultimately the 'group banker', Reid Murray Acceptance (RMA), was formed. A new issue of RMH shares for cash raised about £600,000 and newly listed RMA commenced business with an issued capital of that amount in June 1958. About that time the 5s shares of RMH were selling at around 10s.

Until mid-1960 RMH engaged in an aggressive takeover programme (Table 4.1). By May 1960 its share price had peaked at about 20s (Figure 4.1). No doubt the market premium made it possible to extend the operations of RMH in this way, for vendors would be acquiring listed shares with a record of appreciation. Inspectors were to note later that inclusion of pre-acquisition profits as part of the annual operating profits of the group was to prove misleading and integral to the continuation of a deceptive reported position of the group.[3] We show in Chapter 13 that nearly 30 years later a similar device was used by the Westmex group to inflate its reported profits. And in the mid-1990s there was a legal and accounting dispute over what constituted approximately the inverse case – the initiation of several gold company takeovers were delayed because of the proposed accounting treatment of goodwill acquired in the takeover documents.[4]

RMA was formed as a subsidiary 'banker' for RMH, it seems, with the objective of financing the hire-purchase business of all RMH subsidiaries. The initial capital of RMA (two tranches totalling £2.5 million) came from RMH purchasing shares in RMA. The public provided the source of these funds, with RMH raising additional equity capital. It was the beginning of a circuitous loop between public and private activities within the Reid Murray group, and the beginning of group enterprise rather than entity action. Effectively, RMA acted as an RMH branch. Decisions of RMA were taken informally by the RMH board. According to its first prospectus offering first mortgage debenture stock, that was the 'chief function' of RMA, though it would seek 'any sound finance business available' outside the group.

'Any' indeed! Between July 1958 and May 1962, RMA issued nine prospectuses for stock issues, raising £43 million of new money (equivalent to approximately $900 million in current terms). The net surplus of 'new money' from those issues and retirements of stock was £3 million for the six months of 1958, £12 million in 1959, £12 million in 1960 and £2 million in 1961.

At its peak late in 1959 and early 1960 the company borrowed £3 million every two months. That success in the capital market was against a background of RMH enjoying a glowing financial press in recognition of its reported outstanding financial performance over those years and the appearance in its accounts of going from financial strength to strength.

The nominal amounts of most of the offerings were £1 million, but the company had reserved the right to retain oversubscriptions. The popularity and oversubscriptions of the issues made it almost obligatory to find some use for the money. Curiously, that may have contributed substantially to the sloppiness of its use. Similarities here are obvious with the capital raisings and their use at H.G. Palmer and Stanhill, described in this and the next chapter. Acquired companies brought into the group were allowed to run themselves, in O'Grady's belief that managers could be relied upon to run their companies efficiently. O'Grady's main concern seemed to be to keep the borrowed money coming in.

The level of capital and hence asset valuation were critical determinants of RMA's capacity to borrow and RMH's ability to invest. The first trust deed (July 1958), subject to Equity Trustees Executors and Agency Co. Limited monitoring, limited RMA borrowings to five times the shareholders' funds of RMA – the booked excess of tangible assets (including hire-purchase and time payment debtors, less unearned income) over all liabilities (including tax and dividend provisions), as shown in the audited accounts. Clearly, the higher the asset valuation, the greater the leverage for borrowing more. RMH guaranteed the stock issue. This too was curious, since RMA provided the principal financing of the group.

The security constituted by the deed depended on the value of the assets of RMA – the value of the assets of RMA depended on the book value of the assets of RMH and its subsidiaries. If RMA defaulted and recourse was made

Table 4.1 Takeovers by Reid Murray Holdings Ltd, 1958–60

Date of taleovers	No. of companies	No. of 5s. shares	Cash paid £
July–Dec. 1958	11	4,611,528	166,348
Jan.–June 1959	9	501,071	342,936
July–Dec. 1959	7	191,431	926,219
Jan.–July 1960	9	1,020,900	509,816
Total	36	6,324,930	
	=	£1,581,232	£1,945,319

Source: B.L. Murray and B.J. Shaw (both QCs), *Interim Report of an Investigation ... into the Affairs of Reid Murray Holdings Limited* (Melbourne: Victorian Government Printer, March 1965).

to the guarantor, the guarantee was dependent on the assets of RMH and those of its subsidiaries, which included RMA.

That Byzantine arrangement meant that the incestuous security was, in fact, no security at all. Also, the loans by RMA to RMH were unsecured. Moreover, the borrowing power constraint could easily be overcome. *Groupthink* and group enterprise action began. This approach retains its popularity today, as evident in the HIH, One.Tel and Enron revelations, and detailed in the CASAC *Corporate Groups, Final Report* (May 2000).

At Reid Murray, companies whose ordinary business was not financing could not lend to finance the purchase of their own shares. But RMA could lend, and could thus increase by a factor of five what it could borrow on the strength of new capital. RMA could issue shares to RMH, which could draw its cheque and pay it to RMA. RMA could then lend the same amount to RMH by return cheque, and then borrow forthwith five times that amount on the market. Facilitating this was resort to a now common commercial device – the cheque round robin – a circuitous routing of cheques through related companies so as to obscure the real source of the payment and legitimise its ultimate destination – often one of the entrepreneur's family companies. This group action exemplifies *groupthink* which is discussed further in Chapters 16 and 17. RMA thus became a notable financing innovator, for this circuitous device was to become almost an art form by the 1980s.[5] That mechanism raised £2 million in December 1959, £0.5 million in May 1960, £1 million in August 1960 and £1 million in February 1961. It was pursued on legal advice – advice which the investigators later thought to be 'misconceived'. But pursued it was, though the trustee's monitoring of this aspect of the deed was questioned. Substantially similar unsecured financing practice and alleged ineffective trustee monitoring was to recur during the 1970s and 1980s.

At the management level, the RMH Board was dominated by its founding chief executive. As the inspectors noted in their 1963 Interim Report: 'There is no doubt in our minds that Mr O'Grady dominated the Board completely, but by and large, it was a Board willing, then anxious, and finally (it would seem) determined, to be dominated by him.'[6] This matter recurs in analyses of corporate collapses, yet there seems to be little learned by trustees, other board members or regulators on this score.

The pattern of the rise and fall of Reid Murray is familiar. Figure 4.1 illustrates RMH's share price history[7] and shows what John Argenti described as a trajectory pattern of 'remarkable ascent and rapid demise' – one of three common failure trajectories he identified. RMH's price movement was fuelled by a frenetic growth-by-acquisition policy before its weaknesses were exposed by the externally imposed November 1960 government credit squeeze that lasted until 1962.

Figure 4.1 Reid Murray Holdings Ltd – share price, March 1958 to April 1963

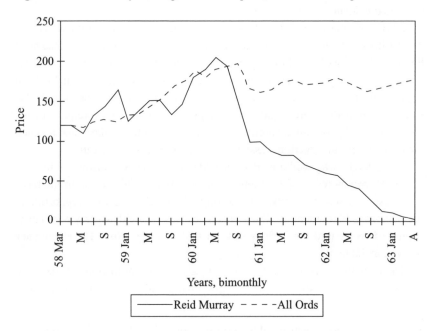

Source: Prices taken from issues of the *Sydney Stock Exchange Gazette.*

In 1959 the group had interests in wholesaling, general retailing, specialty retailing (electrical goods principally), financing and land development. It had diversified into financing land development late in the land boom of the post-war years. By the end of 1960, £7 million was invested in that direction. Diversification was facilitated by the group's capacity to borrow, which in turn was the outcome of the financial esteem it enjoyed, augmented by what the accounts reported. The breadth of that diversification and the credit retailing of consumer durables made the group very sensitive to shifts in economic conditions. Though desperate for liquid funds, RMH's published accounts in the mid-1960s presented a much rosier picture.

Government was already beginning to tighten credit in early 1960 and the business-crunching credit squeeze began with the announcement of Prime Minister Menzies' mini-Budget. That should not have been an outright disaster. Other finance companies, accustomed to regulating their borrowings and repayments in difficult times, seemed to be little affected. But those more adventurous in exploiting asset valuations to increase their apparent debenture trust deed limits, and less discriminating in what they financed, would soon collapse. That exploitation was facilitated by the absence of any requirement for assets to be marked-to-market, a lack of any need for corroboration by externally generated evidence.

RMH had made good use of its bankers and it continued to do so. But in April 1961 the National Bank sought to draw the directors' attention to the need for control over trade creditors, to exercise dividend restraint, and to sell assets or increase equity to reduce borrowing, thereby avoiding any action likely to depress the market price of the company's shares. The National Bank also sought an immediate investigation of the group's affairs on the request of the company's creditors. But apparently the complexity of the group's business and the pressure of other work necessitated abandonment of that inquiry.

The anxiety was well founded as RMH's gearing was always – in conventional, commercial expectations – 'uncomfortably high', even on the basis of its suspect asset valuations. B.L. Murray QC and B.J. Shaw QC, reporting to the Victorian Parliament in 1963 on the causes of Reid Murray's collapse, expressed concern at the parlous state of the group by 1961. Their summary is given in Table 4.2.

Their analysis revealed an exceedingly high proportion of external borrowed funds relative to the group's own funds – £53 million to £13

Table 4.2   Inspector's summary of the 1961 position of Reid Murray Holdings Ltd

Group assets	£	£
Current assets	53,886,811	
Fixed assets	12,348,138	
		66,234,949
Group liabilities		
Debentures and secured borrowings –		
Due within 1 year	4,911,156	
Due after 1 year	28,128,624	
Registered and other deposits –		
Due within 1 year	1,915,707	
Due after 1 year	2,923,758	
Convertible Notes	698	
Amount due in respect of development projects –		
Due within 1 year	823,805	
Due after 1 year	2,507,634	
Bank overdrafts	5,837,647	
Trade creditors, bills payable and accrued liabilities	6,152,057	
		53,202,086

Source: B.J. Shaw, *Final Report of an Investigation ... into the Affairs of Reid Murray Holdings Limited* (Melbourne: Victorian Government Printer, 1966), p. 71.

million. This was exacerbated when the nature of some of the 'group assets' was exposed. The inspectors, for instance, were alarmed by the 'complete lack of reality' shown in the 1961 accounts:

> ... either the published reports and accounts of the group must have been deceptive or inaccurate or that [advisors to invest in Reid Murray] were either incompetent or negligent. We do not think the latter is the case ... We believe that ... the accounts of the group must have fallen short of their supposed objective – namely that of presenting *a true and fair view of the state of affairs* of the group and *the results of its operations*.[8]

They concluded that the defects in RMH's accounts were partly responsible for the collapse. It is interesting to note Murray's and Shaw's observations that the accounts purportedly were to present 'a true and fair view of the state of affairs' of Reid Murray's financial affairs. This tone implies a belief that *that* objective is axiomatic with respect to published financial statements. Nearly 40 years later, arguably that axiom has been ditched (by those responsible for overseeing implementation of Australian legislature) as an essential qualitative criterion applicable to primary financial statements, to provide investor protection (see Chapter 19).[9] Though in the wake of HIH, One.Tel and Harris Scarfe affairs, there is growing pressure for it to be reinstated.

RMH's fourth annual report, dated 31 August 1961, showed a substantial decline in consolidated net profit after tax – from £1,545,340 in 1960 to £895,892. Those 1961 accounts were given a clean audit report, notwithstanding that the auditors were acutely concerned about some features of them.

Later the inspectors were to criticise vehemently the reported results. In general, they were concerned about the overvaluation of land, the improper capitalisation of interest and the understatement of bad debt provisions. Within those categories there were five elements in the accounting without which the reported 1961 result would, according to the inspectors, have been a loss of £67,120:

(a) A change to the use of the Rule of 78 for the calculation of
    unearned income, increased the reported result by   £382,607
(b) A change in the method of calculating rental income of Radio
    Rentals to anticipation of the rental receipts, yielding   £136,016
(c) A change in the method of accounting for the profit on land sales
    by a WA subsidiary, taking 'instant' profits, and yielding   £85,084
(d) a transfer to profit of a trading stock valuation provision
    previously made on the acquisition of a subsidiary   £25,000

(e) An increase in a provision for doubtful debts out of
     reported unappropriated profits (rather than as a charge
     in calculating profits), yielding   £350,000
                                              Total: £979,707

Concern was more than warranted. But it has to be noted that each of the above accounting practices, of themselves, accorded with accepted practice then, and some even today. For example, the Rule of 78 was the accepted method of apportioning interest on term (say, hire-purchase) contracts. This disguised the traditional interpretation of the accounting principle of 'matching' – the idea that the 'revenues' and 'costs' attach to one another in an artificially simulated physical sense. What the market indicated was that the current worth of the physical assets, subject to hire-purchase and the actual receipt by the hirer of interest payments, was taken to be of little consequence. Consolidation accounting practices were also questioned. And justifiably so, for there is considerable evidence that the assumptions and techniques of consolidation accounting are far from conducive to the accumulation of financial data showing the aggregate wealth and progress of related companies. On the contrary, the inherent complexities of consolidated financial statements have been an incorrigible means of deception without any intent to deceive. Arguably, by virtue of their association with corporate group failure, they have exacerbated investor losses.

Forty years later, response to revelations at Enron would rekindle interest worldwide in group accounting issues.

Back to RMH: reporting real estate development projects (£9.6 million) as a current asset (as 'inventories') in the consolidated accounts was seriously questioned by the RMH investigators. That ploy exploited the different valuation rules as they applied to 'fixed' and 'current' assets and the impact of increased closing inventory valuations on the conventional profit and loss calculation. Differential valuation rules remain. If, indeed, all the physical assets were reported on a 'mark-to-market' basis and the changes were brought into the profit calculation, the artificial, financial effect of classification would disappear. The misleading nature of the 1961 report led to the extension of further credit to the group by trade suppliers and to the lending of more money to the group by the public.[10] Critically, capitalisation of interest charges increased the 'book value' of the projects. Recourse to the market at the time would have revealed them as potentially false, though consistent with the 'costs attach' idea, endemic in conventional accounting.

In fact, the last two prospectuses (December 1961 and May 1962) continued to give the impression that the funds of the group were invested in 'comparatively short-term investment, mainly in hire-purchase and instalment debtors', suggesting that the debts were in some sense secured. Even so, often the value of the security (under the tightened conditions) was less than the tangible assets reported. That form of disclosure masked that the bulk of the borrowings of RMA were in fact invested in unsecured debts of other companies in the group (£33 million of the £37 million 'current assets' shown in the accounts of February 1962).

The 1962 accounts of the group were unavailable. In January 1963 the trustees had receivers appointed to RMA. With the acquiescence of the directors of RMH, the affairs of the group were made subject to the receivers of RMA, and on 16 May an order was made appointing liquidators to RMA and RMH. From a high of nearly 20s in May 1960, RMH shares had fallen to 3d by 14 May 1963 and 1d by 31 May. The liquidators recommended another scheme of arrangement which was eventually accepted.

RMH's rapid expansion through exploiting physical asset valuation without regard for other limitations on growth – in this case, especially failing to plan for peak borrowings maturities – was, and continues to be, a generic recipe for failure. With regard to debt, RMA accepted public subscriptions seemingly without discrimination. Apparently there was no plan for repayment of debentures except by further borrowings from the public.[11] Summing up the causes of the company's failure, inspectors Shaw and Murray concluded: 'The simple fact is that the business of the group was badly run. It borrowed without thought and invested without wisdom.'[12] They might equally have added that its accounts never faithfully reported its true financial position.

Borg, a director of a Reid Murray subsidiary, Paynes Properties, was found guilty of fraud and sentenced to nine years' gaol. Importantly, the investigators found no evidence of fraud by other main players. Some directors were fined minor amounts for prospectus offences (see Table 3.1 in Chapter 3). O'Grady was eventually fined the sum of £400 for having made untrue statements in a debenture prospectus dated 9 May 1962 and issued on 30 May 1962. In that prospectus, which raised a total of £920,000 from the public, O'Grady had stated:

> ... profits were lower than for the corresponding [previous] period ... However, reorganisation ... is being successfully carried out, and with an easier economic climate now prevailing, trade and profits should gradually improve ... [Regarding] real estate ... current values are substantially in excess of the book values.[13]

It is worth noting that if the accounts had incorporated the financial effects of the current money's worth (selling prices) of the real estate (and been verified as a matter of course), no such statement need have been made. More importantly, its truth or falsity would have been obvious – public knowledge for all to see and to include in their assessments. But, as accounting stands in 2002, it would be no more obvious now than when O'Grady made the statement. The day after this prospectus was issued, Reid Murray Holdings made its first interest payment default.

A significant feature of this 'still-born' failure depends largely upon how one interprets two pieces of evidence: one a public datum – the company's accounts; the other anecdotal and highly subjective – the personality of O'Grady. Sykes describes Ossie O'Grady as a 'visionary',[14] a 'charming man' and a 'local hero in South Australia'.[15] While this immediately brings to mind the 'charismatic' chief executive so central to many earlier and modern failures, O'Grady was never in the same league as, say, in the 1920s, Lord Kylsant of the Royal Mail; in the 1960s, Stanley Korman; the 1980s entrepreneurs Alan Bond and Robert Maxwell; or the 1990s crowd, Williams, Adler, Schneider, Ebbers and (say) Lay.

The inspector's final report concluded that O'Grady was innocent of any fraud, but was an artless victim of his own incompetence. The group's managers were adjudged as at best 'second class', while others 'were worse'.[16] O'Grady's 'no-management theory' was blamed for many of the group's problems, as he left full responsibility for operating the group's operating subsidiaries to others whose 'talents were insufficient for the task'.

The inspector might also have added the observation that the entirely inept practices of the (then) conventional accounting failed miserably to inform and thereby protect directors from being a financial risk to themselves and to investors. Another of the inspector's comments highlights the seductive role of accounting in inducing investors to participate and hence exacerbate the consequences of the collapse:

> It was the spirit of the late '50s which encouraged the public (enchanted by the *spectacular growth* and *apparent profitability of the Reid Murray group as shown in the published accounts*) to pour into Reid Murray Acceptance much of the money which was subsequently lost … Easy availability of huge sums of public moneys … and the acceptance of the view (both inside and outside the group) that such sums … could be indiscriminately used to construct and expand the group were necessary pre-conditions for the losses which followed …[17]

The importance of Reid Murray cannot be underestimated. Commentators still refer to Reid Murray, suggesting that little has changed in the way of corporate *group* business dealings and business ethics. Also, many of the subsequent related-party transaction mechanisms, and the use of a subsidiary as 'group banker', share similarities with the operations of the Reid Murray group. Partly because of the complexity and obfuscatory nature of the group dealings, the Reid Murray receivership continued some 30 years on as Australia's longest corporate administration.

Many features of the Reid Murray affair were repeated soon after in the Stanhill collapse. Commingling public and private affairs with deleterious public consequences was even more graphically evident in Stanhill, as were the deficiencies of group accounting coupled to accounting for related-party transactions, and the perennial failure to mark (assets) to market. The notorious *Korman Round Robin* is reproduced as a *Postscript* to this chapter as it further highlights the complexity of many corporate affairs making the process of audit verification a 'mission impossible'.

Postscript – Korman Round Robin

What curious webs our corporates weave. The round robin device
emerges and produces 'unjust enrichment of the Korman family [which]
was effected at the expense of the public company, SCL and indirectly
at the expense of the public company, SDF' ...

P. Murphy (1967, p. 121)

When Polish-born Stanley Korman emigrated to Australia it was unlikely he
could have predicted that he would become, like many subsequent European-
born immigrants-cum-entrepreneurs, a household name in his adopted country.
His commercial expertise initially lay in textiles, an area which flourished after
World War II, taking Korman and Stanhill with it.

Korman is reported to have been a man of boundless energies and vision
– 'Short and dapper in a pinstripe suit and meticulously trimmed pencil
moustache ... an exciting, highly persuasive salesman and an aggressive,
ruthless fighter/negotiator',[18] though whether some of those characteristics
are necessarily commercially virtuous is another question. Such a description
evokes comparisons with contemporary immigrant entrepreneurs, Alan Bond,
Christopher Skase, George Herscu and the 1980s textile king Abe Goldberg,
and say, Rodley Adler in the 1990s – all smart enough dressers and successes
in their time, too.

As so often happens in the corporate collapses detailed here, a complex
group structure (Figure 4.2) provided the medium in Sydney Guarantee and
Stanhill[19] for a bewildering array of commercial transactions, masking their
occurrence and scrambling the reporting of their financial outcomes. The first
edition of *Corporate Collapse* detailed the history of Korman's empire building.[20] Only one aspect of that failure, the notorious *round-robin* transaction,
is discussed below.

Korman's round-robin mechanism earns him a place alongside the *best* of
the corporate commercial innovators, for it has been used to 'good effect' in
subsequent financial *causes célèbres*. Korman was also an early exponent of
seeking to have a close relationship with regulatory bodies. He was reported
to have made an initial contribution towards the financing of the Australian
Accountancy Research Foundation when it was formed in the mid-1960s.

A major factor in the Stanhill Group's demise was the Chevron Sydney
Hotel project. The Stanhill Group 'banker', Stanhill Development Finance
(SDF), in the prospectus related to the Chevron project, raised substantial

Figure 4.2 Stanhill Consolidated Ltd group structure

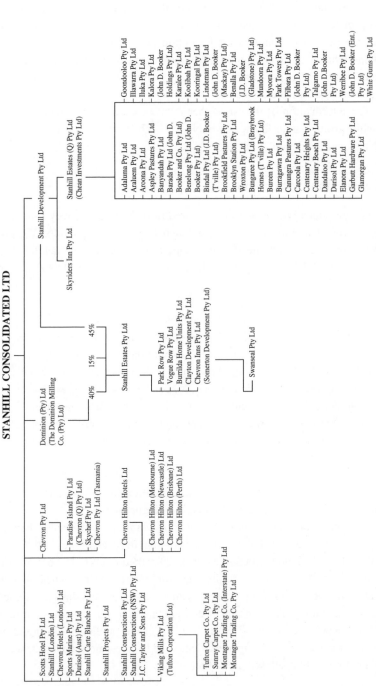

Note: All wholly owned except as shown. Former names are shown in brackets. This structure excludes the Factors Limited Group structure.
Source: P. Murphy, *Interim Report of an Investigation … into the Affairs of Stanhill Development Finance Limited …* (Melbourne: Victorian Government Printer, November 1964), Appendix A at p. 82.

monies. No property of any kind was acquired by SDF up to 31 October 1960, yet almost the entire prospectus funds of the company had been diverted into other related companies needing the cash. The cash transfers were consistent with the peculiar 'all-in-the-family' notion of a 'corporate group', justifying actions which otherwise should have been open to grave doubt. Groups and group (consolidated) accounts have been a major tool of financial obfuscation, as discussed in Chapters 16 and 17.

The introduction of the November 1960 economic adjustments meant the Stanhill group was in financial trouble. As with Reid Murray, a cheque round robin was to be Stanhill's saviour.

The Korman round robin

Companies stuck with properties acquired from Chevron Sydney Limited, and the associated debt the acquisitions entailed, had to find a quick fix. The private family companies badly needed an escape route. The answer was the cheques round robin of 17 February 1961. It was made to measure! As Peter Murphy QC, the official inspector, explained:

> It is not difficult to see why the [round robin] was negotiated by Stanley Korman
> in a furtive manner. It was, in effect, a refined arrangement whereby money was
> taken from the public company, SCL [Stanhill Consolidated Limited], and paid
> to Stanhill [Pty Ltd]. This unjust enrichment of the Korman family was effected
> at the expense of the public company, SCL, and indirectly at the expense of the
> public company SDF [Stanhill Development Finance] ... The only interest
> considered at the time was the Korman family companies, and it did not matter
> that two public companies suffered, provided that the Korman companies were
> to be benefited.[21]

Its effect was to reconstruct the legal relationship of the participants. Its mechanism is depicted diagrammatically in Figure 4.3.

The round robin affected the takeover of Dominion and Stanhill Estates by SCL. Stanhill and Park Lake thereby were able to receive in cash their profits on the sale of the land to Stanhill Estates, repay their debts to Factors, and divest themselves of further responsibility regarding the real estate owned by Stanhill Estates and Dominion. Unquestionably the transaction was designed to benefit the Korman family. The consequences were that SDF was owed £2.3 million by SCL (almost the amount raised by SDF from the public in 1960) and, most importantly, the family companies' debts had been repaid – consequences that were not publicly disclosed at the time.

Figure 4.3 17 February 1961 round robin cheques

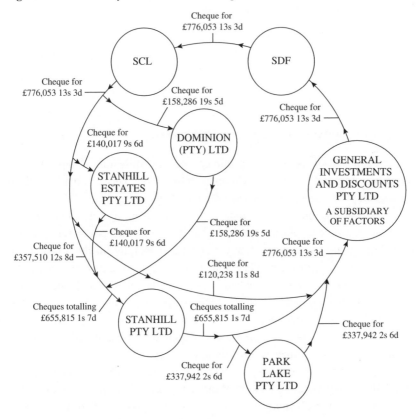

Source: P. Murphy, *Interim Report of an Investigation … into the Affairs of Stanhill Development Finance Limited …* (1964, p. 41).

Nearly two years later, on 14 February 1963, upon the trigger of a debtor's judgment for £2,113,219, a receiver was appointed to SDF, leading to the financial facts being publicly revealed. SDF's Statement of Affairs as at 6 December 1963 showed a deficiency of £1,902,641. The public arm of the Stanhill group had collapsed. SCL and its subsidiaries, Stanhill Estates and Dominion, ended in liquidation and a Victorian government inspector was appointed to examine the group's dealings; Chevron Sydney went into receivership, the hotel was sold and the other assets were distributed to claimants. Inspector Murphy QC estimated the losses of the Stanhill group to be approximately £24 million (or nearly $500 million in current terms):[22]

(i) Subscriptions for share capital, including Factors' purchase of Rockmans Ltd shares	£9,168,208
(ii) Losses by Debenture and Note Holders	£6,584,748
(iii) Creditors	£7,994,513
TOTAL	£23,747,469

Corporate games – Korman's kindergarten?

The rise and fall of the Stanhill group contains many features similar to later Australian corporate collapses. Complex transactions between a labyrinth of private and public companies became a common technique. The ability to mask poorly performing individual companies by various group-related accounting techniques became the norm, particularly as land and other assets were shuffled around the group companies, often with profits (generally for the private companies) and losses (for the public companies) being recorded at each shuffle. It was a good ponzi scheme, antecedent of events in the 1970s, 1980s and beyond. The ponzi technique recurs in this volume. A 'ponzi' scheme was named after a 1920s US market operator, Charles Ponzi. Such schemes promised high returns on risky assets and their success depended on maintaining investors' belief that the assets' prices would continue to rise forever.

That few, if any, major lessons appear to have been learned from the Stanhill saga is disturbing. Inequity and moral (arguably legal) impropriety in the round robin transaction, realising profits for the Korman private companies, as well as repayment of Korman private company debt to the public companies, was a valuable lesson to be learned. Seemingly it was not. The allegations related to group financing and asset shuffling at HIH and Enron would reasonably draw such an inference.

Using a public company as a 'cash-cow' (Factors) was virtually identical in method, and consistent in motive, to later corporate manoeuvres – for example, the alleged 'cash-cow' role played by Bell Resources in the Bond Corporation group's desperate moves in 1989 to stave off insolvency. In both instances, it is arguable that directors of a recognised group of public companies acted commercially as if there was no legal distinction between each separate company comprising it. The effects on shareholders, especially minority shareholders, and on the creditors of each separate company are potentially dramatic.

Some of Stanhill's contemporaries fell just as heavily. None hit the wall any harder than electrical and whitegoods retailer H.G. Palmer.

CHAPTER 5

H.G. Palmer:
'Gilt' by Association*

Did H.G. Palmer (Consolidated) Ltd (receiver appointed) ever make
a true and fair profit?

Anon (1965)

Possibly not! Or so it seems from the commercial post-mortem on the House
of Palmer. In its 15 years as a listed public company reported profits totalled
only £5.6 million before tax. In 1965 H.G. Palmer *unexpectedly* reported what
was then Australia's biggest-ever annual loss of £10 million (approximately
$220 million in current terms). Following the first report of the receiver's
investigation into Palmer's collapse, the financial editor of the *Sydney Morning
Herald*, Tom Fitzgerald, stated that, after retrospective accounting restatements,
'H.G. Palmer has never been a truly profitable business since it came on to the
Stock Exchange in 1949.'[1] Of critical importance is why it took 16 years to find
that out, for the 'retrospective accounting restatements' could have been made
contemporaneously had accounting regulation been different.

Fitzgerald's observation begs the question as to what 'never truly profitable'
might mean. To virtually everyone (at least to those outside of the accounting
fraternity, it appears) it would ordinarily mean that the company's wealth had
decreased year after year, resulting in the aggregative losses revealed in the
eventual liquidation of H.G. Palmer. The problem is, conventional accounting
does not calculate periodic profit (or loss) in terms of an increase (decrease) in
the wealth period by period. Invariably it isn't until the end of a company's life
that it becomes publicly known how it fared financially year by year.

Palmer's collapse and the concurrent demise of Cox Brothers were two major
1960s retail disasters. Both were rude shocks to Australia's retail establishment.

Palmer's founder, Herbert George Palmer, was a salesman, not a financier.
He learned his selling techniques during the Depression,[2] successfully hawk-
ing radio sets from door to door in Sydney's suburbs. Conventional retailing
commenced in 1932 in a rented shop space in the Sydney suburb of Bankstown.
A year later he opened his own retail store in Bankstown, thereby expanding his
sales of radio and electrical equipment.

In 1938 operations expanded by opening a branch on the south coast in
Wollongong. This was the start of his big assault on the electrical retail market. 'Herbie' Palmer was switched on in a big way. This was the beginning

of growing for broke – much like what would occur with Harris Scarfe and HIH decades later.

There is no doubt that Palmer was well thought of during those years: to everyone he was a respectable business person. He was the prototype of many indigenous entrepreneurs who were to follow. Palmer possessed style. He was well known as a man-about-Bankstown in Sydney's West. The press reported at the time of his fall from grace that Palmer 'until quite recently might have been found in the company of the most reputable men in the community'.[3]

Wartime had limited the availability of electrical products and spare parts. Thus, in the early days the Palmer business was largely restricted to repair work. After the war, supplies of stock improved. There was the inevitable period of general post-war business expansion and Palmer was there to capitalise on it. He had a 'natural' sense of opportunity, a 'nose' for where prospects lay. There were also peacetime benefits of wartime research and development being fed into the appliance market. In 1947 two companies were incorporated to conduct the Palmer retailing businesses: H.G. Palmer Pty Ltd and H.G. Palmer (Wollongong) Pty Ltd. Most sales were for cash, with the remaining hire-purchase sales financed by H.G. Palmer (Finance) Pty Ltd (also formed in 1947). In 1949 Palmer incorporated Remlap Electric Pty Ltd as an avenue for the activities of installing and servicing refrigeration equipment. A refrigerator in the home was a kind of status symbol – iceboxes were passé. The whitegoods boom was about to begin.

H.G. Palmer (Consolidated) Ltd was incorporated as a holding company to acquire interests in these four family companies on 7 December 1949. Clearly Palmer had an eye for the emerging business entity par excellence – the holding company. In this respect, H.G. Palmer was a structural exemplar for failed and successful companies alike in subsequent decades – for, in fact, it is difficult to find a sizeable 'success' or collapse since 1950 which has not embraced the holding company/subsidiary organisational structure.

Palmer was on a common (Argenti *Type II*) failure trajectory from almost day one – rapid expansion by acquisition using debt finance, seeking increased sales without associated increased actual profits. The prospectus (dated 12 December) for the issue of shares in this company claimed that the aggregates of the annual profits (1947–49 years, ending 30 June) of the four Palmer family companies since their date of incorporation were: £1,805, £8,431 and £12,215.

The disclosed aggregate book value of the prospective subsidiaries' net assets was £29,472. After deducting £3,500 preference capital, the equity of ordinary shareholders was £25,972. The consideration to be paid to H.G. Palmer and seven relatives for their shares in the four companies totalled £66,935.16s 8d. Of this, £13,435 was to be payable immediately the contract was finalised. The balance was to remain unpaid for up to ten years if so desired by the purchaser, and in return the vendors were granted an option to take up £53,501 in ordinary shares on or before 1 July 1951. The prospectus invited the public to subscribe for 34,000 5s ordinary shares, payable in full on application. A further 66,000 5s ordinary shares were applied for by the shareholders of the Palmer family companies under identical terms, and official listing on the Sydney Stock Exchange was granted on 5 September 1950. Palmer's move into the public arena was off and running – at full speed.

Typical of many of the other failed companies referred to here, from the day of listing until acquired by one of the largest life assurance companies (the Mutual Life Corporation Ltd in 1963), H.G. Palmer (Consolidated) expanded 'by acquisition'. Palmers swallowed a number of Sydney electrical retailers in its expansion phase. In 1954 it was Crooks (Auburn) Pty Ltd and Crooks (Auburn) Finance Pty Ltd; followed in 1955 by acquisitions of the Manly Electric and Radio Co. Pty Ltd and Manly Television Co. Pty Ltd. In order to give the group an edge in sales tax matters, in 1956 Crooks (Auburn) Pty Ltd became H.G. Palmer (Wholesale) Pty Ltd. Other group companies also underwent name changes to generate the H.G. Palmer legend. A Canberra register was achieved through the incorporation of Music Masters (ACT) Pty Ltd in 1957. Music Masters Pty Ltd (Qld) was acquired in 1958, as was Downie Pty Ltd (Vic.); it had been reported to the Sydney Stock Exchange that the main reason for this takeover was the acquisition of a retail site.

The Palmer group did not so much add corporate value as acquire value that already existed. Growth by acquisition was the name of the game. It was easy and there for the taking. Downie was voluntarily wound up in 1960. Two other companies were incorporated in Victoria and the Australian Capital Territory and H.G. Palmer (Consolidated) Ltd had a total of 11 subsidiaries, all wholly-owned except for some holdings of preference shares. The group soon comprised approximately 150 retail outlets in New South Wales, Victoria, Queensland and South Australia. Expansion had been frenetic – sensational, but unstructured, more of it by accident than by design. If there was an electrical retailer for sale, then H.G. Palmer bought it. In this respect, Palmers were moving along a similar, but not identical, failure trajectory to that of Reid Murray. As it turned out, the paths proved equally slippery.[4]

Late on the afternoon of Monday, 8 April 1963, the MLC Ltd made a takeover offer for the issued ordinary capital of H.G. Palmer (Consolidated) Ltd. The MLC was then the second-largest life office in Australia. H.G. Palmer was the largest retailer of electrical appliances in the country. Publicly it had the appearances of a perfect union. The share exchange bid was calculated to be worth 21s for each H.G. Palmer stock unit, 5s more than the latest market price.[5]

The bid was a 'bolt from the blue',[6] at least for many members of the public. There seemed little doubt in the minds of at least some financial commentators

that H.G. Palmer was very prosperous. 'H.G. Palmer sets records.'[7] Only a
few weeks earlier the reported growth of H.G. Palmer had been described
as 'the most heartening ... of the success stories of Australian retailing'.[8]
Those assessments are in stark contrast to Tom Fitzgerald's comments referred
to earlier.

That raises doubts that the market generally is in the know about such
things. Importantly, it exposes that nothing is as seductive as reported success
backed up by corroborative financial statements. At least some in the market
were very much in the dark, but did not know it. By virtue of thinking that they
knew all they probably were worse off than those who were aware that they did
not. That feature has been endemic of many Australian corporate failures
discussed in this book.

The MLC's purchase of H.G. Palmer was the first plunge by an Australian
life assurance company into retailing. But the feeling in the market was that the
acquisition promised to be profitable.[9] It certainly enhanced the commercial
status of Palmers. Within a very short period, it failed to turn out that way.
Again, many experts were wrong. Perhaps this was not surprising, for ultimately even experts are left to draw their financial inferences primarily from
published financial statements chock full of creativity – as seductive to the
expert as to the layperson.

Financing

Successful growth in H.G. Palmer sales of electrical goods has been attributed
to its reliance on borrowing.[10] And, of course, its capacity to borrow was
boosted by the illusion of the group's profitability contained in its audited
financial reports. Analysis of Palmer's debt and equity raising history is
instructive for the insight it gives to the manner in which alternative financing
resources were tapped one by one. It also points to gross misunderstanding
regarding the worth of the asset cover for the accumulating debt. Conventional
accounting then, as now, facilitated recourse to 'book values' – artifacts of the
bookkeeping system – rather than to current selling prices of the assets pledged.
As many before and many since have done, when one finance source dried up,
H.G. Palmer moved on to yet another. Possibly the market did not disseminate
the news about the rejected lines of finance as efficiently as one might have
expected. Nor apparently was the market overtly cognisant of the uselessness of
'book values' when it came to assessing the security for debt. Both aspects are
matters which contemporary market commentators ought to contemplate.

We might presume that the reliance on Palmer's perceived profitability
drove the financial support it received. It is hard to imagine that, had the financial truth been known, investors would have been so forthcoming. Between

incorporation in 1950 and the appointment of the receiver in 1965, the issued equity capital of H.G. Palmer increased from (approximately) £25,000 to £6,824,082. Generally, the equity issues were to 'finance the expansion of the subsidiary companies'. Acquisition of most of the subsidiaries was effected through share issues – for example, the takeovers of Music Masters Radio Pty Ltd (Brisbane) in 1958 and Manly Electric and Radio Company Pty Ltd (Sydney) in 1960. Again, none of that may have occurred had the audited accounts disclosed Palmer's true financial state. However, during the early 1960s equity issues served another role. In June 1964, 500,000 20s 7 per cent cumulative 2nd preference shares were issued to the MLC in order to provide cash for the 'maintenance of liquidity'. During October 1964 the procedure was repeated: another 500,000 20s cumulative 2nd preference shares were issued to the MLC.

Thus, £1 million had been injected by the MLC in a space of four months. Six months later, another rescue bid was undertaken by the MLC upon the discovery, by one of its officers, of at least £2.5 million in bad debts at H.G. Palmer, with possibly another £1.5 million problematic. Good money poured after bad – a fatal managerial strategy. To cover the loss, 4 million 20s 'A' class cumulative redeemable preference shares were issued. The MLC subscribed £3,625,000 and the Palmer family company, Palfam Investments Pty Ltd, put up the residual. Unfortunately the group was within six months of receivership, but nothing in the reported financial results gave indications of it (Table 5.1).

Palmer's scenario, like many others here, included accelerated growth under a charismatic leader, coupled to a quick, unexpected collapse. And further, like those others, conventional accounting practices did not get in the way – indeed, they were most accommodating, not of a kind likely to disclose in a timely fashion Palmer's precarious financial position.

As with most financial intermediaries, prior to 1956 major debt financing came from bank overdrafts and trade credit. Palmer's first public debt raising was in August 1956.[11] Thereafter, 15 issues to the public of notes and debentures were made. Borrowing ceased with the recall of the prospectus issued on 15 January 1965 because of the alleged misstatements it contained.

As early as the 1960s, the difficulties in interpreting the disclosed financial information by Australian public companies, even without management manipulation, were commonly acknowledged outside the professional accounting ranks. Chroniclers of financial institutions Hirst and Wallace had noted:

… adherence to historical cost conventions … means that the accounting reports of companies provide measures of periodic surplus and funds employed which are meaningless as indicators … [They] do not contain the information needed to convert reported profits and funds employed to current values, [hence]

Table 5.1　Palmer's reported trading results, 1950 to 1965

At 30 June	Approximate turnover £	Debtors balance outstanding £	Reported profits £	Dividend rate Preference Interim %	Final %	Ord. %
1950	214,000	84,199	6,403	–	–	10
1951	1,044,000	165,798	31,317	–	–	10
1952	1,398,000	197,807	31,729	6	–	10
1953	2,400,000	342,087	72,092	6	–	10
1954	3,400,000	1,757,842	100,676	6	–	10
1955	3,350,000	2,326,962	101,536	6	7	10
1956	3,300,000	2,378,735	96,170	6	7	10
1957	4,400,000	3,128,307	131,318	6	7	10
1958	8,400,000	4,606,832	250,147	10	–	10
1959	10,010,000	8,533,320	301,494	10	–	12
1960	13,800,000	12,291,095	413,246	10	–	12
1961	14,100,000	15,302,972	421,596	10	–	12
1962	14,300,000	18,547,916	428,746	10	–	12
1963	14,400,000	20,903,869	431,624	10	–	12
1964	13,700,000	23,920,221	408,371	10	–	12
1965	15,000,000	22,184,606	(4,350,091)	5	–	–

Source: H.G. Palmer, *Statement of Affairs.*

shareholders and investors are not able to choose between alternative avenues of investment on a rational basis.[12]

Nonetheless, in the Palmer case choose investors did, seemingly undaunted by that general warning and warnings from many others.

Buoyed by their reputation, created, or at least corroborated by impressive reported financials, borrowing seemingly was easy for Palmer during that period. Palmer prospectuses were issued by the banker for the group, H.G. Palmer (Consolidated) Ltd, but cross-guaranteed by all the subsidiaries when required to set up the floating charge securing the debenture issues. Over-subscriptions at this time were common and legally retained. For example, the August 1956 issue of £100,000 in fixed deposit notes (in multiples of £25) produced £2,004,642; in February 1959, £250,000 was offered and resulted in an increase in debt of £3,763,710 (net of the proceeds required to redeem maturing debt); in June 1960 the first issue of mortgage debentures was followed closely by further offers in November of that year and April 1961; £1,500,000 was asked for and £5,684,575 was received by June 1961. The retention pattern continued, for legislation did not prevent retention of over-subscriptions. Obviously, many in the market must have viewed H.G. Palmer favourably. Following the introduction of the 1961 *Uniform Companies Act*, oversubscription retentions were limited by the terms of the prospectus. Over-subscriptions were still common in the early 1960s raisings. Between July 1961 and June 1965, £35,181,382 had been borrowed.

When a receiver was appointed to the group on 25 October 1965, outstanding borrowings raised by prospectus issues stood at:

	£
Debentures (secured by a floating charge and the assets of H.G. Palmer (Consolidated) Ltd and subsidiaries)	41,701,270
Registered Unsecured Deposit Notes	7,316,374
Registered Fixed Deposit Notes	5,690,548

– an equivalent of over $1 billion in current terms.

It is not surprising that continued borrowing was easy for the Palmer group. It enjoyed a more than favourable press, almost right up to the time of the appointment of the receiver. Indeed, as already indicated, the financial press was most exuberant in its praise. For example, under the 'H.G. Palmer share-holders on clover'[13] accolade sat this positive assessment:

[In spite of the November 1960 credit squeeze] to record an increase in profit, albeit small, was a mark of a highly flexible merchandising technique ... [Palmer] may strengthen more than ever its grip on a market whose boundaries are set by replacement sales and the natural growth, because the end of the TV boom means the passing of a mushroom of 'fly-by-night' retailers.[14]

and under the caption, 'Palmer Progress': 'If Mr Menzies' credit squeeze did nothing else it did at least indicate where the quality lay. Among those to show out with a *nicely gilded fleece* has been H.G. P.'[15] It would seem that, like beauty, quality is in the eye of the beholder – almost certainly influenced, however, by what is being reported about the wealth and progress of the company under assessment. And, of course, all that glitters is not gold, although conventional accounting certainly injects the alchemist's touch.

Shareholders, noteholders and the like were more likely on quicksand than clover! Reputable, knowledgeable broking houses were just as eulogistic. Per-haps on the basis of their presumed superior financial knowledge, share prices rose steadily from a low of 3s in 1952 to the end of 1963 when they stood at 22s. It seems that those presumed to be in the know had created H.G. Palmer

as a 'legend in their own mind', and were quite sanguine regarding the difficulties other retailers were experiencing. Palmer's management was perceived
by many to be one of only a few who had not lost the plot.

Trading activities

Selling electrical appliances on credit terms was the major source of revenue
for the group. Credit contracts were entered into mainly through H.G. Palmer
Pty Ltd and H.G. Palmer (Vic.) Pty Ltd. Transactions were financed internally
by H.G. Palmer Pty Ltd, Hire Purchase Securities Ltd, Mutual Acceptance
Corporation Ltd and Control Securities Ltd. Record sales were the main
revenue source of the Music Masters Pty Ltd stores in Queensland, reputed to
have the largest business of that type in the state.

Goods sold on credit prior to 1965 accounted for approximately 90 per cent
of the group's business. Those goods usually were the subject of a credit sale
agreement under the *Credit Sales Act* in New South Wales and similar legislation in Victoria and Queensland. In contrast with sales under hire-purchase,
property in the goods legally passed to the purchaser upon entering into the
agreement, which provided for not more than eight payments to be made over
the period of 12 months for which credit was given. Interest rates ranged from
10 per cent for short-term contracts to 12 per cent over a longer period.
Presumably (as usually was the practice) the credit sale agreement entered into
was designed to avoid the requirements of the *Hire Purchase Act*. Private
arrangements often executed between H.G. Palmer and customers enabled
payments to be made over a period longer than the 12 months specified by the
Credit Sales Act – a good strategy for showing reported sales growth, but
questionable for ensuring long-term survival. Not surprisingly, Palmers were
moving the goods at a time when the other retailers in general, and whitegoods
dealers in particular, were struggling.

Although many products had an H.G. Palmer brand name, Palmer
companies did not manufacture. Component parts were imported in most cases
and assembled under contract for H.G. Palmer (Wholesale) Pty Ltd by various
Australian companies. Faith in the Palmer group's financial stability proved
costly. On liquidation, Palmer's Statement of Affairs disclosed large (at the
time) debts to well-known manufacturers and distributors, including:

	£
Email Limited	72,505
Kelvinator Limited	96,751
Simpson Pope Group	235,087
Kriesler Limited	38,639

Hoover (Aust.) Limited	37,920
Philips Elect. Ind. Ltd	39,266

Little difficulty was experienced by H.G. Palmer in establishing those credit facilities, which was not surprising given its sales and profit records. Nor, apparently, was there any problem raising debenture moneys from many institutional investors, possibly for the same reasons, especially so after the MLC acquisition. Money poured in from the big institutions, including AMP which provided £825,000; National Mutual Life, £405,000; the NSW GIO, £500,000; and MBF of Australia, £210,000. In current dollars this equates to approximately $40 million, but, more importantly, it was a sizeable amount at the time.

Financial measures of the volume of H.G. Palmer business are contestable. Disclosure of turnover figures did not become mandatory in Australia until the beginning of the 1970s. However, there are some clues that assist its approximation. Turnover in this instance should be taken as a composite of sales of goods for cash, or credit, finance charges apportioned to the Profit and Loss account via the application of the Rule of 78 and proceeds from service contracts and maintenance services.

Employees reported that a net 3 to 4 per cent profit on turnover was aimed for in budget preparation; hence this percentage could be applied to the reported profit figures to approximate turnover. Second, Sir Norman Nock, in his Chairman's address at the annual general meeting for the year ended 30 June 1958, stated that 'turnover now exceeded £8 million'. The profit reported in 1958 was £250,147, which represented approximately 3 per cent of Nock's disclosure. So it appears that the rough formula passed the test. Applying the 3 per cent rule, the turnover for the ten years to 1964 shows a steady trend in sales growth from approximately £3.4 million in 1955 to £14 million in 1961. The rate of growth then dropped greatly to level the turnover at approximately the £14 million to £15 million mark by 1965 – approximating $330 million in contemporary dollars.

The levelling out after 1961 could have several explanations. First, the credit squeeze of 1960/61 put a brake on the sale of consumer durables. Second, the saturation point of television sales, which had picked up where the white-goods left off in the mid-1950s, had been reached. And third, colour television, which Palmer expected to be the saving white knight, had failed to arrive on time. Possibly there was a mixture of all three.

Yet Palmer's growth in assets, sales and debt finance, then and subsequently, was apparently premised on the belief that the market would expand forever. A familiar pattern of entrepreneurial behaviour had emerged. Similar beliefs in respect of investment in securities and real property were integral in many of the 1970s and 1980s collapses.

Returning to Palmer, signs which many in the industry were noting eluded Herbie Palmer's gaze, as well as those of his admirers in the press gallery. The growth at Palmers is instructive. From 1950 onwards the number of stores opening yearly had increased; averaging four a year until 1958 when 21 were opened (NSW seven, Victoria nine, South Australia two and Queensland three). The expansion continued in 1959 with 17 stores being opened, in 1960/61 (14), 1962 (25), 1963 (25) and 1964 (25). By January 1965, 146 retail outlets existed under the Palmer name, yet retailing was having a hard time.

Palmer's financial reports were out of line with the public signals of retailing's woes. It was a victory for 'accounting fiction' over 'financial facts'; fiction that was duly audited and presumably passed on to the market as if it were fact. The failure of the market to consider more closely the public signals is curious, but definitely not a one-off occurrence.

It would seem that few knew of – or if they did, heeded – the notorious 1950s deeds in the United States of Tino De Angelis, where records revealed that reported increases in De Angelis's companies' holdings of vegetable oils exceeded the US Department of Agriculture's production figures; likewise, again in the United States, when Billie Sol Estes embarked upon his 1960s grain frauds; and continuation of the 1972 reported growth in Equity Funding's life policies, which meant that within the next decade it would have insured more people than currently resided in the United States; the derivatives, futures and foreign exchange trading fiascos of the 1990s (e.g. at Barings, Sumitomo and Daiwa) similarly suggest that it is too much to expect these financial lessons of history to be transmitted across countries, let alone across decades within the same country.[16]

Palmer's public, seemingly unquestioning, support is a compelling example of the apparent public preference for the representations in duly verified accounting reports, favourable press and 'gilt' associations, over other externally available information. It also points to the failure of accounting to be structured in such a way that it corresponds to the financial and the related physical facts of the market.

'Gilt' by association

Between mid-1963 and early 1965, H.G. Palmer (Consolidated) Limited issued several prospectuses strongly featuring a photograph of the MLC's head office and emphasising that H.G. Palmer was a wholly-owned subsidiary of the MLC.

According to the evidence given in 1966 at the committal proceedings against officers of H.G. Palmer, the company's liquidity problem had been identified in mid-1964. The court was told of the apparent need of approximately £6 million at that time to meet the repayment of borrowings which were then due. The company was incurring a net outflow of cash. Palmer was

An example of an H.G. Palmer prospectus cover dated 31 July 1964

Source: Sydney Morning Herald, 20 November 1965. Reproduced with approval from John Fairfax & Sons Ltd.

informed that the company was living beyond its means. 'The chief accountant had prepared a set of figures which showed that [Palmers] were living at the rate of $140,000 a week over and above our inflow. This relates purely to cash.'[17]

However, the liquidity problem was relieved by the oversubscribed July 1964 issue of 1st debenture stock. Oversubscriptions were so heavy that a reduction of creditors was effected and the accommodating finance from the MLC Ltd was repaid prior to 30 June 1965. The remaining £1 million cash surplus was loaned to the MLC. Perhaps the MLC had earned special treatment, for Palmers were riding high on the MLC bandwagon of financial strength and respectability. It was a case of 'gilt by association'. Some perceived benefits of the interaction between the MLC and H.G. Palmer are provided by:

[a]n anonymous Newcastle widow of modest means [who] wrote to *The Sydney Morning Herald* ... 'I had intended to reinvest [H.G. Palmer debenture redemptions] elsewhere, but under the umbrella of the MLC's great strength and reputation – and strongly urged by my broker – I reinvested in H.G. P. debentures.'[18]

This was a view apparently shared by many. H.G. Palmer advertised in its prospectus (see above) that the MLC had a 100 per cent interest, implying that the MLC would support H.G. Palmer. Consider this extract from a letter to the *Australian Financial Review* under the caption 'Palmers a good buy': 'In making the investment it is comforting to know the MLC insurance group owns the ordinary capital of Palmers.'[19] Comfort it may have been, but it was to be short-lived. The Newcastle widow's umbrella metaphorically quickly blew inside-out when Palmer collapsed suddenly.

The growth of Palmer's 'debtors' was at a greater pace than that of turnover, and any thoughts that another liquidity problem would ensue should have been anticipated, since borrowings were intended (according to the prospectus) to redeem maturing issues of like securities.

Accounting magic

Reported trading results (Table 5.1) provide a glowing account of the prosperity of the group; profits increasing nearly every year from a humble £31,317 for the year ended 30 June 1951 (the first full year of trading) to £408,371 at 30 June 1964. Particularly noteworthy is that just over a year before being placed in receivership H.G. Palmer recorded its highest reported profits of more than £431,000 (approximately $9 million in 2002 dollars).

Nobody – shareholder, debenture holder or note holder – went short during those heady years: Table 5.1 shows that the constant stream of preference dividends of 6 per cent and 7 per cent to 1957 and 10 per cent thereafter – and 10 per cent ordinary dividend to 1958 and 12 per cent thereafter – continued to the year ended 30 June 1964.

From the date of its formation the group paid out a total of £2,472,348 in dividends. This amount exceeded the amount estimated to be available (according to the Statement of Affairs) to meet the unsecured creditors of the group at the time the receiver was appointed.

Several aspects of the preparation of the accounts and associated financing are noteworthy:

- Little credit control existed. In evidence before Mr Scarlett SM it was reported that branch managers were required to keep rejection of contract proposals down to 2 per cent of the proposals received. Credit was granted therefore, if this is to be taken as indication of the group policy, on a mathematical basis rather than by an investigation of the creditworthiness of the would-be customer.

  Estimated sales were the result of budget projections prepared by the branch manager, proven salespeople and, although each branch had an accountant, their duties were restricted to bookkeeping activities. The basis for the budgetary system was the desired 3–4 per cent net return on sales noted earlier.

  Each branch manager was allocated a proportion of fixed expenses and by adding the expenses peculiar to their branch area, a total expense figure was ascertained. A gross margin of 28 per cent was required. Thus, expenses were to be approximately 24–25 per cent of the total revenues. An anticipated (in fact, essential) sales figure was then projected by multiplying the expense figure by four. Credit policy was tailored to guarantee the sales volume.

The expansion of the amount of credit extended is evidenced by the path of the growth of debtors' balances outstanding, as shown in Table 5.1.

- Hiring charges were apportioned on the basis of the Rule of 78; no allowance was made for: (a) probability of collection; or (b) a hedge against inflation.
- No provision was made for doubtful debts, despite the evidence of difficulty of collection. Mr Davis Hughes referred to this difficulty in a speech to the NSW Legislative Assembly on 9 September 1964, when he disclosed that of 26,000 actions in the Bankstown Small Debts Court in 1963, 18,000 were at the suit of H.G. Palmer Pty Ltd.

Board of directors' reports had not mentioned the bad debts to that point. However, in 1965 the chairman reported:

Bad Debts which are proved have been progressively written off from year to year. Reported Loss for the Year Ended 30 June 1965 was £4,350,091. The reported 1965 loss was the result of adverse trading as reported by the Chairman in his address and the writing off of £1,258,876 'bad debts' and the provision for £2,741,124 anticipated to prove 'bad'.

The write-off and provision followed an investigation initiated by the MLC Ltd on the H.G. Palmer group debtors' ledgers on 4 March 1964, before the takeover. This investigation was carried out by the MLC Ltd in response to information received and the general rumour of 'bad debts' in H.G. Palmer Pty Ltd. Rumour was rife at the time in the city, but presumably it did not discourage the many investors trading in H.G. Palmer securities or those recommending them. Subsequently, H.G. Palmer, suggesting that £2.5 million should be written off debts in the 'black ledger' immediately and a further £1.5 million provided for further bad debts, issued a report on 11 March 1964. The 'black ledger', said to have been removed when earlier investigators had arrived to look at the debtors' ledger, subsequently was found located at the Bankstown headquarters in a toilet – not an altogether inappropriate place for it. The write-offs were financed by the preference issue (mainly) to the MLC Ltd.

At the end of September 1965 the preliminary accounts for the year ended 30 June 1965 were released. It was apparent by the end of October 1965 that a substantial breach of the borrowing ratio of the trust deed had occurred. The MLC board acted swiftly. It moved to write off its entire investment in H.G. Palmer – $8.7 million. Then it requested the trustee for the debenture holders, Permanent Trustee Company of New South Wales, to appoint a receiver,

Mr C.H.R. Jackson. Institutional investors at the Circular Quay end of Pitt Street, Sydney, were staggered; elsewhere, thousands of H.G. Palmer's customers settled back with gratitude to watch the hottest household wonder – monochrome TV.

Doubtful debts and a true and fair view

Of significance for accountants in the H.G. Palmer failure is the similarity with the issues that had arisen over three decades earlier in the United Kingdom in the Royal Mail affair. As Sir William Jowitt had so succinctly summed up:

> If the documents convey to a reasonably intelligent person a false impression,
> all the technical rules of accountancy may be observed and at the same time the
> accountants' profession has failed to carry out its primary and obvious duty … to
> ensure that in the documents which are produced a true and accurate account of
> the affairs of the company is given.[20]

Sentencing Herbert Palmer and the auditor John McBlane, Lee J observed: 'Investment by the public in companies plays an important part in the commercial life of the community and it is of the utmost importance that prospectuses … should be true and accurate in the statements they contain.'[21] Those comments ring somewhat hollow against the current downgrading of the true and fair override clause from Australia's Corporations Act. Somewhere along the way since the Palmer debacle the ethos enunciated by Lee J has been crudely abandoned. We have more to say on this in Chapter 19.

There was ample evidence of H.G. Palmer's compliance in some instances to the 'technical rules of accountancy' – for example, the use of the Rule of 78 to recognise income hiring charges accrued but not yet paid and (say) mechanical debtors' write-offs without periodic recourse to their separate money's worth. The reality was that H.G. Palmer had not made an actual profit in any year since incorporation, let alone the record profit levels for 1963 and 1964. A headline in the press captured the perceived deception: 'H.G. Palmer gets 4 years … auditor 3 years – Prospectuses should be true and accurate'. Indeed, all public accounting information should be.

The issue of what represents 'a true and accurate (fair) view' of an entity's state of affairs was to bedevil the accounting profession for the next four decades. Recent events reinforce the importance of that criterion. In particular, problems have been exacerbated through the increase in the number of Accounting Standards. Expanding their capacity to develop artifacts – tax-effect balances, consolidation oddities (like Enron's Special Purpose Entities – see Chapter 16) alternate asset valuation base, in particular – has stretched to the financially ridiculous the technical (in accord with the Accounting Standards) interpretation of the true and fair view criterion.

Two of ASL's 'white knights', Sir Henry Bolte and Sir Reginald Ansett. *National Times*, 10 March 1979, p. 23. Courtesy of John Fairfax Holdings Ltd.

Kenneth McMahon after having charges dismissed against him over a Minsec profit statement. Courtesy of News Ltd.

Battles rage as liquidator fights for time

JOHN BYRNE concludes his series on the crash that cost 8,000 investors $45 million.

J.H. Jamison (left) had been provisional liquidator for only one week when the then Prime Minister, John Gorton, met in Sydney with Minsec's major creditors in an abortive attempt to have them pool their security. *The Australian*, 28 April 1973, p. 12. Courtesy of News Ltd.

PART III

The 1970s

CHAPTER 6

Going for Broke in the 1970s

If ... due to the optional accounting rules available to them, company managers and directors are able to conceal the drift [in financial position] shareholders and creditors will continue to support, and support with new money, companies which are weaker than their accounts represent them to be.

R.J. Chambers (1973b, p. 166)

At last in the 1970s there was an apparent regulatory response. Nonetheless, it was to prove an opportunity lost.

As in the 1960s, notable Australian collapses in the early 1970s prompted extensive public concern. This resulted in the NSW government forming the Accounting Standards Review Committee chaired by the late Professor R.J. Chambers, conventional accounting's most trenchant critic, 'to examine the accounting standards ... promulgated ... or at the exposure draft stage ... and to consider any other standards ... which should be considered in the interest of parties who use published accounting information.'[1] The Review Committee's May 1978 report was extremely critical of the existing system of accounting. NSW Attorney General Frank Walker threatened state intervention in the Accounting Standards-setting process unless the accountancy profession issued sensible and enforceable directives. For whatever reason, little direct action resulted from this committee's report and those threats.[2] Despite the committee's strong criticism of conventional accounting practices, the pervading public concern of the regulators – the government and the accounting profession – was the extent of non-compliance with practices prescribed by the profession. Non-compliance was perceived in all cases to be deviant professional behaviour. The underlying cost-based accounting practices were not deemed the major problem.

Between 1975 and 1977 the NSW Corporate Affairs Commission had reviewed annually 249, 535 and 250 accounts of companies. This revealed 62, 253 and 211 instances of non-compliance, respectively. Monitoring continued after the release of the Accounting Standards Review Committee Report, with an analysis of 8,699 companies between 1978 and 1982 revealing non-compliance with one or more Accounting Standards occurring in 3,428 (41 per cent) of companies. Whereas that result was presented as a serious threat to the disclosure of necessary financial information, it is argued here that just the opposite was equally likely. So many of the non-compliances related to prescribed practices that were counterfactual – providing for depreciation on buildings when the overall market price of property (including the buildings) was increasing; providing for future income tax and booking future income tax benefits without the immediate existence of or any definite prospect that the supposed liabilities or assets would materialise, for example. Of course, any subsequent change in tax rates will affect, often materially, the amount of reported asset or liability balances. This was highlighted with the reductions from 36 per cent to 33 per cent in the prevailing corporate tax rates announced in 1993, and subsequently to 36 per cent, then to 34 per cent and to the current 30 per cent.

At the time of one tax change announcement, a Potter Warburg study disclosed that the likely effect on the already 'reported' asset and liability balances of certain public companies would be to 'boost BHP's net profit after abnormals by more than $200 million … [and] CRA Ltd [by] $93 million … [while] companies which have previously reported significant losses are likely to show high write downs of the [previously reported] tax benefits'.[3] Earlier we referred to the similar potential being seized upon following the corporate tax rate changes in the 1995 federal Budget.

Failure to report the money's worth of physical assets has been shown to be a pervading accounting problem. This is especially so under conventional practice which frequently prescribes the treatment of money spent as if it were still in the hands of the spender – a particular problem when the expenditure is on speculative ventures in, say, mining and property which have had top billing in a number of Australia's 1970s collapses. Exploration holes and high-rise office blocks have more in common than might at first appear. Both cost a lot and promise substantial returns before any revenue rolls in. Until it does, they may amount to a financial loss.

Precipitating the formation of the 1978 Chambers Committee were the mining-cum-investment and property financial dilemmas of the 1970s, aftermaths of the mining boom of the late 1960s and the property boom of the early 1970s. These included: investment traders, Mineral Securities Australia Ltd and Patrick Partners; construction group, Mainline; property-cum-financier, Cambridge Credit Corporation Ltd; the conglomerate, Gollins Holdings Ltd; and the finance-cum-property development company, Associated Securities Ltd (Table 6.1).

Like their counterparts in the 1960s, these unexpected (to many) major corporate collapses in the 1970s created public pressure on regulators to reassess the utility of existing regulatory mechanisms – in particular, the utility of existing professional accounting and auditing practices. For example, Gollins collapsed in 1975 shortly after an interim six-monthly report had revealed a reported profit of $835,192. Inquiries by an official inspector resulted in it being adjusted to a loss of $10,776,606.[4] Construction heavyweight Mainline

Table 6.1 Major company failures in Australia, 1970–79

Year of failure – date administrator appointed	Name of company	Basis of criticism	Actions against auditors/officials
February 1971	Mineral Securities Australia Ltd (Minsec)	Profit had been created by dealings between related group companies.	Directors of Minsec were charged over matters relating to a published 'consolidated' profit figure. All charges were dismissed
August 1974	Mainline Corporation	(i) Borrowing short and investing long in construction projects; (ii) Overgeared.	n.a.
September 1974	Cambridge Credit Corporation	(i) Consolidation practices; (ii) Intermingling of private and public companies; and (iii) Valuation of land and shares.	'Class action'-type civil proceedings against the auditors by the debenture holders resulted in an out-of-court settlement reportedly of approximately $20 million. Criminal actions against directors dismissed.
June 1976	Gollins Holdings Ltd	Reported *profit* statement of $835,192 was subsequently restated as a *loss* of $10,776,606. This was due to: (i) inadequate inventory valuation procedures; and (ii) failure to recognise losses in overseas affiliate.	Civil actions against auditors produced a $6 million out-of-court settlement. Criminal actions against directors saw two gaoled – Gale for 13 years and Glenister for 12 years.
February 1979	Associated Securities Ltd (ASL)	(i) Real estate property valuations; (ii) Capitalising interest costs; (iii) Recognition of income; (iv) Use of equity-accounted profits; and (v) Lack of assistance from controlling company when associate was in financial difficulty.	n.a.

Source: Expanded version of Table 7.1 of A.T. Craswell, *Auditing* (New York: Garland Publishing Inc., 1984).

had also suddenly gone belly up a year earlier. Apt examples – familiar scenarios which are further revealed in the telling analyses of the 1970s collapses at Minsec, Cambridge Credit and ASL.

Setting up the Chambers Committee was a 'politically' shrewd response given the public outcry. Ignoring its recommendations was 'politically' correct, given the profession's public opposition to the Committee's composition and its silence regarding the Committee's recommendations. That nothing came of its report is indicative of the gap between public rhetoric and the private and professional intransigence. That intransigence is inexcusable against a background of the 'accounting irregularities' noted earlier and examined in the following chapters.

CHAPTER 7

Minsec: Decline of a Share Trader*

Mineral Securities Australia Ltd had started slowly enough but once the accelerator went down there was no stopping it.

G. Souter (1971, p. 7)

That observation captured the flavour of Minsec's meteoric rise. 'Ken [McMahon] and Tom [Nestel] … moved like the wind. They never made a wrong move until the end.'[1] Minsec's lifetime operations occupied just over five years – another 'still-born' failure, but one also illustrative of how extreme success can presage failure.[2] As the Rae Senate Select Committee on Securities and Exchange Report noted: 'No company in Australia has had a more spectacular rise and fall than Mineral Securities Australia Ltd'.[3] Subsequent collapses in the 1980s at Westmex, Compass Airlines (I and II), and more recently at One.Tel, would be worthy contenders for that title.

Mineral Securities of Australia Ltd (MSAL) was incorporated as an unlisted company in May 1965 with an authorised capital of $500,000. Its object was to engage in share trading and investment activities as an offshoot of mining consultants and advisors Kenneth McMahon and Partners. McMahon and Tom Nestel dominated the affairs of the company as the chairman and the managing director, respectively.[4] Minsec was listed in 1967 to take advantage of the share market boom of the late 1960s. It achieved rapid growth, using share-trading profits to acquire control of several companies. Minsec and Patrick Partners were reported to be 'the two great success stories … [of Australia's] financial markets … of the late 1960s'.[5] Quickly this adulation would fade.

By June 1970, share capital of Minsec was reported to be $10.2 million and the consolidated net profit for the 1969/70 financial year was $12.7 million (Tables 7.1 and 7.2). Minsec had acquired a significant position in mineral developments in tin, wolfram, rutile, uranium and iron ore. Its share trading activities were of staggering proportions for the Australian market. In 1970 Minsec had purchased $107 million and sold $47 million worth of shares. The Rae Committee placed this in perspective by indicating that the trading volume that year of the AMP Society – by far the largest life assurance company in Australia – involved purchases of $40 million and sales of $8 million. Minsec's share-trading activity certainly was on a grand scale. It was claimed to be 'the heaviest share trader that Australia has known'.[6] But this also presented Minsec

Table 7.1 Mineral Securities Australia Ltd and subsidiaries, Minsec Investments Pty Ltd and Norausam Pty Ltd – 'consolidated' balance sheet as at 30 June and 31 December 1970

30 June 1970		31 December 1970	
$m	Issued Capital	$m	$m
4.5	Ordinary	4.5	
5.7	Preference	5.7	10.2
	Capital Reserves		
13.4	Share Premium	13.4	
2.0	Capital Profits	2.0	15.4
	Revenue Reserves		
–	Tax Exempt		–
10.1	Unappropriated Profits		13.2*
$35.7	Share Capital and Reserves		$38.8
	Represented by:–		
23.7	Current Liabilities – less than 12 months		86.4
	Less		
3.8	Current Assets		23.9
19.9	Net Short-term Indebtedness		62.5
–	Liabilities – after 12 months		–
19.9	TOTAL Net Indebtedness		62.5
52.2	Investments		97.7*
3.6	Convertible Loan to Robe River Limited		3.6
$35.7			$38.8

Note: * Subject to subsequent reduction of $6.8 million in 'Unappropriated profits' and in 'Investments', upon correction of half-yearly profit statement.
Source: Rae Report (1974), Table 14–9, p. 14.87.

with a potential problem, as it ran the risk of being unable to liquidate a holding without causing a run on the market in that stock.

Growing pains

Understandably, Minsec's growth plans required a continuation of favourable annual net profit reports – $1.9 million in 1968; $1.4 million in 1969 and $12.7 million in 1970. However, the share market boom had begun to wane in late 1969 and into early 1970. Indeed, Minsec's managers decided in February not to buy any further trading stock, new issues, placements below market prices or shares involving rights issues. By the end of May the trading portfolio was reduced to three stocks costing $101,000 and possessing a market value of $92,000. Although conditions did not warrant it, the decision was reversed and by 30 June the trading portfolio had increased to 132 stocks costing $13.1

million and possessing a market value of $12.3 million. One stock, Poseidon, cost approximately $4.5 million.

Poseidon was the most notorious of the speculative mining (nickel) stocks during the 1968–72 mining boom. Its share price was on a roller-coaster ride, increasing from $0.80 on 31 July 1969 to $280 on 12 February 1970, falling back to $178 on 31 March, $73 on 30 April and $44 on 31 December 1970. Primarily these variations were driven by what turned out to be 'over-optimistic' reports of geological surveys of 'nickel reserves'.[7] The market had peaked in early 1970 and in the downturn Minsec and its wholly-owned subsidiaries sustained realised losses of $3.1 million and $1.6 million in July and August 1970 respectively.

Table 7.2 Mineral Securities Australia Ltd – summary of consolidated profit items and dividends, 1965/66 to 1969/70 (to nearest $000)

	1965/66	1966/67	1967/68	1968/69	1969/70
Share trading profits	21,000	161,000	1,887,000	1,946,000	12,418,000
Mining profits (*before* deducting outside interests)	–	–	–	–	7,659,000
Mining profits (*after* deducting outside interests, approximate)	–	–	–	–	2,400,000
Interest and dividends received	6,000	28,000	46,000	124,000	415,000
Outside minority interests in group profits	–	–	303,000	523,000	7,220,000
Taxation provision	7,000	–	–	–	61,000
Consolidated net profit	21,000	161,000	1,584,000	1,423,000	12,707,000
Dividends paid					
Preference	–	–	–	61,000	215,000
Ordinary	–	33,000	91,000	221,000	555,000

Source: Rae Report (1974) p. 14.20.

In order to retrieve its position, Minsec initiated a number of policies with accounting consequences. Subsequent scrutiny by the Rae Committee and the inspectors appointed by the NSW government exposed three practices arguably contravening convention: (1) the back-dating of share-trading losses – principally incurred on Poseidon shares; (2) group dealings in Robe River shares, including back-to-back loans; and (3) 'opportunistic' accounting treatment of its investments in Queensland Mines, Kathleen Investments and Thiess Holdings.

Australian accounting practice had never required securities to be marked-to-market in the primary accounts.[8] Accordingly, Minsec back-dated some of the losses on sales related to share trading after 30 June 1970 to the previous year. This was achieved by writing off an amount of $2.1 million from the trading portfolio as at 30 June 1970. Of that amount, $1.3 million was attributable to the mining investment darling of the period, Poseidon. This policy was disclosed (but without quantifying the effect) in Note 10 to the accounts, declaring: 'Market value of the investments of the group has been calculated on the basis of the last sale price of each stock on 30 June 1970, with the exception of one stock which has been further written down in the light of post-balance events to the realised value.' The stock was Poseidon. This adjustment was reflected in the internal accounts for Minsec and its wholly-owned subsidiaries for the month of September wherein the total losses of $4.1 million from share trading incurred up to 28 September were reduced by that $2.1 million figure.

Later, the Rae Committee was extremely critical of this approach, stating:

> If this statement [in Note 10] was referring to the Poseidon transactions, it was
> uninformative or misleading in several ways. It gave no indication of the amount
> involved in the adjustment, nor any indication of the bearing, if any, that the
> adjustment had on the declared profits. It would be taken by readers to apply
> to stocks actually held at 30 June, and not to any stocks that might have been
> bought after that date and subsequently sold at a loss.[9]

However, the inspectors stated that 'the action taken was adequately explained in a note to and forming part of the accounts for 1970'.[10] They might also have said that compulsorily done, on a continuous basis, it made more sense and better informed shareholders of the current position than the existing method did.

That general rubric remained. For example, moves in the 1990s by the Australian accounting profession to have securities accounted for on a marked-to-market basis by financial institutions (ED 59, 'Accounting for Financial Instruments', 1993) met vehement objection from those in the industry as being too costly, too subjective, too unreliable, too volatile, too prone to change, too

Figure 7.1 Mineral Securities Australia Ltd – major investments as at 30 June 1970

MINERAL SECURITIES AUSTRALIA LTD

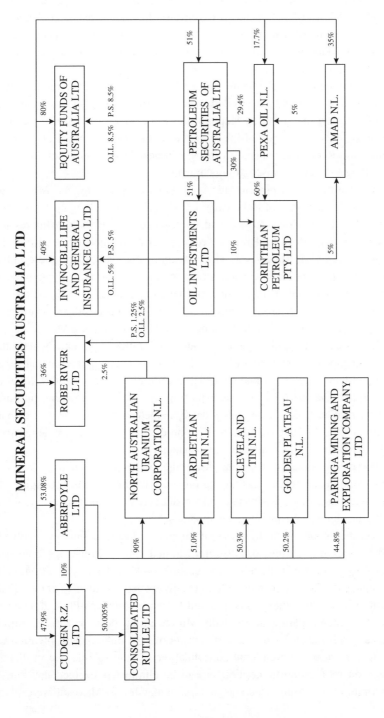

different from the inclusion in 'Notes'. Similar objections greeted the requirements of AASB 1023, 'Financial Reporting of General Insurance Activities',
that investments of insurance companies, akin to their inventory, be marked-
to-market. Marking-to-market is for many a valuation method, it seems, that is
too close to the truth.

Strictly Ballroom, the Australian award-winning movie, captured the excite-
ment of the 1950s which swelled over into the 1960s. Minsec's managers
clearly entered the swing by stepping the Robe River shuffle with deceptive
financial footwork: *Step 1*: Minsec acquiring control of Robe River; *Step 2*:
selling the Robe River shares to intermediaries; *Step 3*: those intermediaries
on-selling to related Minsec group companies.

The shuffle was a ploy to side-step losses on share trading. Minsec had
subscribed to the issue of Robe River Ltd in early 1970, taking up 14.4 million
shares at $1 par value. It also had contributed a $3.6 million interest-free
convertible loan to Robe River. Effectively, as at 30 June 1970, Minsec had
achieved control of Robe River, which meant it was a subsidiary of the Minsec
group. The price of Robe's shares on the market was substantially above par –
largely due to the buying by members of the group (Table 7.3). Minsec resolved
to realise these paper profits. During October–December 400,000 shares were
sold to external parties at a profit of nearly $250,000, reducing Minsec's equity
in Robe River to around 40 per cent. During the following month, Minsec then
acquired another 10 per cent of Robe River – thereby giving it more than 50 per
cent and hence, again, formal control. According to the *Companies Act* at the
time, this made Robe River a subsidiary of Minsec for accounting purposes;
and its profits, which were consolidated, helped to disguise Minsec's share-
trading losses for 1970. All this was within the law, though as we demonstrate
in Chapters 16 and 17 it amounted to financial nonsense.

Perversely, superior financial disclosure being promoted as a virtue of
consolidation accounting was having precisely the opposite effect. Again, this
was an example of professionally and legislatively sanctioned creativity, at least
in the accounts of the individual companies.

Minsec's dabbling in the mysteries of consolidation accounting involved it
and Petroleum Securities of Australia Limited, one of Minsec's subsidiaries,
in selling Robe River shares to the group's brokers, Hattersley & Maxwell.
Hattersley & Maxwell then on-sold to wholly-owned subsidiaries of the Minsec
group, Minsec Investments Pty Ltd and Petsec Investments Pty Ltd. Over the
last three-month period of 1970 the Minsec group dealt with 6.175 million
shares in this manner and 'realised' a profit of $6.6 million. The intention was
to circumvent the conventional consolidation accounting rule that profits and
losses on intra-group transactions are to be eliminated, deemed fictitious, in
determining the group's income or loss. Hattersley & Maxwell were placed

as intermediaries in the deal so that the transactions would not fall foul of the intra-group company elimination rule and the resulting profits thereby could be included in the published consolidated results. At best it is a clumsy rule, inviting smart tactics like the Robe River shuffle. It is to be noted that if assets were marked-to-market continuously and subject to audit verification, manipulations – under- or overstatements of the money's worth of assets – could not go undetected. There would be no need then to assume that all intra-group transactions entailed manipulations and the Minsec–PSAL drama need not have arisen.

The figures in Table 7.3 disclose the impact of the policies of asset valuations and share trading. Ultimately the reported outcome of the deal was reversed, after considerable dispute – inexplicably not over what the shares were worth in the market but whether the transaction was 'intra-group' and thus caught by the consolidation intra-group transaction elimination rule. It was almost as if the financial truth of the outcome was irrelevant – but then it was an accounting issue where financial reality so often, it seems, is given a back seat.

Minsec's shuffling of assets, profits and losses was, to a major extent, facilitated by the holding/subsidiary company organisational structure, the endorsed accounting practice of valuing physical assets at historical cost and consolidating the financial data of group companies. It entailed the compulsory elimination of the financial effect of intra-group transactions. That combination has been a recurrent feature of Australia's post–World War II failures – obscuring financial reality. Shuffling and relocating assets, injecting the aggregated data with fictional assets and equities, reversing the trends in the separate accounts of the constituent companies, and plugging the accounts on consolidation with artifacts of the consolidation process, have contributed significantly to the confusion and have cost some investors dearly in the decades before Minsec and those after.

Table 7.3 Minsec intra-group dealings, October to December 1970

Month	Profit from share trading $	Robe River shares sold $	Profit from Robe River shares $	Profit (loss) excluding Robe River $
October	4,305,874	3,103,000	3,776,947	528,927
November	1,579,090	1,207,800	1,580,548	(1,458)
December	1,055,205	946,000	1,256,223	(201,018)

Source: Inspectors' Report, Vol. 1 (1977), p. 20.

Thirty-odd years after the Robe River affair, the position remains un-altered.[11] Neither the concept of a 'group' comprising a holding company and subsidiaries nor the provision of consolidated financial statements have assisted the securities market to achieve greater confidence or orderliness. Retention of conventional consolidated financial statements in the accounting bag of tricks is as unjustified as it is avoidable.

Financial obfuscation was facilitated also by intra-group and back-to-back loans. Under its debenture trust deed, Robe River was forbidden to lend in excess of 5 per cent of its *total* tangible assets to related companies without the consent of the debenture trustee. Again, asset valuation looms as a major factor. Clearly, as we show here and in other cases, this is an unworkable covenant to monitor or to regulate unless the audited market selling prices of physical assets are disclosed continually. But accounting practice did not require assets to be reported at their market prices then, nor do the current set of Accounting Standards require it universally. If they did, all those *extraordinaries* and *abnormals, one-offs, special items* discussed in Chapter 2 would be less dra-matic when they are reported.

Between 30 June 1970 and 31 December 1970 the borrowing limit of Robe River was approximately $1.5 million.[12] Robe was able to circumvent the limit by back-to-back loans.[13] It would lend funds to an intermediary (on occasions, reputable houses such as King & Yuill Investments or Ord-BT), which would then lend an identical amount to Minsec. The Rae Committee stated that at the end of January 1971 this form of indebtedness was $3 million; at November 1970 it was $4 million, a week earlier $3.5 million, a week later $5.8 million.[14] The committee also stated:

> A knowledge of the financial condition in which Minsec then stood leaves no room for doubt that the loans obtained surreptitiously from Robe River helped materially to finance the process by which Robe River became a subsidiary of Minsec, or that Robe River was being placed at risk in making such loans to Minsec at the time.

Interestingly, those back-to-back financing practices were apparently occurring worldwide, if Charles Raw's account of the way the Vatican Bank and the Banco Ambrosiano defied monetary regulations in shuffling funds in and out of Italy is to be believed.[15] And the Bond Corporation manoeuvres described in Chapter 12 imply that they have contemporary currency.[16]

During this crucial period, Minsec embarked upon other investments. Be-tween September and December 1970 significant stakes in Queensland Mines (QM), Kathleen Investments (KI) and Thiess were purchased. In total these investments cost $30 million – $16.6 million in QM, $10.9 million in KI and $2.5 million in Thiess. These stocks were initially classified as trading stock in

Minsec's internal activity reports. In the November 1970 internal activity report the market gain on all trading stocks was shown as $513,000, including a gain on QM and KI of approximately $1.5 million. At 31 December 1970 the internally recorded losses on QM, KI and Thiess were $3.15 million, $2.15 million and $205,000, respectively. At the end of December, fortuitously, the three stocks were 'reclassified' as long-term investments and therefore not required to be reported with other trading stocks, under the 'lower of cost or market rule'[17] – a variety of bases complying with accountants' conservatism doctrine (which implies it is more prudent to understate the current worth of an asset than overstate it). The inspectors thought the reclassification problematical. Without it, Minsec would almost certainly have had to report a trading loss rather than a profit for the six-month period ending 31 December.

It should be noted that the variant valuation rules for trading stocks and investments existing then effectively remain today. So does the general thrust of the conservatism rule – though how one can continue to justify deliberate understatement any more than deliberate overstatement defies logic. Virtue would appear to lie only in 'telling it how it is'.

Note also the similarity between this impact of classification on the valuation basis to be applied to the asset and the earlier use of classification of property by Reid Murray as a current asset which facilitated not having to inject the profit and loss account with amortisation changes. Clearly it is nonsense to claim that assets are worth more or less, have greater or less value, according to how directors *classify* them.

Unfulfilled ambitions of a mining trader

Despite the difficulties encountered from the falling share market, Minsec did not seek to retreat and strengthen its position. Thirty million dollars had been spent acquiring a position in QM, KI and Thiess. It had also spent a net $7 million expanding its Robe River holding. Minsec's financial positions at 30 June 1970 and 31 December 1970 reveal how these acquisitions were financed (Table 7.1). At 30 June, current liabilities stood at $23.9 million and current assets at $3.8 million. At 31 December, current liabilities had jumped to $86.4 million and current assets were only $23.9 million. Of the current liabilities, $20.9 million was at call, nearly all unsecured, while a further $31 million comprised short-term obligations – a familiar, precarious strategy of borrowing short and investing long.

In summary, many factors coalesced to threaten Minsec's future. First, the downturn in the prices of QM and KI was a result of suspicions that the Nabarlek ore bodies were not as rich as earlier geological announcements had indicated. Minsec's share price fell to $10 compared with its $23 peak during the previous six-month period. Second, Minsec had received a report from Hill Samuel, its merchant bankers, indicating that significant restructuring would be required if Minsec were to survive. The report continued:

> to form a syndicate to provide additional facilities for MSAL ... would be a distinct danger ... it will be necessary to reveal full information regarding MSAL's current position and commitments, its very great temporary dependence on the market might become widely known and discussed, with the effect that its own operation in this area could be prejudiced.[18]

Third, confidence was further damaged by the disclosure in Minsec's take-over documents showing that the cost of its share portfolio had increased by $34.6 million but was financed with outside borrowings to the extent of $31.2 million. Further, Minsec's loans secured by shares required additional collateral as the share prices fell, which in turn limited Minsec's ability to raise fresh secured loans.

Minsec's main hope of overcoming its liquidity problems lay in being able to report a favourable profit. On 25 January 1971, Minsec announced:

> The consolidated net profit, subject to audit, from both mining operations and share trading of MSAL and its subsidiaries for the 6 months ended 31st December, 1970, was in excess of $3.5 million after deducting the minority shareholders' interests, provision for tax and writing down the share trading portfolio to the lower of cost or market value.[19]

Reporting a profit was dependent upon the three policies discussed earlier – in particular, on the contribution from the dealings in Robe River shares, without which the reported group profit of $3.5 million would become a reported loss of over $3.2 million. In a nutshell, the main issue for the account-ants and regulators was not whether the separate subsidiary companies involved had realised a profit on the back-to-back share deals – the inspectors, the judge and common sense would dictate that a profit existed on these transactions. The real issue was whether under conventional consolidation accounting, a *consolidated profit* could be reported. The conventional treatment of subsidiary profits generated from group transactions would be to eliminate those profits. While not accepted in Mr Justice Taylor's initial 1976 judgment, later on appeal this view prevailed – a most peculiar outcome.

As we noted earlier, the adjudication turned not on what the securities were worth in the market, but upon whether the parties to the transactions were related. They were deemed on appeal to be related – so what was profit when they were thought unrelated, turned into a loss when they were deemed to be related, irrespective of what the market disclosed.[20] It would appear that it was important not to let the actual and observable financial outcomes of the deal get in the way of assessing the accounting profit or loss. And that is an interesting outcome, bearing in mind the obsession in the accountancy profession with advocating the 'substance' and not the 'form' of transactions in determining how to account for them. Accounting convention in the 2000s would continue to imply in the Minsec case that no profit was earned, simply because the parties were related.

So, it is likely that exactly the same result would emerge if facts similar to this case were to be heard today. Despite all the substance over form rhetoric, when it comes to unravelling the financial effects of transactions between related companies the form often prevails no matter what the financial substance happens to be.

In addition to its other activities, Minsec established two mutual funds – the First Australian Growth and Income Fund and the Second Australian Growth and Income Fund – early in 1970. Minsec subscribed $1 million and $2.5 million to the FAGIF and the SAGIF respectively. The funds' prospectuses, as noted in the *Rae Report*, confirmed that each fund:

> will be of a 'general' investment type. ... MSAL has now substantially reduced its long-term investments in companies in which it does not have management control ... it is intended that the Fund will direct its activities to long-term portfolio investment not associated with management control ...[21]

Despite those assurances, the *Rae Report* concluded that the funds concentrated the majority of their long-term investment funds in the Minsec group and associated companies.[22]

Minsec also utilised the funds as a source of short-term finance, for Minsec was not an approved money market borrower. Again adopting a 'group' perspective, this was not a problem – as at Stanhill, it was merely a hazard to be overcome. It was circumvented by the use of intermediaries, Minsec's brokers, principally King & Yuill Investments. The Rae Committee stated that 'the combined back-to-back loans from the two Funds passing through King & Yuill Investments to Minsec reached a peak of $7.8 million in mid-June 1970'.[23] Minsec's reported financial position had been obfuscated again by the use of related-party transactions through intermediaries within a group setting.

An unexpected collapse

On 2 February 1971 Minsec was advised by its legal counsel that the profit on the Robe River share transactions should be excluded from the calculation of income for the preceding six-month period ending 31 December 1970. On

3 February Minsec redeemed its shares in FAGIF and SAGIF, realising $2.87 million. Payment was based on valuations of the funds' assets as at that date. Allegedly, Minsec was aware by then of the difficulties it was in and of the probable impact on the funds of the impending announcement of the profit reversal.[24] Clearly this would have had a significant effect on the value of the funds' investments in the group and the redemption value of its shares. Indeed, the collapse of Minsec brought an immediate suspension of redemptions for investors in the funds and losses in excess of $5.5 million on shares which the funds had bought. Redemptions did not recommence until 20 months later.

The next day, 4 February, directors of Minsec issued this statement:

> The directors wish to withdraw the statement made in the Company's circular of 25th January 1971 … directors were advised by senior counsel that 5,193,400 of the Robe River shares purchased by Minsec Investment P/L must be treated as having been purchased from the Company. Accepted accountancy practice requires that profits derived from a sale by a parent company to its subsidiary should be eliminated from the consolidated profit and loss accounts … the profit of $6.63 million earned by the Company on the sale of these shares is to be eliminated from the consolidated profit and loss account, so that the results for the six months will appear as a loss of approximately $3.283 million.[25]

Events moved quickly. Minsec's demise matched its rise. Dealing in Minsec shares was suspended on all exchanges at the company's request. Creditors petitioned the NSW Supreme Court for the winding up of Minsec and Jim Jamison was appointed liquidator on 11 February 1971.

Aftermath – money market dominoes

Minsec's collapse illustrates the inevitable spread of trouble as the financial fallout from a large collapse settles. Minsec owed significant amounts in the official short-term money market and the intercompany market. In Minsec's fall there was the potential for severe economic repercussions. A company domino effect could have developed – companies with significant loans to Minsec failing and falling, with the impact spreading to other related companies. The likelihood of such a flow-on is evident in the reported reaction of business people and politicians who met to consider the possible repercussions for the Australian money market.[26] It might have been amusing to see those captains of finance wringing their hands in despair at Sydney's Kirribilli House. Again we might ponder their thoughts regarding the advice over the years from those in the know. There is no better place to plan damage control than Kirribilli's bush gardens and softening harbour views – Australia's political leaders have been doing it there for years.

Damage control no doubt was necessary. In the longer term it would have been more effective had there been a proposal to discuss how the accounting and other regulatory frameworks had fused to veil Minsec's financial position so effectively.

Those events ring familiar. There were counterparts in late 1973 in the United Kingdom, with the Bank of England's 'lifeboat' rescue of Britain's secondary banks in the aftermath of their ill-fated exposures to property,[27] and in the United States in the 1980s with the salvage package by the US government for the Savings and Loans industry. Again in the United Kingdom, in 1991/92, the Bank of England secretly propped up major banks in response to the potential crisis from their exposure to declining property values and poorly performing loan portfolios. And in Australia in the post-HIH 2002 insurance fallout, federal and state governments were involved in propping up the system against collateral damage. On each of these occasions the threat of a possible domino effect has been used to justify intervention by committed free-market governments. On each of these occasions, too, accounting data have been remiss in failing to warn early insiders and outsiders of an impending crisis.

With Minsec the domino effect was avoided through a consortium of trading banks and other large Australian organisations. A line of credit of $35 million was offered to the liquidator of Minsec. Jamison did not accept it, but the fact that it was made restored confidence until other satisfactory arrangements were made.

Charges

Kenneth McMahon, Tom Nestel and other directors of Minsec were charged in relation to its collapse. The charges mainly related to the publication of the 25 January profit figure. They were prosecuted under section 176 of the *Crimes Act* – which covers the publication of any written statement of account knowing it to be false in any material particular with intent to deceive any shareholders or attempting to induce any person to become a shareholder; under section 73 of the *Securities Industry Act* – which covers the dissemination of any information which at the time it is made or disseminated that person knows or has reasonable grounds for knowing is false or misleading in any material particular; and under section 47 of the *Companies Act* – which covers untrue statements or wilful non-disclosure in a prospectus. Similar legal issues were described in respect of the *H.G. Palmer* and *Royal Mail* cases.

On this occasion, however, all charges were subsequently dismissed. The trial judge, Mr Justice Taylor, stated, *inter alia*:

> if MSAL sold shares, for which it paid a dollar, to Hattersley & Maxwell at $2.50, then in fact and in law, in my opinion, it made a profit ... if the Crown wishes

to establish that this profit statement is false, then it might be expected that they would have produced from an account what they say is a true statement ... there is no evidence fit to go to the jury to consider that this profit statement is false.[28]

A strong point. Indeed, if conventional practices were drawn upon it is unlikely that any such 'true statement' could have been prepared. In many respects the characteristics of conventional accounting facilitated the calculations of profit to which the charges referred. That position substantially prevails today. It would be very interesting to witness a case being made that compliance with the current batch of Accounting Standards could give a 'true statement' of a company's wealth and financial progress. Mr Justice Taylor's challenge for a 'true statement' would have exciting consequences today.

The Crown appealed the decision, not over the acquittals, but to clarify a number of points of law. The NSW Court of Appeal handed down its judgment in June 1979. It found that Mr Justice Taylor 'Fell in error in determining as a matter of fact that the dealings were not sham transactions instead of leaving that question to the jury'.[29] This issue would not have been in question had accounting practice been competent to deal with the situation. It was not, and remains so.

Minsec's rise and fall again highlights the difficulties of properly accounting for profits, losses and asset balances when group transactions are involved. Most of those would not exist if assets were marked-to-market periodically and verified. Minsec's financial problems also evidence the post-balance date dilemma facing accountants and auditors, exacerbated further by the realisation of profit issue. Much of the anguish is due to reliance on cost-based valuations and conventional consolidation procedures. Minsec's virtual control of share trading on the Australian share market created another hitch. Marking-to-market could thus encounter problems of obtaining the externally verifiable market prices of shares to which auditors could refer to corroborate the data presented by directors. Against that it could be argued that this is where the role of the professional would have been significant – the use of judgment based upon the accumulated professional wisdom would have been an imperative.

Finally, Minsec provides another instance of a large, publicly listed company disclosing a substantial, reported profit figure just weeks prior to being placed in the hands of a liquidator. The effectiveness of accounting and auditing, even though within the ambit of existing professional practices and the law, clearly was found wanting.

Four years later, events surrounding the collapse of the Cambridge Credit Corporation group were in many respects of the same genre, a familiar scenario. Plans there for building a financial empire relied primarily on property investment, without sound financial foundations.

CHAPTER 8

Cambridge Credit:
Other People's Money*

Q. Inspector: 'Did you regard Cambridge as a one-man show?'
A. Hutcheson (Director): 'In my opinion most large companies are
dominated by one man, and if that's a one-man show, well Cambridge is
a one-man show.'

Inspectors' 1st Report (1977, p. 24)

Hutcheson's assessment raises difficulties in a public company context. Clearly, Cambridge Credit Corporation Ltd was a 'one-man show', under the direction of R.E.M. (Mort) Hutcheson. He had qualified as an accountant in 1940, receiving his early training in a finance company, and formed R.E.M. Hutcheson Pty Ltd, later renamed Unilateral Services Pty Ltd, to set up and manage a number of small businesses for individual investors. For these services a management fee and a share of the profits were received.

Newcastle Acceptance Company Ltd was incorporated in 1950 with an authorised capital of $200,000. Prior to commencing trading in November 1950, the company took over the Hutchesons' father and son partnership as a going concern. Management was vested in the Hutcheson family company, Unilateral Services Pty Ltd. This arrangement was formalised in June 1957 by a 25-year service agreement, providing extensive management powers, including the right to hire and fire employees. The remuneration for the services consisted of reimbursement of all costs, a commission of 5 per cent of audited net profit before tax, and $3,000 per annum (added later). While this was not unusual it was fraught with temptation. And it bore a similarity to the contingency basis, which determined Lord Kylsant's remuneration from his ill-fated Royal Mail company in the 1920s, and to the Barings Bank and many other flawed *reported profit*-based compensation schemes in the 1990s.

Initially the main business involved hire-purchase financing for all types of durable goods and money lending in Newcastle and surrounding districts and the large country cities of Tamworth and Wollongong. A name change to Cambridge Credit Corporation Ltd was registered in September 1955, by which time it was one of some 100 private and public companies financing hire-purchase agreements managed by the Hutchesons.

After June 1956, several of these companies were acquired by Cambridge, consideration being shares and debenture stock. By June 1957, issued and paid-up capital was $320,000, first mortgage debenture stock totalled $150,000 and deposits with Cambridge amounted to $237,210. Around this time the business

Table 8.1 Cambridge Credit Corporation Ltd and subsidiaries – paid-up capital, borrowings and reported total assets, selected years, 1957–74

Year end 30 June	Paid-up capital $**	Borrowings* $**	Total assets $**	Gearing: borrowings/ total assets %
1957	320,000	387,210	961,444	40.3
1960	1,015,000	7,964,818	9,363,880	85.1
1962	2,362,678	21,558,124	25,429,322	84.8
1965	3,386,000	26,191,000	31,874,000	82.2
1967	3,778,000	30,073,000	36,215,000	83.4
1969	6,365,000	50,148,000	59,564,000	84.2
1970	8,865,000	76,027,000	89,215,000	85.2
1971	10,800,000	88,361,000	104,135,000	84.9
1972	11,800,000	103,288,000	120,934,000	85.4
1973	12,400,000	149,363,000	174,097,000	85.8
1974	12,400,000	188,004,975	215,007,835	87.4

Notes: * Excluding bank overdraft.

      ** Dollar figures in this table represent a 2:1 conversion of reported £ amounts prior to 1966 and the actual reported $ amounts thereafter.

Source: Sydney Stock Exchange Investment Service, C129 (1974).

emphasis shifted to real estate, home financing, property investment and land development.

Official listing on the Sydney and Newcastle stock exchanges was effected in November 1957, with the first public issue of debenture stock in July 1958. Subsequent expansion was rapid, primarily as financier and principal engaged in property trading, land subdivision and lease rental. Despite an increase in debenture borrowings from $2,510,000 to $7,890,726, the group survived the November 1960 credit squeeze – it even achieved an increase in paid-up capital from $1,015,000 to $1,565,000 during the year ended 30 June 1961. Reported consolidated earnings for the financial years 1959/60 to 1961/62 represented 18.7, 18.1, and 19.42 per cent, respectively, on average ordinary capital employed.[1] Cambridge was an *apparent* success, even through those difficult economic times.

Data in Table 8.1 illustrate the group's expansion. The nature of the business medium is revealing. Sometimes unsecured loans were granted to the acquired companies, which in turn built up a substantial equity in Cambridge. On other occasions, joint ventures were undertaken using finance and administrative services provided by Cambridge. Hutcheson's group entity perspective was clearly evident from the outset. Undoubtedly so, for it was an 'accounting way' of arranging business.

Byzantine family structures

From 1966 onwards, Cambridge advanced substantial amounts to subsidiaries or joint venture companies for investment in large tracts of undeveloped land with a view to long-term subdivision and sale, often in working-class outer suburbs of the eastern states' capital cities. Generation of sufficient cash flows to service the projects and the borrowings proved difficult, with Cambridge having to rely increasingly on further borrowings. Undoubtedly the ability to borrow largely depended on reporting satisfactory trading profits, meeting interest, loan redemptions and discharging other obligations, maintaining its share price and *reporting* that it was preserving a capital structure within the limits imposed by the various trust deeds. That was a tall order, though typifying the normal accounting, finance and management bind perennially facing business. But Cambridge managed to sustain an illusion of prosperity for over a decade following its heady start.

By 1962 the company was increasingly enmeshed with private companies substantially owned or controlled by the Hutcheson family. Thus, at Cambridge, the prevailing network of subsidiary and associated companies and joint venture arrangements[2] was woven into the affairs of a complex group structure and accordingly complex financing arrangements (Figure 8.1) – a familiar scenario. Cambridge's complexity mirrors the conglomerate structure at Australia's Adsteam and the UK's Maxwell Communications in the 1980s, HIH in the 1990s and the 1920s Insull Utilities structures in the United States and at the Royal Mail Steam Packet Company in the United Kingdom. Time changes little, it seems, in conducting big business, especially the inadequacy of accountability checks on large, complex organisations.

Apart from the Hutchesons and Davis-Raiss, none of the directors at Cambridge had formal training in accounting or business management. It is not surprising that, in keeping with conventional wisdom, the inspectors reported: 'Mr Hutcheson was the dominant personality in ... the company and the way in which the Cambridge group evolved was the result of his personal ambition and initiative.'[3] Further, 'Mr Davis-Raiss was the only member of the Board apart from Mr Hutcheson who had any real ability but he, too, was dominated by Mr Hutcheson ... [and] had a loyalty to him which infringed upon any independence of approach ... Accounting practices adopted by the group we believe to have been of his devising and initiative.'[4]

Hutcheson, in response to an inspector's question concerning the appointment of outside directors, replied:

Figure 8.1 Hutcheson Conglomerate as at 30 June 1973

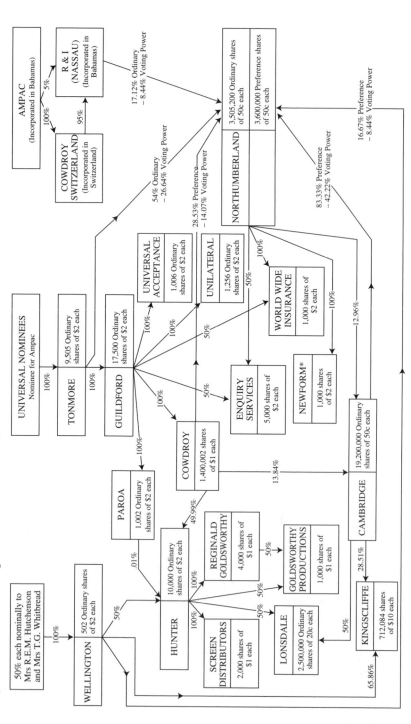

Note: * An additional 1,000 shares were recorded by Newform as allotted to Paroa Investments Pty Ltd on 29 June 1973. This allotment was never taken up, paid for or recognised as an investment by that company. *Source: Inspectors' 2nd Report* (1979) p. 290.

I had the ambition … to make my own name in the city and didn't want an
outside director, whoever or however prestigious he may be, because it was
my determination to build Cambridge up into a large successful company …
In my opinion most large companies are dominated by one man and if that's
a one-man show, well Cambridge is a one-man show.[5]

That was a fair enough comment and one which might have been made of
most of the companies discussed here – certainly of Bond Corporation, Qintex,
Hooker Corporation, Adsteam and Westmex, HIH, One.Tel, Enron, WorldCom
– and, significantly, of many successful ongoing companies. The difficulty for
outsiders and insiders is differentiating the public from the private affairs.

Private and public operations

Throughout Cambridge's history there was a close relationship between the
Cambridge group and an 'amorphous group of private companies' substantially
owned or controlled by Hutcheson. The government-appointed inspectors
formed the view that:

> The conglomerate comprised the two publicly recognised operating groups,
> Cambridge and Northumberland, each ostensibly independent … and the
> Hutcheson family companies. The latter companies were used to disguise the true
> nature and profitability of both … the extent to which public investment by way of
> debentures and unsecured notes (in the case of Cambridge) and insurance
> premiums (in the case of Northumberland) had been used to cover undisclosed
> losses, and to hold assets for the potential benefit of the Hutcheson family. The
> conglomerate members can be conveniently categorised as:
>
> (i)   Cambridge and its recognised subsidiaries.
> (ii) Companies associated with [and dependent on] … Cambridge, used by its
>   management to carry on activities or hold assets on its behalf … primarily
>   comprised Hunter and Wellington … various joint venture companies where
>   the original joint venture partner had ceased to be involved as a result of
>   Cambridge's initiative, or because of insolvency or takeover …
> (iii) Northumberland and its recognised subsidiaries.
> (iv) Companies associated with Northumberland … used by its management to
>   carry on activities or hold assets on its behalf …
> (v)   Companies used for the personal benefit of the Hutcheson family to control –
>   (a) The relatively inconsiderable ($200,000 approximate total book value)
>   private Hutcheson family assets which were in no way connected with the
>   main operating groups …

(b) The ownership of the equity in Cambridge and Northumberland to the extent it was not held by cross-investment between those groups or by the external shareholders of Cambridge ...

(c) The management of Cambridge [by] Unilateral Services Pty Limited (Unilateral).[6]

Northumberland and Hunter

Between October 1963 and October 1969 Hutcheson's direct and indirect ordinary shareholdings in Cambridge increased from 18.2 per cent to 60.25 per cent. Almost all the additional shares issued by Cambridge were purchased by Northumberland Insurance Co. Ltd and Cowdroy Investments Pty Ltd, the latter being used from June 1967 when Cambridge was in danger of becoming a subsidiary of Northumberland.[7]

Northumberland had been formed in 1955 to provide insurance services to Cambridge's hire-purchase customers. Newcastle folklore has it that staff scoured the daily papers for details of accidents and the like in which Cambridge-financed and Northumberland-insured property – motor vehicles, in particular – might have been involved. A good-sized car pile-up might have proven disastrous for Northumberland, allegedly so shallow were its actual financial foundations.

By 31 December 1969, 95.5 per cent of the 2,505,200 issued ordinary 50-cent shares in Northumberland were held effectively by the Hutcheson family interests. Cambridge held 3,600,000 10 per cent cumulative redeemable non-participating 50-cent preference shares, the contention being that such a financing arrangement avoided consolidation of Northumberland in Cambridge's accounts. Critically, Northumberland had operated at a loss for some time, financing its operations from funds originating with Cambridge and channelled through other companies of the group. Using non-disclosed transactions through related parties, from 1971 to 1974 Cambridge management channelled approximately $2.5 million of income to offset Northumberland's accumulated losses.[8] Fortuitously, Northumberland also picked up the insurance of the hire-purchase goods Cambridge financed. It was a matter of business convenience and financial necessity.

Hunter, a private company, was critical to the Cambridge Credit group. Incorporated on 19 December 1955, but inactive from 1961 to 1966, Hunter was 'revived to extricate Cambridge from an embarrassing situation which had developed in its Brisbane branch'.[9] The inspectors were concerned that Hunter was used to quarantine Cambridge's bad debts. The original $2 shareholders of Hunter were Cambridge and Mort Hutcheson. Such an arrangement should raise questions for accountants and auditors, both then and now; in particular, in Hunter's case was it a subsidiary of Cambridge? Although Hunter was passed off as an independent Hutcheson family company, the beneficial ownership of its shares during the relevant period is difficult to determine because of the use of nominees. Notwithstanding this difficulty, the inspectors concluded that:

> Hunter was managed and wholly financed by Cambridge and was no more than
> a device for holding undisclosed Cambridge losses and conducting undisclosed
> Cambridge business ... [I]f Hunter was not a subsidiary of Cambridge it was
> nothing more than an agent of Cambridge or a bare trustee for Cambridge.[10]

For all practical purposes it would have performed as effectively as a Cambridge branch.

That, in subsequent decades and even today, aptly describes the usual roles for many subsidiaries, especially those that are wholly owned:

> Such was Cambridge's involvement with Hunter that ... as in the case of
> Wellington [another family company], Cambridge's published accounts could
> not show a true and fair view of its affairs without incorporating the underlying
> assets and liabilities of Hunter on a line-by-line basis or consolidating Hunter's
> accounts as a subsidiary.[11]

The former might have added clarification, while the latter, contrary to the inspectors' beliefs, almost certainly would have provided further obfuscation.

Accounting practices

Inspectors alleged that the Hutcheson family companies were vehicles used to manipulate the profits of Cambridge so as to preserve borrowing rights. Capital structures were devised to avoid consolidation as Cambridge subsidiaries, yet they operated on funds originating in Cambridge.[12] Eventually group profits were achieved primarily from profits on 'front-end' sales and non-recognition by Cambridge of bad debts in loans to its subsidiaries. Interestingly, Enron (pp. 259–62) would use its Special Purpose Entities and its mark-to-model gimmick to advance revenues to meet the same objectives as Cambridge. None of those accounting tricks are new.

'Front-end sales' – when is a sale really a sale?

One would think it reasonable to presume a sale when property in the goods passes (or the services have been received). A distinction has to be drawn between a gain and loss on the transfer of property and a gain or loss on extending credit to the purchaser. Cambridge made the former, but not the latter.

The generally incisive observations of the inspectors on the matter of 'front-end sales' appear, however, to miss the market price issues:

4.2 Real estate development projects … generally passed through three stages … As a project passed from one stage to the next, it would be 'on-sold' at a price which would show a front-end profit to the vendor. A typical first stage joint venture situation was financed wholly by Cambridge and the only cash flow outwards was in respect of option fees or deposits paid in respect of conditional contracts to acquire the site in question, and agents' and consultants' fees and similar items.

4.3 [In] the second stage … Cambridge was able to negotiate a loan … in its own name on behalf of a new joint venture in which Cambridge and the original co-venturer either participated on different terms or into which a new co-venturer was introduced … *In the second stage joint venture Cambridge normally remained the sole proprietor of the property with sole liability under the mortgage to the outside financier again on behalf of the joint venture* …

4.4 [In] the third and final stage … *Cambridge and its original joint venture partners remained partners in the third stage joint venture and as such accepted liability to guarantee secured loans made to the purchaser by the outside financier as capital partner [taking over] the financing role [previously] performed by Cambridge in the first and second stage joint ventures.* Any front-end profit on the sale between the two joint ventures was brought into account in the same way as in 4.3 above. [Effectively] … Cambridge received full repayment of its advances to the earlier stage joint ventures and depending on the terms … would receive all or part of its share of any front-end profit in cash … in marked contrast to any profit taken at the stage of a sale by a first stage venture, which sale was entirely financed by Cambridge.[13]

Two features of the front-end sale mechanism are worth noting. Both have counterparts in contemporary commercial arrangements. First, the calculation of profit or loss rests there on the historical cost maxim that what is paid for an asset is what it is worth – *good* buys and *bad* buys are not differentiated, even though prevailing market prices might indicate that they should be. Second, Cambridge's joint ventures employed the 50-odd-year-old tactic of *asset pyramiding* – used by, amongst others, Samuel Insull to build his US utilities empire in the 1920s. Then, as now, consolidation accounting is intended to frustrate pyramiding – it does, but does nothing towards having the accounting figures, for assets correspond to their market worths. So consolidation accounting can have exactly the opposite effect to what is intended insofar as it requires the elimination of data, even when they are moving the booked values for assets closer to their prevailing market prices.

From 1970, a significant proportion of the reported trading profits of the Cambridge group was derived from sales of undeveloped land (by companies in which Cambridge had an equity interest) to joint ventures (in which Cambridge also had an equity interest). It was the practice for Cambridge's published accounts to include its full share of the vendor's profits from front-end sales without allowances for, or disclosure of, the proportion attributable to Cambridge's interest in the purchaser.[14] Often, Cambridge had lent the purchaser the necessary finance for the transaction in the first place.

Considerable unease was reported to be occurring within the firm auditing Cambridge regarding inclusion of front-end profits. Specifically,

> it does not seem right for a profit to be 'engineered' simply by moving a small percentage of a project ownership to another party so that it can be said that an actual cash profit has emerged which can be taken in as income in the accounts of one of the original parties to the full extent of the percentage ownership in the project when a major portion of the ownership is still actually retained.[15]

The practice was not limited to Australia.

In 1965 a similar concern had been expressed in the United States by the Securities and Exchange Commission, Accounting Series Release No. 95,[16] and was reiterated in 1975 in Accounting Series Release No. 173.[17] Specified criteria had to be met before the front-end sale could be booked.

Inspectors into Cambridge's operations reported that the national audit partner at Cambridge was particularly eager that the accounting treatment of such profits be disclosed by way of notes to the accounts.[18] Inclusion of approximately $8 million profit arising from front-end sales during the financial years 1973 and 1974 was challenged by the Cambridge inspectors, largely on the basis that the actual transactions were a sham – they lacked substance.[19] Legitimately one might ask, when is a sale a sale?

Profit recognition remains one of the many difficult issues related to accounting for real estate. External bodies, like the then ASX's Statex service and private financial advisory services, attempt to restate (standardise) the raw accounting data of publicly-listed companies to facilitate comparability in financial analyses undertaken by investors or creditors. Transactions of the Cambridge variety, however, are likely to be privy only to the managers and auditors, and therefore unlikely to be the subject of any public adjustments. It is an area that lends itself to increased scope for management manipulation and places auditors at risk. Not marking physical assets 'to market' facilitates misleading data at best and, at worst, outright deceit. Not surprisingly, anomalies in the methods of accounting for real estate are a recurrent theme in this book.

Non-recognition by CCC of bad debts in loans to subsidiaries

Around June 1961, Northumberland commenced to underwrite Cambridge's hire-purchase debtors and losses on investments, whatever their variety. In this manner the Cambridge public group used a technique whereby a loss situation could be carried forward as a claim against an associated company whose results it was not required to bring to account. To 30 June 1966, according to the inspectors, $415,623 had been debited to Northumberland in this manner. Around 1963–64, managerial concern was expressed about credit controls in the group's hire-purchase businesses at Wagga and Brisbane. The Wagga office was closed and in May 1966 Hunter was used to take over several Brisbane electrical retail businesses. Their indebtedness to Cambridge amounted to almost $1 million. Its significance is clear. By June 1966, Cambridge's share-holders' funds amounted to $4,168,568 under conventional accounting, and group profits before tax were reported to be $650,778 for the year.

Another feature of the operations was the level of advances made to joint venture and associated companies within the conglomerate. By 1969 the auditors were uneasy regarding the recoverability of $7 million advanced to the family companies, Hunter, Austral and Carbir, in view of their accumulated losses totalling some $4 million. The problem was easily fixed – the debts were eliminated by the intra-group transfer of profits from Cambridge between 1971 and 1973.[20]

Collectability of a $9 million accumulated debt as at 30 June 1971 owing by Hunter to Cambridge eventually was the subject of protracted litigation. Mr Justice Rogers provided an interim ruling on an application by the plaintiffs (Cambridge) that had the auditors done their duty, shareholders' funds should have been written down or a large provision made for bad debts. The indebtedness of Hunter had increased from $5,129,000 in 1966 to $7,830,000 by June 1970 as a result of repeated trading losses. In an effort to recover some of these losses, Cambridge poured money into Hunter to support investments in production and share trading activities. Both ventures were financial disasters.[21] Rogers J ruled on 27 June 1983, that

> an auditor acting reasonably should have been satisfied that the security and cover for the Hunter debt was doubtful at least in part. An auditor acting with reasonable prudence would have considered it necessary to call for provision against the Hunter debt to the extent of $4,600,000, that being the extent to which repayment was doubtful.[22]

The significance of the Hunter debt is clearly evident from an analysis of the reported undistributed profits and reserves of the Cambridge group for the relevant period: only $780,000 in 1966, $870,000 in 1967, $1,080,000 in 1968, $1,226,000 in 1969, $1,330,000 in 1970 and $1,470,000 in 1971.[23] Writing off the Hunter debt would have just about extinguished Cambridge's reported profits from 1967 onwards.

It was a similar scenario to H.G. Palmer. Had Cambridge ever made a profit since 1967? The inspectors concluded it had not. Although giving the above interim ruling, on 16 September 1983 Rogers J ruled that the plaintiffs, the auditors of Cambridge, were not liable for damages.[24] In a later 1985 judgment the auditors were ruled liable and damages awarded at $145 million, resulting in a reported $20 million out-of-court settlement.

How information hinders

Financial consequences of those accounting practices were particularly disadvantageous for creditors and debenture holders. Especially notable was the regulatory ineffectiveness of the group accounting practices. Cambridge's dealings with Northumberland bear witness to that.

In 1971, Northumberland was in default over the payment of preference dividends to Cambridge. Consequently, these shares attracted voting rights, which it has been asserted meant that Northumberland had become a subsidiary of Cambridge. Share transfers to another family company avoided consolidation, though the total preference shareholding remained booked as a Cambridge investment asset.

Table 8.2 summarises the inspectors' calculation of the conventional accounting effect of Cambridge avoiding consolidation. The inspectors show that as a gross default on Cambridge's part. Whereas the inspectors' assessment of Cambridge's connivance to avoid consolidation may be correct, we would disagree with the implication that consolidated statements were a 'virtue avoided'. Cambridge's asset valuation and income measurement would most likely have been no more reliable and in accord with financial facts with consolidation than they were without it – though, indisputably, they would have been different!

The continuing survival of the group depended on Cambridge's ability to borrow from the public, which in turn depended on reporting satisfactory group profits and maintaining the capital structure prescribed in the trust deeds. Both the debenture stock trust deed and the unsecured notes trust deed (as amended) limited borrowings to the lesser amount of five times the value of shareholders' funds or three-quarters of liquid assets. A similar constraint had been faced by H.G. Palmer. Precise terminology and relevant accounting data are imperatives

Table 8.2 Accumulated shareholders' funds, selected years 1966–73

Year ended 30 June	Reported $	Adjusted $
1966	4,168,658	1,649,846
1971	12,270,104	(2,209,680)
1973	15,672,055	127,623

Source: Inspectors' 2nd Report (1979), p. 278.

in ensuring that those financial constraints are workable. The point was not lost on the inspectors of Cambridge:

> [B]ecause of faulty practices and principles ... coupled with the failure of
> the Board and the auditors to perform adequately their respective duties,
> [a misleading] *outward appearance of viability and growth of assets and profits*
> *was presented to the investing public generally.*[25]

By reason of the alleged overstatement of profits and shareholders' funds after 30 June 1966, the inspectors concluded that Cambridge thereafter had exceeded its borrowing powers. It is to be remembered, too, that the inspectors were still travelling the conventional accountant's route. Had the true market worths of the physical assets been injected, the calculation might have produced an outcome considerably worse than the inspectors claimed – and predictably closer to what the liquidators discovered – as summarised in Table 8.3 and detailed in Table 8.4.

That analysis indicates Cambridge's high-risk, heavy reliance on debt capital to finance long-term investment projects and its need to realise adequate returns to fund the cost of debt and report acceptable profits. Dividends and company taxation paid on dubious profits further depleted the cash resources of the group; these two outflows perhaps were being financed from capital. It was a complex situation requiring tight regulatory mechanisms to ensure investor protection, which neither the holding company/subsidiary structure nor the consolidation accounting for it could have delivered. That regulatory ineffectiveness remains.

In the opinion of the inspectors, five companies, viz. Bremer, Burhead, Dunnoch, Mount Warren and Southern Pacific, were incorrectly treated as guarantor subsidiaries for the purposes of the last two prospectuses. Cambridge's reported profit of $1,970,697 after tax for the six months ended 31 December 1973 was deemed to have been overstated by $3,952,691.[26]

Table 8.3 Debenture profile, 1966–73

Prospectus no. – date	Cambridge share/funds adjusted to exclude overstatement, etc. $	Five times Cambridge shareholders' funds as adjusted $	Debentures in issue $	Excess debentures in issue $
15 – 21/9/66	3,095,019	15,475,095	19,912,082	4,436,987
17 – 2/10/67	3,254,114	16,270,570	22,587,952	6,317,382
19 – 11/10/68	2,629,389	13,146,945	27,512,615	14,365,670
21 – 10/10/69	2,973,965	14,869,825	36,287,969	21,418,144
24 – 6/11/70	4,129,143	20,645,715	46,525,378	25,879,663
26 – 1/11/71	3,046,453	15,232,265	56,016,482	40,784,217
28 – 20/11/72	4,225,753	21,128,765	66,352,471	45,223,706
30 – 12/11/73	6,256,692	31,283,460	69,359,105	38,075,645

Source: Inspectors' 2nd Report (1979), p. 278.

Cambridge's advances to its joint ventures, $88 million as at 31 December 1973 and $102 million as at 30 June 1974, were described in its accounts as 'mortgages and other receivables' and counted as 'liquid assets' in determining borrowing limitations under Cambridge's trust deeds. That was contested – though more in respect to the labels attached to assets than to their financial substance.

From 1969, explanatory notes were included in the accounts, viz. 'Included in "mortgages and other receivables when charges not written in" are secured loans to joint ventures.' At issue was the legal interpretation of definitions contained in the trust deeds. The inspectors observed that, if judgment did not uphold the inclusion of all such advances as 'liquid assets', the company was without borrowing power from around 1969 when the joint ventures commenced.[27]

The Cambridge group's dependency on borrowings to finance expanding investments in projects is apparent from the large and (mostly) increasing deficiency between gross retained cash inflows from trading and increases in total asset expenditure. This shortfall, together with borrowing repayments, was financed from increased debt and/or equity capital. The maturity schedule of 'receivables and borrowings due' confirms the parlous cash position of the group.[28] Basic financial prudence was absent – irrespective of how the assets and liabilities were labelled.

Table 8.4 Cambridge Credit Corporation Ltd – effect of overstatement of assets on various prospectus documents issued during the period 30 June 1966 to 30 September 1974

Prospectus number	15	17	19	21	24	26	28	30	31	Total
Prospectus date	21/9/66	2/10/67	11/10/68	10/10/69	6/11/70	1/11/71	20/11/72	12/11/73	6/5/74	
Details per auditors' report										
Last balance date	30/6/66	30/6/67	30/6/68	30/6/69	30/6/70	30/6/71	30/6/72	30/6/73	31/12/73	
Cambridge shareholders' funds	4,132,028	4,619,387	5,682,660	7,591,784	10,195,509	12,270,104	13,650,797	15,548,634	15,542,206	
Cambridge profits before tax for the										
full year	413,920	434,067	661,345	750,670	674,121	1,534,614	2,387,688	1,864,837	–	
half year								–	1,435,258	
Overstatement Cambridge profit and Cambridge shareholders' funds –										
Amount due from Hunter – Accumulated losses at 30 June 1966 and subsequent losses	1,037,013	326,764	1,291,936	810,467	(981,580)	48,499	(914,148)	(152,819)	–	1,466,132
Issued capital at 30 June 1966 and subsequent increases	(4)	–	(19,996)	–	–	–	–	–	–	(20,000)
Overstatement of investment in listed shares	–	–	–	–	1,367,584	1,939,415	(1,180,141)	(2,126,858)	–	–
Overstatement of investment in film companies	–	1,500	226,689	506,515	587,649	154,511	(3,629)	(1,196,835)	(276,400)	–
Assets not taken up by Cambridge	–	–	–	–	–	–	–	–	171,096	171,096
Amounts written off by Cambridge	–	–	–	–	–	–	–	(1,342,228)	(275,000)	(1,617,228)
	1,037,009	328,264	1,498,629	1,316,982	973,653	2,142,425	(2,097,918)	(4,818,740)	(380,304)	
Amounts due from Carbir and Town and Country	–	–	189,369	247,566	199,894	(85,140)	(551,689)	–	–	–
Mark-up over cost of Kingscliffe and Surfers shares and Burleigh Garden Heights land	–	–	–	–	275,000	1,100,000	2,251,000	482,400	–	4,108,400

Bad debts capitalised as interest-free loan	–	–	–	–	–	–	600,000	–	–	600,000
Front-end profits –										
IRPD	–	–	–	–	–	–	640,255	–	–	640,255
Others	–	–	–	–	–	–	2,684,185	–	3,627,718	6,311,903
Subsidiary company cost of shares reduced by amount finally recognised in the 1973–1974 Cambridge draft accounts	–	–	–	–	–	–	878,798	–	–	878,798
Profit on sale of land to Loftus	–	–	–	–	–	–	–	–	284,973	284,973
Interest income on advance to Elbrook	–	–	–	–	–	–	–	–	40,000	40,000
Overstatement of Cambridge profit	1,037,009	328,264	1,687,998	1,564,548	1,448,547	3,157,285	201,393	(133,102)	3,627,387	12,864,329
Cumulative balance carried forward	–	1,037,009	1,365,273	3,053,271	4,617,819	6,066,366	9,223,651	9,425,044	9,291,942	–
Overstatement of Cambridge shareholders' funds	1,037,009	1,365,273	3,053,271	4,617,819	6,066,366	9,223,651	9,425,044	9,291,942	12,864,329	12,864,329
Adjusted Cambridge shareholders' funds	3,095,019	3,254,114	2,629,389	2,973,965	4,129,143	3,046,453	4,225,753	6,256,692	2,677,877	
Five times adjusted Cambridge shareholders' funds	15,475,095	16,270,570	13,146,945	14,869,825	20,645,715	15,232,265	21,128,765	31,283,460	13,389,385	
Cambridge debentures in issue	19,912,082	22,587,952	27,512,615	36,287,969	46,525,378	56,016,482	66,352,471	69,359,105	77,247,060	
Debentures not capable of issue	4,436,987	6,317,382	14,365,670	21,418,144	25,879,663	40,784,217	45,223,706	38,075,645	63,857,675	

Source: Inspectors' 2nd Report (1979), pp. 330–1.

Table 8.5 Cash flow and debt analysis, 1964 to 1973

Year ended 30 June	Gross retained cash inflows $000	Total asset expenditure $000	Deficiency (cols 2–3) $000	Borrowings at 30 June $000	Capital at 30 June $000
1964	201	2,281	2,080	26,200	3,386
1965	212	1,056	844	27,800	3,386
1966	176	1,103	927	27,200	3,386
1967	172	3,537	3,365	31,500	3,778
1968	217	6,206	5,989	37,300	4,700
1969	237	9,924	9,687	52,000	6,365
1970	342	18,970	18,628	79,000	8,865
1971	481	11,573	11,092	91,000	10,800
1972	636	10,798	10,162	107,000	11,800
1973	1,344	47,227	45,883	158,400	12,400

Sources: Sydney Stock Exchange Statex Service and *Sydney Stock Exchange Investment Service*, C129, (1973).

If the receivables analysis undertaken by Statex had not recognised 'amounts due from joint ventures' to be receivables possibly due within two or five years or some time later, rather than as 'liquid assets', then the actual situation as disclosed in that table would deteriorate markedly.

Incorrect profit figures, bad debts and diversion of irrecoverable funds to associated companies compound the resulting error.

Default – beginning of the end

Similar to the events immediately preceding the Minsec and Gollins collapses, around 12 March 1974 Cambridge issued a press release reporting a 99.9 per cent increase in 'net audited profit' for the six months ended 31 December 1973 ($986,547 to $1,970,697), a high renewal of maturing borrowings and a 'high degree of liquidity'.[29]

Within a few months the group was admitting to serious liquidity problems, intensifying to a crisis by August 1974. Existing financial supporters were unwilling, or unable, to renew loans. Internal evaluation of the liquidity position in October that year indicated an estimated deficiency amounting to $3.5 million if interest and proposed dividends were to be paid. Contracted development costs threatened an accumulated $10.8 million cash deficiency to July 1975.[30]

Incongruously, despite the obvious cash crisis, on 16 September 1974 an unqualified audited statement implied a healthy picture by announcing a profit increase of 33.2 per cent for the year ended 30 June 1974. Strapped for cash, directors of Cambridge held meetings on 25 and 26 September with the Sydney Committee of the Australian Finance Conference (of which Cambridge was not a member), seeking support. It was refused. Not to be denied, the Reserve Bank was notified and Cambridge directors commenced negotiations for overseas borrowings. Borrowings had always done the trick in the past! On this occasion the required lifeline, from either private institutions or public authorities, did not eventuate. On 27 September the shares dropped from 48 cents to 10 cents on the Sydney Stock Exchange, prompting a request from the Exchange 'for information'. Cambridge failed to reply and immediately its shares were suspended. Within minutes the trustee delivered a letter to the company requesting evidence of ability to meet interest commitments due on 30 September. Receipt of a reply on 30 September, indicating the company's inability to meet the payments, necessitated the trustee to appoint a receiver, C.H.R. Jackson of Hungerford, Spooner and Kirkhope.

Receivership and litigation

Cambridge's annual report for the year ended 30 June 1975 was eventually completed on 10 April 1979. Therein directors referred to the extraordinary losses incurred under receivership as due to mortgages and other secured liabilities which became immediately due and payable, and from a need for the receiver 'in the course of their duties, having to dispose of assets of the group at a time when, by virtue of the prevailing economic conditions, the market was in a state of deep depression'. By 1982 accumulated losses exceeded $212 million, leaving a deficiency of nearly $199 million. The receivership continues into 2003. Interestingly, for the financial years 1967 to 1973, approximately $4,618,000 was paid in company tax and $5,184,000 distributed as dividends from *reported* 'profits before tax' totalling some $11,517,000. Inspectors claimed that overstatement of profits for 1966–73 was approximately $9.3 million.[31]

The Cambridge affair proved to be a breakthrough for aggrieved investors, and perversely for directors and auditors too. It spawned a new approach to corporate litigation in Australia – the class action. In a letter to debenture holders, receivers advised of a statement of claim issued by the company (through the Receivers and the trustee for debenture holders), seeking damages against the directors who held office between April 1971 and September 1974 and the auditors. Also forwarded was a notice from the Corporate Affairs Commission containing details of advice given in a judgment regarding individual stockholders' rights to take action as a class against the company and its former directors and auditors.

This was to be the first of several similar class actions taken by regulatory authorities on behalf of many debenture holders in the following decades, including in 1994 the ASC's $340 million claim against the auditor and some of the directors of Adsteam. A decade after Cambridge collapsed, Rogers J awarded the receivers $145 million in special damages against the auditors Fell & Starkey – holding that breaches of their duty were a substantial cause of the collapse at Cambridge. While this judgment was overturned by the Court of Appeal (two to one) in July 1987, the High Court subsequently followed the judgment of Rogers J. Eventually an out-of-court settlement (believed to be approximately $20 million) was paid to the receivers by the insurers of Cambridge.

Action initiated by the regulatory authorities in the case was the start of a new ball game between officers of failed companies, investors and regulators. But regulatory action had been protracted – a point not lost on subsequent regulators such as Henry Bosch, who complained bitterly of his difficulty (as NCSC chief) in getting directors into court in the 1980s.[32] By the mid-1990s several 1980s entrepreneurs had been put on trial and some convicted.[33] For some others, the inordinate prosecution delays would continue, and some remain being chased overseas with the view to extradite.

Cambridge's failure conforms in many respects to a familiar pattern – dominant personality (Hutcheson) in the management of the company seeking to build an empire to satisfy personal ambitions, the company expanding rapidly with substantial short-term borrowings to finance long-term high-risk investments, compounding cash problems by reliance on rolling over its borrowings when due by reporting satisfactory short-term profits and paying tax and dividends thereon, and maintaining the price of the shares on the stock market. That is, keeping the outward (public) signs looking relatively good (certainly not a loss!) for as long as possible. The interaction of an economic downturn precipitated what was to many (though mainly with hindsight) an inevitable failure. Mr Justice Rogers aptly captured the interacting factors:

> Cambridge was *destined* to collapse because financial gearing ... was unable to sustain the aggregate demands ... once the abnormal boom conditions abated ... *low equity ... servicing large borrowings and ... maintaining the myriad of money losing satellites imposed a strain which ...* made Cambridge's financial position insupportable.[34]

Arguably, Rogers J misses a critical point – everybody is entitled to make errors of judgment, including errors of *financial* prudence. There can be no doubt that Hutcheson and his fellow directors wanted the group to be a financial success. They had everything to gain by it. More to the point, along with the privilege to make bad decisions, it is everybody's right to expect accounting to 'tell it how it is', rather than mask the financial facts with the 'jiggery-pokery' or *legerdemain* of the kind which conventional accounting passes off as sophisticated (though mysterious) financial representation. Cambridge's financial position was, in hindsight, 'insupportable', but no more so than the accounting practices used to account for it.

Conflicts between personal and company interests are inevitable in operations using pooled group finance to facilitate related-party transactions between private and public companies. This was clearly the case in the *Reid Murray*, *Stanhill* and other 1960s cases, and would be so in the Bond and HIH cases in later decades. Rules imposed to regulate such conduct are invariably broken or bent. Conventional accounting and auditing practices, by their very nature, provided a vehicle for public deception. Consolidation practices, asset valuation, income realisation and periodic determination, asset and trans-action classification, accounting for (and disclosure of) associated interests and relationships and audit practices are some of the accounting and auditing matters indicated in the Cambridge failure to warrant reform.

The frequency with which these matters continue to arise in episodes of corporate collapse since Cambridge is explicable, but unacceptable. 'Explic-able', by virtue of the prevailing regulatory and accounting orthodoxy and inertia; regulatory mechanisms in vogue, accounting practices in particular, do not ensure a continuous flow of contemporary information on companies' financial affairs. Consumers of published financial information which conforms to the conventional and compulsory pattern put themselves at grave financial risk, a result that is unacceptable, given the frequency of the message.

CHAPTER 9

Uncoordinated Financial Strategies at Associated Securities Ltd*

A lethal mix – the lack of lender-of-last-resort finance, unplanned hedging, mismatched maturities on receivables and borrowings, and an inability of accounting data to inform in a timely manner.

'What in hell's name happened?'[1] This lament appeared as a caption on a letter to the editor of the *Australian Financial Review* in the wake of the Associated Securities (ASL) collapse. Such expressions of disbelief by investors are par for the course upon the sudden, unexpected collapse of a large financial institution.[2] With ASL, such despair was more than justified. Its financial reports had not clearly and unambiguously warned investors of imminent financial disaster.

One account of ASL's problems, published immediately after its collapse, claimed the crash arose because of 'bad property investments ... exchange losses on Swiss borrowings, and the high interest rate structure, far higher than its competitors'.[3] Undeniably these were major factors, but there are other facets of ASL's property incursions which warrant close attention. Five factors are critical:

- The shortening of the maturities structure of ASL's borrowings.
- ASL's failure to match borrowings and receivables.
- The inability of ASL's board, from the late 1950s until the mid-1970s, to obtain lender-of-last-resort facility from a local bank.
- The exacerbation of the financial consequences of those three factors by the unplanned hedging operations in real property.
- And, perhaps the strongest factor of all – the failure of conventional accounting to produce *public* data indicative of ASL's declining wealth, deleterious drifts in its financial position, declining capacity to service and meet its debts, and the paradoxical capacity of conventional accounting to portray precisely the opposite.

At the time the receivers were appointed (8 February 1979), ASL was a mixed bag – a financier, realtor and underwriter of property development. It was the largest non-bank-affiliated finance company in Australia. Assets (at cost or some other variety of book value) totalled $292.5 million. The

Statement of Affairs (March 1979) revealed a deficiency of approximately $12 million in the cover for unsecured ASL creditors. Consequently, there was little likelihood of any return to the shareholders.

The story begins some 50-odd years earlier.

Australian Securities Ltd (the name of ASL was adopted in 1946) was incorporated in Sydney in 1926 with an issued capital of £158,498 (396,245 8s. shares). Prior to 1956, its major activity, consumer finance, was conducted almost exclusively in the Sydney metropolitan area. In November 1956 the directors authorised ASL's first public debenture issue of £500,000. Including oversubscriptions, it raised £726,008. The 1960s cases revealed that this form of corporate capital raising was novel in Australia but that it soon gained *avant-garde* status and was to be the main source of ASL's finance.[4]

By 1960 ASL had begun to diversify and expand its operations across Australia. It was providing consumer finance, finance for transport, mortgage finance, operating finance for sections of industry and finance for capital expenditure, and also debt factoring. At year-end the directors announced the diversification into the financing of real estate.

Those diversifications involved three subsidiaries and nine branches across Australia. ASL appeared resilient, as Table 9.1 shows that the major economic event of the early 1960s, the November 1960 credit squeeze, failed to slow ASL's reported improved performance, asset and debt financing growth.

Exceptional growth was claimed between 1966 and 1974. ASL's assets (at book value) *reportedly* increased by over $300 million and were financed almost entirely from external borrowing. Outstanding liabilities at the end of June 1974 were $347 million. Through a now familiar policy of acquisition and incorporation, ASL had become a diversified company having 22 wholly-owned subsidiaries, and one 95 per cent-owned subsidiary. Activities now included finance (general, leasing and real estate advances), real estate development, real estate investment, investments in securities, trading in securities and general insurances. The apogee occurred in 1974.

However, the salient features of ASL's management and financial structures had potentially put it on a path to failure that would be replicated at Bond Corporation a decade on. Relieved of the accounting subtleties, ASL was in financial difficulties for several years before it finally collapsed.

Dominant management and finance

ASL's management performance is best examined over three distinct periods: 1946–63, 1964–74 and 1975–79. From the late 1940s to 1963, D.H. Currie (chairman) and C.J. Perry (managing director) dominated the operations. They 'guided the company's fortunes with a simple but effective philosophy.

Remarkably they believed in profits first and foremost, profits before size and growth (although they were not averse to these).'[5] This is supported by data in Table 9.1. Currie and Perry confined ASL's activities almost entirely to motor vehicle finance. From 1946 to 1963 they steered annual reported net profits from approximately $10,000 to $1,003,000, and total assets increased from $410,000 to $59.962 million. During this period the traditional form of finance, hire-purchase, was encouraged. By 1963, it accounted for $48 million, or 76 per cent, of ASL's gross receivables.

Table 9.1 Associated Securities Ltd – details of performance, growth and financing, 30 June 1956 to 30 June 1978

Year ended 30 June	Net profit[1] $000	Dividend percentage %	Total assets[2] $000	Share capital[3] $000	Borrowed funds[4] $000
1956	210	15	4,123	1,030	2,057
1957	243	15	5,336	1,030	3,176
1958	291	15	9,419	1,030	6,805
1959	362	15	16,155	1,233	12,787
1960	468	16	29,824	2,686	21,646
1961	861	16	40,250	2,636	28,524
1962	947	16	47,567	3,358	36,700
1963	1,003	16	59,962	3,358	47,436
1964	1,161	16	67,494	4,314	52,309
1965	1,411	16	74,138	4,814	59,196
1966	1,534	16	78,215	4,814	62,641
1967	1,765	16	95,861	6,017	76,384
1968	2,236	16	123,649	7,025	96,443
1969	2,705	16	149,774	9,025	119,078
1970	3,306	16	173,475	12,073	133,706
1971	4,027	16	203,785	13,983	158,699
1972	5,239	16	255,503	18,999	195,013
1973	6,365	16	328,106	21,410	256,812
1974	7,378	10	369,549	25,026	290,667
1975	2,507	8	317,504	25,026	241,728
1976	(5,415)	–	279,253	25,026	214,350
1977	(16,630)	–	235,933	25,026	189,718
1978	178	–	283,942	32,026	226,915

Notes: (1) Net profit after tax, abnormal and extraordinary items; (2) Total assets, excluding unearned income; (3) Share capital – subscribed ordinary capital plus, in 1978, $7 million in preference capital; (4) Borrowed funds consist of first charge debenture stock, second charge debenture stock, term deposits, commercial bills of exchange and bank facilities.
Source: Annual Reports, 1956–78, on a consolidated basis.

With a change in management in 1964 came a change in the direction of ASL's investments, especially into real estate. Moreover, patterns of real estate investment vacillated between home units and land subdivision, often with 'little hope of being rezoned for residential purposes this [twentieth] century, if ever'.[6] Daly recounts the diversity and extent of these real estate incursions, as ASL 'followed the home unit craze' in Sydney, and 'was planning an entire new suburb on 2,308 hectares (in Melbourne) ... even though it was zoned non-urban', and notwithstanding that some of the land 'was resaleable only in 12-hectare lots'.[7]

Perry disapproved of the diversification of the company's resources into real estate financing and ultimately into real estate development. Such a move, however, had the support of Reginald Shanahan (who became managing director of ASL after the death of Currie), as well as the members of the board – in particular, John Darling: '[He] and Reg Shanahan were not the only financiers who believed that property values could not go down.'[8] And, of course, property financiers' accounts generally reflected that view.

In March 1974, Shanahan retired as managing director and was replaced by Eric Upton. His arrival coincided with an emerging liquidity crisis arising from ASL's increasing involvement in real estate investment. In 1976 this was exacerbated when the Royal Bank of Scotland severed a 16-year association with ASL by selling its ASL shares to Ansett. This action, however, heralded the entry of the 'white knights'[9] of Australia's corporate finance to the board of ASL. At the time they all held directorships with Ansett.

The financial consequences of the change in management personnel and their policies post-1963 were immediate and startling. The book value of ASL's assets base and its borrowings both grew by 500 per cent in the period from 1964 to 1974. Analysis of the individual components of the assets and the maturity schedules of ASL's assets and borrowings provides valuable insights into the implications of that growth – increased financial instability and increased risk of failure.

Considerable variability in the composition of ASL's gross receivables prevailed. Prior to 1967, hire-purchase agreements and personal loans represented over half of the total (gross) receivables. Increased investment in real estate in each subsequent year until 1975 reduced hire-purchase and personal loans to only 26 per cent. Then a management rationalisation policy resurrected consumer finance, and by 1978 the proportion was 46 per cent. On the other hand, real estate mortgage finance[10] fell in relative terms from 34 per cent in 1960 to approximately 20 per cent in the mid-1960s, hovered around 25 per cent during the period 1969–71, and then sharply declined to 14 per cent just prior to the receivership.

Table 9.2   Percentage of leasing/gross receivables, selected financial years, 1957/58 to 1977/78[11]

Financial year	ASL	AFC
1957/58	–	0.1
1969/70	14.4	11.6
1974/75	9.4	15.6
1977/78	5.0	25.1

Sources: ASL and AFC *Annual Reports.*

Variability of the components of ASL's receivables is evident in the pattern of the leasing and development projects. Although only introduced in 1964, by 1969 lease finance had grown to 15 per cent of ASL's gross receivables, peaking at 15.2 per cent in 1971 (Table 9.2). Out of favour in the 1970s, it constituted less than 5 per cent by 1978. This trend in the latter years differed from that of other large finance companies operating in Australia.

Diversification peaked in 1974. ASL had attempted to offset its declining leasing activity with investment in real estate 'development projects' as *principal* (rather than financier). Included under the label 'development projects' were lands for subdivision, domestic and commercial construction, and undeveloped lands held for sale. This form of investment began in 1966 (as part of ASL's diversification policy) and was undertaken by a wholly-owned subsidiary, ASL Finance Pty Ltd. Within a decade, development project finance had grown to nearly 20 per cent of ASL's gross receivables.

The first public signs of ASL's over-extension and imminent liquidity problems surfaced in 1973. It is obvious from the share market's response that year that ASL was perceived as not performing well, but that was ten years since it had started its diversification strategy.[12] To forestall ASL's immediate collapse, the directors publicly advocated rationalising its assets – in particular, selling its real estate development projects. But the real estate market had bottomed out, and even by 1978 this rationalisation policy had been only partially completed.

Capital structure and borrowings pressure

Finance companies rely on equity capital and retained profits to a greater extent than other financial intermediaries. Over the ten years to 1973, the average of shareholders' funds to total capital of Australian Finance Conference (AFC) member companies was 14 per cent – a figure which ASL consistently matched. Notwithstanding this shareholder finance base, the majority of finance companies' operations are financed by public borrowing (varying classes of debentures, notes and deposits). To this extent they have to be more careful in their investment strategies than perhaps when capital gearing is lower. While ASL's proportion of public issues to total capital relative to AFC member companies had been lower for a considerable period, by 1978 it marginally exceeded the average of AFC member companies (Table 9.3).

Of course, the validity of those data is contestable. Indeed the prevailing focus in this book is just that. Gearing ratios of this type depend upon the 'valuation' of the assets taken into account to calculate the denominator. Without injecting current market prices through an audited mark-to-market rule, the serviceability of the data is anybody's guess. It is doubtful whether the financial significance of data such as those in Table 9.3 is capable of being unravelled properly. Nonetheless, they were the only available data for making comparisons between the ASL and AFC averages.

One consequence of ASL's adoption of a gearing policy commensurate with other AFC members (albeit slightly lower) during the latter part of the 1970s was the need, between 1974 and 1978, to recover over $20 million annually through its operations (or through successive debenture issues) to meet interest payments.

From 1964, overdraft finance represented between 0.5 and 1 per cent of ASL's total capital requirements, while for the AFC it was between 0.3 and 1 per cent. During the troublesome period of 1973/74, ASL increased its overdraft from $1 million to $10 million − 3 per cent of total capital (AFC: 2 per cent), its highest level since 1964. To overcome the liquidity crisis in July 1974, ASL raised $20 million in the Eurodollar markets with the aid of the Royal Bank of Scotland's guarantee. Bank standby facilities of $50 million were also arranged.[13] That facility and the booked values of the assets no doubt made ASL look financially sound. With hindsight it appears not to have been.

And therein lies another peculiarity of conventional accounting. In hindsight the data provide insight into what the position was not; a curious outcome for an activity whose products are used habitually to assess what the position is at the time and to predict what it might possibly be in the future.

Table 9.3 Percentage of borrowed funds/total capital, selected years 1965–78

Year	ASL	AFC
1965	78.0	–
1970	77.0	82.6
1974	76.0	84.6
1978	79.5	76.2

Sources: Derived from ASL and AFC *Annual Reports.*

Asymmetrical maturities of receivables and borrowings

Table 9.1 shows the aggregated assets (at book value) and aggregated borrowings of ASL. The maturity profile of ASL's assets and borrowings illustrate the
group's financial difficulties more vividly – especially the maturities schedules
of ASL's borrowings and receivables from 1964 to 1978, detailed in Table 9.4.
Several points emerge from analysis of Table 9.4.

- The proportion of ASL's aggregate borrowed funds to receivables was
  increasing, whereas other AFC member companies were experiencing a
  small decline in that ratio.
- During the 1970s, AFC members experienced a shortening of the average
  maturity structure of borrowings. For ASL it was more pronounced over this
  period than for the other companies. The percentage of ASL's borrowings
  greater than five years dropped from 27 per cent in 1965 (AFC: 20 per cent)
  to 7 per cent in 1974 (AFC: 8 per cent) and 1 per cent in 1978 (AFC: 1 per
  cent); while receivables greater than five years remained steady at around
  8–10 per cent from 1964 to 1973 (AFC: 7–9 per cent); with a ballooning
  out to 14 per cent, 15 per cent and 13 per cent in 1974, 1975 and 1976,
  respectively (AFC: 10, 9 and 8 per cent). Reinforcing ASL's seemingly
  'above average' liquidity problem, the proportions of its borrowings due
  within two years increased from 43 per cent in 1964 (AFC n.a.) to 83 per
  cent in 1977 (AFC: 70 per cent); while the proportion due within one year

Table 9.4 Amount and percentage of borrowings/receivables of ASL and AFC
members, selected years, 1965 to 1978

Financial year	ASL		AFC		ASL		AFC		ASL		AFC	
	Total				< 2 Years				2–5 Years			
	$m	%	$m	%	$m	%	$m	%	$m	%	$m	%
1965	$\frac{62}{83}$	76	$\frac{958}{1,429}$	67	$\frac{28}{61}$	46	$\frac{440}{1,059}$	42	$\frac{17}{15}$	113	$\frac{328}{264}$	124
1970	$\frac{142}{205}$	69	$\frac{1,989}{2,901}$	69	$\frac{75}{133}$	56	$\frac{1,000}{2,079}$	48	$\frac{37}{56}$	66	$\frac{661}{614}$	108
1974	$\frac{314}{377}$	83	$\frac{4,704}{6,964}$	68	$\frac{212}{239}$	89	$\frac{2,876}{4,832}$	60	$\frac{80}{85}$	94	$\frac{1,460}{1,419}$	103
1978	$\frac{238}{285}$	84	$\frac{7,976}{12,170}$	66	$\frac{129}{166}$	77	$\frac{5,404}{7,887}$	68	$\frac{102}{90}$	113	$\frac{2,449}{3,162}$	77

Source: Based on data in F.L. Clarke and G.W. Dean, *Working Paper* (1987).

increased from 31 per cent in 1964 to 49 per cent in 1974 to a peak of 54 per cent in 1977.

• In the less-than-two-years category, the ratio of borrowings of finance companies relative to aggregate receivables was increasing steadily from 1964 to 1974, whereas for AFC members the relative increase was significantly slower. In contrast, although for the two-to-five-years category the proportion was decreasing for AFC member companies, for ASL it was the opposite. This mismatching characteristic in respect of the financing and investment strategies of ASL and finance companies in general was described as a 'dangerous convergence' by one scribe.[14]

Although finance companies, generally, were having trouble financing their operations,[15] ASL's position (relative to AFC member companies) was parlous – particularly so in respect to matching maturities of borrowings and receivables due within two years. Liquidity problems were inevitable unless the group could find access to its own banker.

ASL was no Robinson Crusoe in that respect. The inability of ASL to match properly liquid assets' and borrowings' maturities was a common feature of both Australian finance companies and the comparable overseas financial intermediaries involved in the national property booms of the early 1970s (the secondary banks in the United Kingdom and real estate investment trusts in the United States).[16] As such, it is worth contemplating whether ASL's directors were merely following a path of seeking higher returns (in boom conditions) while recognising the higher risks they were taking. If that were so, is it appropriate to criticise their actions with hindsight? But all that begs the question as to whether accounting information provided to directors enabled a proper assessment of the risks. Matching borrowings and receivables maturities was incontestable – straight comparisons of actual amounts of money. If property had been marked-to-market (and verified), related total asset backing, collateral and the like, liquidity and solvency assessments would have been more transparent.

Without knowledge of the contemporary movements in the market prices of ASL's property, the diagnosis that 'bad property investments' were a major factor in the demise of ASL is impossible to confirm or refute on financial grounds. In contrast, the behavioural aspect of ASL's investment policies is a different matter.

Functional transmutation – diversification into real property

Longstanding ideas characterising business activity rest firmly on the proposition that companies are 'going concerns'. Going concern is a firmly entrenched fundamental convention of accounting. Auditors have a primary duty to attest to that going concern status – essentially, whether firms have the financial capacity to continue to do what they are currently doing. Yet the history of business enterprise militates strongly against that. The very use of 'enterprise' evokes the strongest awareness of the function of continual adaptation, speculation, strategic change in operations, expansion or contraction of operations at the margin, as parts of managements' armouries. Frequently, operational changes escape immediate attention by virtue of euphemisms such as 'expansion', 'conglomeration', 'downsizing', 'rationalisation' and 'diversification'. At the same time, those euphemisms tend to disguise the altered direction of business activity. More importantly, managers' use of euphemisms often masks the necessity of adapting other strategic aspects of their enterprise, marketing techniques, advertising practices, public relations exercises and, in particular, operating and financing techniques, to the new circumstances. There is some evidence to support the suspicion that ASL's management may have laboured behind the protection of such screens to deny the reality of things.

The ASL group's increased investment in real estate in general and property development in particular should not be viewed as unusual. It was not atypical managerial action *per se*, nor was it an atypical action by a member of the AFC. The gradual transmutation of ASL from a regular financier of consumer durables to the financing and underwriting of property development was nothing remarkable. In contrast with many companies, ASL's functional change could be considered quite conservative. Irrespective of size, financial structure, market participation, being a price leader or price taker, or public or private status, periodic transmutations of corporate functions are ordinary, everyday events; the essence of going concerns. That is the antithesis of the idea embedded in managerial and financial accounting practices, and underlying a considerable corpus of commercial practices, that firms continue doing the same things throughout their existence. Interestingly, had ASL's move proved successful it would have been attributed to a highly developed business acumen.

Nor was ASL's behaviour different in that respect from the actions of other members of the AFC and by some non-member financial institutions as well. Growth in those companies' assets, in their receivables in particular, was indicative of a common involvement in real property. According to Daly, the property boom was the most significant influence on growth of finance companies' assets between 1968 and 1973.[17] Using Daly's data, real estate assets alone of those companies rose from a reported book value of $684 million to $2,689 million. We would assume that in the rising market the 'book value' was closer to cost than the higher selling price, though it cannot be known for certain on a case-by-case basis. In contrast, the amount of the related debt is unequivocal. Not unexpectedly, the receivables portfolios of finance companies reflected most of the increase. But whereas leasing of real estate was a growth activity during that period, finance companies acting directly as the bankers for developers was more significant, by far. Over the same period, Australian Bureau of Statistics data calculate the 129.7 per cent growth in net receivables of the finance companies to have outstripped that of the trading banks (92.8 per cent), the savings banks (66.1 per cent) and the life offices (25 per cent). Only the building societies' increase of 435 per cent bettered them. But it is noteworthy that the finance companies' net receivables of $5,307 million more than doubled those held by the building societies ($2,510 million), even though the latter clearly held a distinct comparative market advantage in the real estate area.

In contrast, the entry of the finance companies in general and ASL in particular into that market was a maverick action, according to the pervading conception of continuity of business activity. The implications are important for an understanding of the crash. Gottliebsen *et al.*'s post-mortem and conclusion of 'bad property investments'[18] is representative of the view at the time of the ASL receivership. For example, Daly is quick to indicate the significance of 'the movement out of consumer durables' and a critical shortfall in 'managerial skills in the property area'.[19]

But in what sense were those investments necessarily bad, when property was the growth asset at the time and when the banks, life offices and building societies were each competing for as large a share of the action as possible? Nowhere is it explained in those analyses why investments in property by ASL were bad, when similar investments by others who did not fail were (presumably) good. Nor is it shown that ASL's management was generally inferior to that of other members of the Finance Conference, or inferior in particular when it came to property management. In fact, there are some indications that on a number of counts ASL's management was rather conservative relative to others. Not that we would suggest conservatism is a good management trait, though 1990s popular wisdom would appear to rank it above the more risky, 1980s *cowboyish* behaviour.

Prima facie, for a significant time ASL's reported capital gearing was somewhat lower than the AFC average. Irresponsible programmes of rapid and continuous growth in gearing have featured in virtually all the major company failures experienced in Australia since World War II. Many of those companies featured in the expansion of consumer credit in Australia and so have something in common with ASL. Cambridge's adventure into property development forges an even closer link. Moreover, the growth in ASL's share of consumer credit over the period from 1960 to 1970 (2.8 per cent) was on a similar scale to that of a number of other AFC members and considerably lower than some – for example, Finance Corporation of Australia's move from 2.6 per cent to 7.6 per cent.[20]

Unplanned hedging and unserviceable debt –
the role of accounting

More relevant to the peculiar circumstances of ASL's performance and independent of subjective evaluations of the propriety of the move into property
financing is the examination of how it fared in the real estate market. Whereas
holding real estate is an attractive long-term financial proposition during
inflationary periods, such as those between the mid-1960s, the late 1970s and
the mid-1980s, it clearly has numerous pitfalls. It is a paradox that the primary
source of the financial attraction is a major contributor to the most hostile of the
problems which beset developers during periods of price instability.

Inflation has always been the catalyst for the flight from liquidity and
the corresponding investment in physical assets (*Sachwerte*, as the Germans
labelled it in the hyperinflation of 1923)[21] to exploit possible disproportionate
rises in their selling prices, relative to the increase in the general price level. In
nearly every extended inflationary period encountered by Western countries
this century, investment in real property has found strong support. The fortunes of European industrialists and financiers following World War I were
founded on that strategy.[22] Fleeing liquidity and investing in those assets with
the greatest differential increases in their prices compared to the inflation rate
was the normal means. It was good business. Sustained upward movement in
Australian real property prices, ahead of inflation, more than justified ASL's
transmutation. It also exposed ASL and its fellow travellers to the snare of
being seduced into holding property as a hedge against inflation, rather than
pursuing their chosen role of profit takers.

Corporate property holders and developers should be distinguished from
the individuals described by Bresciani-Turroni[23] and Guttmann and Meehan,[24]
in the context of loss mitigation and profit seeking during inflation. Almost
without exception, profitable exploitation of differential price increases has
been by wealthy individuals who purchased property outright, or under conditions in which revenues offset repairs and fiscal charges, including financing
costs. No significant penalty accrues if the property inventory turns over slowly.
Probably it is financially better to hold the property than to sell it, for frequently
the increase in selling prices of properties outstrips the decline in general
purchasing power and more than compensates for having to meet interest and
other period charges. Such investors virtually become their own bankers.

Hedging necessitates self-financing, or at least a near-to-positive cash inflow. In contrast, under a planned profit-making operation, a negative cash
inflow is of little consequence, provided the gestation period is short. Those in
the AFC who had banking affiliates, guaranteed financial back-up, stood in a
similar position to individuals holding property as a hedge. In contrast, ASL

lacked the financial support of a local bank affiliate. Financial backing from the
Royal Bank of Scotland proved insufficient. Unless property could be disposed
of relatively quickly, the cash drain would be too great to service. Property
development is a time-consuming and costly operation. According to temporal
criteria, developers have similar characteristics to those in property as a hedge
against inflation. During the late 1960s and early 1970s the property market
favoured buyers. And in any case, ASL was heavily involved in development
schemes. Perhaps unwittingly, it was forced to adopt the hedging stance.

Without the expectation of a back-up banking facility, ASL was unlikely
to have ever engineered itself into a position of being able to service its debt
portfolio. Sir Reginald Ansett alluded to the critical need for ASL to have the
lender-of-last-resort type of facility that only its own bank could ensure:

> ASL has a magnificent future ... We'll either marry a bank or we (Ansett
> Transport Industries) will buy the lot. That should fix it like a shot out of a gun,
> for once it is wholly owned (by Ansett) there is an enormous amount of freedom
> to solve the problems.[25]

That freedom did not mean that Ansett would *necessarily* support financially its wholly-owned subsidiaries as some commentators had thought. Such
decisions are taken on a commercial, not on a familial, sentimental basis.

Such a statement came far too late to have had any significant impact on
ASL's destiny. It is now well known that a portion of the reported growth
in ASL's assets was the product of capitalising period costs of holding and
developing real estate – a variation on the historical cost theme that money
spent on acquiring and holding physical assets necessarily adds wealth. Even
when the downturn in property prices came during 1974/75, there was no
about-face in the method of valuing ASL assets until a 1976 $12 million write-
down following the takeover of the group by Ansett and the $18 million it
pumped into ASL during the doomed rescue bid mounted during 1977–79.

Prior to 1974, ASL appeared to be well placed to hedge the growing
inflation with its growing property and property-related loan portfolios. The
market perceived it so with its share price at above-average levels. Over 50
per cent of the book value of its assets comprised real estate and real estate-
linked receivables. The 30 per cent shareholding held by the Royal Bank of
Scotland perhaps implied that help was nearby if cash were required quickly.
Some of that expectation materialised in 1974 when $20 million was raised
on the Eurodollar market. A $2.5 million reported annual profit, the illusion
of the strong real estate hedge against inflation and the trust that the Scottish
bank would stand behind the group implied stability – in hindsight, all were
pious hopes.

The Stock Exchange's Statex Service recalculated the 1974 $2.5 million reported profit to have been more like a $218,000 loss, and the disclosed losses from 1975 to 1978 amounting to $22 million to have been closer to $25 million. One of the problems with those kinds of analyses is the general practice of re-calculating by recourse to conventional accounting methods.

Accordingly, often those going on attack cast doubt on the appropriateness of the uncommon accounting practices which perversely make more sense than many of those enjoying the common approbation. Consider the following analysis of one such accounting method used at ASL – equity accounting (the practice of injecting an investor's profit and loss statement and balance sheet with the proportion of the periodic income or loss of another company over which it exercises a 'significant influence' on the latter's activities) – and other techniques to boost reported profits in the 1976/77 and 1977/78 financial years:

> The financial year 1976–77 saw a skimpy net profit of $51,000 … $874,000 for unrealised foreign-exchange losses … was offset only by $666,000 in profits from associated companies brought in through equity accounting'

and:

> [I]n the December half of 1977–78, the adoption of equity accounting increased the group's pre-tax profits by $274,000. If equity accounting had not been used the group would have reported a loss, probably somewhere around $170,000 … Further, the results were inflated by at least one dubious transaction. In December 1977 ASL sold land … to a joint venture for $1.6m. on a deposit of $50,000.[26]

The sale generated a profit of over $500,000 and without it ASL would have recorded a $200,000 loss for the year.

Reporting increased profits is certainly desirable, but keeping out of the red is seemingly a commercial imperative. One is reminded of the desperate manoeuvres of Korman, Reid Murray, Minsec, Cambridge Credit and Gollins several years earlier, and Ariadne, Rothwells, Adsteam, Westmex and the Bond Corporation over a decade later, and the manoeuvres at One.Tel, HIH and Harris Scarfe in the new millennium. However, more germane is that equity accounting is a surrogate, though a poor surrogate, for marking-investments-to-market. The criticism quoted above is contestable.

Paradoxically, some aspects of equity accounting, combined with recognising changes in market prices of physical assets as they occur, have considerable merit. Equity accounting is, in principle, merely a second-best mechanism for assessing the underlying worth of a shareholding. Obviously the best

Source: 'Ansett bales out of ASL', *The Australian*, 12 February 1979, p. 8.
Courtesy of Larry Pickering.

mechanism would be to use the investment's market selling price, were it available. If equity accounting were applied in respect of the affairs of related companies whose profits and losses were based on changes in the money's worth of the underlying net assets, the likelihood is that the outcome would be much more reliable than either the practice of investment valuation in ASL's time or the practice now. And in respect to the land sale, surely the real issue is not the terms upon which the transaction is effected but how it is reflected in the accounts. If the land were marked-to-market in the joint venture, ASL's share in the joint venture would have been adjusted accordingly. That would have brought only a change in the structure of ASL's assets, not their worth.

When Ansett 'baled out' from ASL on 8 February 1979, the irony of that action would fully emerge more than 20 years later when the directors of Air New Zealand would 'bale out' of its wholly-owned subsidiary, Ansett. That example of 'schizophrenic' action by directors – treating ongoing parts of a corporate group as one enterprise, but as separate legal entities when any of the parts get into financial difficulties – would not be lost on observers of corporate groups. With Ansett's bale-out of ASL there was no alternative but for the trustee for the debenture holders, Perpetual Trustees Company, to appoint Gary Warhurst and Tony Koshin of Hungerfords as receivers.

Overdoing a good thing

The real estate vehicle ASL Developments was nowhere near being either equity financed or geared to be an effective hedging medium. As a relatively short-term profit seeker, it had engaged in nearly every conceivable structural error. Its link with Royal Bank of Scotland,[27] ASL's sole remaining hope, was sacrificed in the Ansett takeover – ironically designed as a rescue mission!

Contrary to many of the press reports and other commentaries on ASL, the group's property incursion was neither unusual, nor worthy *necessarily* of the 'bad investment' epitaph. With the onset of inflation and strong expectations of even greater price rises to come, ASL's transmutation conformed to a traditional, historically precedented and often successful business strategy. As it turned out, price movements in 1980/81 somewhat justified those expectations. It is far from clear that the ASL management was inefficient in that respect. Nor is it clear that the management was any less efficient in handling the finance available to it. The difference that the access to bank back-up could have made when ASL was trapped into an unplanned hedge is clear, as is the impossibility of survival in the borrowing conditions at the time, as declining property values restricted the capacity to service current debt, meet maturing principal or negotiate roll-over refinancing. It is a pity that the accounting did not disclose that.

ASL's woes invite conclusions which are *indicative*, rather than definitive. Already we have shown that corporate collapse invariably involves complex arrangements. Autopsies cannot exploit the privilege of working through a catalogue of established, universally agreed, proven, fatal conditions in the manner enjoyed by medical examiners. Nonetheless, failed and non-failed companies often have common characteristics.[28] Painted with a broad brush, they present the same public picture. Published financial data relating to both often report a positive picture, reinforcing that common image.

Notwithstanding that disclaimer, the analysis of ASL revealed aspects of its operations which help to explain critical circumstances of the collapse. The rapid escalation in assets, debt and reported profits in the late 1960s and early 1970s and the prolonged period of languishing (1974–79) is a familiar scenario.

Dangerous shortening of the maturity structure of ASL's borrowings was coupled to the failure to match borrowings and receivables. The inability of the board to secure lender-of-last-resort support from a local bank placed ASL under extreme pressure in its unplanned hedging operations in real property. More than likely, those features in isolation would not be fatal. The performance and survival of other AFC companies implies that. Together, and in the absence of a system of accounting serviceable for exposing their cumulative financial effects, they are a recipe for disaster. Commingled, as they were in ASL, they become a potent mixture – and ASL overdosed.

'Bid to keep Goward bankrupt' – caption adorning this caricature of Russell Goward as he faced perjury charges. *Australian Financial Review*, 15 December 1993, p. 13. Courtesy of David Rowe.

'Adsteam sinks $3.7 billion into red under Spalvins' leadership.' *Sydney Morning Herald*, 29 March 1991, p. 17. Courtesy of Rocco Fazzari.

John Spalvins addresses Tooth & Co. meeting, November 1990. Courtesy of John Fairfax Holdings Ltd.

Ron Brierley and Russell Goward have a beer at the Windsor Hotel, Melbourne. *Age*, 30 November 1983. Courtesy of John Fairfax Holdings Ltd.

Caricature of Alan Bond, *Australian Financial Review*, 16 January 1995, p. 14.
Courtesy of David Rowe.

Alan Bond flies over Sydney (12 June 1986) in his new airship on its maiden voyage.
Courtesy of News Ltd.

PART IV

The 1980s

CHAPTER 10

The 1980s: Decade of the Deal?

Inter-company shareholdings and transactions have given cover to
fraudulent dealings and to legally less serious but financially no less
deceptive mis-statements of results and position.

R.J. Chambers (1973, p. 225)

The 1980s in Australia has been described as a decade of dreams – 'the dream-time casino',[1] a time when the financial system went crazy, when the nation was wooed by the 'decade of the deal', by the call that 'greed was good'.[2] Yet, the collapses that occurred in the 1980s were simply repeats of earlier experiences. The chapter headnote is as apt for the '80s as it was in describing commercial practices of the '60s, '70s and would also prove for the '90s.

More of the same it certainly was. But the scale was different. Financial hangovers on the morning-after demonstrate that without doubt the 1980s hosted a corporate party to remember. Many do, but not fondly. Receiverships and liquidations of publicly listed companies were at record levels, with nearly 500 companies delisted because of the appointment of a liquidator or receiver during the period 1986 to 1995, approximately equal to the total number of such delistings over the previous three decades. They were to be a portent of what would occur in the first years of the new millennium.

Capturing the flavour of those corporate excesses and the paranoia regarding them was the assessment:

> So what went wrong in Australia? Close your eyes! In reality, that is what went
> wrong … Everyone [bankers, lawyers, accountants, regulators and directors] had
> their eyes closed … Some directors fraudulently abused their trust … Some
> directors negligently *or even innocently abused their trust* … Unfortunately
> … some honest directors … closed their eyes and slept.[3]

Those comments were to be made again – a decade later.

The problem is, the paranoia clouded the focus of the corporate observers, blinded *them* to the real issues, and generally let the regulators and the accountancy profession off the hook. 'Bankers, lawyers, accountants and directors', the dishonest and the innocent alike, have been judged through the false perception that most regulatory mechanisms were apt.

Table 10.1 Updated report on the ASC's 1991/92 '16 National Priority' investigations, plus miscellaneous investigations

Company	Official under scrutiny	Action
1. Bond Group	Alan Bond was charged over an alleged dishonest matter relating to Rothwell's. Subsequently, different charges were laid against Bond and other directors pertaining to transactions between Bell Resources and other BCH group companies. In July 1994, Alan Bond was charged with breaching his duties as a director, furnishing false information to fellow directors and providing misleading information to auditors over the *La Promenade* art purchase and its 1988 sale, contiguous with BCH's acquisition from Sotheby's of Van Gogh's *Irises*.	Alan Bond was gaoled for a year on the Rothwells charges but released after three months on appeal. He was acquitted on the retrial. In 1996 Alan Bond was found guilty of fraud charges relating to the *La Promenade* transactions. He was sentenced to two years' gaol on one count and one year on another. Bond, Antony Oates and Peter Mitchell were committed for trial on charges related to the Bell Resources matter. Bond and Mitchell were found guilty – Bond was sentenced to four years gaol – increased to seven on appeal. Mitchell was sentenced to 4 years; Oates is still appealing extradition.
2. Budget Group	Directors Robert Ansett and Stanley Hamley and two others were committed in November 1994 to stand trial. The two other officials had charges dismissed in October 1994.	All were charged over information in a 1989 Budget Corporation Ltd prospectus. Ansett and Hamley were tried and the jury was discharged after failing to reach a verdict.
3. Duke Group	Proceedings brought by liquidator over experts' report in respect of the reverse takeover of the Duke Group in June 1988 by Kia Ora Gold Corporation. ASC concerned over possible criminal matters, ultimately resulting in three directors being charged in 1993 for allegedly failing to act honestly under sections 229(1) (b) and 129 of the former Companies Code.	Three former directors charged by ASC with allegedly breaching duties under section 229(1) (b); two directors charged with breaching section 129, involving Duke Group Ltd financing dealings in its own shares. In December 1994 all parties were committed for trial.
4. Entity Group	Directors Gary Carter, Dennis Vickery, Christopher Blaxland were investigated by ASC and briefs sent to the DPP. Charges laid against Carter, Vickery and Blaxland in 1991 who were committed for trial in May 1992.	Carter subsequently was gaoled for four years. In July 1993, Entity's auditors appeared in court charged with making false or misleading statements in an Investigating Accountants' report – in August 1994 those charges were dismissed.

5. Equiticorp	Concern over alleged transfer of funds out of the group by former chairman of Equity House Limited, Allan Hawkins.	In June 1993, Hawkins was charged but the case was dropped upon his release from six years' imprisonment in New Zealand on another matter.
6. Estate Mortgage	Concern over alleged misleading advertising. Also concern over a possible secret commission payment. Multiple charges.	Richard Lew is gaoled for two years (15 months suspended). Carl Davis was gaoled for eight months; Reuben Lew was gaoled for three years (suspended sentence for two years), and a valuer received a suspended one-year sentence.
7. Girvan Corp.	ASC sought appointment of liquidator to preserve assets.	No charges laid.
8. Golden Bounty Resources	Investigation into suspected market manipulation by Golden Bounty – civil action initiated by the ASC.	Court found that defendants 'ramped' share price and ordered that the shares be forfeited.
9. Halwood (Hooker) Corporation	Analysis of circumstances surrounding failure. No basis for criminal or civil action.	On another matter, managing director George Herscu was gaoled for five years in respect of a secret commission.
10. Independent Resources	Directors Michael Fuller and Joseph Cummins were alleged to have made improper use of their position in three IRL Group companies.	13 charges against directors and intervention by ASC in a series of civil actions.
11. Interwest Group	Concern over the group's collapse at the end of 1989 after reporting excellent profits and proposing a healthy dividend.	15 charges. Criminal prosecutions started against chief executive John Avram in May 1994, and chairman, Stanley Schneider and Interwest shareholder, P. Jordan, relating to placement of 25 million Interwest shares.
12. Linter Group	Warrants issued in respect of alleged *window dressing* using related party transactions authorised allegedly by former chairman Abe Goldberg who is currently in Poland, a country with whom Australia does not have an extradition treaty covering a Polish citizen.	Goldberg charged with breaches of director's duties, engaging in fraudulent transactions and issuing misleading statements. Also the former company secretary and finance director, Katy Boskovitz, was charged on 11 counts relating to related party transactions between the 'banker' company and other Linter satellites. Extradition proceedings against Goldberg continue.

Continued

Table 10.1 *Continued*

Company	Official under scrutiny	Action
13. Metrogrowth Property Trust	Several matters investigated.	DPP did not pursue matters raised. Records of interviews released to assist civil litigation.
14. Qintex Group	Criminal charges against former Chairman Christopher Skase for allegedly 'improperly' using his position involving $10 million of company funds. For nearly ten years the Australian government sought Skase's extradition from Spain.	Criminal prosecution initiated. Extradition application to bring Skase from Spain was initially granted in September 1994 but then overturned on appeal in December 1994. Actions to extradite Skase continued till his death in 2001.
15. Rothwells	Directors Laurie Connell and Peter Lucas and the auditor, Louis Carter, were suspected of conspiracy to defraud.	105 charges laid; 63 were laid against Laurie Connell. Connell died during the proceedings in 1996.
16. Spedley Securities	Brian Yuill investigated by ASC over alleged misuse of position to transfer $17 million from Spedley Securities to his family company. Other directors were alleged to have improperly used their position.	Criminal prosecutions resulted in 16 charges laid. Yuill was found guilty and sentenced to three years and nine months imprisonment. Another former Spedley's director, James Craven, was gaoled for nine months.
17. Westmex Limited	CEO, Russell Goward was charged over an alleged false and misleading press statement about Westmex Securities.	Goward was found guilty of market manipulation and sentenced to 2 years, 10 months gaol.
18. Southern Cross Holdings	Douglas Reid, Deputy Chairman, was charged over an alleged false accounting, theft and other matters involving 'failing to act honestly as a director'.	Reid was found guilty of market manipulation, sentenced to ten years gaol. He appealed the conviction.

Sources: Summarised primarily from data disclosed in the 1991–92 *ASC Annual Report*, pp. 40–1. 'Of the 13 matters referred [in Table 10.1] to the DPP for possible criminal charges, [several] have resulted in the commencement of criminal prosecutions. One matter was successfully resolved by civil action undertaken directly by the ASC (Golden Bounty). In the Duke Group matter the ASC was given leave to appear in a civil action which was subsequently settled … In the Hooker Corporation matter the ASC decided there was no basis for further action. Seven of the 16 matters [as of June 1992] involved civil action as well as investigation of possible criminal conduct (Bond Group, Girvan, Independent Resources, Duke Group, Rothwells, Spedley Securities and Golden Bounty)' (pp. 5–6, *ASC Annual Report*); amended on the basis of information reported in subsequent ASC *Annual Reports*, the latest being the 2000–01 *Report*.

Entrepreneurs such as Bond, Skase, Goward, Ansett, Connell, Parry, Judge, Hawkins, Goldberg, Yuill, Herscu and Spalvins were at one time described as the heroes, the icons of our financial system. The aftermath of the 1980s boom produced public inquiries into the actions of many of those business people (see Table 10.1). In some cases their business reputations were irreparably tarnished, some were exposed to be inept, some were deemed outright villains – though perhaps equally victims of the financial reporting systems guiding their actions.

The 1980s were significant also for public acknowledgement of the extent of complex corporate structures and related-party transactions. Of course, such disclosures were not new. They had existed informally, and some were more of a kind publicly noted in previous decades. But the 1980s revealed more publicly than before the extent of those structures and transactions and their scope for corporate devilment. They are here to stay, as was evidenced a decade later. A commingling of Australian public companies was further facilitated by the actions of a corporate vehicle, Australia 2000 Pty Ltd, formed by a group of business people allegedly to prevent the takeover of some of Australia's oldest blue chip companies. A 'white knight' cross-shareholding strategy was employed to defend those companies. That further blurred the notion of a separate legal entity. While the aim may have been laudable, the consequences of similar related-party arrangements proved dramatic, as revealed in the accounts of several 1980s cases below.

During this period, 'substance over form' became the in-phrase of regulators – in particular, of the Accounting Standards-setters. While compulsory Statements of Accounting Standards were intended to provide 'authoritative guidance' on matters of accounting measurement and disclosure, the necessary exercise of professional judgment appeared to take a back seat to the cookbook of rules. In this setting, paragraph four of AAS 6, 'Accounting Policies: Determination, Application and Disclosure', acknowledged the substance over form concept as being one of five overriding criteria to be considered in choosing appropriate accounting policies.[4] The difficulties of identifying the substance of transactions, either with or without legal form, have been evident in the earlier accounts of events preceding failure in the 1960s and 1970s. That is demonstrated further in the following 1980s *causes célèbres*. However, it is difficult to contemplate the usefulness of accounting for the substance of a transaction without there being legal form. The 1990s would see this issue revisited.

Public experience with Reid Murray, H.G. Palmer, Stanhill, ASL, Cambridge, Minsec and the like should dispel the suggestions that the 1980s experiences were unusual, as should events in the mid-to-late 1990s. In respect of many matters pertinent to commercial practice and corporate failure, it was definitely more of the same. Mixing the financial affairs of public and private companies within complex group structures facilitated share transactions, property dealings and other asset transfers via extensive use of related-party, often round robin, transactions and occasionally back-to-back loan arrangements.

Our conventional standard accounting practices were unable to cope with the complexities. Primarily they failed because of their ad hoc, one-off orientation – methods drummed up as a *quick fix* for a current anomaly, the current object of complaint, the subject of current pressure on the accounting, irrespective of whether they meshed or conflicted with other practices or financial common sense.[5] Whereas the 1980s was the 'decade of the deal' for the entrepreneurs, it was the 'decade of the quick fix' for the Accounting Standards-setters. Attraction to the quick fix continues. By the mid-1990s, the professional bodies worldwide had set in place Urgent Issues Groups (UIGs) to come up with a speedy fix to urgent accounting problems. It was an interesting approach to the systemic defects of current practice – the old reductionist process and its one-off 'solutions' continued, and with as little hope of success in improving accounting data generally as the well-intentioned efforts in the past.

The Australian UIG's capacity for the *ad hoc* and quick fix is indisputable. Its 1996 handling of Pacific Dunlop's use of the inverse-sum-of-the-years'-digits method (ISOYD) to amortise goodwill (more slowly than the straight line method) clearly illustrates that. Unable to muster convincing argument why the ISOYD method was 'wrong', the UIG went straight for the jugular of the complaints levelled at Pacific Dunlop: it declared the method unacceptable, implied it was wrong, but then let bygones be bygones and allowed the company's past practice to stand, although it prohibited it in respect of future transactions. That was a strange outcome. If the ISOYD method was wrong, then the UIG should have required PacDun's accounts to be recast; and if the ISOYD's method was acceptable (not wrong by implication) in the past, then it ought not to have been outlawed in the future. This episode and subsequent ones suggest that the UIG engages in a very peculiar practice indeed.

In the 1980s, misleading or untrue statements caused by balance date adjustments, market rigging or insider trading were sometimes facilitated by the judicious use of financial window-dressing – misleading accounting.

Again, complex business structures and questionable group accounting practices were to the fore, and the sudden, unexpected collapses of public companies continued. Take Ariadne Australia Limited, for instance. For the year ended 30 June 1987, Ariadne had announced a record profit of $142 million. Incredibly, a year later, Ariadne reported it was in financial difficulty, having announced what was then a record Australian corporate loss of $640 million.[6] Interwest was another, as it reported a record operating profit of $25 million in September 1989, only to be placed in receivership three months later. Similarly, in the aftermath of Rothwells' 1988 collapse, according to an estimate by Deloitte Ross Tohmatsu, Rothwells made a loss each year instead of the profit it had reported. In 1987 it declared a profit of $28 million, when its actual result was a loss of $107 million.[7]

Whereas criticism has not been confined to Australia,[8] concern over the way Australian accounting and auditing function is more than justified.

Contrary to the pervading rhetoric, during the 1980s the *form* of transactions ruled over the *financial substance* in accounting's depiction of certain entities' financial affairs.[9] Yet, accountants' focus is said to be on the much wider *economic* substance.

Evidence of transactions, some without intent to deceive, others allegedly contrived or sham in the extreme, produced reported profit figures and related asset balances subsequently expunged from entities' financial statements. Some of this has been due to the suspect techniques described immediately above. Some has been the outcome of compliance with professionally and legally endorsed Standards. These include:

(a) questionable asset balance items, such as the ubiquitous FITB, clearly demonstrated, for instance, in Bond Corporation's 1988 half a billion dollar write-off; and the proposed Adsteam litigation involving asset amounts of hundreds of millions of dollars being questioned;

(b) interest expenditure being capitalised – amounts exceeding tens of millions of dollars have subsequently been written off in one period;

(c) formation expenditure being treated as an asset. In (for example) Compass Airline's 1990 accounts, 'formation expenditure' represented over 40 per cent of the total assets of the company;

(d) other types of expenses capitalised and then, several years later, written off to the Profit and Loss account as a one-off charge;

(e) terminological difficulties ('self-sustaining' or 'integrated, dependent subsidiary', etc.) driving the accounting for foreign-held assets and liabilities and periodic transactions involving foreign exchange;

(f) ambiguities regarding whether convertible notes are 'debt' or 'equity'. Again, Bond Corporation's accounts are instructive. In 1987/88, convertible notes classified as equity lowered substantially the debt to equity ratio; and,

(g) the related-party (often round-robin) transaction was a device used by many 1980s entrepreneurs. In evidence adduced in court cases at Spedley, Rothwells and Linter, round-robin transactions are alleged to have been a medium for masking the true state of those entities' affairs at balance date.

Raking over the particulars of the 'accounting' rise and fall of three 1980s collapses, Adelaide Steamship, Bond Corporation and Westmex, shows that many of the financing, accounting and commercial practices of the 1980s were really repeat performances of what had been so well rehearsed in the 1960s and 1970s. In each 1980s case the directors and auditors were the subject of civil litigation. Our analysis is based on the publicly available material. It does not seek to comment on specific matters litigated. Several of the litigations resulted in out-of-court settlements, thus hampering more informed analyses.

CHAPTER 11

Adsteam on the Rocks

The complexity in Samuel Insull's *top-heavy pyramid* in 1920s USA is more than matched by the outcome of the cross-shareholdings within the Adelaide Steamship (Adsteam) group of companies in 1980s Australia. Enterprise action *par excellence*.

'Adsteam a humiliation for the accounting profession', 'Adsteam's $4.49 billion loss is biggest ever.'[1] Those headlines captured the importance of the saga associated with the scuttling of the monolithic Adsteam group comprising numerous less than majority owned (albeit effectively-controlled) companies. Adsteam would prove to be an exemplar, highlighting the integral nature of accounting and auditing. It also entailed one of Australia's largest collapses where fraud was not an issue. A decade after the company was placed in receivership it would result in a significant out-of-court settlement (discussed in the *Postscript*).

At the time of its partial breaking up, Adsteam was arguably Australia's biggest and certainly the most complex conglomerate (Figure 11.1). In March 1991, Adelaide Steamship Company Limited (the parent company) was placed under an informal receivership-style scheme of arrangement at the behest of a syndicate of banks. It took action to restructure, to simplify the cross-shareholding-based conglomerate structure and to pare the Adsteam group's mountain of debt. By the end of 1993, debt within the group had been reduced to around $1.5 billion, but post-1990 group losses had accumulated to nearly $3 billion.[2]

December 1994 saw a class action, initiated by the ASC on behalf of Adsteam, against its 1990 auditor and several of its directors, including the former chairman and managing director, John Spalvins. Adsteam sought damages of $340 million related to an alleged $518 million overstatement of its 1990 reported profit and the consequential alleged improper payment of dividends.

Adsteam's former auditor challenged the validity of the ASC to initiate this action under section 50 of the ASC law. In April 1996 the appeal was upheld. The ASC then successfully appealed that judgment, with the matter finally settled out of court in November 2000. This is discussed in the *Postscript*.

Financial data of the flagship, The Adelaide Steamship Company Limited (Tables 11.1 and 11.2), offer insight into the changing fortunes of the Adsteam

Figure 11.1 Adsteam group structure as at 30 September 1990

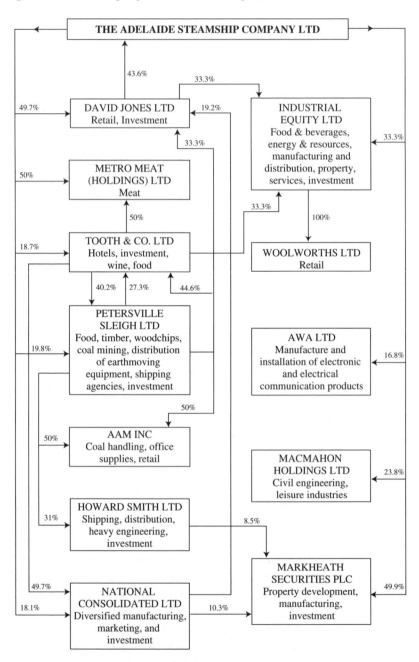

Source: Australian Financial Review, 8 November 1990, p. 18.

group during the 1980s. Typically these reported figures portrayed an incomplete picture of Adsteam's financial affairs.

The Adelaide Steamship Company Limited, one of Australia's oldest surviving industrial companies, had operated passenger and cargo ships since 1875. This activity continues today through the company Adsteam Marine.

By 1995, several years of large reported group losses and its sagging share price indicated Adsteam was only just maintaining that position. Downturns in its initial core activities in the 1960s and 1970s pre-empted a metamorphosis in the company, especially from 1977 under John Spalvins' leadership. Major shipping interests, except towage and port services, were disposed of and a process of extensive diversification begun. The stated goal of Spalvins' leadership was to acquire between 40 and 50 per cent of a target company and hence secure effective control.

Numero uno acquisitions

Changes in Adsteam's share price over the Spalvins era are revealing. Rises occurred in each year from around $1 in 1982 to over $5 in 1987. Dropping to around $4 after the October 1987 crash, Adsteam surged to a high of over $8 in 1989 before declining to between 10 and 20 cents in 1991 and 1992. It remained low into the mid-1990s, as disposal of the empire's assets continued. Adsteam, it must be recalled, was regarded as one of the most active of the 1980s' entrepreneurial companies. Publicly maintaining a strategy of being in basic businesses such as food, ship towage, building and retailing, Adsteam acquired major shareholdings in numerous companies throughout the 1980s. Coincidentally, Table 11.1 discloses a similar pattern of increases in reported profits over that period.

Spalvins' philosophy was to retain only those companies that were an industry's *numero uno*, or at worst number two – a strategy diverging greatly from that followed by another leading 1980s entrepreneurial company, Westmex Ltd.

Adsteam's run began with the acquisition of 'controlling' (though less than 50 per cent) shareholdings in Tooths and David Jones in 1982. Major investments in H.C. Sleigh and the National Consolidated group followed. It culminated in the late 1989 joint venture acquisition by Dextran Pty Ltd of Industrial Equity Limited (IEL). Dextran comprised equal investments by Adsteam's 'public' arms, David Jones, Tooth and Co. and Adelaide Steamship. Acquisition of IEL was possibly a fatal mistake, for it left Sir Ronald Brierley a wounded adversary. He would return at a crucial time in 1990, just when Spalvins needed a breathing space.

Table 11.1 The Adelaide Steamship Company Ltd – Statex balance sheet summary, ratios and profit and loss data, 30 June 1982 to 30 June 1991

	30/6/91 $000	30/6/90 $000	30/6/89 $000	30/6/88 $000	30/6/87 $000	30/6/86 $000	30/6/85 $000	30/6/84 $000	30/6/83 $000	30/6/82 $000
Cash and liquids	174,165	273,072	394,748	181,892	8,017	67,326	59,697	18,998	20,175	51,454
Trade debtors	66,284	156,825	94,948	103,255	45,615	131,306	53,234	48,438	39,034	40,849
Stocks	139,484	135,872	56,959	117,834	54,461	65,129	57,507	52,745	59,896	60,266
Other current assets	108,850	20,855	12,473	39,752	19,552	148,458	5,303	9,273	22,038	18,229
Total current assets	488,783	586,624	559,128	442,733	127,645	412,219	175,741	129,454	141,143	170,798
Bank overdraft	68,162	3,921	2,467	2,911	2,154	2,438	1,722	1,454	1,622	8,262
Trade creditors	19,761	43,011	29,390	44,925	38,638	55,313	21,928	17,116	19,890	40,353
Tax provisions	35,165	2,099	1,076	633	475	6,677	171	353	428	1,918
Debt due in one year	1,078,279	153,707	31,914	37,638	25,852	55,930	28,840	18,464	35,296	36,025
Other current liabilities	44,685	115,781	163,101	59,045	41,710	35,859	48,450	40,218	29,603	25,364
Current liabilities	1,246,052	318,519	227,948	145,152	108,829	156,217	101,111	77,668	86,839	111,922
Net working capital	-757,269	268,105	331,180	297,581	18,816	256,002	74,630	51,786	54,304	58,876
Net plant and property	50,872	57,195	75,170	102,030	70,301	68,040	70,192	89,186	86,503	69,605
Investments	596,493	1,992,727	1,619,984	907,759	767,317	639,982	637,259	424,696	385,939	355,230
Deferred assets	211,667	129,912	118,075	132,114	144,716	28,773	29,012	15,887	10,227	5,746
Total invested capital	101,763	2,447,939	2,144,409	1,439,484	1,001,150	992,797	811,093	581,555	536,973	489,457
Long-term debt	4	743,390	826,345	417,619	165,186	407,594	266,406	147,876	148,895	125,602
Other deferred liabilities	34,347	6,479	3,701	4,218	3,945	2,685	2,169	2,608	2,118	1,997
Minority interest	-75	43,254	29,600	25,798	359	76,604	117,243	117,677	100,811	106,479
Preferred capital	0	0	0	0	0	0	3,000	3,000	3,000	5,000

Ordinary equity	67,487	1,654,816	1,284,763	991,849	831,660	505,914	422,275	310,394	282,149	250,379
Total invested funds	101,763	2,447,939	2,144,409	1,439,484	1,001,150	992,797	811,093	581,555	536,973	489,457
Total tangible assets	1,347,815	2,766,458	2,372,357	1,584,636	1,109,979	1,149,014	912,204	659,223	623,812	601,379
Intangibles	9	55	871	18,416	125	145	166	187	208	105
Total assets	1,347,824	2,766,513	2,373,228	1,603,052	1,110,104	1,149,159	912,370	659,410	624,020	601,484
Balance sheet ratios										
Liquid ratio	0.29	1.43	2.22	2.28	0.68	2.25	1.18	1.00	0.95	1.06
Current ratio	0.39	1.84	2.45	3.05	1.17	2.63	1.73	1.66	1.62	1.52
Shareholders' interest	5.0	61.4	55.4	64.2	75.0	50.7	59.5	65.4	61.9	60.2
% Market/Bk listed inv.	59.3	94.1	101.8	100.0	135.8	168.6	128.4	109.2	138.6	108.6
Net assets/share (adj.)	1.01	4.65	4.83	4.49	3.00	2.28	1.92	1.45	1.34	1.20
Dilution factor used	1.00	1.00	0.72	0.60	0.53	0.42	0.34	0.34	0.34	0.34
Long-term debt/equity	0.0	44.9	64.3	42.1	19.8	80.5	63.0	47.6	52.7	50.1
Short-term debt/equity	1,698.7	9.5	2.6	4.0	3.3	11.5	7.2	6.4	13.0	17.6
Profit after tax, after minority interest (000)										
As per Adel. Steamship Co. accounts	(1,358.21)	220.33	200.85	160.71	64.14	117.22	60.19	41.60	32.69	24.03
As per Statex	(1,358.21)	220.33	200.85	160.71	64.14	117.22	60.19	41.60	32.69	23.08
Sales (000)	312,320	136,738	409,325	388,525	473,324	365,473	244,372	392,695	447,664	354,290

Source: Sydney Stock Exchange Research Pty Ltd, *Statex Service*, Adsteam (A2) run on 7 November, 1991.

Adsteam was the very model of a model conglomerate. Industries penetrated included retailing (David Jones and Clark Rubber), food, meat, wine and smallgoods (Tooth & Co., Petersville Sleigh and Metro Meat Holdings), real estate and property investment (Pioneer Property, W.A. Realty and Markheath Securities plc), its traditional activities of towage and port services (Adelaide Steamship and Petersville Sleigh) and manufacturing (National Consolidated and Ajax Cooke). If diversity gave strength, Adsteam ought to have been a Goliath. Then again, perhaps it was.

Acquisition strategy resulted in an extremely complicated cross-shareholding-based structure. This facilitated loans to subsidiary companies, the recording of interest receivable from those subsidiaries, the inclusion of the ubiquitous company *debit* – the future income tax benefit. It also presented a nightmare for auditors in attesting the worth of the investments in related companies and the collateral underlying Adsteam's loans to them. Adsteam's structure was the seminal example of auditors' worst nightmares.

The maximum amount of shareholdings of any company in other group entities was kept below 50 per cent. That practice, perhaps, is an excellent instance of how the rule-book approach to consolidation accounting imposed by the law and the Accounting Standards *at the time* determined managerial actions. It also, of course, thereby determined asset valuation bases and the 'group' profit calculation at Adsteam. And it created difficulty for anyone trying to unravel the financial significance of transactions between the related companies.

At that time percentage shareholding essentially determined whether control existed and hence whether companies' accounts were to be consolidated, and with that the injection of the consolidation accounting artifacts. Now, under AASB 1024, arguably a broader criterion of 'control' determines whether a company is a subsidiary of another. But the point remains: curiously, how the financial outcomes are reported depends upon the relationship between the companies, not upon the financial facts. Adsteam's cross-shareholding strategy meant that consolidated financial statements were not required, though Adsteam officers publicly provided different reasons for the complex shareholding arrangements. Closing off possible takeover opportunities against Adsteam group companies was advanced, as was the need to use shelf companies to buy and sell shares of Adsteam group companies. To that end, between 1984 and 1987 shelf companies issued preference shares to other Adsteam companies which were then, under the complex arrangement, entitled to all realised profits on the share deals. It was the epitome of group enterprise action.

Whereas many analysts and financial institutions were wary of the resulting conglomerate, untangling it appeared to be beyond virtually everyone. It is far from clear whether Adsteam's management and accountants could do so themselves. Certainly, if they employed something akin to consolidation accounting practices to obtain a clue or two, they were bound to be more in the dark than when they started.

Most of the Adsteam group companies' shares were cross-held, as shown in Figure 11.1. It is understandable that only two or three institutional share-holders appeared in the top 20 Adsteam shareholders between 1986 and 1990. Whatever the institutional view of Adsteam, the cross-shareholding strategy would have kept them out.

Spalvins' management strategy was on the one hand praised, and on the other equally criticised. As with Palmer, Reid Murray, Cambridge Credit and the like, Adsteam was reported in the financial press on numerous occasions as a corporate *success* story. Consider this early 1987 assessment: 'Adelaide Steamship, with its group of companies stands out in the stockmarket as an entrepreneurial company with the best management, backed up with a stringent, highly disciplined reporting system. The credit belongs to John Spalvins.'[3] Table 11.2 supports this view as it reveals increasing profits nearly every year from 1982 to 1990. Another Icarus paradox example suggesting that extreme success is a portent for impending failure? Or, as suggested previously, is it more the case that *reportedly* successful companies relying on creative accounting should be considered likely candidates for failure?

Twenty-five years before, almost identical comments and certainly the same sentiments had been expressed regarding the business acumen of Herbie Palmer. Perhaps it was a foreboding of Adsteam's fate. And then in 1988:

Table 11.2 Summary financial statistics of the operations of The Adelaide Steamship Company Ltd, 30 June 1982 to 30 June 1991

Year end 30 June	Sales (other revenue) $m	After-tax profits $m	Total assets $m	Total debt $m
1982	354	24	601	139
1983	448	33	624	238
1984	393	42	659	228
1985	244	60	912	368
1986	365	117	1,149	566
1987	473	64	1,110	277
1988	389	160	1,603	567
1989	409	201	2,373	1,058
1990	137	220	2,767	1,068
1991	312	(1,358)	1,348	1,280

Source: Sydney Stock Exchange Research Pty Ltd, *Statex Service*, Adsteam (A2) run on 7 November 1991 (reproduced as Table 11.1).

'Spalvins has the market guessing ... Adsteam is basically a strong group with good operating businesses, but the cream on its earnings has come from takeovers and dealing, and Spalvins undoubtedly wants to generate more such cream.'[4]

By 1989 producing 'cream' was proving difficult. But Spalvins went for two ambitious investment plays. One was a miscalculated greenmail investment in Bell Resources at the time of Bond Corporation's move on Bell's cash box. By the time the Adsteam investment had been secured, the now notorious $1.2 billion 'loan' (see Chapter 12) from Bell to several Bond group companies appears to have been sealed. With the cash box emptied by Bond, Adsteam's investment in Bell was looking bad. Spalvins tried several moves to claw back funds into Bell Resources from the Bond group. They proved futile. The second poor investment in 1989 was the IEL acquisition, using Dextran. A syndicate of banks provided the $900 million required. Spalvins apparently was keen to edge out an old adversary, Sir Ronald Brierley.

Adsteam had certainly achieved conglomerate status with this 1989 acquisition. It now had a large finger in many industries – food, retailing, real estate and property, meat, wine, manufacturing, and shipping and towage. Whether because of bad luck or simply the poor investments Spalvins had made to crank up the conglomerate, Adsteam was perceived by its backers to lack collateral. Its plates were cracking – Adsteam had begun to 'take in' water.

Contiguously, regulatory interest occurred on two fronts. The Australian Taxation Office (ATO) and the ASC became interested in certain aspects of Adsteam's Byzantine operations. The ATO would have liked to have lifted the corporate veil. Adsteam's public image was particularly dented by the long-running legal battle with the ATO over disputes involving millions of dollars of tax assessed on capital profits on intra-group share deals by those shelf companies. Adsteam ultimately settled this matter, paying the ATO over $250 million in March 1991.

On the other front, the ASC investigated several transactions between Adsteam and related companies during the 1989/90 period, as well as the propriety of certain asset valuations. This eventually resulted in the ASC launching its class action in December 1994 in the Federal Court against the Adsteam auditor and several of its directors on behalf of Adsteam.[5]

The ASC alleged that related-party transactions between Adsteam, several subsidiaries and other related parties (loans, investments, sales with put options, etc.) were used in order to present the financial state of affairs of the Adsteam group in a better light than it really was. And, that individual entity asset revaluations, related entity profits and dividend transfers, were not in accord with existing Accounting Standards. Specifically, it was alleged that the directors of Adsteam should not have permitted payment of the interim dividend of $131,488,000 and the $97,313,000 final dividend for the financial year ending 30 June 1990. They should have been aware that 'Adsteam's profit for the six months ending 31 December 1989 was overstated in the 1990 interim accounts at least by the sum of $449,985,498', and that 'Adsteam's profits for the year ended 30 June 1990 were overstated in the Adsteam's accounts at least by an amount of $518,981,000'.

Several reasons were advanced by the ASC to support its contentions. ASC's claim suggested that loan asset balances should have been written down and FITB balances written off, and that asset revaluations were selective and not in accord with approved Accounting Standards. Contested was whether a surplus arising from an asset revaluation related to a particular company could be used to allow a cash dividend. The ghost of the 1961 UK case, *Dimbula Valley (Ceylon) Tea Co Ltd v Laurie* appeared in the discovery process. There, Justice Buckley had ruled that, while it may not be prudent, *under certain circumstances* such a cash dividend was legal.

Reportedly, the ASC's argument drew upon the proposition that those related-party transactions masked the true state of the financial affairs of Adsteam as at 30 June 1990. The question of entity versus group enterprise immediately surfaced. Arguments presented in the process of discovery concerned whether 'group' profits were appropriate. This raised the issue of whether 'group' profits exist *per se*.

Also, we would argue that no FITB balance ought to be raised in the first place, physical asset valuation under the Standards is always selective, and related-party transactions do not so much 'mask' as does the conventional accounting for them. The successful appeal by the auditors against the validity of the ASC bringing the class action was overturned on a further appeal by the ASC. Years later a settlement was reached – see Postscript.

Based on the assessments of some commentators, and certainly with hindsight, by the end of 1989 the nadir for this corporate monolith was nigh.

Adsteam's and Spalvins' critics

By April 1989, respected financial writers had contradictory assessments of Spalvins and Adsteam. Discussing an *Australian Ratings* report on Adsteam, Sykes noted: 'The carefully separated accounts of Adelaide Steamship and its associates have only ever shown parts of the picture. The whole doesn't look so pretty ... Investors are suspicious of the group's incestuous interlocking shareholdings.'[6] In contrast, a week later Gottliebsen, referring to Spalvins as 'the king of cross-ownership', claimed: 'While [Spalvins] has been lambasted by his critics and ignored by the sharemarket, Adsteam's chief has been building his billions.'[7] Adsteam's 1988/89 financial statements disclosed total tangible assets of $2.372 billion. But, of course, the more you have, the more there is to lose. In December 1989 Spalvins predicted that Adsteam's interim profits would exceed $100 million, which they duly did, coming in at $131.448 million in February 1990. However, as we noted, this was questioned by the ASC.

Early in 1990, bearish sentiment followed publication of *Australian Ratings*' negative assessment of Adsteam's liquidity and interest rate cover. News reports of the assessment by stockbroker analyst Viktor Shvets (rated by *Australian Business* as the best financial analyst in 1991) certainly did not help – 'under certain conditions, the cash flow of the Adsteam group as a global entity would be deficient by as much as $250 million following the group's takeover of Industrial Equity Ltd'.[8] He also revealed that a large proportion of Adsteam's reported assets were in fact 'non-assets' in many people's reasoning – for example, the questionable FITB item. Adsteam's share price plunged. Spalvins followed a popular strategy when under attack, his bellicose remarks aimed directly at those who doubted the financial strength and viability of Adsteam.[9] But this proved to no avail.

Even towards the end of 1990 the board, in reporting to the ASX Adsteam's preliminary unaudited results, still projected an optimistic outlook for 1990/91:

> For the last fourteen years the Company has recorded a regular improvement
> in profit for the benefit of shareholders. We recognise that 1990/91 is going
> to be another challenge, but believe that the strength of our core businesses and
> the quality and depth of our management will ensure another good result in the
> year ahead.

It was not to be. Table 11.1 discloses that a loss of over $1.35 billion was posted for 1990/91. So much for relying on managerial forecasts!

Commenting after Spalvins' fall from grace, Gottliebsen recalled that 'Spalvins was worshipped by bankers who scrambled to lend him money un-secured ... [and] he believed the [conglomerate] game could go on forever'.[10] Interestingly, those loans were accompanied by negative pledges and corporate cross guarantees. These proved to be of little benefit to many unsecured group creditors here and in other cases, a matter about which we have more to say in Chapter 16.

Possibly the *coup de grâce* was dealt by the archetype investor-cum-entrepreneur, the wounded Sir Ronald Brierley. Spalvins had not satisfied the essential condition if one sets out to 'kill a king' – you 'have to get him with the first shot'. Brierley's compelling negative assessment of Adsteam's financial prospects appeared in September 1990 under this caption: 'Brierley effect puts Adsteam into a freefall'.[11] Brierley's assessment was based on his recast Adsteam's accounts, by applying conventional consolidation practices.

By the end of October the tone of some analysts suggested that the financial position of Adsteam was becoming desperate. Chanticleer noted in the *Australian Financial Review*:

> The major outstanding issue [facing Adsteam's board] is the rationalisation of the convoluted and incestuous group structure. ... Many other valuable assets [than tax losses] are held in artificial 50–50 joint ventures that will be very difficult to unravel. It is a process that will take years to complete and at the end of it there may or may not be any real equity left. I doubt that even John Spalvins knows what he will end up with.[12]

Spalvins on profits

Critical commentaries about Adsteam's accounts appeared in the press: 'Adsteam's accounts are mysterious. Even the most diligent analysts have to admit that this labyrinth of inter-company and local and overseas off-balance sheet complexity defies full analysis.'[13] Particularly interesting was the overwhelming allusion in the financial press to Adsteam's strategy of denying the market the perceived benefits of consolidated financial statements. 'The consolation is that economic entity consolidation [under AASB 1024] might make any future Adsteams easier for analysts and investors to recognise in their infancy.'[14] One wonders how preparing consolidated accounts of such a complex conglomerate would have made anyone the wiser? Conventional consolidation techniques are fraught with problems and anomalies. Despite the push for consolidated financial statements generally towards the end of the 1980s, and more specifically in commentaries on the Adsteam case (and over a decade later in the Enron case), perversely the financial public were almost certainly better off without the additional complications consolidation brings.

Under attack, Spalvins aimed criticism of his own at members of the accounting profession for their shifting position on differentiating 'extraordinary' and 'operating' profits. Reportedly the position he took was 'that what matters is a company's creation of wealth by income and asset appreciation jointly. This includes property and asset revaluations whether they are called "profit" or not'.[15] The crucial issue in this regard is how to determine an asset and its worth.

Undoubtedly this becomes an extremely difficult problem for auditors and directors when related parties, especially wholly-owned subsidiaries and private companies, become enmeshed in transactions with publicly listed parent companies. It was reported that in one financial period, 'an analysis of the trading of the [Adsteam] group showed that an average of 70 per cent of the stock being traded was accounted for by associates of Adsteam'.[16] It is perhaps a little premature to claim that accounting numbers can be signed off as 'true and fair', even though those numbers may not 'bear any relationship with the health of the operating business. In Adsteam all this was done *quite legally*'.[17] Whether it occurs legally is contestable. Curiously, the same commentator earlier had berated Adsteam for not preparing consolidated statements (see fn. 14) – the most notorious vehicle of misleading accounting data. A recurrent theme throughout this book is that if many conventional accounting data were ever extensively tested for financial truth, common sense and fairness in a court, they would fail miserably.

Within months of Spalvins' counter-attack, with Adsteam's share price around $4, it was reported:

> How quickly times change. Just eight months ago John Spalvins was being
> fêted as Australia's most dynamic entrepreneur, having snatched Industrial Equity
> Ltd from under its management's nose in a cleverly executed lightning raid.
> [The investment proved disastrous and] ... today the Adelaide Steamship Co.
> chief is fighting to keep the share prices of his empire afloat as he buys time
> to restructure.[18]

A year later, Spalvins' had departed the boards of all Adsteam companies. Corporate success had immediately presaged failure.

In a perverse twist, Spalvins' outpouring on what represents corporate profits was closer to the mark than many of the pundits of the accounting profession. His comment there struck at the heart of the problem with conventional accounting practice – that it is not directed at measuring the 'wealth and progress' of a company in meaningful, real financial terms. Wealth certainly does comprise the market worth of all assets; income (increase in wealth) has to include all realised and unrealised financial gains and losses; and asset appreciation (*a pretium* – increase in price) has to be included (even if unrealised), as does depreciation (*de pretium* – a decrease in price, equally unrealised). Realisation does not create or consume wealth, it merely changes its form – a physical asset into cash, cash into a physical asset, and the like.

History has the uncanny habit of being repeated. In the United States over 65 years earlier, Samuel Insull had taken on the accounting profession in defence of his depreciation accounting policies which conflicted with the profession's wisdom. Insull only brought to account a decrease in the worth of the assets when it was evidenced in the market. He rejected the idea that regular charges for depreciation created a replacement fund as the conventional wisdom was promoting (much the same as it more or less does today). A charge for depreciation when the market price of the asset is constant or increasing deliberately understates profits or overstates losses, as the case may be. Like Spalvins, Insull made more financial sense on that than the accountants. And for one good reason – uninhibited by the rules and conventions of accounting, he was applying the methods financial calculation, financial evaluation and assessment used in ordinary, everyday, commercial settings. Irrespective of his motives, those methods not only gave him the answers he perhaps wanted, they also gave the answers he should have got, but which conventional accounting could not have given!

Of course, Insull's views were rubbished, particularly by the accounting profession, as were Spalvins'. Even more coincidental is the correspondence in their respective corporate structures. Insull's main tilt at the profession centred on his utility maze comprising several holding and sub-holding companies and hundreds of subsidiaries, without consolidation accounting being employed. In the end, Insull, too, left his empire unceremoniously. Several years later he was found without identification, alone and dead on a Paris Metro station with only a five centime piece in his overcoat pocket. Such might be the unjust fate of accounting reformers!

Insull's complex group structure, labelled by Valance (1955) as a 'top-heavy pyramid', is illustrated in Figure 11.2. Insull had imposed layers of hundreds of holding and subsidiary companies over the utility operating companies with a series of trusts at the apex. As with Adsteam, such a complex structure is likely to engender uncertainty on the part of prospective shareholders as to whose interests are being served by intra-group transactions.

Unjustly, few are likely to acknowledge, or even be aware of, Insull's or Spalvins' efforts to inject the conventional accounting of their times with some financial commonsense.

Returning to the Adsteam saga, a plethora of charges and counter-charges over accounting practices accompanied Adsteam's collapse. They involve several contentious matters, including whether the accounts of various entities comprising the complex Adsteam empire ought to have been consolidated. Eventually, changes to the ASX listing requirements and Accounting Standards and the post-October 1987 legislative developments mandated the production of consolidated financials for situations pertaining in the Adsteam group. The proposed charges contained in the 1994 ASC claim of presenting mislead-ing data in the Adsteam accounts, had they been heard in court, could have elicited a fascinating argument. It would likely reveal if there were any sub-stantive matters, previously not disclosed, in respect of the actual financial affairs of Adsteam prior to its major disinvestments under the informal 1990s receivership.

Figure 11.2 Samuel Insull's 'top-heavy pyramid' (extract)

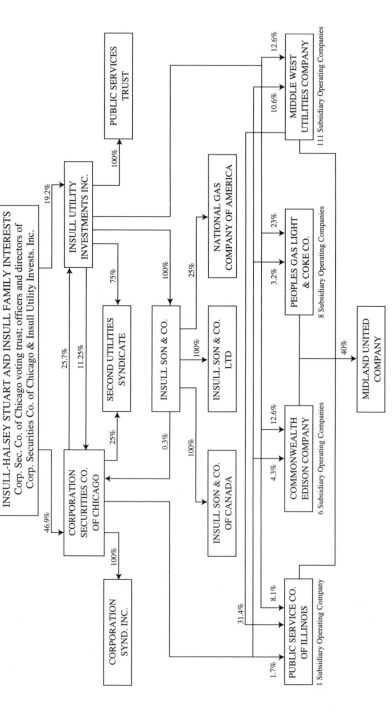

Note: Insull Utility Investments and Corporation Securities Co. of Chicago were trusts. Percentages as at end of 1929.
Source: United States Congressional Record – Senate (1935), p. 8499.

A lay jury drawing upon ordinary financial common sense may well be at odds with the accounting profession on whether Spalvins' views on asset appreciation and depreciation, and the merits of consolidation, were so ill-founded. Certainly it would be embarrassing to the accounting profession and the regulators if virtue in any of Adsteam's accounting practices was to be exposed by the amateurs. Like Minsec in the 1970s (and Insull some 60-odd years before), some of Adsteam's *publicly disclosed* accounting appears closer to financial common sense than the outcomes likely from using the professionally endorsed practices – consolidation, arbitrary depreciation calculations and FITBs, in particular. In accounting, recourse to financial 'commonsense', casual but careful observation of financial affairs, and compliance with the rubrics of monetary calculation are uncommon practices.

Postscript – Beyond 2000

Eventually Adsteam was broken up under the new administration name, Asarco. The main operating companies – Woolworths, David Jones, Metro Meats, National Consolidated – continue to be household names in Australia. The navigation company remains to ply its trade as a profitable listed company, Adsteam Marine.

But the new century heralded a major auditing development in Australia following an out-of-court settlement of the 1994 class action described earlier. In November 2000 ASIC released a press statement to the effect that several of the directors and auditors agreed to a settlement of the class action that ASIC had brought on behalf of Adsteam. The reported settlement figure was $20 million. The settlement announced in an ASIC *Media Release 00/452* contained the following covenants that have significant implications for the future actions of directors and auditors:

> 6. The auditors acknowledge the importance of accounting and auditing standards, and agree that compliance with those standards is essential to the presentation of *true and fair* financial statements. [*emphasis added*]

> 7. The directors and auditors note that in the 1990 Adsteam financial statements they adopted some accounting treatments which they believed were technically available. The directors and auditors note ASIC's views that the 1990 Adsteam financial statements did not present a true and fair view of the position of the company and fell outside of the accepted accounting principles and practices of that time. While they are unable to agree with this view, including for legal reasons, with the benefit of hindsight, the directors and auditors accept that a different accounting treatment would have been appropriate.[19]

This may prove to be a watershed. The settlement is reinforced by developments post-Enron, the HIH Royal Commission, the Ramsay Report on Auditor Independence, the *CLERP 9* and JCPAA *Report 391* Discussion Papers.

It is worth considering in detail some accounting matters referred to in the *Adsteam settlement* covenants. They go to the heart of accounting issues generally, *inter alia*, to whether asset revaluations were valid? whether they generate a profit, especially distributable profit? Had indeed dividends been paid out of capital swelled by the increased asset values recorded as asset revaluation reserves? Further, debate centred on which entity those accounting questions related to – to the individual company, in this case The Adelaide Steamship Company Ltd, or to the Adsteam Group? The uncertainty surrounding the issue aptly illustrates the confusion for both accountants and observers, directors and regulators when discussing financial performance and financial position. They allow their reference to vacillate between the *notional group* of related companies and the *separate companies* comprising *it*.

Of course, similar issues pervade this volume and are summarised in the regulatory reform chapters in Part VI.

We now turn to the Bond Corporation affair, aspects of which evoke similar convictions.

CHAPTER 12

Bond Corporation Holdings Ltd (Group): Entrepreneurial Rise and Fall*

What has been is what will be, and what has been done is what will be
done; there is nothing new under the sun.

Attributed to King Solomon, Ecclesiastes, 1:9

This account of the troubles at the Bond Corporation group remains partial –
an instalment. While many matters were completed by the end of the 1990s,
some major issues involved 'out-of-court settlements', resulting in continuing
uncertainty. The account has been updated from our first edition, drawing upon
public revelations from numerous criminal and civil cases and myriad
regulatory investigations.

While an orderly but informal liquidation of the Bond group of companies
probably began in about 1991, formally the group continued to trade under a
scheme of arrangement from the beginning of 1993 under the name of Southern
Equities Corporation Ltd. The Bond administration was to comprise two phases
– initially a debt moratorium, then the transformation of creditors' claims into
ordinary and preference shares, redeemable periodically until 31 December
1995. The appointment of a liquidator on 23 December 1993 halted those
plans.[1] Revelations continue from the ongoing inquiries over a decade after the
informal liquidation.

We repeat therefore our first edition caveat. Some of what follows is based
on disclosed information, while other matters are necessarily interpretative and
conjectural.

The early life of the group's founder, Alan Bond – signwriter turned multi-
millionaire-cum-bankrupt – has been told by many. Paul Barry notes that
'Smiling, loud-mouthed, uncomplicated, almost always cheerful, Alan Bond
was a rags-to-riches success, a role model for young Australians.'[2] In 1985,
'Bondy' (as Bob Hawke, then Australian Prime Minister, as well as many
others, referred to him) had already been awarded (in 1978) 'Businessman of
the Year'. He had received an Order of Australia in 1984 for services to
'yachting … [being] team captain of the successful America's Cup challenge
in 1983'. Then followed an 'Australian of the Year' award in 1987. Prior to
the aftermath of the October 1987 share market crash, he was presented as the
epitome of Australian entrepreneurial spirit and business acumen – a true
success story. Within five years the sweetness of success had soured. Alan

Bond was declared bankrupt in April 1992, imprisoned in 1993, then released six months later. In 1996, Bond was gaoled over the *La Promenade* purchase and in 1997 faced further court charges over the notorious Bond/Bell Resources 'cash-cow' transaction. He pleaded guilty to fraud over this transaction and was sentenced to four years' gaol – appealed – but had his sentence extended to seven years. He was released early in 2000 and has returned to what he does best, being an entrepreneur – this time in the United Kingdom. His first venture encountered financial difficulties. The auditor of the parent company of the Bond group, Arthur Andersen was sued over its handling of the company's 1988 audit and settled out of court in May 2002 for a reported figure of $110 million.[3]

Bond provides another instance of the Icarus paradox.[4] Success had quickly turned to failure. Adulation turned to derision, some claiming that the reported figures underpinning that adulation were illusory – perhaps even that the decline of the Bond group of companies may have begun as early as 1984.[5]

A 'poor immigrant made good' mantle draped comfortably on 'Bondy' in those heady days of the 1980s. Already he had become a multi-millionaire. His meteoric rise began with the 1956 sign-writing company, Nu Signs Pty Ltd. But the story of the Bond of recent fame begins with the 1967 formation of Bond Corporation Pty Ltd (Bond Corporation, the head of the Bond group), which he chaired from beginning to near its end. A reverse takeover in 1969 of West Australian hardware merchant W. Drabble Ltd (renamed Amalgamated Industries Ltd) was the backdoor means by which Bond Corporation achieved a stock exchange listing. The world, fame and fortune, public awards, national honours, the America's Cup victory, adulation, corporate collapse, bankruptcy, imprisonment and release, a heart attack, memory losses, Liquidator's hearings, another imprisonment and other trials, all lay before its chairman, Alan Bond. It was a crowded agenda.

Growth by acquisition

Bond's *modus operandi* meshed real estate transactions and inter-group dealings. The following is only a slice of all BCH's investments and divestments occurring over 20 years.

The early 1970s witnessed an oft-repeated technique involving Alan Bond's group of public and private companies. Yanchep Estates Pty Ltd, a wholly-owned subsidiary of Bond Corporation, sold its half-interest in 1,450 lots of land in the Yanchep Sun City development project (near Perth) to a Bond Corporation-controlled company, W.A. Land Holdings; the half-interest was then resold to a company within the Bond group. W.A. Land Holdings then concentrated on diversifying its operations by acquiring Shield Life Assurance

Ltd and the Savoy Corporation group of companies. In 1973 Bond Corporation acquired (on instalment) a 46 per cent interest in Robe River Ltd from the liquidator of the collapsed Mineral Securities (Australia) Ltd for $19.6 million.[6]

Each of the related companies within the Bond group owned a piece of the major action of the others while doing its own unique thing on the side. Individual company and group actions were inextricably intertwined. This was convenient, but as revealed in several of the other failures (for example, H.G. Palmer, Reid Murray, Cambridge, Adsteam, HIH, Enron, and the like), the Byzantine configuration had the potential to be a house of cards. And it would prove a nightmare for creditors, auditors, judges and administrators when the pack imploded.

The year 1974 proved interesting. The Yanchep Sun City project was transferred from Yanchep Estates Pty Ltd to a new joint venture company, Yanchep Sun City Pty Ltd, owned by both the Tokyo Corporation of Japan and Bond Corporation. Eventually, Bond Corporation sold its interest to Tokyo Corporation. During 1974 a liquidity crisis emerged. Given the Australian wages and interest blow-out of 1974, Bond Corporation's debt-based expansion had overreached, as was the fate of other large property and construction companies at that time, including Mainline and Cambridge Credit. We have seen how placing the latter in receivership on 30 September 1974 created a panic in financial markets, which did not help Bond Corporation.

On 17 October 1974 the Perth Stock Exchange queried Bond Corporation's and home-builder Landall Holdings' financial viability. Bond Corporation survived the scrutiny.

Recourse to another feature of Bond's operations (and, subsequently Rupert Murdoch's in the early 1990s) then occurred – calling the banker's bluff, to forestall the banks 'calling in their chips'. According to Barry,[7] a frontal attack on the press and the bankers was used. With Spalvins' and Adsteam's critics the manoeuvre failed – as it did eventually at HIH over a decade later. With Alan Bond and Murdoch it worked.

Financial breathing space was achieved and Bond, after this period of expansion, merged Bond Corporation with W.A. Land Holdings. W.A. Land Holdings, the parent company, was renamed Bond Corporation Holdings Ltd (BCH) on 12 June 1975. For this, another recurring technique was used – commingling private (family) company dealings with other public Bond group companies. Bond's family company, Dallhold Investments Pty Ltd, sold all its shares in Bond Corporation to W.A. Land Holdings for $17.6 million. Through a combination of direct and indirect means, Alan Bond remained the largest shareholder in BCH.

Contiguously, BCH reported a loss of $8.95 million for the 1975 financial year, claimed by the *Financial Review* to be 'one of the biggest ever by a local company'.[8] How quickly the 1960s failures had been forgotten!

Towards the end of the 1970s the Bond group changed its investment strategy. It disposed of interests in the Savoy Group of companies. In May 1978 BCH acquired a 24 per cent shareholding in Endeavour Resources Ltd, and in August 1978 a consortium headed by BCH purchased Burmah Australia Exploration from Burmah Oil Australia for $36 million, and changed its name to Bond Mining and Exploration Pty Ltd.[9] Its principal assets were shareholdings in Basin Oil N.L., Reef Oil N.L. and Santos Ltd, a Cooper Basin oil and gas field operator. The next two years produced continued buying and selling of corporate investments. The Santos investment proved to be one of BCH's most successful asset plays. By the end of 1979, BCH had achieved a paper profit of nearly $60 million on this investment.

Diversification and divestment – the name of the BCH game

Retail diversification was the portfolio play in 1981, as BCH acquired a 43 per cent interest in Waltons. Although Waltons Bond diversification was heralded as a 'street-wise' smart move, it proved to be an enormous longer-term financial drain on the group. But adulation is enjoyable and success contagious. Bond was on a deceptive and seductive roll. Everybody, it seems, was happy to be his friend and felt deprived if they were not.

We have drawn attention to the inherent conflicts of interest in conglomerate structures involving family and public companies being a recurring feature of Australian corporate failures. Growth often has been through acquisition using share scrip as the consideration. Extreme diversity in operations is almost inevitable. Frequently, too, top management has neither the experience nor the capacity to control the resulting labyrinths. It has been a common recipe for disaster which the flurry of takeover activity and hubris temporarily disguise, and in respect of which the obscurities of accounting erect a beguiling façade of success.

Whereas Adsteam's operations demonstrated that the true conglomerate has a finger in every industrial pie, BCH was still short of achieving that in the early 1980s. Hence, forays into petroleum exploration were extended, primarily through the licensed area in Western Australia, WA-192P. These would be complemented with further exploration acquisitions in the mid-1980s.

Acquisitions of diverse companies continued in 1982. In July Waltons Bond ACT acquired all the issued capital in Norman Ross Discounts Ltd, with BCH and Waltons Bond each having a 50 per cent interest in Waltons Bond ACT. During 1982, BCH acquired all of the issued capital in The Swan Brewery Company Ltd (Western Australia's only brewer) for a total cost of $163 million. In turn, investments in Santos, Reef and Basin were disposed of for around $180 million. Deckchairs were repositioned, but was the game proving profitable? At Santos – yes. With many others – no. Endeavour Resources Ltd also acquired Northern Mining Corporation N.L. in 1982. Meanwhile, on the retail front, BCH acquired just under 20 per cent of Grace Brothers. But there was no sentiment. Subsequently, Myer Emporium's offer for Grace Brothers was accepted by shareholders, including both BCH and Waltons Bond ACT

Mining investment dominated again in 1983. Northern Mining N.L. and Samcentre Pty Ltd were acquired from Endeavour Resources. This acquisition afforded BCH total direct ownership of the Rhondda Collieries in Queensland. Northern Mining's interest in the Argyle Diamond Mining venture was to prove controversial. BCH sold Northern Mining's 5 per cent interest in the Argyle Diamond Mines to the West Australian government for $42 million. Poor performances continued to plague the operations of Waltons Bond; the conglomerate needed a 'cash cow', but Waltons was turning into a 'corporate dog'.

In August 1983 BCH increased its interest in Pacific Copper to over 90 per cent and also purchased a 31 per cent interest in Austmark International, a listed property developer. The Austmark acquisition was risky: it needed reconstruction and revitalisation, achieved through a cash issue in which BCH stood as principal underwriter.

Indeed, not all was rosy in the BCH group. Acquisition brings growth, but it does not necessarily generate property, increase wealth or ensure ongoing profits. Around this time *Australian Ratings* publicly expressed concerns about BCH's financial viability and re-examined its rating.

Waltons Bond's financial drain continued – it reported losses of $199.2 million in 1982/1983, while Austmark losses totalled $30.9 million that year. It was then that the America's Cup victory put a glow back into the conglomerate for some observers, even if only temporarily. Group reported profits in 1983 were $6.84 million (see Table 12.3 on p. 186). But any feeling of satisfaction was temporary as the next two years produced losses of $13.59 million and $6.99 million (on sales of $365.3 million and $517.8 million, respectively). While financial prudence dictated that this reported performance trend could not continue, the acquisition policy did!

BCH entered the media by purchasing an interest in the Swan Television and Radio Broadcasters Ltd, operating in Western Australia. In early 1984, BCH expressed interest in, and not long after had control of, Winthrop Investments Limited, a company which owned various business properties in Victoria, the North Kalgurli gold mines and the hydrocarbons explorer Petro Energy, and had a controlling interest in Mid-East Minerals (which ran the Greenvale nickel mine).

By then Bond's slow-moving blimp with whirring engines, synonymous with BCH, had become a well-known though annoying sight, especially over the northern suburbs of Sydney. Residents of some of Sydney's prime suburbs in the executive belt, Wahroonga and Turramurra, objected to the snail-like observation platform sliding over their rooftops, interrupting their pool parties. Nonetheless, the blimp did conjure up the image of property and prosperity – evidence of conspicuous consumption – and whereas the locals may not have been in love with the noise, perhaps they regarded its promoter with some affection. It was no surprise when in October 1984 BCH increased its interest in Airship Industries to 82 per cent. Under an agreement with Nissan in Japan, BCH could manufacture (under licence) and sell airships in Australasia. This was to prove one of BCH's poorer investments. Airship Industries reported losses in financial years 1987 to 1989 of $5.2 million, $3.7 million and over $15 million, respectively. BCH eventually sold its interest in Airship Industries in 1991, incurring a substantial book loss.

In January 1985 BCH acquired Queensland Television (the operators of Channel Nine, Brisbane), increased expenditure ($75 million) on the Harnett offshore oilfield near Barrow Island, and in February sold its 6.7 per cent stake in Hooker for a profit of about $2 million. Rearrangement of the deck-chairs continued.

January 1985 also produced an example of a significant related-party transaction:

> Millions of dollars were tucked into private companies such as Shield Enterprises … Shield came to public attention in the mid-1980s [for] receiving $8 million in tax-free profits when another [Bond group] company, Lapstone, with its subsidiary Bond Oil, were sold to Shield for just $100 in January 1985.[10]

Similar asset transfers were facilitated by setting up a legal web of trustee companies and trusts for the benefit of Alan Bond's family. This type of manoeuvre upsets many observers; Australian governments over several decades have been aware of the tactic but have not prevented it. It is an apt instance of regulatory failure.

A 5 per cent stake in Arnott's was purchased in January, followed by a $400 million takeover offer. This was thwarted by the 10 per cent holding acquired by Campbell's Soup Company, eventually to gain control of Arnott's in 1992. Then in June 1985 the interest in Waltons Bond ACT was sold to Waltons Bond.

Alan Bond's *magic* did not insulate BCH from the need to meet the necessary conditions for ultimate financial success. BCH was buying existing assets, often companies, at a breathtaking rate, revaluing them and, on the basis of the revalued collateral, borrowing further to stake up in order to repeat the process with another acquisition. This resembled the 'daisy chain' method so prevalent in US Savings and Loans' operations throughout the early 1980s: on-selling through related companies at ever increasing prices, booking profits on the way, and ratcheting up the capacity to borrow on the security of the higher book value of the assets. It is similar also to Samuel Insull's utilities asset pyramiding mechanisms in 1920s pre-depression America. Without an externally verifiable, continuous, marked-to-market asset valuation practice, it was bound to have much the same result.

A critical link in a growth-by-acquisition strategy using borrowed funds is the market veracity of the valuations of assets pledged as collateral. In that respect, from the mid-1980s onwards, some of Bond's companies, like the more or less contemporary Adsteam, H.G. Palmer two decades earlier, and HIH a decade later, were using cross guarantees and some with negative pledges (covenants protecting existing lenders' security) as part of their standard loan agreements. The need for verified, continual, up-to-date asset valuations was clear, but there are doubts about delivery.

None of those technicalities dampened the pace of the acquisitions. During July 1985 BCH acquired all the issued capital of Castlemaine Tooheys at a cost of $1.2 billion; in February 1986 the US regional brewer, Pittsburgh Brewing Company, was acquired for US$29.8 million; in April the Screen Entertainment Division of Thorn EMI was purchased for £125 million and soon after sold to Cannon (UK) for £175 million. Judicious use of Jersey's tax haven status and subsidiary company dealings produced zero taxes on that deal for British coffers. Barry claims the ploy was repeated many times in the 1980s, often using the Cook Islands tax haven.[11]

Arguably that is good business, just like Bond's legal use of trusts, though commentators seem to want to take the *moral commercial high ground* in respect of it. What is missing in that moral maze is the immorality of fuelling the exercise with asset valuations at odds with the market. While everybody is entitled to arrange their affairs legally to minimise their tax, our view is that nobody can justify asset valuations which market evidence refutes.

During 1986 BCH effectively acquired nearly all of the property owned by its associate, Waltons Bond. Disposals by BCH also occurred during that year, including the sale of Southern Cross Beverages Pty Ltd (a soft drinks business) for $107 million and of British Vitamin Products Ltd (a former investment of Castlemaine Tooheys), and also the disposal of various hotels, which previously had been owned by Castlemaine Tooheys and Swan Brewery, to the Austotel Trust for $326 million.

Next came BCH's move into Australia's fastest growing export industry – education. Bond University, the first private university in Australia, was the vehicle. That possibly was a landmark for BCH too, for here something was created, not just acquired. While Bond Corp would sell its interest in the university it continues to operate successfully in the new century. Figure 12.1 illustrates BCH's complex conglomerate operations around the mid-1980s.

Figure 12.1 Bond Corporation Holdings Ltd group structure as at 30 June 1985

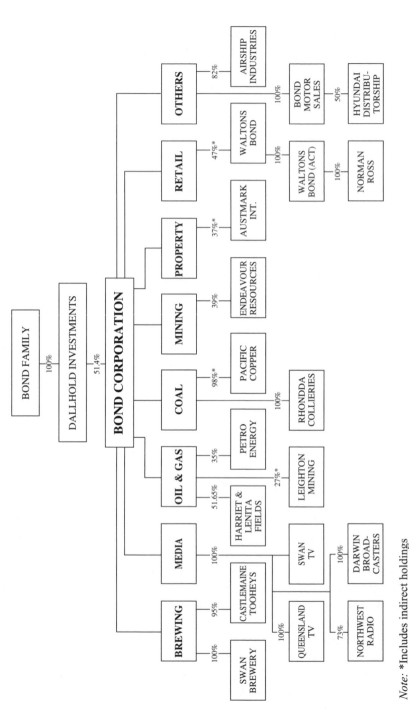

Note: *Includes indirect holdings

Source: *Australian Business*, 13 November 1985, p. 18.

The scale of the acquisitions was beyond anything previously experienced in Australia. Their timing was also important. The 1986/87 and 1987/88 financial years resulted in the greatest scrutiny of the accounting practices of BCH. During 1987 the acquisition binge continued.

BCH spent more than $5 billion on acquisitions – the 'too good to refuse' $1 billion purchase of the Nine Network from Kerry Packer, a US$262 million stake in the Chile telephone company Componia de Telefonos De Chile, an investment in Chilean gold mines and, in September 1987, the US$1.3 billion acquisition of the ill-fated fourth-largest US brewer, G. Heileman & Co. Amalgamation with Bond Brewing produced the fourth-largest brewing operation in the world.

During the middle of 1987 Bond Media was floated, which in turn acquired the remaining media interests of BCH with the purchase of Bond Television. Through its 50 per cent ownership of Bond Media, BCH was able to control the broadcasting licences of television stations such as TCN 9 Sydney, GTV 9 Melbourne, STW 9 Perth and QTQ 9 Brisbane. In addition, BCH had the right to distribute programmes to hotels and motels Australia-wide via use of a satellite on the Sky Channel service.

Not even the unforeseen blimp of the October 1987 stock market crash could halt the heady acquisition programme. With hindsight, perhaps the massive *ponzi* scheme did not allow for a halt.

One month after the October stock market crash, Van Gogh's *Irises* was 'purchased' for a world record of A$61 million, augmenting an already impressive Bond group art collection which included McCubbin's *Finding Time*, Boyd's *Jacob's Dream*, Monet's *La Promenade* and several other Impressionists' works.[12] One can only muse what Vincent would have made of the circumstances surrounding this modern patron of the arts.

Like Adsteam, BCH had now achieved a true conglomerate status. BCH had investments in brewing, wine and spirits, media, communications, property development and investment, minerals, retailing and a burgeoning art collection. Whereas the tactics were familiar, Figure 12.1 shows that the scale of BCH was atypical for all except a few Australian companies, with over 600 subsidiaries operating all around the world and employing nearly 11,500 people. Tables 12.3 and 12.4 reveal that from 1987 to 1989 BCH was able to announce increasing reported profits – on 22 August 1988 it reported a massive increase of 255 per cent to $355 million. This was clearly a useful outcome, given that reliance on debt finance had increased from around $2.6 billion in 1986 to over $6 billion in 1988 and would escalate to more than $9 billion in 1989.

Enterprise v Entity action?

Lonrho acquisition

Early in 1988 came a critical investment decision. A 19.8 per cent stake in the London-based multinational Lonrho for approximately A$700 million. Bond's tilt at Lonrho pitted him against *Tiny* Rowland, the British commercial buccaneer and Lonrho chairman. Rowland proved to be Bond's nemesis, just as Brierley had proved to be for Spalvins at Adsteam. Rowland immediately commanded his financial executives to find a chink in BCH's financial armour. Reportedly, their brief was to gather and disseminate evidence to financial journalists world-wide to the effect that BCH was technically insolvent and financially incapable of completing the Lonrho acquisition. The market *cognoscenti* were reinforcing the importance of the accounting/finance/investment nexus, for, ultimately, the only true test of BCH's solvency was to match the market worth of its assets against the amount of its liabilities. What BCH had *paid* for its assets in various takeover plays was and always would be irrelevant to that assessment.

Interestingly, in the Lonrho joust, 76 million of the 95 million Lonrho shares were not bought by a wholly-owned company within the BCH group, but by a subsidiary of Bell Resources at a cost of A$623 million. This was evidence again of *group enterprise*, not *entity* action in operation, for it must be recognised that Bell Resources was at the time a majority-owned subsidiary of BCH. The intertwining of the interests of the two separate, publicly listed companies would prove controversial in subsequent years, as had similar practices in the Sydney Guarantee Ltd–Stanhill Consolidated Ltd link in the 1960s. BCH effectively was able to bypass the Bell Resources shareholders, who were not even given the opportunity to voice an opinion concerning the purchase. This arrangement benefited BCH, as it left relatively little impact on BCH's balance sheet. At issue is the potential for conflict of interest when the affairs of two public companies whose boards include common directors are so intertwined. Another twist to the enterprise v. entity saga was just around the corner.

Bond/Bell Resources 'cash cow' transaction

The upstream transfer of approximately $1.2 billion from the Bell Resources group's *cash box* to subsidiaries and related parties of Bond Corporation has been described as Australia's largest corporate fraud. Importantly, both Bell and Bond were listed holding companies, seemingly under the control of Alan Bond – Bond Corporation through direct holdings, and by virtue of the holdings of related parties, owned 53 per cent of Bell Resources. Johnson (2000), though illustrating only a part of the fraud (see Table 12.1), provides a window into how complex the 'cash cow' manoeuvres were.

Table 12.1 Details of back-to-back loans used in Bond Corporation Group

Dates	Lender	Intermediaries	Borrower	Amount ($ millions)
Early 1988	Bond Brewing Holding Group	Subsidiary of Markland House.	Bond Corporation Holdings Limited	Not stated
Reason for transactions: Syndicate of banks imposed a condition that revenues generated by Brewing Group were retained in Brewing Group. Bond Corporation Holdings Limited had difficulties in obtaining funds from external financial institutions.				
Between 29 August and 3 November 1988	Bell Resources Limited	Companies in Markland House group. One or two intermediaries were used.	Bond Corporation Holdings Limited	447.5
			Dallhold	55.0
Reason for transactions: Bell Group had given undertaking to bankers that it would not lend more than $25 million to companies outside the Bell Group. Bond Corporation agreed with Bell's financiers only to borrow from Bell Resources and J.N. Taylor for short-term accommodation needs.				
At 15 November 1988 these loans existed	J.N. Taylor Finance	Merchant Capital Limited. Winnington Securities Limited and Markland Investments Limited.	Bond Corporation Finance	101.0
			Bond Corporation Finance	25.8
Reason for transaction: Not stated.				
24 November 1988	Pascoe Limited	DFC Overseas Limited and Catton Finance Limited.	Bond Corporation Finance	50.0
		European Pacific Banking Company and Catton Finance Limited.	Bond Corporation Finance	50.0
Reason for transaction: Rewind back-to-back loans existing at 15 November 1988 and to comply with NCSC requirement and borrowing requirements.				
After 13 December 1988	Bell Resources Finance	Markland House Group Companies.	Bond Corporation Finance	170.2
Reason for transaction: Not stated.				

Sources: Statement of Facts included as a schedule in the case, *The Queen v Alan Bond 1997* (unreported), *Pascoe Limited (in Liquidation) v Lucas 1997* and *Sykes (1994)*, pp. 224–5. This table is reproduced from R. Johnson, 'Back-to-back loans: A fraud in transition', *Australian Accounting Review*, November 2002, p. 66.

Johnson's analysis and Figure 12.1 reveal that the main group 'lenders' were public companies such as: Bond Brewing Holdings, Bell Resources Limited, related companies like Bell Resources Finance, J. N. Taylor Finance (part of the J.N. Taylor group), Pascoe Limited. 'Intermediaries' to the transactions were 'smallish' group companies like *Markland House* and its subidiaries, Merchant Capital and Markland Investments. 'Borrowers' were Bond Corporation Finance, BCH, and Alan Bond's private company, Dallhold Investments.

Drawing on the agreed 'Statement of Facts' in *The Queen v. Alan Bond* (1997), Johnson notes the motivation for the transactions was that: 'Early in 1988 BCHL was having cash flow difficulties and found it difficult to borrow in from external financial institutions'.[13] External financial institutions had lent money to individual companies in the Bond or Bell Resources groups using negative pledges – avoiding those pledges would require some fancy financial footwork. Enter *enterprise* action – namely the use of related parties to move funds between various companies *as if* they were in fact one enterprise.

In January 1995 criminal fraud charges were laid against Alan Bond and two other BCH directors over this transaction. Commencing in 1996, the trial eventually led to Alan Bold pleading guilty to the fraud charge and being gaoled for four years, increased to seven when Bond appealed the length of the original sentence. Interestingly, the shuffling of funds in the manner described arguably strikes at the heart of a fundamental principle of English law, the *separate legal entity principle*, of which we have more to say in Chapters 16 and 17. It is sufficient here to point out that Bond put up his hand for doing what was consistent with the erroneous, but prevailing, view that the *group* is – for all intents and purposes – a real, single entity. Were that to be so, the shuffling of assets between the component parts of the single entity would amount to no more than shifting them from one 'department' to another. But, of course, whereas that view is embedded in conventional consolidation accounting thought, it is contrary to the legal framework in which companies operate. That piece of accounting sophistry lies at the root of more commercial mischief than possibly any other corporate misconception.

Back to the big picture at Bond. The aborted rescue of the late Laurie Connell's Rothwells Limited added to BCH's financial woes and may have been one of the catalysts for the group cash shuffling.

Rothwells rescue – what are friends for?

When Laurie Connell's investment company Rothwells teetered on the brink of collapse in the wake of the October 1987 stock market crash, it was Alan Bond who engineered and led the rescue effort. Reportedly, together with West Australian Premier Brian Burke, Bond hired James Yonge of Wardleys to approach various entrepreneurs for funds. An amount of $380 million was raised, and coupled to an additional sum of $150 million provided by the National Australia Bank. NAB, however, claimed that its advance was covered by a WA government guarantee.[14] Late in 1993 this dispute was settled out of court, reportedly in favour of the bank.

Rothwells' rescue plan entailed the WA government using the State Government Insurance Commission (SGIC) to buy 20 per cent of the Bell group from a Holmes à Court-owned company. BCH likewise was required to purchase a 20 per cent share. In this way, it has been reported that the two entities would have control of Bell Resources and its $2 billion in cash, in return for a relatively small outlay of $130 million each. The Bell Resources cash would then be used to purchase Petrochemical Industries Corporation Ltd from Connell for $400 million. After paying $50 million to his partner, Connell would have $350 million to pay off his poorly performing debts to Rothwells, thereby relieving the WA government of its purported guarantee to the NAB.[15] It had been described as a win–win situation for all. However, arguably there were also negative financial consequences for certain share-holders and creditors, not to mention employees.

BCH director Peter Beckwith reportedly suggested that the SGIC and BCH had in reality acted in unison. Giving an insight into the nature of the trans-action relating to the shareholding in Bell Resources, he explained:

> The Government's involvement in PIL and its shareholding via the SGIC in the Bell Group were from day one enmeshed. The Government, having acquired the stake in Bell Group, proposed to this company [BCH] that the cash strength of Bell Resources be used to buy what was then PIL for a sum sufficient to enable Mr Connell to fund Rothwells to retire the Government guarantee before the Government faced the electorate. From that point forward, the Government continued to invite and induce our participation in this project.[16]

It appears unlikely that the plant was worth $400 million. Indeed, the value of the site is estimated to have been worth varying amounts to a low of $10 million.

A contentious aspect of this manoeuvre to gain control of Bell Resources, and as noted above its 'pot' of cash, was the $1.2 billion which Bell Resources subsequently 'lent' within the BCH group, via a supposed 'deposit' being paid by Bell Resources for the brewing assets of Bond Brewing Holdings.

On investigation, the NCSC perceived the substance of the arrangement to involve associated groups buying 40 per cent of Bell group without making a full bid. It was the decision of the NCSC to ignore the technical (legal) form, which ensured that the two purchases would not be linked. The NCSC ruled that

BCH had to put up $520 million for 80 per cent of the Bell group, in effect forcing the company to make a full bid, while excluding the 20 per cent the SGIC would continue to hold. This meant that the survival of BCH had become entangled with the liquidation of Bell, the Rothwells rescue and the value of PIL and, most importantly, the concurrent battle at Lonrho.

Confluence of these and other matters, such as the battles with the Australian Broadcasting Tribunal over whether Alan Bond was a 'fit and proper person' to hold a TV licence and the Channel Nine settlement, meant BCH's battle-front was expanding. Financial strains meant that the beginning of an unofficial liquidation of BCH was imminent.

BCH asset sales were frenetic during the 1988/89 and 1989/90 financial years as part of that unofficial liquidation. Substantial creditors' repayments were crucial to the survival of the group. Bankers demanded that debt be pared. Assets previously held by the Bell group and Bell Resources were sold for approximately $1.8 billion, including the Lonrho investment at a loss of £110 million. Other major group asset sales were negotiated: $170 million for BCH's Harriet Oil stake; $140 million for the holding in ITC Entertainment; $25.5 million from selling the 10 per cent stake in TV-AM; a 50 per cent stake in the Hong Kong Bond Centre to joint venture partner EIE Development (International) Ltd for HK$1.3 billion; St Moritz Hotel (NY) to creditor FAI Insurances Ltd (it is interesting, as described in note 6 above, how these 'troubled' assets get shuffled); a half-interest in the R&I Bank Building for $108 million; the remaining half-share in the St George's Hospital site in London for about $100 million; and the Australian coal mining operations to FAI for $199 million.

This was restructuring on a massive scale. As always, creditors' obligations had to be satisfied with cash or its equivalent. All the mythical book values and the artifacts of conventional accounting – the FITBs and other 'deferred' bookkeeping debits – would count for nothing in that exercise.

Unfortunately, the desirable impact of the 1988/89 asset disposals was mitigated somewhat by several significant purchases during the same period. A 56.25 per cent interest in that notorious West Australian petrochemical plant consumed $225 million. Another $182 million was spent on a further stake in the Chilean telephone company, and $40 million on purchasing a number of coal mines from BHP. But divestment of the Chilean venture in 1990 yielded an estimated profit of A$90 million. Outflows continued as a controlling stake in J.N. Taylor Holdings Ltd was achieved with an additional share purchase for $39 million late in 1988. And the outcome, as Nolan notes: dealings between J.N. Taylor Holdings Ltd (the 'cash box') and related companies of the BCH group, especially the Bond family company, Dallhold Investments Pty Ltd, which are the subject of legal action and regulatory investigation.[17] More may unfold on this aspect if the investigations and legal actions are completed and eventually disclosed to the public.

Exacerbating matters for BCH, the Lonrho misadventure was just around the corner.

Lonrho – tears of death

Table 12.2 shows that towards the end of 1988, BCH's share price began to slide. That proved irreversible. However, BCH continued to spearhead a take-over of the international trading house, Lonrho. The *raison d'être* was familiar. The plan was to use the cash and asset power of Lonrho to buy the British brewer Allied-Lyons and use the latter's cash flow to venture into the field of telecommunications. This strategy had worked for BCH in the past.

Emerging in 1985 from a critical period of market pessimism, the share price moved along steadily with the general market upsurge in 1986 and 1987. While suffering initially from the October 1987 crash, the price stabilised between $1.50 and $2.00. Downward pressure increased in early 1989 with further institutional selling of BCH stock. A manoeuvre was hatched and the counter-attack on Lonrho was mounted, causing the share price to rally temporarily. Directors of BCH – one suspects, especially Alan Bond – clearly had not properly predicted Tiny Rowland's response. Rowland vigorously and publicly questioned BCH's financial credibility to such an extent that, ultimately, BCH retreated.[18]

Table 12.2 Bond Corporation Holdings Ltd selected last trade daily share prices, 1985/86 to 1989/90

	Month beginning					
Year	1 July $	1 Sept. $	1 Nov. $	1 Jan. $	1 Mar. $	1 May $
1985–86	1.23	1.80	2.20	1.80	2.50	3.85
1986–87	3.38	3.25	2.82	2.56	2.70	2.60
1987–88	2.49	2.75	1.50	1.80	1.65	1.85
1988–89	2.28	1.95	1.86	1.85	1.58	1.19
1989–90	0.92	0.47	0.29	0.13	n.a.	n.a.

Source: Stock Exchange Research Pty Ltd, *Stock Exchange Investment Review Service*, Bond Corporation Holdings Ltd, B191.

The Lonrho joust is instructive. As well as illustrating BCH's penchant for enterprise rather than entity action, it illustrates a certain style of decision-making at BCH, especially in the latter stage of its life. Some have alleged that the BCH board ratified decisions of the three-man executive committee *ex post facto*, that there was little documentation backing some major investment decisions, and that there was an inadequate mechanism for communicating information about them to lower operational managers.[19] Decision-making in respect of Lonrho prompted this comment by Mr Justice Sir Nicholas Brown-Wilkinson in assessing the 'need-to-know' philosophy of the three-man executive running BCH:

> It is a very remarkable phenomenon when you have a company that had by that stage invested 360 million pounds-odd (now A$781 million) that not a single piece of paper is available supporting that fact.[20]

That comment is *déjà vu* for those familiar with the international dealings over 60 years earlier of another corporate buccaneer, the Swedish match-king Ivar Kreuger. He is reputed to have kept most of the financial details of his multinational conglomerate, Kreuger and Toll Inc. and its international match empire, in his head![21] This, of course, made auditing that colossus a difficult exercise. Whenever information is released only on a 'need-to-know' basis, a similar difficulty arises.

Back to BCH. The 93-page financial document, 'The Bond Group of Companies: A Financial Analysis by Lonrho plc', selectively released worldwide on 28 November 1988, contained criticisms of BCH's accounting and managerial practices. It concluded that BCH was 'technically insolvent'. It was circulated to financial houses and bankers around the world – corporate dirty tricks at its best. Yet, despite its apparent financial sophistication, its analysis is problematic to the extent that it relied on conventional historical cost data.[22] However, it has been suggested that without the tenacity and resources of a Tiny Rowland, it is unlikely that the extent of the BCH group's complex intra-group arrangements would eventually have been revealed to the public.[23] If true, placed with the obfuscation previously noted (at, for example, Adsteam), such a state of affairs is surely cause for concern, as it strikes a body-blow to claims of market efficiency and the adequacy of regulatory checks and balances. We return to this aspect of 'the system' in the final four chapters.

Lonrho's document produced, amongst the overseas community of investment analysts, a general consensus that the looseness of Australia's Accounting Standards was to be blamed for allowing BCH to deviate and engage in creative accounting, a line of reasoning that appears, in respect of several major publicly disclosed transactions, to have been unfounded.

Clearly, the implication of that consensus was that tighter enforcement rules would have saved the day. In reality, being able to depart from the Standards or to interpret them idiosyncratically is potentially a force for the good. Contrary to general belief, with respect to several instances of misleading data and contested interpretation, the evidence is that BCH generally complied with the Accounting Standards and legal accounting requirements rather than deviated or departed from them.

Irrespective of whether the Lonrho document was accurate in depicting BCH's financial state, the convergence of several factors and Rowland's attack was fatal. BCH's share price fell rapidly during the latter part of 1989. Those other contributive factors were varied. In the first week of May 1989, *Australian Ratings* announced that BCH would be downgraded from a B credit rating to CCC, signifying 'poor debt protection levels'. BCH responded to this news by selling a major asset, its remaining half-share in the Bond Centre in Hong Kong. It also began a buy-back plan of its shares in an effort to prop up its share price. Further bad news occurred when the Australian Broadcasting Tribunal announced its findings on 26 June that Alan Bond was not a 'fit and proper person' to hold a TV licence. And the ASX suspended trading in Bell Resources. A triple whammy had hit the Bond empire.

The extent of the damage was implicit in the 1989 Chairman's Report: 'Over the period spanning the 1985 to 1988 financial years total group assets grew more than seven fold and operating revenue grew eight fold ... substantially financed by debt'.[24] Such debt-financed growth was unsustainable, even if the assets were worth their book values. Conjecture continues as to why the banks had maintained financing for it. The relationship between Alan Bond and BCH's bankers has become legend.[25] Apparently, normal prudential limits were by-passed, and this was further exacerbated in the early 1980s by Alan Bond's introduction to Michael Milken and BCH's dubious financing trifecta: negative pledges, cross guarantees and junk-bond financing.[26]

That fateful day on which the public at large was to read of Bond's collapse in the *Financial Review* had arrived. Shortly thereafter, on 29 December 1989, trading in BCH securities was suspended following the appointment of a receiver to Bond Brewing Holdings Ltd. The receiver was removed three months later but liquidation was looking ever more likely.

During 1990 BCH staggered towards a formal liquidation. Then, in early 1991, Alan Bond resigned as chairman, with the group's creditors effectively administering BCH's affairs. Initially, under an informal arrangement, a formal scheme commenced in August 1991 and, finally, a liquidator was appointed in December 1993.

BCH's *ponzi* scheme had run out of acquisition options. At every turn in this commercial saga the BCH numbers men and the practices of accounting had played their vital role.

Accounting's temporary survival kit

BCH relied primarily on debt to engineer its earliest investments. Even after the October 1987 stock market crash, BCH was able to go on a multi-million-dollar investment spree. It was revealed that BCH continued to finance acquisitions with debt (Table 12.3). Not surprisingly, the largest of international bankers and financiers, all presumably part of the 'informed' financial market, were caught when BCH finally went under, including Hong Kong and Shanghai Bank, American Express Bank, Standard Chartered Bank, Salomon Bros, Midlands Bank, Drexel Burnham Lambert's clients, Barclays Bank, First National Bank of Boston and the local banks, NAB and Westpac.[27]

Following the October 1987 stock market crash, other entrepreneurial companies were winding back their operations, yet BCH was expanding.

Table 12.3 Summary financial statistics of the operations of Bond Corporation Holdings Ltd (consolidated data), 1982–91

Year	Sales (other revenue) $m	Statex adjusted profits $m	Total assets $m	Total debt $m
1982	244.1	4.3	447.2	237.3
1983	308.7	6.8	531.1	276.7
1984	365.3	(13.6)	700.4	473.9
1985	517.8	(7.0)	1,221.2	874.1
1986	1,600.7	76.7	2,771.7	2,190.2
1987	2,281.9	104.7	4,115.6	2,690.4[2]
1988	4,616.9	338.6	9,015.3[1]	6,378.2[2]
1989	7,666.1	(834.7)	11,703.8[1]	9,168.9
1990	9,073.9	(1,069.0)	2,215.9[1]	2,594.8
1991[3]	339.3	(642.5)	526.8	1,822.9

Notes: 1 Intangible items were negligible before 1985; thereafter they were $486.9 million (1986), $486.5 million (1987), $2,460 million (1988), $2,897.5 million (1989) and $396.1 million (1990).

2 Total debt excludes Convertible Notes amounting to $457.5 million (1987) and $707.5 million (1988).

3 For nine months' operations only.

Source: Based on Stock Exchange Research Pty Ltd, *Statex Service* (B191), run on 16 December 1991 (reproduced as Table 12.4).

Questioned on the incongruity of it all, Bond responded that BCH had a solid 'cash flow' to see it through the difficult times. Such queries continued throughout the latter part of the 1980s. Some in the market clearly were concerned. The share price of BCH declined to around $1.80 from its $3 pre-October 1987 price. It levelled off in 1988, peaked again in mid-1988 at $2.28 and then slipped further in the aftermath of the Lonrho affair. By September 1989 it had fallen to 47 cents per share, nearly half its July price. Obviously the market was nurturing major reservations about the viability of BCH by this stage. For BCH to survive, drastic surgery to its debt levels was necessary. Sale of the brewing assets was essential. But the sale dragged on over many months. Uncertainty and unease over the group's prospects increased.

BCH's growth strategy has many parallels with Reid Murray and Stanhill in the 1960s, the Cambridge Credit Corporation and Gollins sagas, and many others in the 1970s and 1980s. Borrowings growth needed to finance BCH's type investments relied on its public image of wealth and progress, on its ability to report increased profits and growth in net assets. Clearly the role of accounting was crucial. Accounting Standards did not force the reporting of continuous, rather than *ad hoc*, audited market values of physical assets. To a substantial extent the application of many Standards prevented it. Reinforcement of the significance of the holding company/subsidiary structure, and the validation of consolidation accounting and injection of accounting artifacts thickened the financial morass. Singularly and collectively, the Standards ensured that the generic defects of conventional accounting differed little from the positions prevailing in respect to similar matters decades earlier. In some senses the importance of that role may have been exacerbated inadvertently; the existence of the increasing number of Accounting Standards perhaps created a sense of false security for the investing public – a façade of protection from the generic problems.

Tables 12.3, 12.4 and the following analysis of specific practices during the period 1986–88 disclose the significance of chosen accounting treatments publicly disclosed by BCH. Interestingly, the audit litigation in respect of this period has failed to reveal any more public information than was revealed at the time the first edition of this volume went to print. Not being privy to the detailed matters outlined in the claim or in the evidence against BCH's auditor, what follows passes no comment on them. Suffice it to say that there was a reported $110 million out-of-court settlement (with no acceptance of any fault) made by the audit firm in May 2002.

Financial statements for 1986/87 and 1987/88

BCH's financials received mixed assessments from financial observers. Early in 1987 financial journalists Meagher and Chong had made this assessment:

Table 12.4 Bond Corporation Holdings Ltd – Statex balance sheet summary and ratios, 30 June 1982 to 30 June 1991

	30/6/91 $000	5/10/90 $000	30/6/89 $000	30/6/88 $000	30/6/87 $000	30/6/86 $000	30/6/85 $000	30/6/84 $000	30/6/83 $000	30/6/82 $000
Cash and liquids	11,845	43,700	609,100	473,500	288,501	192,641	196,559	55,528	56,344	12,499
Trade debtors	1,791	63,400	451,600	486,600	117,126	113,096	31,055	21,702	15,141	22,420
Stocks	33,349	93,100	380,300	254,500	164,066	100,364	37,251	26,738	22,029	17,894
Other current assets	53,965	229,400	544,500	900,200	793,933	502,831	163,855	64,998	18,300	11,640
Total current assets	100,950	429,600	1,985,500	2,114,800	1,363,626	908,932	428,720	168,966	111,814	64,453
Bank overdraft	5,534	9,500	82,300	50,700	24,906	28,559	8,435	2,984	6,295	5,187
Trade creditors	9,834	77,500	695,900	481,800	150,812	201,431	87,222	39,624	25,430	28,611
Tax provisions	38,886	32,000	423,000	41,300	28,105	141,768	29,469	19,033	5,354	8,670
Debt due in one year	1,535,357	2,101,800	2,811,200	1,505,700	402,610	490,174	103,547	68,251	78,596	61,077
Other current liabilities	210,914	289,500	461,100	231,100	58,923	67,378	62,399	18,670	8,061	10,295
Current liabilities	1,800,525	2,510,300	4,092,800	2,310,600	665,356	929,310	291,072	148,562	123,736	113,840
Net working capital	-1,699,575	-2,080,700	-2,107,300	-195,800	698,270	-20,378	137,648	20,404	-11,922	-49,387
Net plant and property	122,956	540,000	3,639,300	1,889,600	760,459	372,913	189,219	141,253	133,031	135,485
Investments	229,926	670,800	1,870,600	1,219,300	1,073,060	474,512	274,237	209,118	160,242	186,343
Deferred assets	73,008	179,400	1,310,900	1,331,500	431,924	528,456	321,895	166,933	121,376	59,345
Total invested capital	-1,273,685	-690,500	4,713,500	4,244,600	2,963,713	1,355,503	922,999	537,708	402,727	331,786
Long-term debt	7	84,500	4,900,800	3,619,800	1,911,603	1,247,929	575,397	321,263	148,336	122,479
Other deferred liability	22,367	-315,100	175,300	456,800	113,482	12,990	7,649	4,116	4,603	990
Minority interest	0	89,700	1,908,500	1,029,400	220,924	100,143	80,134	11,745	13,706	414
Preferred capital	0	0	0	0	0	0	49,103	49,103	49,103	0
Ordinary equity	-1,296,059	-549,600	-2,271,100	-861,400	717,704	-5,559	210,716	151,481	186,979	207,903
Total invested funds	-1,273,685	-690,500	4,713,500	4,244,600	2,963,713	1,355,503	922,999	537,708	402,727	331,786

Total tangible assets	526,840	1,819,800	8,806,300	6,555,200	3,629,069	2,284,813	1,214,071	686,270	526,463	445,626
Intangibles	0	396,100	2,897,500	2,460,100	486,548	486,898	7,152	14,145	4,601	1,621
Total assets	526,840	2,215,900	11,703,800	9,015,300	4,115,617	2,771,711	1,221,223	700,415	531,064	447,247
Balance sheet ratios										
Liquid ratio	0.03	0.13	0.40	0.82	1.87	0.89	1.38	0.97	0.76	0.42
Current ratio	0.05	0.17	0.48	0.91	2.04	0.97	1.47	1.13	0.90	0.56
Shareholders' interest	245.9	25.2	4.0	2.6	25.9	4.1	28.0	30.9	47.4	46.7
% Market/book listed inv.	123.4	103.6	98.6	83.5	91.3	131.9	86.1	76.7	57.6	70.8
Net assets/share (adj.)	−2.01	−0.85	−3.40	−1.28	1.23	−0.01	0.62	0.65	0.80	0.89
Dilution factor used	1.00	1.00	1.00	1.00	1.00	0.69	0.48	0.30	0.30	0.30
Long-term debt/equity	0.0	−15.3	−215.7	−420.2	266.3	−22,448.8	273.0	212.0	79.3	58.9
Short-term debt/equity	−118.1	−384.1	−127.4	−180.6	59.5	−9,331.4	53.1	47.0	45.4	31.8
Profit after tax, after minority interest (000)										
As per Bond Corporation Holdings Limited	(642,491)	(1,065,900)	(814,100)	354,700	117,720	86,611	(5,647)	(13,585)	6,837	4,299
As per Statex	(642,491)	(1,069,000)	(834,700)	338,600	104,649	76,684	(6,990)	(13,585)	6,837	4,299
Sales (000)	339,269	9,073,900	7,666,100	4,616,900	2,281,932	1,600,710	517,815	365,270	308,653	244,091

Source: Stock Exchange Research Pty Ltd, *The Statex Service*, BCH (B191), run on 16 December 1991; data are on a consolidated basis.

'Bond's two biggest moves – the Castlemaine Tooheys purchase and Packer buyout – have collected prime assets and cash flow that leave the group in a comfortable position.'[28] Following the October 1987 crash, Philip Rennie was having a bet each way in this assessment:

> At any other time of share market crises in the past 15 years Bond Corporation would have been one of the first companies subject to disaster rumours. Yet there are none after the worst stock market crash in history. Some property companies that were put into receivership in 1974 were rumoured to be more solvent than Bond Corporation.[29]

A somewhat more sombre assessment appeared early in 1988 by accounting professor Bob Walker, who exposes the perverse nature of accounting:

> … one could not expect to find many gains or losses from the sale of businesses treated as extraordinary items because Bond Corp specifies that the 'primary operations' … include 'the disposition of assets acquired during the period or held for trading purposes from prior years.
> … 'normal operations of the group … include operations … of material once only transactions'. Readers are advised that 'while relatively few of these transactions may be completed in any one year, their effect on the group's results is not regarded as being abnormal nor outside the principal operations of the group' … extraordinary items which to Bond Corp are just ordinary items.[30]

Terminological niceties were used to veil what was occurring, all under the rubric of compliance.

Two weeks later, under the caption 'Window dressing at Bond Corporation', Walker this time commented on two other technical accounting matters – one relating to tax effect accounting, and the second relating to the treatment of convertible bonds. Both these items were accounted for in a manner which, according to Walker, maximised 'the impression of growth and liquidity'.[31] Another accounting treatment having a further positive effect on BCH's financial outcome related to foreign currency. These three treatments and their effects on the 1986/87 and 1987/88 accounts are of great significance, for they invited inferences regarding BCH's financial stability from the only publicly available financial information at the time – BCH's published financial statements. They provided valuable insights into the role of accounting information and, in particular, with respect to the matter of compliance with Australia's Accounting Standards.

Reminiscent of the reliance placed upon usual or standard practice in the 1920s Royal Mail accounting saga in the United Kingdom, there was no categorical claim that BCH had not complied with the Standards. Certainly the accounts were duly audited as such. No doubt they would be claimed to offend 'the spirit' of the Standards – but 'the spirit' resides as much in the opportunity for alternative interpretations, the looseness of and omissions in the Standards, as in what they state. With H.G. Palmer the court also revealed 'omission of material particulars' – specifically, failure to make *adequate provision for bad and doubtful debts*, which produced a reported profit of £408,371 in 1964 and a year earlier a profit of £431,624. Whether accounting at BCH was creative or feral, whether material particulars were omitted from the accounts, whether parties are brought to book for any actions, has still not been definitively determined by the court deliberations, judicial actions and the out-of-court settlement. The published accounts from those inquiries imply a mixture of all.

On the matter of BCH's 'cheques in the drawer'

BCH's 1986/87 financial statements reported the proceeds from $457 million in convertible bonds as having been received prior to the balance date. On this matter the use of *notes* to the accounts is instructive. They were 'noted' to have been approved by shareholders at an extraordinary general meeting on 26 June 1987 and the proceeds (amounting to US$200 million and £80 million) not to have been received until 9 July 1987.[32] The convertible bonds transactions thereby qualified as a significant 'post-balance date event'. Such a treatment was actually applied in the 1986/87 accounts in respect of the issue of A$250 million worth of convertible bonds to Monstrot Pty Ltd, a company in which Alan Bond had 'a substantial financial interest'.[33] These treatments appear to have complied with Accounting Standards, at least to the auditor's satisfaction.

Professor Walker argued that there was a parallel between BCH's treatment of its post-balance date convertible bonds receipts and the more common commercial problem of the 'cheques in the drawer'.[34] Possibly this difference of opinion says as much about the looseness of Accounting Standards as the use BCH made of them. BCH's subsequent treatment of those convertible bonds drew upon 'assumption' rather than fact. Boom periods allow a company's directors to argue that its convertible bonds should be counted as part of equity capital, *in anticipation* that subsequently they would be converted into shares. Quite curiously, many Accounting Standards explicitly countenance the injection of the products of directors' conjectures into the accounts.

When the market crashed in October 1987 the exercise price of BCH's convertible bonds sat well above the company's share price and the probability of their conversion into shares became remote. Arguably, by 1987/88, it would have been more realistic to treat the convertible bonds as a form of debt to be redeemed at the option of the holder, for the only chance that the bonds had of being converted into ordinary shares was if BCH's share price recovered to above the conversion price of $2.89.[35] During 1986 and 1987, conversion was a possibility since the conversion price of the bonds was marginally above the market price of the shares. However, during 1988, bondholders were faced with a substantial premium if they decided to convert their bonds into shares. Financial commonsense would have dictated that the convertible bonds would not have been converted into shares. An even more commonsense approach would have been to 'tell it like it is' and not impute private conjecture incapable of corroboration by public fact.

The effect of that imputation was to artificially strengthen the 1986/87 balance sheet in two ways. First, it decreased the ratio of total liabilities to total shareholders' equity – by treating convertible bonds as part of shareholders' equity. This succeeded in increasing shareholders' equity and decreasing liabilities for 30 June 1987. During 1986/87, the debt to equity ratio was noticeably strengthened ('liabilities' fell from approximately three times to double shareholders' equity). Second, the balance sheet also looked better by virtue of doubling the current ratio. BCH applied the yet-to-be-received proceeds of the issue to 'repay certain term advances' with only the balance augmenting the amount of receivables. Thus, current liabilities were decreased by $299.9 million, while current assets (receivables and other current assets) were increased by the residual, $157.5 million.[36] This method contrasts with the usual, but not mandatory, treatment of convertible bonds being reported as a liability, which has a relatively small impact on the current ratio, since both current assets and non-current liabilities are increased, effectively offsetting one another.

Preparation of the 1987/88 accounts was subject to a new Schedule 7, and to the protestations of the NCSC that it would be scrutinising company accounts even more closely. This regulatory call is repeated seemingly after every economic downturn and its associated *unexpected* large corporate collapses. Predictably, following the HIH and One.Tel revelations, the ASIC has declared an all-out war on non-compliance with the Accounting Standards. Yet there is no evidence that non-compliance with the Standards had contributed to the unexpected failure of those companies.

Back in 1987/88 the revised Schedule 7 prescribed mandatory treatment of convertible bonds (and other debt securities which could be converted into shares) by specifying that they had to be shown as long-term borrowings in the accounts, come what may.[37]

Recasting the 1987/88 accounts in accord with the new Schedule 7 requirements would have resulted in BCH's shareholders' equity being reported at $1.92 billion, rather than the $2.63 billion. Conversely, total liabilities would have risen from $6.39 billion to $7.10 billion, producing at 30 June 1988 a ratio of total liabilities to shareholders' equity of 3.69, rather than the figure of 2.43 – a substantial blow-out.

BCH reported convertible bonds as a separate line item, between liabilities and capital. Terminological concerns bring back memories of the notorious omnibus classification evident in the account of the Royal Mail saga some 60 years earlier: 'Balance for the year, including dividends on shares in allied and other companies, adjustment of taxation, reserves less depreciation on fleet, &c.' Classification uncertainty had been cleverly exploited by Lord Kylsant in those Royal Mail accounts. Aggregated figures and related ambiguous reporting terminology (facilitated by a complex group structure) were used to hide transfers from secret reserves, thereby masking current period losses, to in fact imply current profits.

The classification of the convertible bonds was changed in BCH's 1988/89 accounts, with directors stating that it was their expectation that conversion of these bonds into ordinary shares would be unlikely. Convertible bonds were reported as part of non-current liabilities. Overall, a use of creative accounting at its best!

The 'benefits' of tax effect accounting

BCH, like many other companies, used the deferral method in accounting for its tax obligations, in accord with then Australian Accounting Standard AAS 3, 'Accounting for Income Tax (Tax-Effect Accounting)'. However, in the 1986/87 financial year there was a change in accounting policies involving the 'provision of group tax relief'. Significantly, it appears that in neither the notes themselves, nor in any other part of the accounts, was there disclosure of the rationale for this change in accounting policy. Walker has argued that this change in accounting policy apparently referred to the adoption of section 80G of the *Income Tax Assessment Act 1936*, thereby allowing BCH to set off losses from its wholly-owned Australian subsidiaries against the profits accruing to its other subsidiaries.

Notes to the 1986/87 BCH accounts disclosed the reduction of future income tax benefits (asset) and deferred income taxes (liability) by $156 million each during 1986/87. Further, the notes disclosed that had this accounting policy change been applied in 1985/86, the above two items in that year would each have been reduced by $59.6 million. BCH was an effective user of tax credits. And while these accounting policy changes were not hidden, being disclosed in the notes their overall effect is not easy to determine, as Walker demonstrated:

Some $156 million was taken from the liability item, provision for taxation, and also from the asset item, future income tax benefits ... it is not clear how $96.4 million of the $156 million arose during 1986–87, and how this would affect the balance of future income tax benefits. What is apparent is that the change reduces a current liability (provision for income tax) with a corresponding change in a non-current asset (future income tax benefits).[38]

In fact, the reported tax position was even more contestable than that. BCH had reduced the liability with amounts drawn from 'tax-effect' balances that are mere artifacts, fictions from the bookkeeping mechanism described earlier in Chapter 2. None of that could have occurred had the FITB not been raised in accord with AAS 3. Compliance meant that a balance with financial substance was reduced by an amount without any substance at all. Thus one effect on the 1986/87 BCH accounts of the convertible notes and tax effect accounting treatments was to portray a current ratio at 2:1 instead of 1:1, a far less impressive indicator of liquidity.[39]

The illusory nature of the 'tax-effect' debits and credits was evident in the write-offs made in the 1988/89 annual reports. With either the greater attention to detail prevailing in the 1988/89 financials, or changed circumstances, BCH's reported 1988/89 loss of $980 million included a $453.4 million write-off of a future income tax benefit. The FITB recorded in compliance with the prescribed professional Accounting Standard on tax accounting was now unceremoniously dumped, again in accordance with the Standard! One might justifiably claim this to have been, substantially, a seminal example of *compulsory creativity*.

Forex accounting – compliance was more help than hazard

In the 1987/88 accounts, the treatment of foreign exchange translations was significant in determining the reported profitability of BCH – with 38 per cent of the operating profit being foreign exchange gains. Accountants and others were obliged to comply with ASRB 1012, 'Foreign Currency Translation', on this matter. And of course they did.

BCH's 1987/88 financial statements contained a change in accounting treatment of long-term monetary items with fixed or ascertainable lives, in order to comply with the new currency translation requirements of ASRB 1012. Therefore, in addition to short-term monetary items and forward exchange contracts, gains or losses on long-term monetary items were now brought to account in the profit and loss account as they arose. Again BCH would appear to have complied and, as a result, legitimately ceased to recognise any exchange fluctuations as extraordinary items. Hence, the 1987/88 profits included a $149.9

million foreign exchange gain, a figure substantially more than the one recorded in 1986/87.

However, $59.2 million of that total foreign exchange gain was attributable to the conversion of the above convertible bonds into Australian currency. While recognised, since the directors had stated in the 1986/87 accounts that a fixed exchange rate would be adhered to, a provision was offset against this gain. In addition, BCH also had $3,208.6 million worth of foreign currency borrowings that would have benefited from the appreciation in the Australian dollar in the period ending 30 June 1988 (comprising $611.4 million worth of current liabilities and $2,597.2 million worth of non-current liabilities). When these loans were converted into Australian currency, the resulting 'gains' were included in the reported profit figure. In BCH's previous year's financial statements, by following AAS 20 these gains had been amortised (spread over a number of accounting periods). Again much of the backing and filling in BCH's profit figures was the result of following the professionally or legally prescribed Standards, through which clearly it is difficult to discern the financial truth of the matter. At about the same time, Tiny Rowland distributed that notorious financial analysis document.[40]

Others also dissected BCH's 1987/88 accounts. Sentiments were far from positive. Journalistic attention centred on a windfall gain of $88.2 million in terms of post-extraordinary equity-accounted after-tax profits. That was possible since restatement flowed from Bond being 'one of the fullest reporters in Australia'.[41] The comment reinforced how Bond Corporation's profits were delivered by complying with the Accounting Standards, though that point was lost in rehashing the conventional equity-accounting debate.

More analysis of that kind was forthcoming. Investigatory work by the Australian Broadcasting Corporation's 'Four Corners' national TV team led to some further contentions regarding the 1987/88 accounts. Specific queries related to the alleged 'overstated profit figure' from, inter alia, inclusion of profits on two asset 'sales': the Porta di Roma land deal and the Hilton Hotel sale. Questions surfaced over Arthur Andersen's unqualified 'true and fair' audit report.[42] Barry notes:

> The Institute of Chartered Accountants in Australia had been less than impressed with Arthur Andersen's work. Following the 'Four Corners' report, the Institute had asked a senior non-practising accountant to investigate whether Bond's 1988 accounts complied with Australian Accounting Standards; his conclusion was that they did not.[43]

Perhaps the courts may have an opportunity to examine this aspect thoroughly. We suspect it is likely that the Standards provided the opening

– an accounting window of opportunity – for innovative, some might allege *feral*, accounting, just as it had done years earlier in the Minsec Robe River shares affair.

Despite reportedly 'looking increasingly like a basket case',[44] the chairman of BCH remained ebullient. Even the release of the 1988/89 financial accounts could not dampen his optimism. These accounts were scrutinised closely both prior to and after their late release. They disclosed at that time the largest ever corporate loss in Australia of nearly $1 billion. Alan Bond reportedly suggested that the loss was largely made up of non-cash items, in particular:

> ... $330 million depreciation, future income benefits [$454 million] ... the write down in shares included $200 million in non-cash. Foreign currency adjustments of $120 million were non-cash ... We have been writing our brewing assets down at $950 million book value, the difference between the real value and book value of $1.5 billion, which belongs to the shareholders.
>
> ... We are not insolvent because we have a huge net worth. The Chile Telephone company is written down at $250 million less than its worth and our properties have not been revalued – they are worth $250 million.[45]

Perversely, it had been increases in non-cash items that had been so heavily relied upon in generating BCH's profit figures as collateral for borrowings for several years. That, too, seems to have been lost on many commentators, as was the linkage between the vagaries of conventional accounting practice – especially its artifacts – and the failure to disclose generally for all physical assets their market worths (continuously updated and duly audited), and the significance of verified up-to-date asset valuation in financing BCH's expansion.

The half-a-billion dollar question was: 'What do Bond's words, "real value" and "worth", mean?' Unless they mean current money's worth – that is, what the assets could be sold for – then the numbers reported were of limited use for those making financial assessments, especially *Tiny* Rowland's insolvency claim.

Much has been written about the rise and fall of BCH. Most often it has examined Bond's personal fortunes and misfortunes. But the real sting in the BCH tale is its similarity with many of the previously described (and subsequent) failures and the associated regulatory, accounting and ethical deficiencies. Some financial warnings were there, as the comments of several financial commentators above clearly indicate. However, the use of accepted accounting techniques, especially in the context of *enterprise* action, masked the true failure path which BCH was travelling. Further, our overview of selected publicly disclosed accounting treatments, in respect of foreign currency, deferred tax and convertible notes, suggests considerable compliance with the specifics of individual Accounting Standards.

Because of the lack of publicly available data, due in part to the 2002 out-of-court settlement in the Bond civil litigation case, there remains an open verdict as to whether there was, as in the UK *Royal Mail* case (and others), a failure to disclose to investors any 'material particulars', and if so, to what extent not doing so was due as much to compliance with the Standards as to deviation from them.

How serviceable was BCH's accounting compliance, especially in pro-ducing the 1987 and 1988 consolidated accounting data? The complex BCH corporate structure, with over 600 subsidiaries, many registered overseas, facilitating dealings with related parties including family companies of the founder, again raises the question of whether society is well served by such structures and the conventional, standard accounting for them.

There are myriad examples of transactions similar to those at BCH – albeit perhaps not on that scale, but generically identical – in the annals of corporate failure both in Australia and overseas. Likely as not in respect of corporate success, too! The latest revelations in the HIH Royal Commission regarding group enterprise dealings more than confirm this.

Ultimately, virtually none of the pumped up financial outcomes of BCH's actions would have gone undetected for as long were assets to have been marked-to-market continuously and duly audited, as a matter of what one might reasonably expect to be essential mechanisms of accounting and auditing best practice.

CHAPTER 13

Westmex Ltd: The Security Façade of Cross Guarantees

[The rationale of an indemnity or cross guarantee is] that the interests of creditors would be protected if the holding company and the 'relieved' subsidiaries entered into a Deed of indemnity and, in the event of insolvency of any company party to the Deed, the creditors could look to the assets of the other companies party to the Deed.

Mr Justice McLelland (1992)

How convenient it would be were deeds of cross guarantee to give that protection in practice. However, they do not. In the aftermath of many group liquidations in the early 1990s came the cry for reform of the system governing borrowing arrangements that had exacerbated many of the 1980s excesses. One area of interest relevant to our theme is whether groups and consolidation accounting, meshed with negative pledge, cross guarantee and (sometimes) junk-bond financing, provided an effective means of operating and informing investors. This issue would return to the fore in the 1990s and be the subject of a CASAC discussion paper and report (CASAC 2000). It underpins this analysis of the rise and fall of Westmex.

Westmex began life on 30 June 1969 as a base metal explorer in Western Australia. When mineral operations waned during the mid-1970s, Westmex became a cash box. Diversification into real estate and share trading was followed by moves into earthmoving contracting in 1976 and 1977. It was back to resource exploration as the resources boom of the late 1970s and early 1980s came and then went. By the mid-1980s Westmex's investments had been directed mainly in option and share trading, with its mining investments concentrated on gold.

Events surrounding the collapse at Westmex reveal a dramatically changed set of operations following the arrival of the new CEO, Russell Goward, in 1986. During his time at Industrial Equity Limited (IEL), Goward had been described as a 'miracle of technology with his year-round tan and permed hair [whose] charm and enthusiasm were infectious [*sic*]'.[1]

Early in 1986 a young Russell Goward, then CEO at Sir Ronald Brierley's IEL, seized an opportunity. He acquired a controlling stake in Westmex Limited, reorganised it and re-listed in March 1986 on the industrial board. Westmex, post-1986, comprised a substantially different group of entities, under the influence of Goward's dominance, charismatic appeal, and the group's dramatic asset growth increase. Deceptively, it seemed he had the Midas touch.

Quick to perceive a *quality* performer, the financial press described Goward, one of the youngest of the 1980s Australian 'entrepreneurs', as a 'magician', a 'whiz kid', and 'a curly-haired investment genius'. As with many such assessments before and after, that acclamation proved premature. Subsequent to the equally fast descent of the Westmex empire during 1989, the fickle press penned less favourable nomenclatures – 'failed tycoon', 'bankrupt businessman' and 'grounded high-flier'.

Perhaps the acclamation was undeserved from the start. Recent accounts of Goward's days at the helm of IEL are equally less sanguine. It is now claimed that even his mentor, Sir Ronald Brierley, was said to have grown tired of Goward's desire to claim the attention of the press, and that IEL's investments under Goward proved to be less than raging successes.[2]

The right time for an idea

Goward's seizure changed the direction at Westmex, resulting in an enlarged capital base (see Table 13.2). Investments were now in entrepreneurial entities, primarily in Australia and the United Kingdom. Perhaps Goward felt this was one of those times right for a new idea. In the United States Michael Milken had already perceived the 1980s to be the right time for his junk bond financing.

In Australia the stock market was booming, entrepreneurial stocks were fashionable, bank finance was readily available, and negative pledge and cross guarantee arrangements were common in-group financing, though why that should have engendered great optimism and comfort for creditors and some financial commentators is questionable. Twenty-five years earlier, cross guarantees of a similar sort had not provided adequate security for H.G. Palmer's creditors.

Westmex's first major investment, in June 1986, was a 52.3 per cent stake in the ailing listed UK company, Charterhall plc. Several of Westmex's directors were appointed to its board. The venture into Charterhall enabled Westmex to springboard into the United Kingdom and the United States. Charterhall's operations were transformed from that of an independent exploration and production company in the North Sea into a specialised investment group.

Although Westmex had begun corporate life as a mineral explorer, by 1986 it had been transformed into a specialised investment group, primarily a retailing and exploration venture. In the six months prior to Westmex's acquisition, Charterhall had posted a loss of £6.248 million. Within six months of Russell Goward being at the helm, Charterhall had returned to the black. Three years later, a six-monthly profit of £4.587 million was reported. Profits, assets and debt growth are summarised in Table 13.1 and detailed in Table 13.2.

Table 13.1   Westmex Ltd – reported growth in profits, 30 June 1986 to 30 June 1989

Year ended 30 June	Reported profits $	Revenue $	Dividends cents/share
1986	355,550	717,000	n.a.
1987	9,952,402	47,232,000	5.0
1988	17,448,168	192,224,000	10.5
1989	27,015,417	377,344,000	12.5

Source: Sydney Stock Exchange Statex Service, Westmex Ltd (W190), run on
31 December 1989 (reproduced herein as Table 13.2).

By 30 June 1988, Westmex's investments comprised two main operating
groups, under the umbrella of CAL Resources (formerly Charterhall Australia)
and Charterhall plc in the UK. CAL Resources had petroleum interests, including Australian Petroleum Fund (Auspet), Pancontinental Petroleum Ltd
(100 per cent) and IOL Petroleum. In the UK, Charterhall plc had investments
in retailing (80 per cent footwear) and petroleum.

The aura of success was promoted, and accounting again had its role to play.

The large financial institutions certainly did not miss the opportunity to be
on the ride. Undoubtedly they did not foresee it was to be on a roller coaster
destined to crash. So, when Westmex was placed in liquidation in early 1990
the list of creditors in the Statement of Affairs included major Australian banks,
some overseas banks and many of the other major Australian financial houses.
The *cognoscenti* had been caught again. Of course, it could be claimed that
they had priced their exposure according to the high risk involved. However,
Westmex's accounts gave their usual impression of truth and fairness, undoubtedly masking the higher level of financial risk involved.

Goward's 'whiz kid' appeal, aided by impressive reported growth in profits
and assets, undoubtedly drew the small punters to Westmex, with 9,000
individual shareholders on the register at 30 June 1987. The next year this grew
by 27 per cent to 11,500. A large multinational group had been formed with
over 50 companies. A 'closed group'[3] of 36 companies indemnified under a
cross guarantee instrument was interposed within that structure. The implications of that arrangement may be gleaned from the extent of transactions
within the 'closed group', illustrated in Figure 13.1.[4]

On a roller coaster

Westmex's fast descent followed seductive increases in reported profits and
asset growth from its newly acquired worldwide corporate empire.

Figure 13.1 Inter-company commercial dealings between Westmex 'closed group' companies ($000)

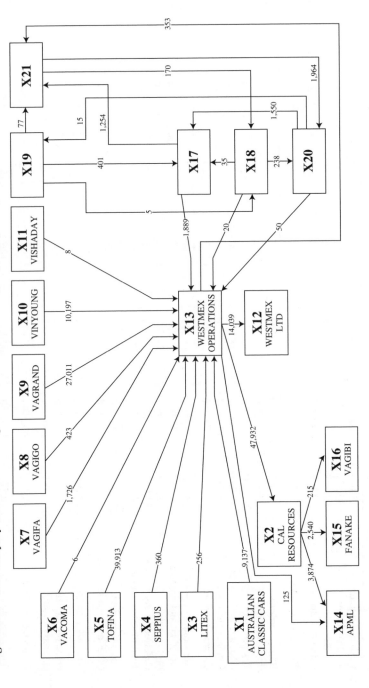

Notes: Xn = company number as in Table 13.3. Direction of arrow indicates the amount of inter-company debt from company Xi to company Xj (e.g. X1 owes X13 $9,137,000).

Source: Reconstructed from data provided in the Liquidators' Affidavit to the NSW Supreme Court, in *Westmex Ltd (in liq.)* ... February 1992.

Table 13.2 Westmex Ltd – Statex balance sheet summary and ratios, 30 June 1983 to 30 June 1989

	30/6/89 $000	30/6/88 $000	30/6/87 $000	30/6/86 $000	30/6/85 $000	30/6/84 $000	30/6/83 $000
Cash and liquids	35,698	38,416	5,833	2,257	1,532	0	1,750
Trade debtors	30,137	4,627	139	41	37	59	19
Stocks	67,833	9,382	0	0	0	0	0
Other current assets	39,107	22,231	26	970	1,417	2,086	0
Total current assets	172,775	74,656	5,998	3,268	2,986	2,145	1,769
Bank overdraft	14,057	4,314	179	115	0	2	34
Trade creditors	27,503	2,229	2,378	1,728	338	1	13
Tax provisions	0	0	0	9	50	19	109
Debt due in one year	78,038	48,512	18,674	0	0	94	0
Other current liabilities	78,780	16,531	0	0	11	71	5
Current liabilities	198,377	71,586	21,230	1,852	399	187	161
Net working capital	−25,602	3,070	−15,233*	1,417*	2,587	1,958	1,607*
Net plant and property	66,433	11,987	237	123	0	0	0
Investments	82,659	80,607	93,591	3,560	0	0	0
Deferred assets	21,003	6,479	308	195	195	433	564
Total invested capital	144,493	102,144	78,903	5,295	2,782	2,391	2,171
Long-term debt	224,082	49,244	0	0	0	0	0
Other deferred liabilities	2,893	834	0	0	0	0	0
Minority interest	70,001	15,237	0	0	0	0	0
Preferred capital	0	0	0	0	0	0	0
Ordinary equity	−152,483	36,829	78,903	5,295	2,782	2,391	2,171
Total invested funds	144,493	102,144	78,903	5,295	2,782	2,391	2,171
Total tangible assets	342,870	173,730	100,133	7,146	3,181	2,578	2,333

Intangibles	239,497	18,307	0	0	0	50	50
Total assets	582,367	192,037	100,133	7,146	3,181	2,628	2,383
Equivalent fully paid shares	172,566	113,900	91,178	59,285	12,735	12,735	12,735
Balance sheet ratios							
Liquid ratio	0.56	0.97	0.28	1.88	7.48	11.57	13.88
Current ratio	0.87	1.04	0.28	1.76	7.48	11.45	10.96
Shareholders' interest	24.0	30.0	78.8	74.1	87.5	92.7	93.1
% Mark/book list inv.	59.6	100.0	100.0	100.0	100.0	100.8	0.0
Net assets/share (adj)	−0.70	0.23	0.48	0.18	0.03	0.03	0.02
Dilution factor used	0.84	0.66	0.53	0.36	0.16	0.16	0.16
Long-term debt/equity	−146.9	133.7	0.0	0.0	0.0	0.0	0.0
Short-term debt/equity	−60.3	143.4	23.8	2.1	0.0	4.0	1.5
Profit after tax, after Minority interest (000)							
As per Westmex accounts	27,015	17,645	7,294	355	163	45	126
As per Statex	27,015	17,645	7,294	355	163	45	126
Sales (000)	312,064	79,540	8,203	n.a.	n.a.	n.a.	n.a.

Note: *Rounding errors; figures as per original.

Source: Stock Exchange Research Pty Ltd, *The Statex Service*, Westmex Ltd (W190), run on 16 December 1991; data are on a consolidated basis.

In the 30 June 1989 Chairman's Report the exponential-like growth in reported profits and revenues was well exploited by CEO Goward:

> Your company's continued prosperity during these adverse times is evidenced
> in the Accounts by the record 1988/89 profits (the fourth consecutive record
> year) and the substantial increase in the underlying value of the Group's core
> businesses ...
>   Westmex's achievements over the past few years were recognised by two
> independent bodies.
> 1 *Australian Business* magazine gave Westmex its 'Acorn Award' for outstanding
> new entrant to its list of Australia's Top 500 Companies.
> 2 The Australian Stock Exchange Research Department ranked Westmex as the
> No. 1 performing company in Australia over the past five years ...
>   'Institutional' shareholders increased their ownership of Westmex from 22%
> one year ago to 31% today.[5]

As with Alan Bond's assessment of Bond Corporation's fortunes near its nadir, and John Spalvins' of Adsteam's performances, it all depends on what is meant by Goward's words 'profits' and 'value'.

Many analysts during the mid-to-late '80s certainly thought Westmex was a good investment. If luck lasted, its 'diversified investor' investment strategy would soon find its way into the DIY recipe books of management gurus – another management fad to join the long list which includes diversification, decentralisation, stick-to-the-core operations, just-in-time, EVA, downsizing, zero-based budgeting, total quality control, benchmarking and then total quality management, theory X, theory Y and finally, perhaps, theory Z.[6]

'Diversified investor' aptly described Westmex's operations. According to Goward, Westmex was 'an investment company, a divestment company and an operator of businesses'.[7] Westmex's disclosed corporate objective captured its investment philosophy:

> To optimise long term returns to shareholders ... by maximising the dividends
> paid and the wealth created ... through the identification, acquisition and
> development of well managed operating businesses in chosen industries with the
> potential to show outstanding returns (operating profits plus increases in business
> value) ... where those businesses can be acquired at an immediate discount on
> underlying business value and on-sold when they reach their full potential.[8]

'Where' indeed! Many of Westmex's investments were in unlisted companies. Unfashionable, fragmented industries were sought for acquisition. The purported rationale was that companies in those industries could be acquired on a far lower price–earnings ratio and therefore offered scope for the greatest gain. This was possibly true, but it also carried the risk of the greatest loss.

Usually the companies acquired became subsidiaries, often wholly-owned. While primarily in shoe retailing in Britain via the Charterhall group, and stationery in Australia, the diversification strategy also thrust Westmex into textiles in the United Kingdom. Petroleum, printing, classic car production and other miscellaneous industries were targeted in Australia. At a time when the prevailing management rhetoric suggested a move towards 'sticking to the basics', or 'sticking to one's knitting', Goward was steering the opposite course. Some analysts observed that Goward's 'counter-cyclical conglomerate investment acquisition approach' created 'an interesting and possibly unique company ... [while] many investors remain unconvinced that the conglomer-ate concept can achieve lasting success. Westmex is dedicated to disproving that.'[9] Such conjectures are grist for the mill of those suggesting there is no theory of management.

Regarding reported profits, it appeared that Goward had Westmex proving to be the exception to the rule. He was receiving a better than good financial press:

> Russell Goward's Westmex Ltd was another company that emerged from the chaos of last year's [October 1987] sharemarket crash in fine shape. Profit for the latest half-year was up $13.5 million, to $15.4 million.[10]
>
> Goward's magical P/E formula: since Black Tuesday the market was impressed, first with the jump in profit [for the six months to December 1988] from $1.1 million to $7.9 million, and second with the fact that Westmex, although expressed as an entrepreneurial stock, had seen the crash coming and reduced its exposures.[11]
>
> Westmex: Acorn award – outstanding new entrant: According to the Stock Exchange Research Department Westmex has been the best-performing investment among the larger stocks over the past five years and the sixth best performer during calendar 1988. It would be hard to argue that Westmex is not an appropriate winner of the Acorn Award for Outstanding New Entrant.[12]

Hard indeed, given the audited evidence. And those are the same types of sentiments expressed in favour of others previously, when H.G. Palmer, for example, was reporting performances contradicting those being experienced by its peers in the wake of the November 1960 credit squeeze.

Not all financial observers were as impressed with Westmex's performance. Just prior to the October 1987 crash, Henry Bosch was one who was publicly critical of the way Westmex Limited calculated its profits. Bosch is reported to have said the 1987 Westmex report was 'more akin to a public relations exercise than to the presentation of a true and fair view of the company's financial affairs'.[13] But then a cynic would suggest generally that this is not all that different from most annual reports and no different from the calculation of profits virtually everywhere, then and especially now, given the alleged accounting irregularities at Enron and HIH! Specifically, it would appear that Bosch's concerns were that, at least publicly, in respect of companies taken over, Westmex had inflated profits by including an incremental value attributed to acquisitions over their cost. In his defence, Goward insisted that he was simply applying accounting practices used previously at IEL under the direction of Sir Ronald Brierley.

That is an interesting observation in itself. It seems that Goward learned some tricks of the takeover trade, though it would be unwise to pin too much on his explanation of where his school was. Wherever it was and whether by accident or design, Goward's idea of bringing to book incremental changes to the worth of assets is spot on, provided he was referring to their independently verifiable changes in selling prices. But of course we would argue that this should be done annually and that, without exception, it must be subject to an audit in the usual manner.

We would expect that Bosch's complaint was directed at unrealised profits being brought into account, for that is not in accord with conventional practice's *realisation principle*. But conventional practice runs counter to commonsense on this point, for, at the same time, it compels approximations of decreases in selling prices (depreciation) to be brought to account, even though they are unrealised too. Goward (and it seems his mentors at IEL) all (unwittingly, we suspect) made significant contributions to accounting thought through these tilts at conventional practice. Whatever their motives, on that score they were talking more commonsense than their critics, in much the same way as had Samuel Insull and John Spalvins.

Eventually Westmex changed its incremental valuing practice. Pointing to a much wider problem with the accounts, Westmex's auditors, Mann Judd (after resigning from the audit in 1987), are reported to have described Westmex accounts as 'bordering on the fictional'.[14] Whether it was only *the realisation issue* that they regarded as fictional, and if so why, has never been publicly debated. The action by the auditors is exceptional, for it appears to be the only (at least publicly acknowledged) case in the 1980s where an auditor from one of the major auditing firms resigned when a dispute between the auditor and directors of a publicly listed company could not be settled. An alternative explanation is that all such matters were mutually agreed.

Interestingly, in 1996 two events occurred that might shed light on Westmex's 1988/89 accounts. First, the Companies Auditors Liquidation Board suspended the 1988/89 auditor of Westmex for five years for failing to carry

out or perform adequately and properly the duties of an auditor.[15] This provided
fresh impetus to a suit lodged in 1992 by Bankers Trust and several shareholders claiming $60 million damages under the *Trade Practices Act 1974*
against the auditor and his partners at the time of Westmex's liquidation. The
claim was made under section 52, claiming negligence, and misleading and
deceptive conduct.[16] Whether and, if so, how these accounts were 'fictional'
potentially could have been revealed in this action were there to have been a
judgment. An out-of-court settlement reduced that likelihood. Subsequently,
one of the participants in that action put on the public record some of the
details, which we now consider.

John Fielding, a litigant in that action, put on the public record via the
Internet his observations on what was reported in Westmex's published financials for 1998 and 1989. He obtained additional information under 'discovery'
but was unable to reveal any of that.

Westmex's annual reports for the years 1987–89 (Table 13.2) contained
many contentious accounting practices, each of which had the effect of increasing Westmex's reported profits or assets, even if only in the short run.
These included on a consolidated basis (1988 financial year) capitalisation of
expenses for intangibles (goodwill) of $5.6 million; other expenditure of $19.12
million made up of exploration expenditure $2.87 million, future income tax
benefit, $2.48 million, and trade and brand names, $11.6 million. In 1989
'intangibles' had increased from $18.307 million to a staggering $239.497
million. 'Deferred assets' had risen to $21 million from $6.479 million. Fielding's Internet analysis lists several accounting practices that he regarded as
questionable. These related to AASB 1013 on goodwill, Westmex's use of consolidation accounting and its use of a 'provision for integration and rationalisation' account against which losses in Westmex's acquired Stationery Division
were debited. Fielding alleged those acquisition losses were never publicly disclosed.

But, as with many of the accounting practices at Bond Corporation Holdings and others, arguably those individual practices may have been in accord
with the Accounting Standards. Whether they, in conjunction with other accounting practices, accorded with the Companies Act's 'true and fair' view override,
in toto, is debatable. One financial commentator has described Westmex's
accounts as:

> a castle of sand almost from the start, based on elaborate sale and lease-back
> arrangements, with vast sums set aside for the goodwill of the companies
> purchased, and with cash flow dependent on selling things off; $28 million of the
> company's $38 million 'profit' [before tax] in its last year of operations [1989] was
> from the sale of assets, leaving $10 million to service $300 million worth of debt.
> 'In the end he [Goward] just ran out of things to sell', says a UK analyst.[17]

This account provides an interesting contrast with the final months at Bond Corporation. BCH was financially incapable of maintaining asset purchases. Cash purchases and on-selling to related companies, rather than sales to outsiders, were critical in maintaining BCH's *ponzi* scheme.

All of this has to be balanced against the detail contained in the Westmex Ltd annual reports for 1987–89. As with Bond Corporation, the level of disclosure was extensive – detailed notes to the accounts, segmental reporting, extensive disclosure of accounting policies – all the good Accounting Standard stuff, but seemingly not serviceable one iota.

Similar to many other collapses, the latter stages of Westmex's demise occurred suddenly.

In September 1989 Russell Goward had provided a positive assessment of Westmex's prospects in his Chairman's Report. The share price was around $1.20, and net assets of the company (including intangibles) were reported at $87.014 million, or approximately 50 cents per share. Fortunes nosedived. Around this time the AMP insurance company off-loaded six million shares with predictable effect. Westmex's share price plummeted – to 80 cents by November, then to 30 cents in late December. It was now in free-fall. By January it hovered around 15 cents. Throughout this period Goward was an aggressive acquirer of Westmex stock, but to no avail. But Goward also sold some of his Westmex shares just prior to Westmex's collapse early in 1991. He would be prosecuted and in 1998 gaoled for misleading statements made to the Sydney Stock Exchange at the time of those sales. That period of incarceration followed an eight-month stay at Her Majesty's pleasure for giving false evidence at a bankruptcy examination. Goward had been declared bankrupt on 2 January 1991 after the Westmex group was placed in provisional liquidation in February 1990. The parlous position of the creditors of the Westmex group, especially the 'closed group' subject to cross guarantees, is shown in Table 13.3.

Deregulation and cross guarantees – a security façade?

Following the NCSC's mid-1980s deregulatory push under Henry Bosch, Westmex was one of many publicly listed companies to take advantage of the NCSC Class Order Deed of Indemnity. This guarantee arrangement was claimed to be the NCSC's major deregulatory administrative initiative, purportedly providing cost savings to business by granting parent company relief from the accounting and auditing requirements of their wholly-owned subsidiaries.[18]

To achieve this, under the covenants of the deed the parent company and the relevant subsidiaries within the 'closed group' agreed 'to severally, unconditionally and irrevocably' guarantee each other's debts. Additionally, directors

Table 13.3 Westmex Ltd 'closed group' particulars

Exhibit 1: Assets and liabilities of companies subject to Westmex Class Orders (in $000s)

Company identifier	Company name	Est. realisable value	Inter-company debtors	Total assets	Secured creditors	External creditors	Inter-company creditors	Third party guarantees	Total liabilities
X1	Aust. Classic Cars	150		150		−1,015	−9,137		−10,152
X2	CAL Resources		47,932				−6,629	−17,893	−24,522
X3	Litex						−256	−12,517	−12,773
X4	Seppius						−360		−360
X5	Tofina						−39,913		−39,913
X6	Vacoma						−6		−6
X7	Vagifa	1,090		1,090			−1,726		−1,726
X8	Vagigo						−423		−423
X9	Vagrand	9,733		9,733			−27,011		−27,011
X10	Vinyoung	6,051		6,051			−10,917		−10,917
X11	Vishaday						−8		−8
X12	Westmex Ltd		14,039		−12,517	−175,804		−86,783	−275,104
X13	Westmex Ops	439	91,726	439		−116,764	−62,449		−179,213
X14	APML		3,999						
X15	Fanake		2,540						
X16	Vagibi		215						
X17	Miscell. 1		1,986				−3,143		−3,143
X18	Miscell. 2	3	175	3			−294		−294
X19	Miscell. 3	307	15	307		−2	−483		−485
X20	Miscell. 4	661	2,203	661		−8	−1,625		−1,633
X21	Miscell. 5	1,668	1,684	1,668		−418	−2,134		−2,552
		20,102	166,514	20,102	−12,517*	−294,011*	−166,514*	−117,193	−590,235

Note: *External creditors total $294,011,000, third party guarantees plus secured creditors $129,710,000, hence the 'total' liabilities of closed group companies ($590,235,000) comprise these two amounts added to the $166,514,000 of inter-group company creditors.
Source: Extracted from liquidator's affidavit on behalf of appellants in the *Westmex* case.

provided attestations of solvency in respect of relieved companies. To the officials of the NCSC, these arrangements were perceived to be a means of improving the efficiency of the market mechanism. Effects on equity for various 'closed group' creditors has proved less certain. Those effects are still uncertain following the outcomes of 1990s court cases and compromises or schemes of arrangements that applied to several 'closed group' administrations. They include J.N. Taylor Holdings, Halwood Corporation (formerly Hooker Corporation), Westmex, Equiticorp, Adsteam, Tricontinental, Brash Holdings and Linter.[19]

Westmex and 36 of its wholly-owned subsidiaries covenanted to produce the Westmex 'closed group' under NCSC Class Orders 613 and 633 during 1988/89. A characteristic of those deeds is to limit investors' and creditors' access to public sources of the financial data relating to subsidiaries comprising a 'closed group'. Without access to the subsidiary companies' accounts, the consolidated data of Westmex became the public bulwark for creditors of any of the 'closed group' companies seeking financial information pertaining to the security of their loans. How this informed those creditors is anybody's guess.

Of course, creditors have the opportunity to seek out whatever information is necessary from any source at their command – itself a function of the relative bargaining powers of these contracting parties. But this begs the question as to whether the law should countenance certain creditors being privy to differential data in respect of a legislatively created corporation.

Westmex Ltd's 1987–89 consolidated accounts, prior to the appointment of the liquidator in February 1990, disclosed the sensational 1986/87 reported growth in assets – $7.146 million to $100.133 million. Short-term debt had increased from $1.8 million to $21.23 million without any recourse to long-term debt. By 1988 the total book value of assets had increased to $192.037 million and current liabilities were now $71.586 million, but this time with a significant increase in long-term debt to $49.244 million. Westmex presented as a truly outstanding performer. It was this type of performance which attracted the 1989 Acorn Award for outstanding new entrant to its list of Australia's Top 500 Companies by *Australian Business*, as well as the Australian Stock Exchange Research Department's ranking of Westmex as the No. 1 performing company (on a share price return basis) in Australia over the past five years based on an annual compound return to shareholders of 113 per cent. Such evaluations invite anxiety regarding the capacity of the analysts and the financial community to withstand the seduction of conventional accounting data. Repeatedly it appears that few can.

However, the quicker and higher the rise, the further and harder the fall.

Naively one might have thought that the conventionally calculated consolidated asset cover for those debts in the financial year ended 30 June 1989 (an excess of $87 million, including intangibles, but excluding minority interest) would have been adequate. Final audited financial statements appeared in September 1989. And quickly, any perception of such security was to be shown to be unwarranted. Within four months of those statements, all companies within the Westmex 'closed group' had been placed in liquidation – an exemplary group domino effect.

Summary data provided by the liquidator in affidavits before the courts (Table 13.3) disclosed an alarming discrepancy between the publicly reported consolidated financial position of the Westmex 'closed group' of companies and that revealed on liquidation. All companies within the 'closed group' were insolvent and the group deficiency was around $280 million. Recall that the last financials had disclosed an excess of $87 million! And all that within the space of four months? Well, probably not!

Court decisions regarding 'closed group' liquidations have cast doubt on the efficacy of the cross guarantee arrangements in group liquidations subject to NCSC-approved Deeds of Indemnity. Mr Justice Debelle's judgment in the South Australian Supreme Court case, *Re J.N. Taylor Holdings Ltd (In liq.) (No. 7)*,[20] that the indemnity arrangements did not apply when all companies were insolvent, was a portent that the purported protection afforded to creditors may be illusory.

In October 1991 a compromise scheme of arrangement was put to creditors at Hooker Corporation based, one imagines, on reservations of the Debelle J type. It was suggested to creditors to avoid crystallising the guarantee. Whither creditor protection based on *ex-ante* certainty of outcome?[21]

Our analysis suggests that Westmex's rise and unexpected demise was a seminal example of regulatory and accounting failure. Westmex exposed the fragility of accounting's most complex bag of tricks, consolidated financial statements and other conventional practices.

Curiously, the accounting profession would most likely regard consolidation accounting to be one of its, if not *the*, most sophisticated mechanisms for showing the wealth and progress of companies. Complex – yes. Sophisticated – doubtful; informative – rarely; illusory – virtually always! Accounting Standards-setters appear impatient with history. Few appear to heed the persistent way in which collapse is accompanied by questionable consolidated accounting data. Perhaps they view the correlation as spurious. Apparently a major shift in thinking is needed. In particular, there needs to be a reconsideration by regulators of the way corporate business is conducted through webs of parent companies and the companies related to them, and how conventional consolidation accounting is incapable of portraying financial outcomes. This matter is addressed in the 'Regulatory Reforms' section below.

PART V

The New Millennium –
Life in the Farce Lane

CHAPTER 14

2000 and Beyond: Crisis in Accounting and Audit

This period exposed Dr Alan Greenspan's 'irrational exuberance' and
John Kenneth Galbraith's 'inventory of undiscovered embezzlement'.[1]

The post-2000 world has witnessed the nadir of the longest stock market boom of the twentieth century, largely driven by the hype and investment in technology stocks from the mid-1990s. The Dow Jones Index tumbled dramatically. It had risen nearly continuously (except for some glitches like Black Monday, 19 October 1987) from 776.92 on 12 August 1982 to 11,908.50 during 14 January 2000. Declines in the Wilshire 5000 Index (which provides a broader, all encompassing tracking of US publicly traded companies) was even more dramatic. It dropped nearly 50 per cent from around 15,000 on March 24, 2000 to just above 8,000 on 18 July 2002 – reflecting a massive US$7 trillion reduction in share values.[2] Subsequently, there have been significant oscillations on a weekly basis, drawing ominous analogies with general share price movements in earlier recessions, including the 1929 Depression.

Dramatic financial aftershocks occurred in those two years and even more are possible. It should be noted that the falls in the securities markets in Australia since April 2000 have been much smaller – around 10–15 per cent – albeit they still represent a substantial decline causing most Australian investment fund managers to report negative returns in 2001 and 2002. It has been noted that the correlation between Australian share market indices and indices of Australian reported corporate profits also is much more positively aligned than their US counterparts – during the 1990s the level of reported corporate profits was much higher in the United States.

As in previous decades, the financial system went on a crazy roller-coaster ride. Market *bears* were in the ascendancy. Initially, in the broader market, the bulls retreated gradually after the April/May 2000 tech-wreck with the associated increase in insolvencies. That retreat would gain pace and become a rout a year later when myriad corporate scandals involving alleged 'accounting irregularities' were revealed. In Australia many dot.coms, including One.Tel and Opentel, had their market capitalisations eviscerated in late 2000 and early 2001. Their cash hungry, up-front operations, coupled to minimal prospects for immediate revenues, were juxtaposed against a market that in April/May

2000 had suddenly turned off the 'cash spigot'.[3] A similar fate would await several major corporates – like HIH, Ansett, Pasminco, Harris Scarfe and Centaur. Other large corporates experienced financial difficulties.

And the story was repeated in the United States – hundreds of dot.coms,[4] and leading telcos such as Global Crossing and Qwest Communications, became financial flotsam. More significantly, some of the United States' mainstream companies like Enron, WorldCom, Tyco and Xerox either collapsed or suffered financial embarassment on a gigantic scale, after disclosing alleged 'accounting irregularities' entailing billions of dollars.

During 2001 and 2002, questionable accounting and auditing practices would become daily media fodder. It was a worldwide phenomenon. The 'dull and boring' images of accountancy were supplanted by even less favourable ones. Accountants became the brunt of talk-show hosts' jokes. Front-page caricatures adorned mainstream and business media. The 'Big Five' accounting firms became the *Big Four*. Andersen was hit by a fatal torpedo. It took the brunt of the criticism of auditors and auditing as it proved to be the ultimate focus for the media. Andersen's alleged questionable audits of Enron (with the notorious document shredding), WorldCom, Waste Management, Sunbeam, The Baptist Foundation of Arizona and others in the United States saw it reportedly 'cut loose' by the Big Four survivors.[5] In Australia, a similar fallout was associated with Andersen sagas at HIH and Bond Corporation (specifically Andersen's reported $110 million May 2002 out-of-court Bond Corp settlement). The revealed particulars of perceived accountability deficiencies caused some financial commentators to argue that there had been a loss of confidence in the securities market being a 'fair game'. Others observed that accounting and auditing was in a 'state of crisis'.[6]

However, as this volume has shown, it is arguable whether the game has *ever* been fair. And the crisis existed long before the current epidemic of 'accounting phobia'. Anyone who had bothered to look into the earlier episodes of corporate failures would have realised that. The accounting issues that emerged in the 2000s included the capitalising of expenses, revenue recognition issues, disputes about solvency, questions of inappropriate asset valuations. These were not new found issues.

It was simply more of the same. Yet, many repeatedly asserted that, especially in Australia, the scale of the financial dilemmas was different. Table 14.1 data contest those assessments.

Regulatory responses

Since publication of the first edition of this book, the name of the major corporate regulator has changed from the ASC to the ASIC. More resources

Table 14.1 Company *losses** in nominal and scaled dimensions, and % of losses to GDP*

Year	Company	Loss in nominal $m*	CPI ^{2000}m	Loss in ^{2000}m	GDP $ billion	Losses as a % of GDP
1963	Reid Murray	47	14.1	416	17,601	0.00027
1990	Adsteam	2,100	100.0	2,619	351,933	0.00060
1990	Bond	5,330	100.0	6,647	351,933	0.00151
1990	Qintex	1,260	100.0	1,571	351,933	0.00036
1990	Hooker	1,960	100.0	2,444	351,933	0.00056
1990	SBV	2,700	100.0	3,367	351,933	0.00077
1991	SBSA	3,150	105.3	3,730	384,710	0.00082
1993	CBA	2,976	108.4	3,423	406,427	0.00073
1993	Westpac	6,367	108.4	7,324	406,427	0.00160
1993	ANZ	4,690	108.4	5,395	406,427	0.00115
2001	HIH	5,300	124.7	5,300#	593,311	0.00089
2001	One.Tel	650	124.7	650	593,311	0.00011
2002	Ansett	1,500	124.7	1,500	593,311	0.00025
2002	NAB	3,900	124.7	3,900	593,311	0.00066
2002	News Corp	12,800	124.7	12,800	593,311	0.00215

Sources: CPI and GDP data are taken from Catalogue item 6401, ABS, 2000; 1990 base year = 100.

HIH estimated losses and 'writedown losses' for One.Tel, Ansett, NAB and News Corp are in 2001 dollar terms. Other amounts in this column have been restated in ^{2000} equivalent purchasing power terms.

* 'Loss' data are taken from T. Sykes, *Bold Riders*, 1996 and Clarke, Dean and Oliver, *Corporate Collapse*, 1997; and financial press regarding asset writedowns.

were obtained for the regulator. There have been numerous investigations and several actions taken. Table 14.2 details some of those actions and the results to date. At the beginning of 2002 the Australian press led with the claim that Australian 'judges face a busy time as watchdogs pounce'.[7] Again, for regulatory agencies, finding a scapegoat is crucial. But whither the system?

In that regard, the legislative responses have been predictable. The JCPAA released a report in August 2002 that followed inquiries into 'noteworthy collapses both in Australia and overseas … to explore the extent to which it may be necessary to enhance the accountability of public and private sector auditing'.[8] Contiguously, the Treasurer, Peter Costello, released discussion paper *CLERP 9* with the proviso that more changes may follow the likely

Table 14.2   Major company failures in Australia 1990s–2002

Year of failure – date administrator appointed	Name of company	Major criticism	Actions against auditors/officials
April 2001	HIH	Issues of solvency determination True and fair view of insurance reserves Related-party transactions Netting off related-party assets and liabilities of HIH's licensed insurance subsidiaries Complex groups	Civil penalty proceedings under Corporations Act against former directors, Rodney Adler, CEO Ray Williams, Dominic Fedora. Found guilty of breaching directors' duties. Adler and Williams were banned from being involved in company management for 20 and 10 years respectively. They were held jointly liable to pay compensation of more than $7 million.
May 2001	One.Tel	Complex groups Related-party transactions Proper books of account	Civil penalty proceedings have been commenced against certain former executive directors seeking remedies of banning, fining and compensation – in excess of $75 million.
2000	Harris Scarfe	Improper accounting for inventories Capitalising expenses	Criminal charges against former CFO, Allan Hodgson, resulting in a six-year gaol sentence.
2002	Centaur		Pending charges.
2001	Pasminco		n.a.

Source: ASIC *Annual Reports* 2001–2002; D. Knott, Monash Governance Research Unit Inaugural Lecture, 17 July 2002.

release of the HIH Royal Commission Report early in 2003. The matters raised therein included proposals relating to: auditor independence, the interaction between audit and non-audit services, auditor liability, accounting standards, analyst independence, continuous disclosure, and fundraising. Claims were made Australia's legislative responses were 'lighter' than their US counterparts – that they were, however, 'principles-based' rather than 'black-letter-law-based'. These matters are discussed in Chapters 18 and 19.

Revisiting the observations made in Chapter 10, the paranoia of today's press, regulators and others has again clouded the focus of the corporate observers, continued to blind them to some real issues, and generally let the regulators and the accountancy profession off the hook. As we said in Chapter 10, '"Bankers, lawyers, accountants and directors", the dishonest and the innocent alike, have been judged through the false perception that most regulatory mechanisms were apt'. To this list can be added the ineffective and seduced financial media, the mutual fund managers, and the share analysts whose assessments in the US allegedly were affected by conflicts of interest. In such an atmosphere, investing was more likely to be part of a process that John Maynard Keynes had described as a 'casino', than what efficient marketers' claimed was an 'efficient allocating mechanism'. Has there ever been a greater opportunity for accounting to act as a countervailing force – as the impartial disclosing mechanism? One that would act as a brake on what appears now to have been the unfettered market activities of various vested interests?

What follows strengthens the arguments made in preceding chapters, that reforms to accounting need to address many of the commercial practices that have emerged in this latest boom/bust period. These include: mixing financial affairs of public and private companies within complex group structures, undertaking property dealings and other asset transfers via extensive use of related-party transactions (again sometimes entailing round-robin transactions) using share options to reward managers with the hope of aligning longer-term interests of shareholders and managers, and using debt and off-balance sheet financing in the form of financial derivatives. The annals of finance during the latter part of the twentieth century would reveal new forms of derivate financing techniques, collateralised debt obligations (CDOs – allegedly used by some banks to assist some corporate loans being kept off their balance sheets). It has been reported that post-2000 the debt-to-GDP ratios (at least in the United States) are at record levels. This, coupled to the extent of CDO portfolios being exposed to WorldCom's US$30 billion of debt, makes potentially for a dangerous mix.

Unfortunately, within this complex scenario conventional standard accounting practices proved no more able to cope effectively than in the past.

Somewhat serendipitously, the current bankruptcies at Enron and WorldCom in the United States and HIH in Australia, *inter alia*, involved the same major auditing firm, Andersen's. That resulted in considerable talk of a need for inquiries into audit independence. Parliamentary and regulatory agencies' inquiries would emerge on cue, premised on a desire for better (higher quality, in the new millennial jargon) information for investors. Executives were to be made more accountable. Stronger, more accountable auditing systems were to be developed. But, as in the previous upheavals, after big name corporates crashed the major push has been for more rules and regulations of the kind already ill-performing. There were calls to prohibit the joint provision of audit and non-audit services, calls to mandate audit committees and auditor rotations.[9]

The tenor of many of those demands mimics the rhetoric surrounding Roosevelt's New Deal reforms following the 1929 crash in the United States, and received with approbation by those in the United Kingdom still miffed by and outraged by the Royal Mail scandal.[10] Similar financial affairs included: in the United States – the Penn Central and Equity Funding crises of the 1970s and the S&L fiascos in the 1980s and '90s; the unexpected collapses of Minsec, Mainline, Gollins and Cambridge Credit Corporation in Australia in the 1970s, of Bond Corporation, Westmex, Qintex and Adsteam, for example in the 1990s; and in the UK collapses of Pergamon in the 1970s, the Maxwell Corporation and BCCI debacles of the 1990s.

However, some newer reform measures have included: (i) proposed additional supervisory boards of accounting and audit practices (presumably to augment existing regulatory oversight); (ii) audit firms voluntarily adding new in-house monitoring committees to ensure ethically-based best practices are being undertaken by all auditing staff; and (iii) stiffer criminal sanctions against fraudulent reporting and negligent auditing practices.

So the story continues. Revelations have led many to question the usefulness of audited accounting data as a sound basis for financial assessments and evaluations by investors, regulators and other interested parties. Misleading or untrue financial statements have involved balance date adjustments, and other practices, such as deferring expenses, advancing revenue recognition, and judicious use of complex business group structures. These practices were described in the post-2000 euphoria as being 'aggressive', and they were justified again by managers who argued that they were better able to assess their appropriateness. The quality control and neutrality aspects of a professionally qualified accountant determining how to account for transactions seem to have taken a back seat. Directors were allowed to be the scorekeepers! The Chairman's Foreword to the JCPAA 2002 *Report 391* observed that 'there has been a change in the profession over time from an emphasis on professional ethics to a more business-oriented focus'.[11] This is examined further in Chapter 19.

Yet, again on the cusp of an economic bust, the common experience was the sudden, unexpected collapses of large, public companies. While many, have argued that no necessary relationship exists between accounting and corporate collapses *per se*, few still fail to be alarmed at an accounting system (worldwide) that fails repeatedly to report on a timely basis downwards drifts in corporations' financial positions prior to their ultimate collapse. This inability of conventional accounting to be a reliable instrumentation system is highlighted in the cases that follow – including, HIH in detail and case vignettes at Patrick/MUA, Ansett, One.Tel and Enron. Other collapses could have been examined in detail, for example: Pasminco, Harris Scarfe and (say) Centaur. We have been content with noting them in the context of the bigger picture.

The latter chapters of Part VI demonstrate the myriad responses to the familiar claims of accounting inadequacy, and the concomitant similar proposals for regulatory and professional reform, are likely to result in only cosmetic changes. They are likely to have minimal effect in preventing the types of large unexpected collapses that produced the type of wealth redistributions presaging those reforms.

CHAPTER 15

HIH – Unfettered Hubris

HIH may prove to be the exemplar corporate collapse – lashings
of hubris, *groupthink*, creative and alleged feral accounting, alleged
insider trading, lengthy regulatory inquiries, press concentration on
the individuals, a judicial scalp or two and a flurry of proposed reforms.
But the financial reporting system remains relatively untouched. Whither
the lessons from history?

Analysing HIH's trajectory to failure is of national and international significance. It was the second largest insurance company in Australia and it is now
reportedly the subject of one of the largest corporate collapses in Australia.[1]
The statements of claim lodged by the HIH Administrator, Tony McGrath,
launched a $5.6 billion lawsuit against Australia's federal government and the
national insurance industry watchdog APRA (initially the ISC), before proposed changes to Australia's negligence laws could obfuscate such actions. The
proposed claim alleges that the government and its prudential regulator were
negligent in allowing HIH to collapse in March 2001. The upshot of this claim
will make riveting reading and possibly a good telemovie! The characters will
certainly be well known.[2]

The actual circumstances leading to HIH's demise are unfolding as investigations of the Royal Commission[3] into the Group's business affairs continued
in the latter part of 2002. More will be revealed when the Commissioner
reports in early 2003. The following account is preliminary and partial, drawing
mainly on newspaper accounts, annual reports and existing Royal Commission
evidence.

Public records show that HIH fits Argenti's *Type III* failure trajectory –
characterised by periods on successively lower plateaus. But, if one were to
take the acquisition of FAI in late 1998 as creating a new 'enterprise', then
the 'Group' failure is more like Argenti's 'still-born' *Type I* trajectory – with
the enterprise being in declining mode from nearly day one.

The extent of losses suffered by the community is unlikely to be fully
evident for some years.[4] Some civil cases have been completed, others continue and criminal cases are likely.[5] Financial commentator Mark Westfield
appositely captures HIH's significance for the themes we are pursuing:

> HIH's main sin was its failure to publicly disclose its deteriorating position.
> Listed companies are obliged by law to warn the market of material information
> that might have an impact on their share price. HIH told the market the exact

Nicholson's 16 May 2001 depiction of the perceived need to find a scapegoat. Cartoon by Nicholson from *The Australian*. (www.nicholsoncartoons.com.au)

opposite, claiming as Williams did in a letter to insurance brokers last June that HIH was 'rock solid'. Investors were trading HIH shares in an information vacuum. Policy-holders would continue to buy or renew policies that would become worthless.[6]

But, of course, that is not only HIH's 'main sin', it has been the main sin of corporate failures throughout Australia's annals of finance. Events at HIH emphasise the importance of fully understanding what is meant by notions of *solvency* and *going concern* and the virtual impossibility of using the usual mechanisms for making informed assessments of them within the context of conventional accounting information. The role of auditors in grappling with creative and perhaps feral accounting, and pressures on management to show companies in the best light possible, appear evident in this case. Set within the context of an alleged inept and under-resourced prudential regulator,[7] and alleged executive improprieties, HIH has the lot!

HIH – exemplar of corporate groupthink

Comprising over 240 separate companies, the HIH Group at one time operated in five of the world's continents, with companies incorporated in 16 countries – including the United Kingdom, the United States, New Zealand, Hong Kong,

Argentina, Malaysia, Sweden, Greece, Russia, Fiji, Papua New Guinea and the Philippines, as well as Australia. Figure 15.1 shows several Australian insurance licence-holding companies that maintained ubiquitous insurance cover for Australians, including personal and domestic, workers' compensation, small business, rural and commercial, travel, builders' warranty, sporting and life insurance.

The seeds of group enterprise were sown in 1968 by the formation of a small company by an Australian entrepreneur Ray Williams (and a colleague, Michael Payne). British-listed C.E. Heath plc took over that company in 1971; C.E. Heath International was listed on Australian Stock Exchange in 1992 with a stock market capitalisation value of $240 million. In 1995 growth continued via C.E. Heath's CIC Insurance acquisition, meshed with a partnership agreement with the leading Swiss insurer, Winterthur. HIH Winterthur was born. Or was it to be 'still-born' in Argenti's trajectory terms?

We digress. It has been claimed by assistants to the HIH Royal Commission (HIHRC) that at all times Ray Williams played a dominant CEO role at HIH. Dominant CEOs have been a feature of several cases in this volume. Whether it is always a sign of potential corporate difficulties is a matter of conjecture. It is to be recalled that Argenti perceived it to be a 'weakness' for calibrating his *A score*. But then, dominant CEOs are also frequently features of highly successful companies. Perhaps it is more the case, as revealed in several cases previously, that dominant personalities can make bad situations worse.

Back to HIH's growth. Overseas expansions in the United Kingdom (Cotesworth and its links with Lloyds Insurance) and the United States have been claimed by many appearing before the HIH Royal Commission to have been significant factors in the Group's eventual demise. In particular, the acquisition of activities undertaken by California Insurance and the quagmire of US workers' compensation insurance into which it plunged, proved critical to the Group's dwindling fortunes.

A group enterprise philosophy seems to have underpinned many of HIH's activities. Interestingly, the HIH Administrator's claims against the partners of the now defunct firm, Andersen, and HIH's long-standing actuary allude to this groupthink approach, drawing on data revealed at the HIHRC. It is reported that the claim:

> also criticises Andersen for allowing HIH's licensed insurance subsidiaries to 'net off' related party assets and liabilities when calculating solvency as defined by APRA for insurance licence purposes … [Further, the HIH Royal] commission has heard that that if gross transactions had been disclosed to APRA, one subsidiary would have failed the solvency test for insurance in 1999 and 2000, and a second in 2000.[8]

Reinforcing groupthink was HIH's continued use since 1992 of ASC regulatory-approved corporate class order deeds of cross guarantees. At that time C.E. Heath adopted them presumably to assist with reducing group financing costs and to reduce group reporting costs. Various Deeds of Assumption and Revocation followed in the mid-1990s – some deeds appear to have been retained even after the FAI acquisition in 1998. That acquisition is nearly universally attributed to have been HIH's Achilles heel – euphemistically described as HIH's *Trojan Horse*!

Consider the diagrammatic illustration (Figure 15.1) of the HIH Group prepared by the HIH liquidators for a Report to Creditors, dated 3 April 2002.

FAI – HIH's Trojan Horse

Counsel assisting the HIHRC early in its proceedings invoked the Trojan Horse analogy. Several leading players at HIH have attributed a similar significance. But the finding is open at this stage. It has been suggested by others that the

Figure 15.1   HIH Corporate Group Structure as at April 2002

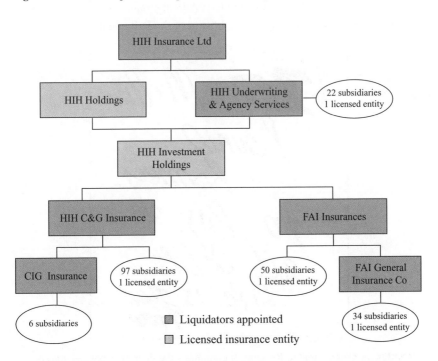

Source: KPMG Report to Creditors, 3 April 2002.

single biggest contributor to the collapse was a failure of processes relating to the provision of future claims – the under-reserving and related reinsurance issues. Additional critical risk factors included: exposure to several high-risk insurance activities, such as UK film investments, 'long tail' (higher risk) marine insurance business that was written from approximately the mid-1990s, damages claims from the major hailstorm in Sydney, the 1999 Florida typhoon and overseas workers' compensation claims resulting from the industry deregulation in California and altered court-awarded benefits. And then there were the financial effects of the 'poor' investments arising from the FAI acquisition – the St Moritz Hotel in New York's Central Park and Perth's Swan Brewery site. FAI's Rodney Adler had purchased both assets from the carcass of Bond Corp in the early 1990s. Just another case of 'problem assets' doing the rounds of entrepreneurs in financial difficulties.

HIH's rise and demise thus produces a seminal mix of technical causal factors – bad business decisions, failure of the actual financial outcomes to be reflected in the financial statements, the alleged failure by the regulator to heed information from whistle-blowers or otherwise to identify how HIH's position differed from industry norms; and alleged negligence by almost everyone – HIH's directors, auditors, actuaries, and the prudential regulators – at least according to claims lodged within the HIH Administrator's suits. And of course the inevitable press concentration on the cult of the individual.[9]

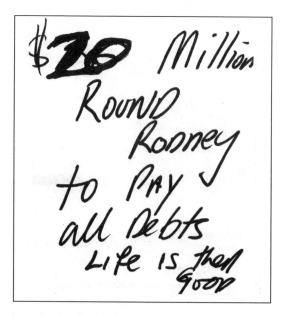

Alleged memo from 'Brad to Rodney'. It epitomises the interest in the activities of individuals at HIH. Courtesy AAP Image.

At the time of writing there have been more than 150 days of examination at the HIHRC – with over 200 witnesses, 19,000 pages of transcript and 1.6 million exhibits. Deliberations have centred on whether FAI was insolvent when acquired, FAI's accounting practices, and more effective due-diligence by HIH. In issue is whether the prudential regulator and auditor could have exposed FAI's black holes, and HIH's subsequent recording of FAI's Goodwill on Acquisition. The FAI acquisition is said to have presented HIH with a 'magical box' in which it could either enter or extract profits or losses at its discretion. Concern has been noted in the HIHRC that the proportion of HIH's net assets represented by intangibles such as goodwill had increased substantially from 1997 to 2000.[10] Below and elsewhere we lament that those intangibles should be reported *at all* in a statement of financial position.

The KPMG Report commissioned by the HIH Board canvassed the possibility that HIH may have been trading while insolvent. After the first 90 days of inquiry at the HIHRC, financial journalist Trevor Sykes noted that 'one of the most disturbing aspects of the HIH Royal Commission has been the emerging spectre that large insurance companies may have been able to operate below minimum solvency levels over long period of time without being detected by the public, or apparently by the regulators'. Further, in a submission to the HIHRC on 18 July 2002 counsel assisting the Commission, Martin, QC noted that because of financial difficulties with FAI, HIH *might* have been insolvent as early as two years prior to its March 2001 collapse and associated $5.3 billion deficiency. It will be interesting to read Commissioner Owen's assessment.

Liquidation revelations

HIH was placed into provisional liquidation in March 2001. Initial estimates of the maximum losses by the administrator were $4 billion, subsequently revised to more than $5.3 billion. The administration occurred, incongruously, not long after HIH had reported the 'apparently' successful purchase of FAI for $300 million in 1999, followed by a 112 per cent rise in profits in the first half of 2000. Although detailing an 'emphasis of matter' opinion in note 13 of the *Notes to the Accounts*, HIH's auditors had provided an otherwise unqualified opinion in respect of the financial accounts in June of that year, showing a surplus of net assets of $939 million. That exposes the curious state of the auditing game. An 'emphasis of matter' of opinion, though obviously indicative of a reservation entertained by the auditors, is not regarded as a *qualified* opinion. But clearly, it is entering a caveat that could be drawn upon as a defence if the need arises, were the 'clean' report to be challenged later. Auditing is a very peculiar practice, indeed.

Not that such anomalies had not been exposed before. Consider the examination of 'Mr Moreland', the Price Waterhouse auditor of the Royal Mail company, in Lord Kylsant's trial in the early 1930s, which provides the greatest insight to the way in which conventional professional thinking runs on such matters. At issue there was whether 'secret reserves' were a legitimate source from which dividends might be paid. The short answer was 'yes'. The long answer was 'yes and no!' Lord Plender (the president of The Institute of Chartered Accountants in England and Wales, and chair of the London-based firm of Deloitte, Plender and Griffiths) offered the opinion that the 'materiality' of the amount is what mattered. We might take it that in the same way that non-disclosure of the source of the Royal Mail's dividends did not negate a true and fair appellation by the auditor, nor does the 'emphasis of matter' comment negate an unqualified audit opinion today. In respect of a clean audit report, Lord Plender's 'materiality' safe harbour played the same role as the current 'emphasis ...' plays today. Putting this audit matter into context, it is worth considering the financials of HIH for the financial years 1999 and 2000, as shown in Table 15.1.

There is a view that the 'emphasis of matter' opinion should have alerted any interested parties to possible risks at HIH. Counterbalancing this, the Royal Commission inquiry appears to have revealed questionable accounting practices. We await with interest Justice Owen's considered assessment of these matters.

The lore is that HIH was under-reserved.[11] The issue of assessing the amount of an insurer's liabilities is inherently difficult – as many witnesses to the HIH Royal Commission have attested. HIH's provisioning policy did not provide for an adequate prudential reserve margin in respect of its future claim obligations, but rather it sought reinsurance to cover the risk. Allegations before the HIHRC suggest there were undisclosed (at least to many), questionable 'reinsurance side letters' that may have meant that certain reinsurance rearrangements would have been, in effect, loans. If so, reported profits would have been reduced and liabilities would have been higher.

Concerns also were raised of an alleged attempt to prop up HIH's share price by a series of related-party transactions. It was alleged that during 2000 $10 million was used to fund related-company transactions – including the 'on-market' purchase of about $4 million of HIH shares by Pacific Eagles Equities, a subsidiary of HIH. In relation to those transactions, ASIC laid charges against three former HIH directors, implying that the funds were improperly used.[12] Those charges were to be found proven and one director, Rodney Adler, was disqualified from acting as a director for 20 years; another, CEO Ray Williams, was disqualified for ten years; while there were fines against HIH's finance director, Dominic Fodera, as well as Adler and Williams.

Table 15.1 HIH Insurance Limited – extracts from the financial reports for the year ended 30 June 2000

	Parent entity		Consolidated	
	1.7.99– 30.6.00	1.1.98– 30.6.99	1.7.99– 30.6.00	1.1.98– 30.6.99
Profit and Loss Statements	$m	$m	$m	$m
Operating profit before abnormal item and income tax	54.1	104.6	61.9	102.0
Abnormal item before income tax	–	–	(6.0)	(50.0)
Operating profit before income tax	54.1	104.6	55.9	52.0
Income tax attributable to operating profit	(4.0)	(2.2)	(17.9)	(14.7)
Abnormal tax expense	–	–	(18.8)	–
Operating profit after income tax	50.1	102.4	19.2	37.3
Loss on extraordinary items	–	–	–	(50.1)
Income tax attributable to loss on extraordinary items	–	–	–	–
Loss on extraordinary items after income tax	–	–	–	(50.1)
Outside equity interest in operating profit	–	–	(0.8)	(8.4)
Operating profit/(loss) after extraordinary items and income tax attributable to members of the parent entity	50.1	102.4	18.4	(21.2)
Retained profits/(Accumulated losses) at the beginning of the period	19.3	3.1	(26.5)	89.9
Total available for appropriation	69.4	105.5	(8.1)	68.7
Dividends and other distributions provided for or paid	(33.3)	(86.2)	(49.4)	(95.2)
Retained profits/(Accumulated losses) at the end of the period	36.1	19.3	(57.5)	(26.5)

Notes: Comparatives. The economic entity changed its financial year-end from 31 December to 30 June, as at 30 June 1999. These financial statement extracts have been prepared to provide financial information and statements for the year to 30 June 2000 with comparatives stated for the 18-month period to 30 June 1999 drawn from the HIH Annual Report for 2000.

continued

Table 15.1 *cont'd*/HIH Insurance Limited – extracts from the financial report for the year ended 30 June 2000

| | Consolidated | | Consolidated |
Balance Sheet	30.6.00 $m	30.6.99 $m	31.12.97 $m
Current Assets			
Cash	461.6	638.7	203.7
Receivables (Note 11)	1,603.6	1,400.7	739.2
Investments	624.4	803.5	580.5
Reinsurance recoveries receivable	431.6	415.5	169.5
Deferred acquisition costs	304.3	278.3	139.8
Other	25.0	33.8	16.4
Total current assets	3,450.5	3,570.5	1,849.1
Non-current assets			
Receivables	0.6	35.0	–
Investments	1,753.1	1,908.8	1,165.3
Plant and equipment/Land and Bdgs	164.6	147.8	65.6
Reinsurance recoveries receivable	1,383.3	986.7	276.6
Intangibles (Brand Names/Goodwill)	494.4	346.5	42.1
Other (including FITB)	244.4	191.7	115.8
Total non-current assets	4,045.4	3,616.5	1,165.4
New South Wales Workers Compensation Statutory Funds	831.2	864.1	472.2
Total assets	8,327.1	8,051.1	3,986.7
Current liabilities			
Accounts payable	381.0	563.7	224.6
Borrowings	19.6	164.5	–
Provisions	83.7	46.3	51.7
Outstanding claims	1,423.4	1,415.5	734.9
Unearned premiums	1,069.4	1,038.9	540.2
Other	49.2	33.9	43.5
Total Current Liabilities	3,026.3	3,262.8	1,594.9
Non-current liabilities			
Accounts payable	14.5	–	57.9
Borrowings	504.4	335.8	76.5
Provisions	4.1	6.0	3.2
Outstanding claims	3,007.5	2,636.0	1,221.7
Total non-current liabilities	3,530.5	2,977.8	1,459.3

continued

Table 15.1 *cont'd*/HIH Insurance Limited – extracts from the financial report for the year ended 30 June 2000

Balance Sheet	Consolidated 30.6.00 $m	Consolidated 30.6.99 $m	Consolidated 31.12.97 $m
New South Wales Workers Compensation Statutory Funds	831.2	864.1	472.2
Total liabilities	7,388.0	7,104.7	3,426.4
Net assets	939.1	946.4	560.3
Shareholders' equity			
Share capital	697.9	684.2	80.8
Convertible notes	65.3	65.3	65.3
Converting notes	213.1	213.1	–
Reserves	8.7	(1.0)	321.9
Retained profits/(Accumulated losses)	(57.5)	(26.5)	89.9
Total shareholders' equity attributable to members of the parent entity	927.5	935.1	557.9
Outside equity interests in controlled entities	11.6	11.3	2.4
Total shareholders' equity	939.1	946.4	560.3
Note 11 – Receivables			
Trade debtors	613.1	497.5	328.7
Less provision for doubtful debts	(8.8)	(19.8)	4.0
Trade debtors net	604.3	477.7	324.7
Amounts due from reinsurers, other insurers and statutory bodies	377.8	360.7	91.9
Accrued premiums	526.4	470.0	295.5
Accrued interest, commission and other income	8.4	5.9	7.0
Other debtors	86.7	86.4	20.1
Total current receivables	1,603.6	1,400.7	739.2

Source: Annual Reports, HIH 30 June 2000 and 30 June 1999. FAI was acquired in 1998.

Those actions are being appealed as this volume goes to press, but there is also press speculation that the ASIC may be pursuing criminal actions in respect of those transactions.[13]

One needs to consider other items in the financial statements that are apposite in assessing the auditor's report containing its 'emphasis of matter' opinion. Further, the rise in HIH's reported profits to June 2000 was contested. It was alleged that the company had been able to report an increased profit partially because it had relied on several generally accepted accounting practices – including the capitalisation of expenses such as deferred acquisition costs, deferred information technology costs, and other 'bookkeeping debits' such as future income tax benefits and goodwill.

Let us consider one of these, the upward revisions of the calculation of the purchased goodwill in the HIH acquisition of FAI amounting to between $300 and $400 million, instead of the less than $100 million originally recorded in the 1998 HIH accounts. Booking *goodwill* is highly contestable at the best of times. Under conventional accounting, goodwill is the excess of the amount paid over and above the *fair value* of the assets acquired. *Fair value* is the market-evidenced selling price of the assets. So, the booked goodwill is taken into account for (at best) the expectations of the purchaser regarding above-normal future earnings from employing the asset, and (at worst) the capitalisation of the loss incurred on a 'bad buy'. HIH's acquisition of FAI was an allegedly 'bad buy' at $300 million. It has been alleged that $100 million would have been nearer the mark. On that score the FAI acquisition incurred an immediate loss. But the important point to note is that conventional accounting, by an Accounting Standard (AASB 1013) on how to account for goodwill, provides the possible legitimate circumstance in which the worth of goodwill becomes a contestable issue, rather than a non-event. There also have been claims of further problems in the way that insurance provisioning was actuarially calculated. However, all of these adjustments accounted for somewhere between $1 to $2 billion of the $5.3 billion eventual deficiency. A large deficit remains unaccounted for and we will return to this matter when analysing HIH's accounting and auditing practices.

These matters, in particular, illustrate the fragility of conventional accounting practice that induces error, by virtue of, *inter alia*, not having recourse to market prices. Whereas considerable discussion has addressed how much HIH should have paid to purchase FAI, were assets to have been marked-to-market a significant portion of the $1 billion of HIH assets related to intangibles would *not* have been reported, and HIH's likely insolvency at the time may have been exposed earlier.

HIH had adapted its operations in early 2000, suggesting to some that it was in financial difficulties. What has emerged since then is that in August 2000 HIH sold a controlling share of its Australian general insurance business in order to meet the APRA's new guidelines; in September 2000 HIH announced that chief executive Williams would resign; in February 2001 its shares were suspended; in March 2001 the Board of HIH was warned by consultants, Ernst and Young, of fatal problems with its accounting practices; and approximately one week later the group was placed into provisional liquidation.[14]

Relativity of HIH collapse[15]

There is no doubting the enormity of the collapse. Much has been written about its scale. But data in Table 14.1 and the previous case analyses in this volume imply that there have been many other large, certainly some larger, corporate crises and collapses in Australia.

In terms of regulatory failure it is misleading that so much focus attends the liquidation of companies. For what is most important is not whether companies fail to survive, but the incidence of *involuntary* redistributions of shareholder and stakeholder wealth occasioned by corporate crises. We suggest 'involuntary', insofar as it is unlikely that those whose wealth is dissipated by the redistributions would have been willing travellers had the companies' financials disclosed earlier their perilous states. Accounting failure induces regulatory failure – facilitating audit failure, executive failure and ethical failure. Events at HIH aptly illustrate that.

Involuntary wealth transfers by shareholders and creditors listed in Table 14.1 are usefully compared with HIH on two bases. First, in real terms – the equivalent of the losses expressed in terms of current general purchasing power. Comparing the *number* of dollars lost in each event serves no good purpose when the general purchasing power of the currency has changed. It does not give any indication of the relative size of the fallouts. Second, it is instructive to compare the losses in each failure relative to Australia's GNP at the time they occurred. For, if we take the GNP to be an indicator of the level of economic activity at the time, the percentage of the reported losses with their respective GNPs provides an (albeit rough) indication of the relative significance of the losses in terms of the national economy. Relative comparisons with some notable past failures and HIH and One.Tel are set out in Table 14.1. Also revealed are loan write-offs by the banks in the early 1990s and the $12.8 billion write-off by News Corp (primarily related to its investment in Gemstar). These are taken, for the sake of argument, to be within our definition of 'losses' – though the survival of the companies to which the write-offs relate is a matter of history.

Those data show that, though the estimated HIH loss is undeniably large, others in the small sample shown in Table 14.1 outscore it in terms of the benchmarks we have used – some on both counts. It is reasonable to conclude that the HIH fallout is no more demanding of radical action than were those earlier failures. Perhaps HIH is the 'straw that has broken the camel's back'.

A point of departure might have been reached. However, the need for radical reform of the corporate regulatory system, particularly its information flow mechanisms, was as critical in the past, in the wake of the 1960s, 1970s and 1980s, as it is now. With hindsight, perhaps even more so. For had the systemic defects been eradicated in the past, perhaps the size and spread of HIH's financial fallout might have been less. Recall our Chapter 6 leader where nearly 30 years ago iconoclastic, Ray Chambers opined:

> If ... due to the optional accounting rules available them, company managers and directors are able to conceal the drift [in financial position] shareholders and creditors will continue to support, and support with new money, companies which are weaker than their accounts represent.[16]

Analysing HIH's accounting and auditing practices

Royal Commissioner, Justice Owen was asked to inquire into the collapse of HIH to determine the extent to which actions of HIH's directors, officers, auditors, actuaries and advisors contributed to the failure of HIH. Further, the Commissioner was charged to seek evidence of undesirable corporate governance practices and to assess the adequacy of prudential supervision arrangements for insurance companies. However, missing is any explicit direction to inquire into the adequacy of the Accounting Standards and generally accepted accounting principles upon which HIH prepared its annual accounts. Though, this may be implicit in the issues related to auditors and their governance role and in assessing solvency.

Australian Accounting Standards are proposed by the Australian Accounting Standards Board. The Commonwealth Parliament gives them legal backing. Accountants are obliged to implement approved Accounting Standards when preparing company financial statements. That seems to imply that where the compulsory accounting practices are found inadequate as an instrument of corporate governance, the trail of responsibility leads back through the accountants and auditors to the regulators enforcing compliance with the Standards, those who were involved with the drafting and enactment of the legislation embracing the Standards, to, possibly, those who developed and recommended the Standards in the first place. This speculation is one that neither regulators nor Accounting Standards-setters are likely to contemplate with comfort.

HIH's published accounts followed the standard prescription path. On 16 October 2000, external auditors attested that HIH's accounts for the year ended 30 June 2000 were prepared in accordance with Accounting Standards and gave a 'true and fair view' of its financial position. The following extract from that report, as contained in the 30 June 2000 financial statements, illustrates the form of the 'emphasis of matter' opinion discussed earlier.

INDEPENDENT AUDIT REPORT

To the Members of HIH Insurance Limited

Scope

We have audited the financial report of HIH Insurance Limited for the financial year ended 30 June 2000 as set out on pages 24 to 74. The financial report includes the consolidated financial statements of the consolidated entity comprising the company and the entities it controlled at the year's end or from time to time during the financial year. The Company's directors are responsible for the financial report. We have conducted an independent audit of the financial report in order to express an opinion on it to the members of the company.

Our audit has been conducted in accordance with Australian Auditing Standards to provide reasonable assurance whether the financial report is free of material misstatement. Our procedures included examination, on a test basis, of evidence supporting the amounts and other disclosures in the financial report, and the evaluation of accounting policies and significant accounting estimates. These procedures have been undertaken to form an opinion whether, in all material respects, the financial report is presented fairly in accordance with Accounting Standards, other mandatory professional reporting requirements and statutory requirements, in Australia, so as to present a view which is consistent with our understanding of the Company's and the consolidated entity's financial position, and performance as represented by the results of their operations and their cash flows.

The audit opinion expressed in this report has been formed on the above basis.

Audit Opinion

In our opinion, the financial report of HIH Insurance Limited is in accordance with:

a) the Corporations Law, including:

i) giving a true and fair view, of the Company's and consolidated entity's financial position as at 30 June 2000 and of their performance for the year ended on that date; and

ii) complying with Accounting Standards and the Corporations Regulations; and

b) other mandatory professional reporting requirements.

Whole of Account Reinsurance

Without qualification to the opinion expressed above, attention is drawn to the following matter. As indicated in Note 1(t) to the financial statements, the consolidated entity enters into whole of account reinsurance contracts to protect its underwriting portfolio. The realisation of benefits arising from a contract entered into during the financial year are dependent on factors described in Note 13. [*emphasis added*]

Note 13, which related to the 30 June 2000 Reinsurance Recoveries Receivables balance amounting to $1.8199 billion (1999 balance was $1.4022 billion), stated:

Consistent with industry practice, the consolidated entity has entered into whole of account reinsurance contracts to protect its underwriting portfolio. In the current year, the consolidated entity has entered into a further whole of account contract for a period of five years. Included in reinsurance recoveries receivable above is $220 million of discounted recoveries relating to this contract. Of this amount the recovery of $120 million is dependent upon the performance of the contract, in line with the expectations over the life of the contract. The principal factors influencing performance include:

1. Investment performance of the underlying experience account.

2. Claims payments patterns.

3. Continuity of the contract.

These events are inherently uncertain and the ultimate performance of the contract and the realisation of the benefits of the contract may differ from expectations. The net financial benefit of this contract for this financial year was $84 million after taxes. [*emphasis added*]

Faced with this 'emphasis of matter' audit opinion, it is instructive to consider the plight of the HIH policyholders, shareholders, creditors, other interested parties and, given the HIH Administrator's litigation claims, the regulators. Recall the events and lessons of the previous cases – Cambridge, Adsteam, Bond and Westmex. How could a company ('consolidated entity') that had received this apparently clean bill of health in its audited accounts for the financial year to 30 June 2000 collapse generally *unexpectedly* within nine months, with what was initially estimated as a $4 billion (then adjusted to $5.3 billion) deficiency of funds? This appears fundamental to the administrator's statement of claims lodged against the government, the prudential regulator, directors, auditors and actuaries.

Such a question would come as no surprise to those with even a limited knowledge of what underpins conventional accounting practices. A major confounding factor is that Accounting Standards routinely yield statements of financial position and performance that are at odds with ordinary financial commonsense and financial experience. They are based on conventions, principles [*sic.*] and doctrines such as the 'going concern, the monetary convention, the matching principle, and the conservatism doctrine'.[17] They lead to financial statements that are prone to be misleading, deceptive and not of 'merchantable quality'. It may be that superimposing the problems of conventional accounting upon the inherent difficulties of assessing liabilities of insurance companies created a fatal mix.

HIH – the tyranny of surprise

In HIH's failure, like those preceding it, the dominant element has been the surprise attending the collapse of the company. Although numerous commentators have, *ex post*, implied that the failure of HIH did not surprise, the facts remain that the company's critical financial state was not apparent from either the contents of its published financial statements to 30 June 2000, nor from the usual commentaries on corporate matters. *Surprise* in respect of corporate matters is not reasonably assessed according to what those supposedly 'in the know' are apprised of, or what is talked about in the bars around town, but what can be assessed or gleaned from the publicly available information. That is the function of published financial statements, the ASX's continuous reporting regime, the obligation on auditors to report anomalies, and the like.

Yet HIH failed at a time when Australian corporations are experiencing the greatest volume of regulation in Australian corporate history. Not only are there regulatory agencies, ASIC and APRA, general oversight by the ASX, and organisations such as the Australian Shareholders' Association, but there are more Accounting Standards and Auditing Standards than ever. It is reasonable to expect that the corporation laws entail the latest legal mechanisms to regulate the activities of corporations *per se*, their directors, managers, accountants and auditors. HIH's failure thus occurred in a climate of a crescendo of talk regarding corporate governance following the collapses of the 1980s, and where audit committees *are* commonplace. HIH is reported to have had an audit committee in the periods prior to its collapse. It also had non-executive directors. Yet the characteristic surprise that greeted HIH's failure was no less than has been shown in this volume when H.G. Palmer, Stanhill and Reid Murray failed in the 1960s; or when Minsec, Mainline, Cambridge Credit and Associated Securities Limited failed in the 1970s; or when Bond, Westmex, Adsteam and Qintex fell over in the 1980s. There may well have been *some* who knew of, or suspected, the difficulties HIH and those other companies were experiencing, but that matters little for the *majority* of the punters if the public information avenues are blocked.

HIH's solvency

Considerable debate, comment and speculation have arisen regarding whether, and, if so, at what point, HIH became insolvent. Of critical importance also is whether, and, if so, at what time, might HIH's directors, individually and (or) collectively, have become aware, or ought reasonably to have been aware, of it. Further, as noted, the HIH Administrator reportedly has lodged a claim against the prudential regulator, APRA (and its predecessor, the ISC) and partners of the now defunct auditing firm, and its long-standing actuary, stating that they should have known of the insolvent states of FAI and HIH (and some of its licensed insurance subsidiaries) some time prior to the HIH collapse.[18] This type of action against a regulator is a first for Australia.

It has been argued elsewhere (Clarke and Dean, 1992) and here in Chapter 2 that the questionable serviceability of conventionally prepared financial data hinders the task for all concerned. The potential trail of responsibility for what appears in the published financial statements could be, as we suggested earlier, a tortuous path.

Clearly the financial management literature in general, and the accounting literature in particular, are replete with explanations of solvency. Notwithstanding the debate over what are the critical tests ('balance sheet' or 'cash flow' tests) of solvency and insolvency, there is general agreement that the notion of being solvent entails having the capacity to meet 'debts' as they fall due. Laypersons might properly expect that in an orderly, well-regulated corporate environment, the data set out in a company's financial statements would be pertinent to, and serviceable for, such an assessment.

Insurance companies clearly present idiosyncratic problems in respect to solvency, especially on the liabilities side. The HIHRC transcripts relating to the actuarial calculations underpinning the estimation of the likely value of future claims HIH might have faced make good reading.[19] Of particular note therein is the discussion regarding capital adequacy measures.

Of greater immediate interest are the means of obtaining serviceable accounting data where the money's worth of assets and liabilities is objectively determinable at specified dates. Conventional accounting in accord with the current suite of Standards mainly ignores such means or, in limited circumstances, makes the employment of them optional.

Assessment of solvency entails predictions regarding the likely capacity to meet liabilities when they become due for payment in the future. Claims on insurance companies are a case in point; neither when they will arise nor how much they will be is known at a particular balance date. Actuarial calculations are the best shot in the dark.[20] It has been reported that HIH's data were disputed on actuarial grounds and the opinion conveyed to APRA. Indeed, APRA Chairman Jeffrey Carmichael is reported to have attended the conference where a paper was presented. Subsequently it was circulated within APRA. No action appears to have been prompted by that assessment.[21] The assessment of solvency requires the determination of financial position – the nature, composition and money's worth of a company's assets and the settlement amount of its liabilities at a specified date. That requires that all physical assets be stated at their current selling prices, *marked-to-market*, for that is the best indication of financial resources they embody, their current money's worth at that time. And, in respect of physical assets, no other datum is serviceable for determining solvency at that date. It is difficult to understand how an insurer can satisfy the requirements under the Insurance Act for an insurer to meet specific asset and liability ratios without using a marked-to-market approach for all its assets and liabilities – but apparently it can.

Financial position, like all *positions*, is unique to a specific date. In most circumstances only the present financial position can be determined and therefore only the current state of solvency. The prediction of future states of solvency requires estimations of likely future financial positions. No reasonable prediction of future financial positions, or of the cash resources likely to be in hand, or to which there might be access through pledging or selling physical assets, is possible *without knowledge of the present financial position* from which all future such positions will be departures. For the most part, a comprehensive use of the Accounting Standards does not produce data from which financial position in those terms can be determined.

Overall, the Standards are not geared to producing the data necessary to determine financial position as described above, notwithstanding the recent departure from the term *balance sheet* and adoption of the term *Statement of Financial Position* in AASB 1040. For, whereas the Accounting Standards contain some instances of specifying current market prices for certain assets, for the investments of general insurance companies (AASB 1023, for example), it frequently is optional (AASB 1041). In respect to general insurance companies it is to be noted that notwithstanding the specification of market prices for investments, operational assets are not required to be marked-to-market. We find the distinction between *investments* and *operating assets* curious, and the different valuation rules applicable to them serve no useful purpose.

Conventional *historical cost* accounting is a 'capitalisation-of-expenditure model'. And the current Australian Accounting Standards remain *primarily* within the historical cost paradigm. Commentators on the recent financial problems in the United States do not appear to understand this. Thus, we find the Australian approbation of the US commentators' and regulators' horror at WorldCom's alleged capitalisation of costs rather strange. Almost every Australian company will have capitalised costs – it is almost compulsory. *HIH certainly did*. Every company with *goodwill* on its balance sheet has capitalised costs; every company that reports 'start-up costs' as assets – *HIH apparently did*; every company that reports physical assets at their historical *cost* (or that amount amortised) has capitalised expenditure – that is what 'cost' means. The amortisation regime required under AASB 1021 implies that 'cost' has been capitalised and is to be leached into the calculation of income periodically according to expectations; every company that uses the *accrual* system capitalises costs, and indeed revenues, in order to supposedly 'match costs with revenues'; every company that reports a *deferred tax debit* (under the new tax-effect accounting regime of AASB 1020) has capitalised an expense for financial reporting purposes – *HIH apparently did*. The conventional system in accord with the Accounting Standards is riddled with capitalisation opportunities and obligations; indeed, capitalisation of expenditures is endemic to the historical cost system. *It appears it was so at HIH*.

Asset and liability particulars in Table 15.1, above, would allow lay persons to assume that at 30 June 2000 HIH had $8,327 million worth of assets to meet its reported debts of $7,388 million at that time. But those book value dollar amounts of HIH's resources did not necessarily represent any equivalence to the financial, the monetary, resources HIH had, or would have, to pay its debts.

Under conventional accounting, in accord with the Accounting Standards, assets arise when an expenditure provides the prospect of future benefits. Those benefits are deemed to be worth what they cost – under the historical cost doctrine that is translated into being the *value* of the asset. That disputes everyday financial experience. If the benefits materialise it will be in the future, not at the date of the financial reporting. Contrary to SAC4, the company has the asset, not the benefits. It only has an expectation of them. Common experience of lay persons is that at each point in time the current money's worth of a physical item is not what was paid to acquire it, but what it could be sold for. It defies all the experience in markets to assume otherwise. As with most balance sheets, HIH's assets at 30 June 2000 were a mixture of the financial resources HIH had at that date, or had almost immediate access to (for example, Cash $462 million and Receivables $3,424 million), and money it no longer had by virtue of having spent it to acquire assets (for example, Plant and Equipment, shown at written-down cost of $165 million).

Clearly, a number of the financial representations of those asset items are not serviceable for assessing HIH's solvency at 30 June 2000. The *written down cost* of the plant and equipment is irrelevant to the assessment, though what the items could be sold for obviously would be, were it to have been reported.

A closer look at three other components of HIH's total assets is revealing. Those assets are all referred to in the HIH Administrator's litigation claims. The *deferred acquisition costs* item relates to sums expended in the past to acquire another business. Under the conventional rubrics it is defined as an 'asset' and gradually 'written-off' as its 'benefits' are deemed to have been received. But the $304 million reported has gone. Much the same can be said about *goodwill* ($475 million). Likewise the *future tax benefit* ($228 million). In each case those amounts do not have any real world manifestation. They exist only in *accounting*, and do not represent anything that necessarily can be converted into cash then, or necessarily in the near future. Recent evidence before the Royal Commission relating to the raising of 'goodwill' on HIH's acquisition of FAI has exposed just how subjective the goodwill figure can be. HIH's 'future tax benefit' is an artifact arising from the Accounting Standard (AASB 1020) prescribing tax-effect accounting – conventional accounting's *hocus pocus* at its subliminal best!

Adjusting the June 2000 HIH balance sheet for those three dubious assets (totalling $1,007 million) reduces the total assets figure to $7,320 million. That is, $68 million less than reported debts. And, according to that, *cet. par.*, HIH would be 'technically insolvent' if the 'balance sheet' test were to have been applied. But as matters stand, a conclusion that HIH was insolvent at that date, identifying who might have known it and predicting what HIH's solvency might be at future times is impossible without data indicative of the money's worths of all of HIH's assets and liabilities at 30 June 2000.

The critical prius to assessing solvency then and predicting it in the future is not forthcoming under conventional accounting in accord with the Standards. This applies equally to the affairs of companies that have not failed as it does to those, like HIH, that have.

Interestingly, examining these items reveals that the product of complying with GAAP produces amounts far in excess of those involved in transactions that have been the major bone of contention at the Royal Commission inquiries to date. Of note in this respect are the purported FAI 'reinsurance' transactions with those notorious and questionable 'side letters', the uncertainty associated with estimating HIH's (or its licensed insurance subsidiaries') future claim obligations and deliberations concerning the value of the net assets acquired by HIH in its FAI purchase. This further reinforces our belief that the Royal Commission's terms of reference were too limited. We await with interest to see if the Commissioner will make any recommendations in respect of accounting matters redolent to solvency.

HIH and auditor independence

Working within that framework for the enforcement of compliance with questionable corporate structures and Accounting and Auditing Standards, the alleged failures of ASIC, APRA and the audit mechanism are (perhaps) explicable. Yet that is not how the regulators appear to see it. The recent November 2000 settlement of the ASC claim against the auditors of Adsteam (see pp. 167–8) illustrates that. There it was noted that the covenant entered into by KPMG and ASIC ensuring enforcement of the Accounting Standards as part of the deal was a questionable development.[22] But for reasons different from those we offer. In the context of the HIH Liquidator's action against the APRA and the predicted action against the Commonwealth, consider the ASIC's position were the Standards to be deemed to produce misleading information as we argue here. Suggestions that making more such covenants in the future should be perceived as progress is problematic. It almost ensures that auditors' independence will be as shackled to the Accounting Standards in the future as it is now.

Rather than the regulatory rules and sanctions creating an orderly commercial environment, in their current form they militate against it. It would be interesting were the Royal Commission to contemplate whether mandated audit committees, rotating audit firms or partners, and greater-resourced regulatory agencies could achieve their objectives with the *system* as it is. A sizeable part of the media coverage on aspects of the HIH audit has been directed to drawing out connections between a non-executive director and former partner in Arthur Andersen, and the Arthur Andersen firm, the auditors of HIH. In many respects this has been fuelled by the Andersen firm's Enron-related woes. HIH certainly augmented the worldwide anxiety over the issue of auditor independence. Here, the Arthur Andersen firm was caught in the groundswell of concern regarding the US partner's alleged involvement in the Enron affair, Sunbeam's fall, the troubles at Waste Management, problems with The Baptist Foundation of Arizona and the like. Consistent with the contemporary audit paranoia, the concern was whether the Arthur Andersen auditor at the time HIH collapsed failed to entertain the necessary level of auditor independence, given the current and past personnel connections with the firm. The firm also provided non-audit services to HIH, as the US firm had at Enron. One might argue that such closeness with a company's affairs could provide 'an industry edge' not available where audit is the only professional activity provided. Primarily by virtue of a distorted understanding of the notion of auditor independence, those perceived advantages of multiple professional activities being undertaken by the auditor on behalf of the client receive equivocal responses.[23]

The (essentially *financially* driven) notion of auditor independence, to which the comments refer, is perceived to be the primary hazard in respect of audit. A likely more fruitful question is whether the manner in which auditors are directed by the Corporations Act, the Accounting and Auditing Standards, indeed facilitates any independence of the kind embraced by professionals. For the essence of professionalism is that practitioners are able to ply their skills, devise their processes and procedures, by drawing upon their specialised knowledge, vast experience in the field and the accumulated wisdom it brings. Contestably, the regulation of audit procedures falls well short of permitting that.

Peroration

We were cautious with our analysis of Bond Corporation, noting it was an *open verdict* on several issues – as even more than ten years after its demise there were still ongoing inquiries and some facts had remained hidden due to out-of-court settlements in some matters. This applies even more so with HIH as the Royal Commission continues, and many civil and criminal actions are pending as this book goes to print. Much has been revealed in the HIHRC inquiries but undoubtedly there will be more. And we have not had the benefit of being able to digest Justice Owen's considered assessment against that often contradictory evidence.

But some things seem clear. A reported 2000 financial year asset surplus of nearly $1 billion was eviscerated not long after producing an estimated 'black-hole deficit' under administration of more than $5 billion – a more than $6 billion difference! The reliance on general-purpose accounting numbers for assessing the capital adequacy of HIH (as for all insurance companies) was rejected by the regulator, APRA, and recourse was had to asset and liabilities ratio data required under the *Insurance Act*. But those data drew heavily upon Australian GAAP.

The regulator has accepted that it failed to monitor effectively HIH's capital adequacy as it was understaffed and under-resourced. That is not contested here. The point is, even with many more higher skilled staff and greater resourcing we question whether the conventional accounting data presented then (and likely to remain unchanged substantially after the Royal Commission and other inquiries are complete) would have assisted an informed monitoring of HIH's financial affairs, especially an adequate monitoring of its solvency.

Further, even if all the agreed structural 'best practice' corporate governance mechanisms are in place – audit committees, audit firm or auditor rotation, non-executive director/executive director balance – there needs to be some independent information oversight mechanism. There needs to be a quality, reliable, serviceable, information reporting system – an effective instrumentation system to act as the 'super independent' governance mechanism.

Finally, the revealed events at HIH confirm the corporate use of *groupthink* – a contentious aspect explored in the next two chapters.

Postscript – HIH Royal Commission Summing Up

The final submission of the Counsel Assisting the HIH Royal Commission should have sent a chill through corporate Australia with the suggestion that there *might* be more than 1,000 breaches of the law at HIH and FAI. 'Heads on poles day' lived up to expectations. 'Gloves were off' as Martin QC, Whyte SC, O'Bryan SC catalogued myriad 'adverse findings', including:

Name	Position	Critical Comments	Possible Breaches include:
Rodney Alder	FAI CEO and HIH non-executive director	Might have acted dishonestly on numerous occasions and might have failed to discharge his duties.	Might have breached four sections of the Corporations Law relating to use of his directorship to benefit himself, HSI and Cooper. Might have breached two sections of the Crimes Act. Eleven possible breaches of the Corporations Law relating to share trading. Eight possible breaches relating to improper use of position and information.
Ray Williams	HIH founder and CEO	Conduct might have been grossly improper, involved in possibly undesirable corporate governance and might not have met professional standards.	Might have breached 16 sections of the Corporations Law relating to dealings with the board and accounts. Twenty possible breaches related to HSI, dealings with the board, FFC transaction and the Ness transaction. Six possible breaches relating to the Allianz deal, the Hannover deal and loans to Frank Holland.
Brad Cooper	Entrepreneur	Conduct might have been grossly dishonest over a long period.	Might have breached 10 sections of the Corporations Law and seven possible breaches of the Crimes Act relating to HSI.
Dominic Fodera	HIH Chief Financial Officer	Might have been dishonest, might have breached his duties and might have been involved in undesirable corporate governance.	Might have breached up to 19 sections of Corporations Law relating to failing to ensure accounts were accurate, failing to inform board and auditors. Twelve possible breaches relating to deals with Hannover, Société Générale, General Colgne Re and National Indemnity.
Tim Mainprize	FAI Finance Director	Might have been involved in undesirable corporate governance relating to Project Firelight.	Might have breached two sections of Corporations Law relating to Project Firelight. Four possible breaches relating to FAI's Part B statement. Three possible breaches relating to duties.
Charles Abbott	HIH non-executive director	Might have been involved in undesirable corporate governance related to potential for conflict of interest.	Might have breached two sections of Corporations Law relating to payment of $1 million to Blake Dawson Waldron. Might have breached two sections of Corporations Law relating to consultancy payments to his private company. One possible breach relating to a Brad Cooper introductory fee.

continued

Name	Position	Critical Comments	Possible Breaches include:
Bill Howard	Head of HIH Financial Services and Investment Manager	Might have been involved in undesirable corporate governance.	Might have breached five sections of Corporations Law relating to failing to inform auditors. Two possible breaches of Corporations Law relating to Blake Dawson Waldron. Eight possible breaches of Corporations Law if deemed an 'officer' and one possible criminal charge in relation to HSI.

Source: Based on summary data from 'Counsel assisting's key submissions', *Australian Financial Review*, 17 January 2003, p. 56. Commissioner Neville Owen has stressed that the counsel assisting's submissions are not final recommendations. Parties noted here subsequently rejected the Counsel's submissions. The Commissioner's Report is still to emerge.

Quite properly, the final submission exercise sought to identify who *might* have been responsible, to detail the plethora of misdeeds, by ineptitude allegedly of many individuals – directors, accountants, advisors, actuaries, associates, regulators and the like. Subsequently those named have responded denying any wrongdoing. The Commissioner has made no comment as yet on the claims and counter-claims. Yet the full significance of this incredible document will be lost if the 'cult of the individual' obscures the deeper significance of its 4,236 pages. There are more significant implications for corporate Australia than the potential knee-capping of some of its previous high-flyers – high-flyers in the 1980s and earlier were also knee-capped – no doubt others will be in the future.

Underpinning each of those actions and inactions lies exposure of the folklore of conventional practice. The practice of how directors go about their business, and auditors theirs; how accountants, lawyers and financial advisors interact with their clients; how the Stock Exchange monitors listings; how (and the criteria by which) the corporate and prudential regulators (ASIC and APRA) function; the apparent ease with which Accounting Standards can be manipulated; and the questionable serviceability of the audited products of those Standards in disclosing the wealth and progress of companies even when manipulation is absent.

However, the HIH Royal Commission has revealed particulars that provide a rare insight into the generic defects in the corproate system. Systemic defects persist in the way corporate officers function, and in the system of accounting intended to disclose the financial outcomes of their actions. Reconstructing HIH's published financial statements on a mark-to-market basis would expose the folly embedded in the current 'capitalisation-of-expenditures'-based financial reporting system with which current Accounting Standards accord. Further, the perceived demotion of the 'true and fair criterion' and the consequences of audit reports being based upon compliance with those Standards would be revealed as placing even competent auditors on a 'mission impossible'; their 'independent state of mind' when preparing their 'audit opinion' could be shown to be highly contestable; the impossibility of determining corporate solvency with conventional accounting data would become apparent; and audit committees charged with ensuring Standards compliance would be exposed as most likely doing more harm than good, as would regulators pursuing the same objective.

PART VI

Regulatory Reforms

CHAPTER 16

Groupthink: Byzantine Structures*

… almost any economic goal that can be achieved by the creation of
a subsidiary can be equally well achieved by the creation of a division.

M.A. Eisenberg (1992, p. 4)

Paradoxically, one of accounting's grandest inventions to achieve financial clarification is its most virile medium for deception. From its introduction, giving special status to a *group* of related companies and the methods of consolidating its accounts has facilitated financial deception. Equally paradoxical, rather than abandoning it as its role in corporate crises has become obvious, both the regulatory bodies and the accounting profession have preferred 'patching-up' consolidation accounting. In the post-Enron reforms, the patching up continues. Indeed, there is no evidence that proscribing the group structure and consolidated financial statements has ever been considered seriously.

Ramsay and Stapledon[1] demonstrate that big business in Australia operates primarily through groups of companies related to one another through shareholding, common directors or managers, and other controlling or influencing mechanisms. For decades, corporate groups with their complex structures and their idiosyncratic consolidation accounting have been the somewhat protected vehicles for obscuring corporate misbehaviour and the means of public deception, often unintentional, sometimes deliberate.

Connecting many companies to create a financial empire certainly appealed as much to the 1980s' and 1990s' entrepreneurs as it had throughout the 1960s, the 1970s and earlier years. And the attraction continues in the post-1990s, if, for example, the well-publicised HIH, One.Tel, Ansett, Enron and WorldCom affairs are any indication.

Financial commentary on corporate collapse often refers to the simultaneous failure of a number of related companies – the corporate domino effect. Prized for the promise of managerial synergism, groups of holding, subsidiary and associated companies (in the current idiom: chief entity and controlled entities, etc.), have proven to be a mechanism of financial obfuscation in many of the cases referred to previously. Yet, curiously, even now the Corporations Act does not define a corporate group, other than in terms of itself – circumlocutiously as a structure, rather than an entity with specific financial, economic and social dimensions. It remains a vague concept, the exact function of which is equally indeterminate. Judicial dicta, for example, Mason J in *Walker v. Wimborne* and Murray J in *Re Enterprise Gold Mines NL* suggest 'corporate groups' comprise: 'two or more corporations that are affiliated in a manner that depends in significant part on stock ownership ... an affiliation ... typically structural and not so easily terminated'.[2]

In reality, a multiplicity of factors underpins the development of corporate groups, as Eisenberg explains: 'unlike many or most business structures they frequently do not represent an adaptation to economic forces',[3] and: 'almost any economic goal that can be achieved by the creation of a wholly-owned subsidiary can be equally well-achieved by the creation of a division'.[4]

Nonetheless, most corporate business is done through groups – holding companies and their subsidiaries – often extremely complex group structures at that. Apart from being such a useful device for financial deception, one is virtually at a loss to identify any other necessary purpose for them (excluding taxation considerations, applicable mainly in the past), other than to exploit a divisionalisation of the limited liability privilege that corporations enjoy. The claim that it is necessary to further economic risk-taking is difficult to accept, given that the limited liability benefits would already apply with a single company using divisions or branches

Anglo-American financial history is replete with organisations having complex group structures, often comprising hundreds of subsidiaries (as in the cases examined here), many wholly-owned. Governing legal rules are varied, but ultimately they are always geared to enable the collective entities to take on the appearance of, and act as, a single company. And that potentially is at the peril of those dealing with *it*.

Beneath the veil

Whereas commentators have suggested financial markets are becoming more complex and sophisticated,[5] the late 1980s, throughout the 1990s and beyond have been little different from the 1960s and 1970s (even 1890s Australia), when it comes to avenues for exploiting group structures and their accounting. Perhaps the increasing complexity of financial instruments has exacerbated the exploitation.

Essentially the *modus operandi* has been common. Assets have been threaded through the web of related companies – backwards and forwards, round and about. The origins of the transactions in many instances are almost impossible to trace. Adding an international entity to the exercise completes the complexity. In the 1980s, Bond Corp's dealings with the Porta di Roma land via an off-shore-related entity, the back-to-back loans integral to the Bond/Bell

Resources 'cash cow' transaction[6] and others – for example, one Bond Corp transaction reportedly involved 25 companies – the Rothwells, Linter related-party transactions, Spedley Securities' round robin and Adsteam's inter-company share and loan transactions, all bear witness to that. So too did Stanhill's land sales and round-robin payments, Minsec's dealings with Robe River shares and Cambridge Credit Corporation's myriad international company deals, decades earlier.[7] In the 1990s that practice continued and, human nature being what it is, it will into the future as long as the existing group structure is permitted. Development and the standardisation of consolidation accounting techniques have not removed the capacity to obscure financial consequences of group transactions. To the contrary, they have given them an undeserved legitimacy.

Contrary to the view held by some that the changed 1990s regulatory environment provided adequate checks and balances, private companies have continued to be the intermediaries through which assets are shuffled, money is funnelled and then used to purchase shares in, or otherwise trade with, the prime public company. Transactions in 1990 between Coles Myer Ltd and related entities associated with the 'Yannon' transaction, and those later in the decade between HIH and its related entities, were indicative of the way in which the perception is, as noted in the 'leader' to the 1960s' *Reid Murray* case, that private and public interests may become entangled.

Granted, some particulars of the 1980s and subsequent cases may have been slightly novel due to the use of put and call options on asset transfers and a greater use of trusts registered in overseas tax havens; and in current cases like Enron the use of derivatives and special purpose entities. However, the generic characteristic – the lack of public disclosure – underlying the concerns is not novel.[8] Ultimately group structures and the idiosyncratic consolidation accounting for them have been perennial vehicles for masking corporate misbehaviour, the archetypal means of public deception (see fn. 15, Chapter 17).[9]

Despite the image of size, solidarity and perpetuity generated by large corporate groups, history shows that once one of the related companies topples the rest may fall like a line of dominoes. Westmex in the 1980s and HIH and One.Tel in the 1990s were seminal Australian examples. But, it is also possible for any solvent company within a group to walk away from the obligations of the insolvent if they *legally* can, as occurred with the MLC at H.G. Palmer in the 1960s and Air New Zealand with Ansett in 2001. Corporate solidarity is a financial and legal myth. Sentiment does not get in the way of corporate business. That is a major reason why corporate cross guarantees generally, and the ASC Deed of Cross Guarantee specifically, came into existence, and CASAC's proposals *opting-in* selected subsidiaries were developed.

Figure 16.1 Royal Mail global trade routes and related corporate shareholder linkages (%)

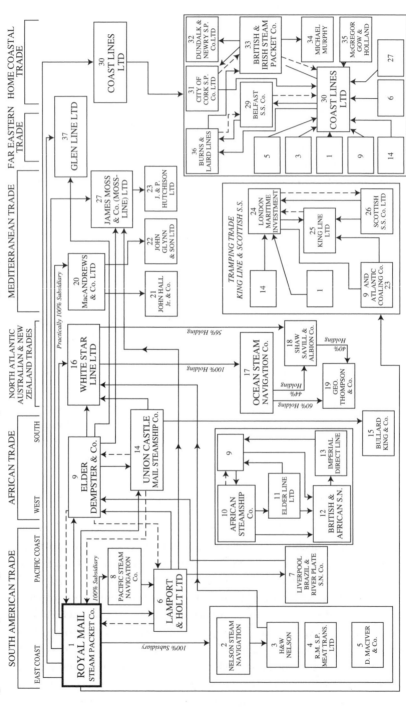

Note: Numbers in the diagram refer to Royal Mail related companies operating on various trade routes. Full details appear in *The Economist*, 5 March 1932, p. 525. Further details of significance of the structure to the secret reserves manoeuvres are outlined in Green and Moss (1982, especially Chs 5 and 6). *Source:* Anon, 'The Royal Mail scheme', *The Economist*, 5 March 1932, pp. 521–5 at p. 525.

Modern commercial arrangements through groups have a long international lineage. Complex trust-based administrative and financial arrangements in the United States in the early 1900s, the group structures and the special methods of accounting for them, were fellow travellers. So were utility and other investment trust companies in the 1920s. Samuel Insull's inverted pyramid of gas and electric light companies, Ivar Kreuger's complex international match empire, and Lord Kylsant's secret reserve manoeuvres through the Royal Mail subsidiaries in the United Kingdom, for instance, are notorious examples of the exploitation of corporate groups for purposes of obfuscation.

The significance of the aggregation of assets through the complex group structure and the financing avenues this opened at RMSP (Figure 16.1) is appositely summed up as being: '... the facility it offered for maintaining in power men who had ... become mere personal money-spinners, their personal position and gain being secured to them.'[10] That comment aptly captures the essence of *groupthink*. It has a virtual timeless applicability, as applicable equally to the complex arrangements in the 1890s British and Australian land and mining boom vehicles as it is to the 1920s US investment trust combines, pre–World War II Japanese *zaibatsus* and post-war *keiretzus*, and Korean *chaebols*. Intertwined corporate webs facilitated round-robin and back-to-back loan transactions in 1980s corporate Australia and the myriad inter-group transactions by HIH.

The issue of groupthink was integral to the 1995–96 Rothwells' conspiracy case where it was claimed by the prosecution that round-robin transactions at balance date between a private company, L.R. Connell and Partners and the two public companies Spedley Securities and Rothwells Limited were used to mask the true state of the financial affairs at Rothwells. As Chapter 12 revealed, the notorious Bond/Bell Resources 'cash cow' transaction had all the hallmarks of *enterprise* rather than *entity* action underpinning its *modus operandi*, irrespective of whether fraud was the motive.

Entanglements of companies have featured in the most notorious of Australian collapses. Consider the publicly disclosed outcome of such entanglements in the 1990 complex loan arrangements under cross guarantee at Hooker Corporation. Figure 16.2 only illustrates the internal debt relationships – there were more than $1.5 billion of external debts also to be unravelled at Hooker. Administrators took nearly ten years to unscramble this financial morass and determine the amounts the separate creditors were entitled to and due from which companies. And then this was only achieved through compromise, relying on *ad-hoc* methods and ignoring the cross guarantees![11]

Even with modern-day computer power it is virtually impossible to track through those types of corporate mazes, let alone determine unambiguously the financial implications of transactions within them. An essential feature of

Figure 16.2 Internal loans between the Hooker Corporation 'closed group' companies as at date of provisional liquidation

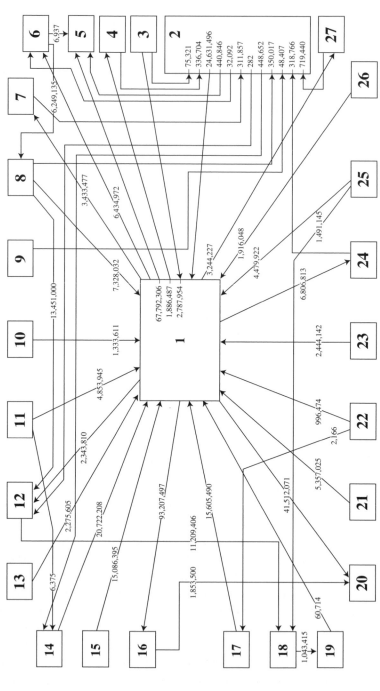

Note: The above arrows and amounts depict outstanding loan balances between subsidiary companies within the Hooker Corporation 'closed group,' at the time of the Hooker Scheme of Arrangement in 1991. See also p. 289.

Source: Based on Hooker *Statement of Affairs* dated 30 June 1990.

groupthink is that only the parties to the transaction really know, and believe *only* they need to know, the intricacies. Consolidation accounting, in many ways, helps to obscure them to outsiders and, we suggest, perhaps to most of the insiders too.

The 1990s' WA Inc. Royal Commission examining the 1989 Rothwells collapse provides ample testimony of this. There were more than 44,000 pages of transcript. Regarding Rothwells, 80,000 exhibits alone were prepared by investigators and a summary investigators' report 'commissioned to piece together Rothwells accounts' amounted to a staggering 2,500 pages. Consider the difficulty facing those attempting to untangle numerous related-party transactions in the 1995–96 Rothwells conspiracy case. There, over 29,000 financial exhibits were computer imaged to assist in that task. Similarly, the complexity of the transactions pertinent to the Linter group case was revealed with the disclosure that 120,000 pages of documents had been computer imaged for ease of access in the proposed hearings.[12] Clearly, financial analysis for ongoing or collapsed firms was never meant to be easy. In the Linter case parties were spared the possible embarrassment of publicly trying to unravel this matter when it was settled out of court. Notwithstanding Laurie Connell's death, the Rothwells conspiracy case continued, creating even greater headaches for those trying to understand what happened.

The 2002 HIH Royal Commission has revealed similar complexity, alleged intrigue, and obfuscation characterising the company's collapse. The scale of that Commission mirrors the WA Inc. Rothwells Commission – the number of exhibits exceeds 1.5 million. In particular, what has been revealed to date shows that the auditors' and regulators' tasks appear no easier now than they were in previous decades. Arguably, the incongruities characterising groups and the accounting for them exacerbate the difficulties. Everyday association with group financial data does not have the luxury of years of inquiry and hundreds of analysts to undertake those tasks. Our *mission impossible* tag remains apt.

Even more disturbing is the problem of assessing which of the transactions between related companies are genuine. For ongoing companies, conventional consolidated accounting techniques purportedly make that easy – the consolidation elimination rules pertaining to related-party transactions have only to be applied without letting the financial truth of the transactions get in the way. Under consolidation procedures, all within-group transactions are assumed 'from an economic group perspective' to be shams. It is mandatory that data relating to those transactions be eliminated from calculation of 'group' profits and losses, and 'group' financial position. But that is as useless a way of getting at the financial truth as assuming that they were all genuine simply because there was normal documentation. What is needed is an accounting mechanism by which the actual financial results of the transactions are truthfully presented, irrespective of whether collusion occurred.

At the heart of the matter is the fictional notion of 'the group'. Taking a contrary view, group trading has caused many to question the separate legal entity principle that underlies corporate identity and commercial practice. There is a suggestion within legal circles that it be supplanted by the group enterprise model in which the related companies become an identifiable enterprise.[13] At issue is the divergence between the traditional legal treatment of groups and purported commercial reality.

Some lawyers have asserted that 'there is evidence of a general tendency [on the part of the judiciary] to ignore the separate legal entities of various companies within a group, and instead to look at the economic entity of the whole group'[14] – (as Lord Denning said) to 'draw aside the [corporate] veil', to 'pull off the mask'.[15] However, Professor Baxt has observed that, generally speaking, the courts are reluctant to ignore the corporate veil in order to ascertain the 'true' financial or commercial position.[16] This is a view shared by others,[17] as recently confirmed in Baxt and Lane.[18] At best, the commercial position is confusing.

Divergence between commercial practice and legal dicta has created increasing pressures for change. So much so that Rogers CJ Comm. Div. observed 'that the whole issue of the separateness of the corporate entity be re-examined in the context of the modern commercial contract'.[19] Further challenging the conventional wisdom, Rogers CJ has noted: '[I]t may be desirable for Parliament to consider whether this distinction between the law and commercial practice should be continued?'[20] This was not the first time that he had found the distinction troublesome. In 1989 he had referred to the law's 'scant regard to the commercial reality'[21] – a similar judicial comment to that which had appeared in the UK context even earlier.[22] Analysis of the regulation of corporate groups in Australia perhaps justifies a similar stance.[23] But disagreement over what that commercial reality *is* underlies all such comments. For the essence of groupthink being touted as commercial reality seems to be anything but that. Groups are being presented as commercial reality. Yet most of the financial, social and legal settings in which groups operate clearly indicates they are not.

Material canvassed in CASAC's *Corporate Groups' Final Report* (2000), including the controversial *ex ante* lifting of the corporate veil contained in the 'opting-in' proposals, as well as Australia's *CLERP 9* (2002) reforms, augment the debate.

A push for reassessment is evident in the 1992 changes to Australian insolvency administration procedures. Changes to the then Corporations Law required directors of a parent company to be held liable for any debts that a subsidiary company incurs from trading when insolvent.[24] Also, in certain cases, sections 588V-X deem the holding company liable for debts incurred by a subsidiary when it was already insolvent or the directors of the holding company would have expected it likely to become insolvent. That assessing solvency continues to be problematic is illustrated in the HIH case.[25]

An emphasis on solvency and its accounting measure has become of primary importance to directors in their general administration of companies. The solvency statements they have to make each year under the Corporations Law (subsection 301 (5)) places them at considerable risk if the data upon which they rely for that purpose are not indicative of their company's capacity to meet its debts.[26] Clearly, directors face a considerable risk in respect of individual companies and an exacerbated risk in respect of 'closed groups' of related companies where cross guarantees are in place.

Cross guarantees and 'closed group' accounting relief

Unease in that confused setting has spawned the *avant-garde*. It has encouraged regulatory bodies – and, with recent changes to the Corporations Act, the legislature – to circumvent the separate legal entity principle. This is most explicit in the way that commercial arrangements have been formalised by NCSC, ASC and ASIC Class Orders for standard-form, regulatory-approved indemnity or cross guarantees between a holding company (chief or parent entity) and its wholly-owned subsidiaries (controlled entities). As noted in the previous chapter, initially under an NCSC Class Order Deed, relief from the accounting and audit reporting requirements was granted to wholly-owned subsidiaries, so long as there was compliance with certain deed-imposed constraints. The purported security *quid pro quo* was that parent and subsidiary companies enter into indemnity arrangements – to 'severally, unconditionally and irrevocably' guarantee each other's debts. By contrast, no such guarantee existed *between* the subsidiaries of the 'closed group'.

However, relief was conditional upon the directors of the holding company including in the Directors' Statement a solvency statement 'as to whether there are reasonable grounds to believe that the guarantor company will be able to meet any obligations or liabilities to which it is, or may become, subject by virtue of the deed'.[27]

Those arrangements initially proved very popular (Table 16.1), though post-1991 anecdotal comment suggested a decline in their use. However, subsequent empirical work by two of the current authors indicates that the initial popularity has been maintained.

When introducing the indemnity (cross guarantee) and relief arrangements in 1985, the NCSC claimed that there would be very large savings to

Table 16.1 Wholly-owned subsidiaries' class order, 1986/87 to 1998/99

Financial year	No. of deeds	No. of subsidiaries granted relief	Financial year	No. of deeds	No. of subsidiaries granted relief
1986/87	219	1,155	1994/95	71	442
1987/88	244	1,525	1995/96	50	342
1988/89	299	1,737	1996/97	113	812
1989/90	306	1,700	1997/98	53	321
1990/91	220	1,650	1998/99	80	534
1991/92	208	2,674			
1992/93	273	2,488			
1993/94	89	808			

Source: Prepared from copies of original deeds supplied by officers of the ASC. Data for 1994/95 to 1998/99 is still to be confirmed. They exclude Assumption Deed and Revocation Deed data.

business, especially to the thousands of wholly-owned Australian subsidiaries. This would be achieved without sacrificing investor protection where the holding company was prepared to guarantee the debts of those subsidiaries.[28] An ASC rationale for extending the creditor cross-claim indemnity to a cross guarantee by all companies within the 'closed group' was to ensure that a wholly-owned subsidiary effectively 'pools its assets and liabilities with its holding company' when a winding up occurs.[29] The ASC also stated that consolidated accounting data would provide investors and creditors with the most useful data in respect of a 'closed group'.

Faith in the virtue of consolidation accounting seems unrelenting. Both the accounting profession and the legislature have sought to tighten the rules relating to consolidation accounting. Yet neither appears to have canvassed the idea of dumping consolidation practices. The Corporations Legislation and the Accounting Standard AASB 1024 have broadened the base of the 'economic entity' to which consolidation accounting applies – every parent entity that is a reporting entity and controls one or more companies or business entities is required to prepare a consolidated balance sheet, consolidated income and consolidated cash flow statements, and entities other than companies are now required to be consolidated if they are *controlled* by the parent (or chief) entity. Though what such an entity actually comprises is far from definitive, as was aptly demonstrated in a 1993 dispute between Washington H. Soul Pattinson (WHSP), the Australian Stock Exchange and the ASC over whether the 49.84 per cent share of Brickworks Ltd gave Soul Pattinson control and hence should be consolidated. Reportedly the directors agreed to the ASC's request to consolidate Brickworks' accounts with WHSP, adding the disclaimer that:

> such a consolidation inflates the profit and net tangible assets of WHSP so as to be misleading to its shareholders and to potential investors in WHSP ... [Accordingly, Directors] disclaim any responsibility to shareholders and/or investors who may suffer loss as a result of relying on such misleading information, the responsibility for which rests wholly with the ASC.[30]

This was a strange twist to the general principle of *caveat emptor* and similar disclaimer clauses. We wait with interest to see the outcome of the first test case.

Other forms of group accounting reporting are no longer permitted. The prior companies legislation in the 1960s, 1970s and 1980s permitted a variety of combinations of the separate statements of constituent companies and consolidated statements. But the basic tenet of consolidation, that it is a means of ignoring the separate legal entity by accounting for the 'economic group', has been retained. Retained too are the basic consolidation procedures, which have been in vogue since about the 1930s following the appearance in the United Kingdom of Garnsey's celebrated 1923 *Holding Companies and their Published Accounts: Limitations of a Balance Sheet*.[31] And, it is suggested, retained also is the potential for obfuscation regarding subsidiaries' activities:

> The ... extra corporate layer reduces the likelihood that someone will even detect the wrongdoing, much less bring suit to correct it. ... reporting requirements ... demand little disclosure of subsidiary activity. The parent ... may consolidate information about the financial performance and condition of the subsidiary into its own financial statements.[32]

Debate concerning creditors' and shareholders' rights in group liquidations (especially in 'closed-group' liquidations) exemplifies the incorrigible entanglements which consolidation accounting helps to mask. There, it is crucial for directors to be able to assess the solvency of each company within a corporate group. Enter the wonder-world of *accounting's groupthink* – consolidation accounting.

Prior to entering that uncertain world, it is rewarding to examine some recent cases to illustrate the continued application of groupthink, and that the capital boundary problem persists. They also provide support for Baxt and Lane's (1998) claim of 'directors' schizophrenia'. We analyse briefly: the 1998 Patrick/MUA dispute, Enron's implosion in 2001, One.Tel's overextending and Air New Zealand's 2002 casting off of Ansett.

MUA/Patricks' intra-group therapy

Elements of the Patrick/MUA dispute are tentatively unravelled from the limited data publicly available on the Patrick's 1997 *September Transactions*.[33] Leading corporate lawyers Baxt and Lane observed that:

> [the Patrick/MUA] example highlights the issues that arise and the problems posed for directors of different companies within a group. This scenario, which will no doubt return to the court in due course will be a fascinating one against which to measure some of the [*CLERP* and other] proposals for reform and the way in which the law has developed.[34]

Industrial and legal disputes in the 1990s provide illustrations of the complexities resulting from selective recourse to the *group* and *separate legal entity* notions in the management of corporate affairs. They highlight the *capital boundary* problem. Examples involving the entitlements of employees from insolvent operating companies include employee dismissals at Cobar and Woodlawn mines, Steel Tank and Pipes, and the attempted dismissals at Patrick Stevedores.

Press speculation suggests a situation similar to that at Patrick Stevedores had occurred in the Australian textiles industry in 1990. On that occasion it was reported that employees in a Gazal group company discovered after a 'major event' that 'a separate company that had no assets and only massive debts' employed them.[35] Allegedly, the employees were frustrated from obtaining suitable financial redress against any specific 'asset rich' separate legal entity within the Gazal group due to the separate legal entity impediment to accessing the 'pool' of group assets. This impediment is endemic to the holding company/subsidiary company's structure, which is a feature of Australia's corporate sector.

The Patrick affair is a prominent example of the effect of restructuring on creditors' rights and the limited potential for their protection through provision of consolidated accounting data and the potential protection afforded by group financing cross guarantees.

Patrick: Creditor exposure

What follows illustrates the ease and legitimacy with which assets can be relocated within a corporate group to the detriment of the creditors. It reveals how approximately $228 million of bank finance raised by one or more companies within the Patrick and other sub-groups was used legitimately for transactions within the parent, Lang Corporation Group. It shows that consolidated accounting data do not reveal any shuffling of funds between those group companies. To the contrary, the consolidation mechanism eliminates all evidence of it. Obfuscation of the domicile of the assets and liabilities of the separate companies is characteristic of consolidated accounting data – indeed, it is an essential outcome of applying the group entity concept. In accord with the group convention, Notes to Lang's 1997 Accounts (p. 25) reveal that security for the externally raised finance included charges over tangible and other assets of the *various* entities within the economic entity. This arrangement further demonstrates the ongoing potential for and practice of a commercially motivated selective balancing of the separate and group entity principles.[36]

Consistent with legislatively and professionally endorsed practices, consolidated accounting statements neither revealed *which* companies within the larger economic group or the smaller Patrick Stevedores sub-group owed moneys to one another, nor *which* of the related companies were in debt to external financiers. What is disclosed in respect of the parent's accounts is the *aggregate* of loans made to and from Lang Corporation Limited to its subsidiaries. Regarding the consolidated accounts, all intra-group transactions are eliminated as part of the conventional consolidation process. Though in accord with professional Accounting Standards, legislation and the ASX's continuous disclosure requirements, it is contestable whether that variety of disclosure is properly described as providing continuous relevant disclosure necessary to achieve an informed market.

The Patrick/MUA affair suggests that the propriety of corporate restructuring and selectively bankrupting an 'employer' subsidiary with limited capital, when other group companies are relatively 'asset rich', is questionable. It highlights the capital boundary problem. Such selectivity can produce a scenario in which an 'employer' subsidiary becomes insolvent, and its employees dismissed in circumstances likely to deny them financial satisfaction of their holiday, superannuation and leave entitlements.

Bend it like Enron!

Enron was adept at bending convention. Predictably the group structure and the accounting intrigues it facilitated were a feature of Enron's dramatic and, for most it would seem, *unexpected* collapse late in 2001. The demise of Enron, then the seventh-largest listed US company, has had major ramifications for the United States and other major capitalist economies and was a major factor in the disintegration of the Andersen audit firm.

Enron's collapse spawned a new financial condition, 'Enronitis', referring to the securities market's loss of confidence due to concerns that accounting practices were being abused, that the market was not being fully informed.

Enron was an exemplar conglomerate. Prior to its financial demise it was the leading energy trader in the United States, innovator of new wave energy contracting. Formed in 1985 by a merger between two state-based natural gas companies, its main activity was to operate interstate gas pipelines. Its early share price reflected those beginnings and it was not until the early 1990s that its share price nearly doubled to around US$20. It then began a meteoric rise as the US stock market also soared in the mid-to-late '90s. Enron's shares peaked in 2000 at around US$89. It enjoyed corporate celebrity status. Ex Harvard Business Review Editor, Kurtzen refers to Enron as that 'great radical innovator'. Only a year later its share price would dive to under US$1.

By then, Enron had diversified into trading non-energy-related commodities – including new weather derivatives. Its buying and selling activities extended into bandwidth and numerous e-business operations. It was by then significant on the world's energy stage. Its investments resulted in a complex group arrangement with hundreds of subsidiary and other related entities, including Special Purpose Entities (SPEs), as illustrated in Figure 16.3

The major transformation in the mid-1990s into e-business activities, such as Enron online, also resulted in Enron being a major user of derivative financing. As the group diagram suggests, those activities and their financing were undertaken through myriad corporate entities – some consolidated, others not – numerous limited liability partnerships (LLPs) and joint ventures – the

Figure 16.3 Diagrammatic illustration of the Enron Corporate Structure

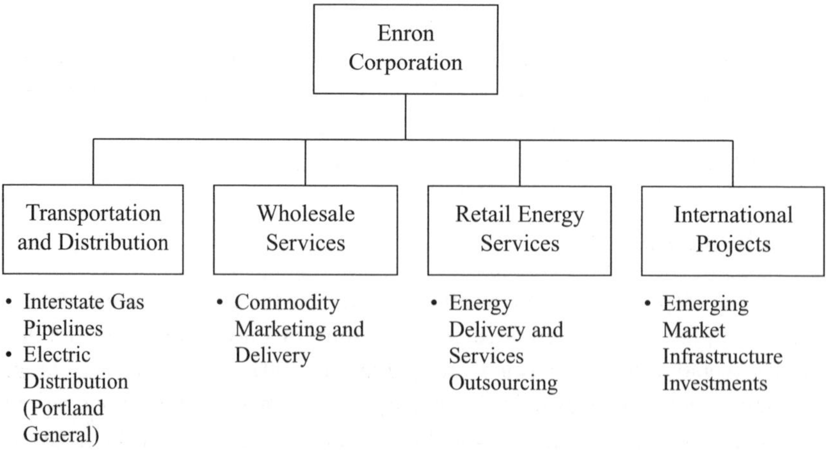

Source: Enron Corporation Organizational Meeting, December 12, 2001, New York, NY, Presentation to Creditors, Powerpoint Format
(www.enron/com/corp/pressroom/chapter11/creditorpresentation.ppt)

SPEs. In typical failure fashion, it would be the inability to service Enron's burgeoning debt that brought about its fall. It had been able to continue to raise significant tranches of debt financing by continuously reporting profits. But *reported* as opposed to *real* profits differed dramatically.

Enron, it is claimed, *bent* the applicable US GAAP group accounting rules. A well-publicised aspect of Enron's operations was the use it made of those SPEs, allegedly to keep debt off the group consolidated balance sheet and to hide numerous losses. This was possible because US GAAP worked within an ownership criterion to determine which entities are subsidiaries and when their financials had to be consolidated. It was relatively easy for Enron to manipulate the ownership level of the SPEs below the statutory 3 per cent benchmark. It is to be noticed that that *deconsolidation* tactic is similar to mechanisms that supposedly were employed by Spalvins in respect of Adsteam. Then, as recently with Enron, the weight of the criticism has been more directed at the alleged manipulation of the rule, than at the ineptness of the rule being so manipulable, and in any event with consolidation not having any direct relationship with showing the financial consequences of transactions between the related entities.

Enron's SPEs served the same purpose as Adsteam's judicious use of controlling shareholdings. They also achieved a similar end to Cambridge's interposing of an intermediary. Each facilitated taking debt off the balance sheet. But they did not bring Enron undone financially.

Enron's so-called mark-to-market (its mark-to-model) front-end loading of profits (just as had occurred at Cambridge) on long-term energy contracts (some over 20 years) allowed it to book 'profits' as 'earned' upon the contract being signed. The SPEs thus channelled 'profits' into Enron, allowing it to borrow externally. When the contracts fell over, so did the SPEs and in consequence, Enron.

Enron's use of the phrase 'mark-to-market', in respect of its basis for the valuation of its energy contracts, is misleading. Fusaro and Miller explain that in 1991 Enron picked up and applied to its energy futures the technique of the financial industries in marking-to-market securities, on the basis of the existing market prices. They explain:

The mark-to-market approach is standard operating procedure for a financial institution that invests in stocks ... The problem that Enron faced is that many of its contracts were very difficult to value – there was no price in an active market to use as a reference point. The alternative, which was also common use on Wall Street, was to value the contract using a computer model, a process known as mark-to-model. Indeed, in many investment-banking circles, bankers would lapse into the illusion that computer-model-generated prices were real prices and misleadingly refer to mark-to-model prices as mark-to-market prices. Enron not only fell into the same trap, but as its competition caught up with it and profits were harder to come by, it would manipulate the [discounting-based] models to its advantage.[37]

The distinction between mark-to-market and mark-to-model techniques has important financial implications. Whereas the former draws upon the corroborable evidence of actual market prices, the latter is purely a calculation that entails the estimate of future revenues and expenses and more often than not the discounting of them to derive their 'net present values'. It appears that besides investment bankers, other observers have also fallen into the 'trap' that Fusaro and Miller speak of. Loren Fox, for example, is highly critical of Enron's use of 'mark-to-market' valuations.[38] In using the booking of 'paper-profits' on movements in share prices, he clearly mistakes Enron's model-based 'synthetic' prices for real market prices. Since Enron had used the mark-to-model basis from 1991, it would appear that the SEC and other regulators did not understand the critical distinction either!

Claims have been made that Enron's use of the SPEs to hide the group's aggregative outside debt could not have arisen were the United States to have had a *control* criterion governing groups, as in Australia's AASB 1024. The idea is that those aspects of Enronitis could not happen here. At best that is a simplified view of matters. Were the SPEs to have been consolidated by Enron, outside debt would have emerged on the consolidated balance sheet, but to whom and by how much each member of the group was a net outside debtor would be no clearer than when the aggregate outside indebtedness was unknown. Further, in the absence of cross guarantees, aggregative outside indebtedness is largely irrelevant, for it is the individual companies and other entities comprising the group that are indebted, and not the group *per se*. Knowing the total outside indebtedness on a group basis under the Australian consolidation criterion is of questionable financial significance. And we should note that were the SPEs to have been consolidated, the indebtedness between the group members would be eliminated in the process.

Consolidation then would provide information of aggregative outside indebtedness that has no particular significance in the absence of cross guarantees, and would obscure information regarding inside indebtedness. A sensible financial analysis requires information on both the internal and external indebtedness of the group members, from which it can be determined which are net internal or external debtors or creditors, and in respect of whom. This aspect is explored in the Appendix to Chapter 17.

One.Tel's overextending

One.Tel was the creation in the mid-1990s of Paul Barry's 'Rich Kids' entrepreneurs, Jodee Rich, Brad Keeling, and Mark Silbermann, with financial assistance facilitated by, *inter alia*, Lachlan Murdoch and James Packer.[39] Launched in Sydney, Australia in May 1995, it was described as a global tele-communications group with more than 200 companies offering a fully inte-grated product list including low-cost international and national calls, Internet services, prepaid and post-paid calling cards, plus GSM mobile phone services.

In the 1960s' boom, conglomerates were all the rage. Peters and Waterman's KISS had not emerged. The 1980s was the era of the entrepreneur. In the 1990s telcos were the vehicles to exploit the market upturn as the cash spigot from stock market punters was turned on.

One.Tel's stellar rise and demise was an exemplar. It was a typical Argenti *Type I* 'still-born' corporate trajectory. One.Tel's failure epitomises the con-sequences of overtrading, overcapitalisation, marketing ploys that entailed cash outflows impossible to sustain, and the problems endemic of *recognising* revenues ahead of the likely related cash flows. With these tactics, One.Tel simply over-reached its cash flows. Exacerbating those cash problems appears to have been an inadequate customer billing system. Cash management issues proved critical at One.Tel, as they do in all failures. Further, it has been alleged that there the board were provided with incorrect internal cash flow data, there-by exacerbating One.Tel's financial fate. Irrespective of the veracity of those claims, it is clear that what is needed is an accounting system (producing both internal and externally available data) that tracks cash or cash equivalent flows. These data are critical in any solvency assessment.

One.Tel's accounting practices have been under examination in respect of other matters. Mention has been made that its spectrum license was valued at the 'cost' amount of over $500 million, notwithstanding dramatic changes in the telco sector and the spectrum license market in particular, since the license was acquired. Then there was the issue of a $90 million prepaid advertising asset. Reportedly, the administrators have written-off this 'asset'. The question really is when or if expenditure on advertising should be reported as an asset? A further weakness at One.Tel was an alleged inadequate internal management accounting system, causing One.Tel to cost its products improperly – a recipe for financial disaster.

The full particulars of the collapse will undoubtedly be revealed after assessment of matters unearthed in the ongoing inquiries.

Orphaning Ansett

By clipping Ansett's wings, Air New Zealand brought about a curious confluence of circumstances. Chapter 9 described how in 1979 directors of Ansett
Transport Industries had cut loose its 49 per cent owned satellite Associated
Securities Ltd without any concern that it was ASL's major shareholder and, for
all intents and purposes, its *parent*. In that respect it acted entirely within the
law, as indeed had the MLC with respect to its subsidiary H.G. Palmer over
a decade earlier.

Ansett was placed in Voluntary Administration on 12 September 2001. As
part of the administration, early in 2002 Ansett was orphaned by Air New
Zealand. But, the circumstances were said to be such that the relationship
between the two was greater than that between most parent companies and their
subsidiaries. They were said to share many functions – including accounting
and other financial operating arrangements. It was alleged that they shared
maintenance regimes and spare-parts inventories. They functioned in the
same industry.[40] Clearly, when push comes to shove, legally the capital boundary is unequivocal. Air New Zealand and Ansett were separate companies –
though they shared functions, the ownership of assets lay where legal ownership resided; debt lay with the company against which it could legally be
enforced. In orphaning Ansett, presumably the major shareholder of Air New
Zealand, the New Zealand government, acted in the best interests of its company. Such actions, however, raised concerns that Ansett may have continued
to trade while insolvent, and that there may have been some conflicts between
the actions of the directors of Ansett and Air New Zealand.

Again, despite all the misleading talk of *group* assets, liabilities, revenues
and expenses, and against the background of all the assessments of *group* –
profits and losses, rate of return, earnings per share, and the usual *group*
financial indicators – the separate legal entity principle of *Salomon v Salomon*
prevailed. Perhaps that was convenient for Air New Zealand, as earlier it had
been for the MLC, Patricks, and those others over time that had sought the
refuge within the capital boundary. Ironically for Ansett, it now found itself
quite properly outside the boundary fence. It would seem that Baxt and Lane's
'directors' schizophrenia' is clearly evident here.

The circumstances led ASIC to investigate. It concluded that it was unlikely
that evidence could be adduced to suggest that there was any impropriety in the
actions of Ansett's directors. They noted in a press release:

> On 14 September 2001 ASIC commenced a wide-ranging investigation into
> the Ansett collapse. Since that time, extensive enquiries have been conducted
> in Australia, New Zealand and Singapore involving a comprehensive review

of company records and examinations of directors and other officers. Counsel
on a variety of issues has provided legal advice. ASIC has now reached the view
that based on the evidence currently available there is no realistic prospect for
successfully prosecuting the directors of Ansett for breach of their general duties
of care under the Corporations Act or for insolvent trading. Senior Counsel
confirms this view. The factors contributing to this conclusion include the steps
taken by the Ansett directors to obtain financial support from their parent
company, Air New Zealand Limited, including a letter of comfort for $400 million
for working capital commitments in August 2001.[41]

It is now time to enter the wonder-world of *accounting's groupthink* –
consolidation accounting.

CHAPTER 17

Groupthink – Group Therapy: Consolidation Accounting*

It is ... misleading to imply that a group can have a state of affairs or can earn profits... no set of consolidated accounts can give a true and fair view of anything.

Accounting Standards Review Committee (1978, pp. 128–9)

Whether consolidation accounting practices should be tolerated is contestable. Accounting data are reasonably expected to reflect financial reality in its legal, social and economic contexts. And whereas reality might be less than transparent, consolidated financial data cannot by any stroke of the imagination be considered a realistic reflection of the aggregative wealth and progress of the related companies. For conventionally prepared, consolidated accounting data are pseudo aggregations of their separate conventional accounting data – some as they appear in the originals, some adjusted to accommodate presumed, often counterfactual, characteristics of the transactions between them.

Continued support for consolidation accounting proceeds more by default than design. Perhaps misunderstanding within both the accounting and legal professions of the nature and financial significance of the information in consolidated statements is the primary contributor to that default. Specifically, it is contestable whether the ASC's (as it was then) assertion that 'consolidated accounts ... [provide] more meaningful information for users of the accounts' is sustainable. Equally contestable is the claim that enforcement of these 'new requirements' by the accounting profession will ensure that 'most of the major and well-used opportunities for the manipulation ... under the previous Companies Code will disappear'.[1]

In supporting a mandatory legislative requirement to prepare consolidated accounts, some of the judiciary and members of the accounting profession have claimed that consolidated data best reflect group operations as a single economic or business entity. That is claimed to be the substance of the transactions between the related companies. Though supported by critics who wish to reduce conformity with the separate legal entity principle,[2] consolidation might also be contested against a background of corporate strategies which have bestowed considerable advantage through exploiting it. At the heart of these allegiances lie the differential accounting outcomes that emerge. Yet, despite the rhetoric, a 'group' of companies is neither a single entity under the present general interpretation of the law, nor (usually) reasonably identifiable as a separate economic unit. Thus aggregative representations of the outcome of the so-called group operations and its financial position are a financial nonsense. Contrary to what is claimed, consolidated financial statements are the product of relying on the purported economic form, rather than the legal form and its consequential financial substance.

It is assumed (but not evidenced) that consolidated reporting gives interested persons information on the overall financial status and current financial performance of group companies 'as an economic unit'. Distinguished legal opinion, for instance from Professor Gower, explains that the UK legislature has:

> recognised at least since the *Companies Act 1948* ... where there is a relationship between companies such that one, the parent or holding company, controls the others, the subsidiary or sub-subsidiary companies, then, for certain purposes, including *especially presentation of financial statements*, all must be treated as one ... *The most important of these [qualifications to the separate entity principle] relate to accounts* ...[3]

Judicial dicta support this view. Lord Denning MR declined to treat a wholly-owned subsidiary, Fork Manufacturing Co. Ltd as a separate legal entity.[4] And his dicta in *D.H.N. Ltd v. Tower Hamlets* explained: 'We all know that in many respects a *group* of companies are treated *together* for the purpose of general accounts, balance sheet and profit and loss account. They are treated as *one concern*.'[5] And Mason J in *Industrial Equity Ltd v. Blackburn*, while rejecting Gower's proposition and championing the separate legal entity principle, noted (in *obiter*) that the purpose of consolidation is to:

> ensure that the members of, and for that matter persons dealing with, a holding company are provided with accurate information as to the profit and loss and state of affairs of that company and its subsidiaries within the group.[6]

In the early 1990s the 'group' notion was endorsed in an ASC Media Release, *Public Hearing: Accounting Relief for Wholly-Owned Subsidiaries*. On the basis of a presumed commonality of interests of all 'closed group' companies, it was suggested that 'consolidated accounts would more accurately reflect commercial realities'.[7] *How* was not disclosed, though from these observations it would be reasonable for lay persons to expect consolidated statements to contain an aggregation only of the data in the separate companies' accounts, perhaps adjusted to avoid double counting, but neither including data not sourced in those accounts nor excluding data which are. Whether reasonable, that is far from the reality. Consolidation accounting does both.

Groupthink remains virulent today. And consolidated financial statements are the group therapy being prescribed. However, there is good reason for concern over the serviceability of consolidated financial statements. The 1992 Royal Commission inquiry into the $2.2 billion bale-out of the State Bank of South Australia alluded to its doubt on the matter when referring to 'the different accounting practices which can be applied to consolidated, group, equity and aggregated accounting.'[8] The CASAC (2000) Corporate Groups Report and the revelations at the HIH Royal Commission confirm the currency of those concerns.

It is not only a problem of variant accounting practices. More fundamentally, the proposition that group accounts are prepared to reflect accurately the operations of the group as a single economic or business unit runs contrary to the historical development of consolidated accounting. Any allusion to consolidations being the product of an evolutionary refinement is in error. Equally questionable is the proposition that consolidated or group accounts can:

> ensure that the members of, and for that matter persons dealing with, a holding company are provided with accurate information as to the profit and loss and 'state of affairs' of that company and its subsidiaries within the group.[9]

On several occasions we note that if the group is representative of neither a legal nor an economic entity, how can it be said to have a state of affairs?[10] Critical to that issue is what is meant by 'state of affairs', particularly as it applies to related companies, their members and their creditors. Money is the primary concern of all parties. Legally, one of the imports of the separate legal entity principle has been to isolate the fund that belongs to the company from the fund that belongs to its members. The company fund is liable for the company's debts and the member's fund is liable for the member's debts. In that setting, consolidated accounts are more likely to be a source of deception than illumination for the users of accounts in general, for the creditors and those dealing with the separate companies in particular.

Fuzzy financials

It is far from universally agreed what function consolidation or group accounting serves. In Australian consolidation prescriptions, AASB 1024 and the relevant sections of the Corporations Act, it is presumed that the function is to 'depict the affairs of an economic entity or group' of companies. AASB 1024 broadens the base of the consolidation process. However, Walker's (1976) comprehensive history of consolidated accounting exposes that numerous functions were posited initially, though few supported the current rationale being offered:

[In the 1920s, UK] consolidated statements were not regarded as primary reports. Nor were they thought of as depicting the affairs of an 'economic entity' or of a 'group' of companies ... In the 1920s, consolidated statements were regarded as supplementary remedial reports (p. 77).

... U.K. accountants were concerned with amplifying the reports of holding companies and to *overcome the limitations* of conventional cost-based methods of accounting for inter corporate investments (p. 353, emphasis added).[11]

Consolidating the separate financial statements of the parent company and its subsidiaries in effect lifts the corporate veil as if the accounts of each were those of the mere branches of one. Aggregated data are thereby presented to be more informative than disaggregated data. A curious proposition, for virtually everywhere else in human endeavour, disaggregation and deconstruction are being proposed as the window on enlightenment. But the idiosyncratic consolidating mechanics make those *aggregations* even less capable of meaningful interpretation than their components are in the separate financial statements of the controlled entities.

Consider the general proposition driving consolidation techniques – the notion of a 'group' comprising the parent (chief) entity and its subsidiaries or controlled entities. So much of the debate underlying (and deemed to support) Australia's AASB 1024 and the sections on consolidation accounting in the Corporations Act address superficial niceties regarding the artificial group entity to which the consolidated statements refer – how to identify a parent company, a subsidiary; how to eliminate the 'effect' of intra-group transactions and the like, rather than the inherent conflict between the 'group' notion and the separate legal entity principle.

Consolidated statements report on a fictitious structure, the group, which lacks legal capacity generally to exercise property rights, to sue or be sued, to incur physical or financial damage or impose it upon others. The statements contradict the legal, social and financial essence which their constituent corporations enjoy. By virtue of legal incapacity, *group* assets and *group* liabilities are an impossibility unless the legislature intervenes, for example, by introducing covenants such as apply under a Class Order Deed of Cross Guarantee, or through the courts' resolving liquidation disputes by ordering *ex-post* a pooling of group assets. Recourse to the group notion does, however, facilitate the labyrinths that have proven so friendly to corporate finagling. Despite being paraded under the 'accounting politically correct' substance-over-form banner, consolidated data are not user-friendly.

The 'substance-over-form' safe harbour is an accounting fetish, with a history dating from the 1920s. In essence, the objective is to prescribe that accounting captures the financial substance of transactions. But, in the context of consolidated statements the substance-over-form criterion offers no shelter. For the legal (and hence financial) substance is that the assets and liabilities included in the consolidated balance sheet are those owned and owed by the separate constituent subsidiaries, whereas the form is that they are presented to be assets and liabilities of the mythical group entity. Consolidated income or loss is the adjusted aggregate of the separate companies' profits and losses of the parent company and its subsidiaries. Consolidated statements are a particular instance where, contrary to the profession's dictum, the form is forced upon accountants in preference to the legal substance.

Conformity with other Australian Accounting Standards in the consolidation process exacerbates that effect by requiring specific adjustments of the data originating in the separate financial statements of the constituent companies. In the ordinary course of events, those Standards create artifacts of their own – compulsory amortisation of the price paid for fixed assets, creation of tax-effect balances, and the carry-forwards of various types, are examples. Some data appearing in the accounts of the separate entities are expunged from the consolidated financial statements; others are modified in a variety of ways once the same Standards are applied to the aggregative data under the consolidation rubric.

For example, compliance with AASB 1020 (*tax-effect accounting*) in relation to eliminated profits and losses on intra-group transactions (on the grounds that they are *unrealised* – from the *economic entity* point of view) injects consolidated financial statements with data that have not appeared in the accounts of any of the constituent companies. Superimposed is the impact of consolidation techniques, creating data exclusively the province of consolidated statements, goodwill on consolidation, discount (premium or capital reserve) on consolidation, adjustments to consolidated fair values, consolidated assets and equities, creation of future tax benefits, and provisions for deferred income tax not in, or opposite to, those in the constituent companies, and the like. These are mere artifacts of the consolidation process. Through applying AASB 1024 and the relevant sections of the Corporations Act, consolidated balance sheets have usually contained data for which no corresponding amount appears in the constituents' balance sheets. Using the lower of cost-or-market rule to book inventories may (in the aggregate) not correspond with the prevailing outcome of complying with the rule by the constituents. The change from balance sheets to statements of financial position does not change that.

Many of the consolidated balances do not have any counterpart elsewhere in the framework of conventional accounting. *Goodwill* and *discount on consolidation* are purely consolidated artifacts. Nor do they necessarily have any relevance to the financial assessments and evaluations habitually made in commerce. The genuine financial impact of transactions between companies within the group is eliminated irrespective of the validity of the data according to the evidence of the market. The outcome is curious – artifactual data only generated by the consolidation process are inserted in the consolidated statements, whereas genuine transaction data are excluded. Consolidation processes manage to nurture the worst of both sides of creative accounting.

Elimination of the financial impact of legally binding transactions (e.g. sales and purchases) between group members is a prescribed mechanism. Similarly, legally determined profits and losses made by the separate entities by virtue of transactions with other group subsidiaries are deemed to be fictitious, not at 'arm's length', *from the economic-entity point of view*. It is implicit in the claims made that under the new legislative prescriptions the consolidation process negates the possibility of assets being shuffled around group companies at ever increasing prices.[12] This is debatable in principle, and evidenced to the contrary in practice. There is a long history of asset shuffling, even in recent times. The experiences discussed in Chapter 16 of the Patrick Stevedores' employees finding their employer company in the Lang Group being asset poor and initially unable to meet their termination entitlements during the 1998 *Patrick Stevedores v. MUA* is a case in point. Arguably, the group structure facilitated this. It would seem also that Bond Corp's milking of the Bell Resources' *cash box* was made all the easier because of the group structure.

In consolidation accounting within a historical cost accounting framework, the purchasing company would report the asset at its cost (or deemed cost) and the selling company book its profit (or loss) on the sale; both are presumed fictitious in the group context and hence adjusted in the consolidation process. Of course, both the sale and consequently the purchase may be contracted on a genuine and commercial basis. Assets are 'worth' what they can be sold for, not what they cost to purchase. A 'view from the market' would dispose of the 'arm's length' problem. A 'view from the group' cannot.

Counterfactual reasoning encourages *corporate groupthink*. Separate companies and related entities are deemed to be *de facto* branches of the parent company. Indeed, early consolidation procedures were labelled the 'branching of profits and losses … depicting the affairs of a holding company and its subsidiaries as if they were a single organisation or *as if* the subsidiaries were merely *branches* of the parent'.[13] It seems that, in the context of accounting, what is declared or stated often enough becomes part of the received wisdom. All analyses of major corporates are undertaken on the basis of the consolidated data – rates of return, solvency, gearing, asset backing, earnings per share, overall financial performance and financial position, even though none of those absolute or derived financial indicators is meaningful outside the context of the separate individual subsidiaries comprising the groups.

Dispensing with the legal status of the constituent companies and other entities is mischievous and tampers with commercial and financial reality. The separate companies have an unquestionable separate legal status bestowed upon them by virtue of incorporation and nothing short of liquidation can deprive them of it.

Consolidation techniques entail recourse to the counterfactual: notions of group profits and losses, group rate of return, group gearing and the like, imply that the profits and losses of the separate entities will filter ultimately (through dividend payments or liquidation distributions) into the ultimate parent entity; notions of group solvency implies that the assets of the entities comprising the group are separately and collectively available for the discharge of the liabilities of one another. Reference to asset backing in respect of the group data implies that those with a shareholding in the ultimate parent are shareholders in the subsidiaries; and the idea of group liquidity implies that the cash boxes of each are there to be raided by the others. If all that were *really* the case, cross guarantees would be unnecessary. Expositions in techniques are presented as mathematical formulae, to be applied, without regard for the subsidiaries' separate legal status, to achieve the level of aggregation required. Notions of a distributive flow of wealth through the subsidiaries to the ultimate parent entity, with leakages to the subsidiaries' shareholders with a non-controlling share holding, are embedded in those formulae, though rarely disclosed to be what they are. That evokes an obvious question: if the desire is to report the activities of the separate (especially wholly-owned subsidiary) companies as if, from the group point of view, they were mere branches of the controlling company to be operated as branches, why have them as separate companies in the first place?

An answer is less obvious. Eisenberg has noted that economic grounds were not driving the formation of most, if any, corporate groups. And there cannot be any accounting argument in favour of the holding/subsidiary company structure. For if a branch structure were to be employed, the outcome would agree in broad objective – data aggregation. Idiosyncrasies of the legislatively prescribed reporting requirements of the Corporations Act and relevant Accounting Standards promote the substantial differences in the reported data that emerge. But, whereas the defects of historical cost accounting would remain, the aggregation of the branches' data would not require the fabrication of accounting artifacts as occurs in the professionally and legally prescribed consolidation process.

Consolidated data are accounting's fabrications *par excellence*. The aggregates for the assets, equities, revenues and expenses of the constituents are virtually certain to vary from those in the consolidated statements of financial position or financial performance. Consolidated income or loss will vary even further from the aggregate of the constituents' results by virtue of compliance with processing Standards, requiring the amortisation of the excess of the cost of the investment over the proportionate amount of the subsidiaries' equities acquired. Supposed indications of the solvency of the group, debt-to-asset cover, asset backing and other ratios conventionally calculated, are almost certain not to correspond to the aggregation of those for the separate companies. By virtue of the compulsory elimination technique, neither aggregate sales revenue nor aggregate expenses (by class or in total) necessarily equal the total of those of the separate companies.

Combining the elimination of intra-group transactions and tax-effect accounting exacerbates these anomalies. It frequently introduces data to the consolidated statements without counterparts in the separate accounts of the constituents – deferred tax asset balances appear as a consequence of applying the tax-effect rules to the reduction of the supposed unrealised profit component in asset balances arising from the elimination of intra-group transactions. Deferred tax liability balances emerge from the combined effect in respect to the elimination of intra-group losses, and similar adjustments to tax effect any deficiency or excess amortisation attached to the unrealised profits or losses in respect of non-current asset sales and purchases within the group. Yet neither deferred tax asset nor liability may appear in the accounts of any of the constituent business entities. And when they do appear, they may well be in the opposite direction to the aggregate of those represented in the consolidated balance sheet.

It is doubtful if anybody can make financial sense of such outcomes. Certainly they defy commonsense. Unbundling them in a group comprising hundreds of related companies is nigh impossible. Yet it all is done purportedly in the name of disclosure and clarification.

It is a matter of chance rather than design if data so contrived, so removed from real world referents, inform of the wealth and progress of the constituent companies, either individually or collectively. Yet, despite the financial obfuscation they facilitate, their counterfactual underpinnings and the resulting artifacts, surprisingly consolidated financial statements are perceived by legislative drafters, by many legal practitioners, by the courts and by many accountants, to be the means of providing greater financial insight, for lifting the corporate veil. To the contrary, they achieve precisely the opposite.

It is futile to expect progress by tinkering with the Standard on preparing consolidated accounts. The reasoning for this view has a long history and has been detailed elsewhere.[14] Perhaps what is required is a *Gestalt* shift, a recourse to lateral solutions – either (i) proscribe wholly-owned subsidiary companies and account for the decentralised operations *as if* they were branches; or failing that, (ii) require an aggregation of group assets based on the market prices of assets. Each promises data more serviceable than any in conventionally preferred consolidated statements.

Alternatives to consolidation accounting

Proscribe wholly-owned subsidiaries with recourse to branch operations and branch accounting

Proscribing wholly-owned subsidiaries would be an extreme approach.[15] Manipulations through the group structure have a long history. Lord Kylsant's shuffling of the Royal Mail's secret reserves in the 1920s was a seminal example. More recently, Bond's draining of Bell Resources' cash box showed how it was done, as mentioned above.

Financial chicanery within Robert Maxwell's public/private entanglement provides an apt justification of the need for radical reform. His corporate monolith of over 400 public companies, intertwined with 400 *Maxwell* private companies, was further complicated by their incorporation across several national jurisdictions.[16] The structure shown in Figure 17.1 effectively denied regulation.

Regulatory impossibility has not gone unnoticed – just not acted upon. A joint report in 1995 by international regulators in the banking, securities and insurance fields, *Supervision of Financial Conglomerates*, noted that where complex company entanglements impede effective supervision, power should be given to regulators to prohibit those structures. This response was similar to that following revelations about the US utility holding/subsidiary company abuses in the 1920s (see Chapter 17 fn. 15) and the perceived abuses in respect of the major Japanese *zaibatsus* resulting in their enforced break-up by US authorities after 1945. Such a response is long overdue in the general corporate arena. But little by way of real reform has emerged.

Earlier we noted 1990s amendments to Australia's corporations legislation addressing abuses related to insolvent subsidiary trading. CASAC's 'May 2000 opting-in' proposals contained in its *Corporate Groups Final Report* are similarly directed.[17] Sanctioning the bypassing of the fundamental principles of company law is a precedent likely to turn and *bite* the regulators. Lifting the corporate veil, stepping past the separate legal entity principle on occasions of financial stress, invites the inference that the holding company/wholly-owned-subsidiary structure is failing the 'net benefit to society' test. Compromising the principles of company law, the legislative lifting of the veil would be unnecessary were subsidiary companies to be prohibited.

Corporate abuses through group structures are evident in the fallout from corporate failures and dilemmas repeated each decade in Australia since

World War II.[18] Erosion of public confidence in the Australian capital markets resulting from the large 'group' collapses in the 1960s and 1970s, was repeated in the 1980s. Commenting on the collapses of the 1960s and early 1970s it was noted that 'inter-company shareholdings and transactions have given cover to fraudulent dealing and to legally less serious but financially no less deceptive mis-statements of results and position'.[19] That observation equally describes events in the 1980s, 1990s and post-2000.

Many well-known 1980s Australian entrepreneurs reportedly used related-party transactions, especially round robins. In particular, the reported deals prior to Rothwells' collapse and then also in its ill-fated rescue; deals between a Spedley Holdings shelf company, P152, and a related public company, GPI Leisure Ltd;[20] and deals involving intermingled private and public companies within the Linter[21] and APA/Unity groups respectively. The holding/subsidiary company structure certainly appears to have facilitated more than hindered those deals. It also effectively shielded them from the public gaze and scrutiny.[22]

Similarities with events at Stanhill Consolidated, Reid Murray Holdings and at Minsec and Cambridge Credit Corporation decades earlier are all too clear. Commercial practices such as these have a disorderly, sometimes chaotic effect on confidence in the securities market in particular and the capitalist system in general. In the United Kingdom, echoes of Prime Minister Heath's 1970s lament can be heard clearly in the aftermath of reported shuffling of assets within the Maxwell empire prior to its collapse to the detriment of thousands of pensioners dependent on the Maxwell Pension Funds. Even more recently, the bewildering financial merry-go-round that, from the HIH Royal Commission's revelations, appears to have been a feature in the HIH affair gives the impression that the skill has not been lost. It is demonstrable that groups can be a mechanism for manipulation.[23]

If wholly-owned subsidiaries are in effect *de facto* branches, and if consolidation accounting is intended to simulate branch accounting, the common-sense answer is to make them branches. Proscribe wholly-owned subsidiaries and be done with it. This would avoid the confusion generated by the regulatory imposition of the *avant-garde* ASC Class Order Deed of Cross Guarantee and CASAC's proposed 'opting-in' arrangements.

Consistency and also commonsense support a similar hard-line approach regarding partly-owned subsidiaries. Now that *control* is the subsidiary criterion, partly-owned companies are, in effect, no more than inter-entity investments. Possibly, the total deletion of subsidiaries, or at least any justification for a special accounting treatment regarding them, would be too radical for the corporate sector. But investments in the shares of other companies and unincorporated entities have the same nature, irrespective of the differential power of control or other privileges they might bestow.

Figure 17.1 Maxwell group structure

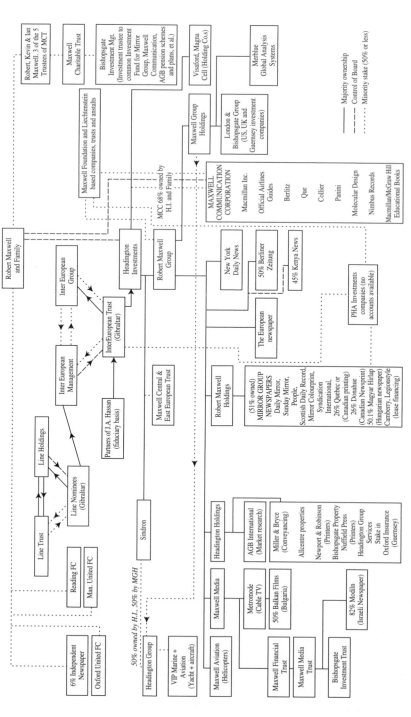

Source: Bronwen Maddox, *Financial Times*, 6 November 1991.

Distinguishing between investments according to the degree of control exercised over the investment is no justification for differentiating the basis for its valuation, though it might well justify differences between their market prices. Whether there *is* control would have an impact on the prices the respective shareholdings would fetch in the market. The market might reasonably be expected to unravel that. Accordingly, investments in the shares of other companies ought to be reported at their current market prices too. In our proposal, the financial affairs (assets, equities, revenues and expenses) of what now are known as wholly-owned subsidiaries would be absorbed completely as the financial activities of 'branches' of the primary company. Shares in what are now part-owned subsidiaries would be accounted for as investments in securities, and would be stated at their current market prices. As such, the accounting for them would be identical with the accounting for all shareholdings in all other companies to which no controlling significance attaches. If the market does not accord the investment any market worth, then the accounts ought to report just that! It would seem reasonable to produce schedules of assets and liabilities of the partly-owned subsidiaries, as outlined in a later section discussing an alternative market-based system of accounting for wholly-owned subsidiaries.

That contrasts with accountants' and the legislatures' attempts to restructure corporate relations to alleviate the effects of commercial abuses worked through holding/subsidiary company structures. Patching up reporting by groups has kept many busy for a long time, possibly at considerable cost – but ultimately the outcomes appear to have fostered (or at least left untouched) the precise irregularities they were intended to remove.

Market price accounting for groups

A commonly declared overall objective of conventional consolidation is a greater insight into the wealth and progress of related entities than provided by their acquisition cost. Clearly conventional consolidation accounting sidesteps the *Salomon v Salomon* separate legal entity principle through the aggregation of the separate entities' assets and liabilities, revenues and expenses, injecting consolidation-specific data and adjusting legitimate transaction data, under the umbrella of a supposed group (economic) entity. In the wash-up, consolidated data fail miserably to achieve their stated objective.

In 1967 Chambers wrote complaining of that failure – 'Consolidated Statements were not really necessary', though the sort of information they sought to present had some significance for the evaluation of the financial outcome of intercorporate investments. His proposal drew upon his preferred general framework for the form and content of statements of financial performance and financial position – Continuously Contemporary Accounting (CoCoA). The posited new form of group accounts would comprise: a statement of financial position of the parent company and a statistical summary detailing the nature, composition and aggregative money's worths of its related entities' assets and the amounts of their liabilities. The key features of his CoCoA system are: all assets will be stated at their current cash equivalents (for vendible physical assets generally best indicated by their market selling prices at the reporting date); income is all-inclusive, including all gains and losses arising in the worth of assets during the period under review. Gains and losses in the general purchasing power of money are brought into the income calculation by means of an annual capital maintenance adjustment. Accordingly, all inter-corporate and other investments would be stated at their current cash equivalents – that is, they would be marked-to-market.

Markets are never perfect. Information is never complete. But the market prices of items are as objective an evaluation of their contemporary money's worth, of their current contribution to the wealth of their owners, as can be found. The better the information, the better the evaluation, the better the financial assessments, the better – should be – decisions to invest and disinvest. Properly informed securities markets require accurate information of the current wealth and past financial progress of companies. Share prices might reasonably be expected to capture not only their companies' current financial position and an understanding of how it arose, but also impound all the expectations and fears for the future that the information might evoke. A rational economic perspective would suggest that.

Even if wholly-owned subsidiaries were proscribed, as suggested in the previous section, the great problem of accounting for investments in shareholdings remains. If subsidiaries remain, the problem is exacerbated. Whatever the case, it seems critical for an orderly securities market that all shareholdings be accounted for on the same basis. Differences in circumstances attaching to the shares – giving or not giving control as the case may be – would be impounded in their prices. If that were so in properly informed markets, perceptions of the relative degree of control and other advantages or disadvantages attaching to a particular shareholding would be transparent.

Were there to be a professional and legislative rethink of how to effect the capital boundary in relation to what are currently defined as related companies, Chambers' alternative presentation of the aggregative data provides a workable solution. His aggregative data are *relevant* to the interests of those who desire some aggregative financial overview of the related companies and other controlled entities; they are more *reliable* than present consolidation information since no manipulation of the data is required to effect the aggregations; because of their contemporary and non-manipulated nature they are *comparable* with the aggregations on both inter-firm and intra-firm bases; and readily *understandable* by dint of the aggregated data being in the same general form and having the same financial significance they possessed in their separate financial statements.[24]

Underpinning consolidation calculations is a peculiar line of reasoning that contradicts the separate legal entity principle of company law. It implies mathematically that the investor company has immediate uninhibited access to the assets and responsibility for the discharge of the liabilities of the entities it is *deemed to control* – 'deemed to control', for it is a subjective matter of interpreting from the attendant circumstances whether control actually exists. That determination is very important. For now in the Australian context the group is to include controlling interests in incorporated and unincorporated enterprises. Yet we know that control, *per se*, is insufficient to facilitate legal access to the resources of a controlled entity. And we must presume that consolidated statements are intended to reflect legal compliance. Consider, for example, the criticism of the back-to-back loans by a Bond Corporation related entity through which Bond Corp is alleged to have siphoned Bell Resources' cash box into the Bond Corp group. Not only was there 'actual' control, and the access it facilitated deemed insufficient to effect legally the transfer of assets via related group entities, it brought a custodial sentence for Alan Bond. That leaves no doubt that the cash of Bell Resources was not legally a resource of the Bond group.

A working assumption underpinning the alternative we present is that for the share price to be useful the market must be informed with accurate financial information of the wealth and financial progress of the companies in which the shares or ownership interests are held. Currently, the market is uninformed or misinformed to the extent that conventional income statement and balance sheet data are drawn on to assess financial performance and financial position. Periodic statements of financial performance and statements of financial position need, therefore, to simulate properly the only kind of calculation that can determine the financial outcome of a business venture over its entire life – a comparison between the sum of money with which it commenced and (in like terms) the sum of money or its equivalent with which it finishes – for that is all that periodic financial statements can reasonably achieve. It is the function that they properly can be expected to serve.

The current financial impediments to having wholly-owned entities liquidated and the assets transferred to the investor are accepted. Also accepted is the need for financial information in respect of what underlies substantial investments in other entities. The recent events at Enron, HIH, WorldCom, Ansett and the like evidence clearly that conventional consolidation exacerbates the inherent defects in conventional accounting prepared in compliance with the Accounting Standards. Even were the group structure to be retained, there is a critical imperative that the accounting for it be improved. We propose a form of accounting for inter-corporate investments that removes the defects of consolidation but achieves the objectives attributed to it.

First, in accord with Chambers' CoCoA, all the assets would be stated at either their face cash amount (debtors and cash) or their cash equivalent, best represented by their current selling prices verified by the auditors (non-current assets, inventories). Second, unlisted shares in subsidiaries would likewise be stated at the proportionate amount of the underlying money's worth (approximate selling prices) of the net assets in those entities. Third, had the controlled entities been listed companies, the investment in them would have been entered at the current selling price of the quoted shares – the proportionate equity in the net worth of the underlying net assets would be noted in parentheses at the balance sheet entry. This captures both the current selling price of the stock and the extent to which the listed price reflected *ex ante* assessments by the market of the company's future prospects in comparison with its current financial position. Fourth, all amounts in the statements would either be indicative of actual amounts of money or the equivalent thereof, as best indicated by the current selling prices of vendible assets. No amounts would, or could, be stated for non-vendible items – many of the intangibles currently reported in conventional standards-based financial statements. Thus, all the data would be denominated in monetary units of the same current general purchasing power dimension, contemporary as at the reporting date and therefore financially homogeneous, capable of having mathematical operations performed upon them to yield arithmetically valid and interpretable products.

There is no place in such a schema for any artifacts of the system, no place for data not indicative of actual amounts of current money or its equivalent, no place for making charges (such as for depreciation) unless they are sub-stantiated by the observable financial implications (i.e. declines in the assets' selling prices), and no necessity to concoct rationales that no sensible person would accept in respect of their own financial affairs.

Not only do the data then *tell it how it is*, as can best be determined at the time, they also tell it in terms of the common and established understanding of financial matters outside of accounting. In that setting, accounting can be a financial instrument effectively meeting the reasonable information functions accorded it, and assisting in improving the corporate governance mechanisms.

Enron's financial reporting shenanigans confirm the potential usefulness of our group accounting proposal. For whereas some commentators have contended that those capers highlight the need for a wider application of conventional consolidation accounting to all types of entities, the impotence of such a proposal was exposed earlier. Only disclosure of the market worths of the SPEs, or alternatively the market worths of their separate assets and the amount of their separate liabilities, would provide the financial information of the kind the critics seem to have sought in vain. In essence, in what is proposed here the deleterious effects of the financial obligations of Enron's SPEs would be reflected in the assessed market worths of their net assets and reported in our proposed group accounting mechanism, through both the statistical annexure and the inter-entity indebtedness matrix. Of course, where undetected fraud is involved in the manipulation of asset and liability balances, no accounting mechanism can be expected to provide reliable information.

The prescription described here and illustrated in the Appendix[25] is an accounting mechanism in which periodic statements of financial position contain data from which aggregations of the money and the money's worth (selling prices) of the physical assets and the amount of the liabilities can be determined, and articulated income statements produced. Adjusted for changes in the general purchasing power of money, income or loss automatically calculated as the change in the company's net wealth (stated in constant terms) then quite properly becomes the approximate increase or decrease for the period in the general purchasing power attributable to the company's net wealth. Conventional accounting complying with the Accounting Standards falls far short of that. Consolidation procedures inject their own fictions into the conventional accounting system, fuelling the information shortfall. In the end a necessary condition to reporting share prices data entails a restructuring of accounting.

If that were to be so, the reporting for share investments in unlisted companies, for wholly-owned subsidiaries, for other unlisted companies and unincorporated entities, falls into place. A reasonable surrogate for a company's non-existent share price or a proportionate share in an unincorporated entity's equity would be the proportion of its assets and liabilities (accounted for as above). At least those data are indicative of what underlies the shareholding, irrespective of whether it amounts to a controlling interest or to the merest of a minority interest. If subsidiaries were to remain, or if for substantial shareholdings disaggregated data were deemed necessary, they could easily be provided in supporting schedules of the various classes of assets and liabilities of the companies in which the investments were held. Indebtedness, intercompany sales and purchases, expenses and the like, and the double counting they may entail in bland aggregations of those data between related entities, can be disclosed in easily constructed schedules. The veil is drawn over such information by the elimination rule in conventional consolidation accounting; precisely the opposite of what is intended.

Our approach partly accords with the view that:

> [t]he larger and the more diverse the group, the greater is the need for the disaggregation of consolidated accounts to show the performance and worth of operating subsidiaries, entities or divisions within the group.[26]

Reporting the selling prices for physical assets automatically corrects in the balance sheet of the purchaser, for the consequence of transactions that have not been at arm's length. Related businesses could trade assets at whatever prices they chose and, separately, properly report the consequential profits and losses; avoid the financial solecisms in consolidated financial statements, avoid the counterfactual assumptions underlying consolidations' procedures, eliminate the complex and contradictory calculations endemic of the consolidation process as part of conventional accounting practice and provide all the necessary aggregated and disaggregated data which it is said consolidated financial statements are to give – but which they fail to deliver. The general structure of the alternative proposed appears in the Appendix.

Perversely, this alternative achieves the information objectives claimed for consolidated financial statements, without their sophistry, without their make-believe. Some of the scope for the manipulations so evident in many unexpected corporate failures is removed. Consumers of the data can treat the related businesses as single entities if they choose. They can aggregate and disaggregate as they like. The necessary data necessary would be there. They can group, sub-group and re-group, as they see fit, without artificially lifting the veil of incorporation. They can peep under the veil or peer through it if they wish without offending the separate legal entity principle, for so long the foundation of 'British'-based company law.

Improved Corporate Group Accountability*

The commonly declared overall objective of conventional consolidation accounting is to provide greater insight into the wealth and progress of related entities than that provided by their investment cost at the date of acquisition. We have contested that conventional consolidated data can achieve the objectives attributed to them: show an aggregative financial position of the related entities, assess their overall solvency, determine their potential cash flows, or otherwise evaluate their overall or individual performances. We have suggested that were there to be a professional and legislative rethink of how to effect the capital boundary in relation to what are currently defined as related companies, Chambers' alternative presentation of the aggregative data provides a workable solution. The overall effect of the features of his CoCoA is to remove most of the causes for the creative accounting that we have identified elsewhere. His system is now illustrated by example.

Imagine statements of financial position drawn up along those lines (see Table 17.1). Suppose that H Ltd has a 75 per cent interest in A Ltd and a 60 per cent interest in B Ltd, while A Ltd has a 20 per cent interest in B Ltd.

Not only do the data tell it how it is, as can best be determined at the time, they also do so in terms that draw on the common and established understanding of financial matters outside of accounting. In that setting, accounting can be a financial instrument that effectively meets the reasonable functions accorded to it. It will assist in improving the governance mechanisms related to the corporation.

H Ltd's statement of financial position and the statistical annexure to which Chambers referred could appear as in Table 17.2.

Comparing a conventional consolidated accounting financial statement with the H Ltd statement of financial position above, the accompanying statistical annexure and inter-entity indebtedness (cross claims) matrix highlights several features of each:

    (i)   With the proposed mode of reporting, the fictitious notion of a group entity, with rights and obligations similar to those attending incorporated bodies, is

Table 17.1 Hypothetical statements of financial position, H Ltd, A Ltd, B Ltd, as at 30 June 2005

	H Ltd $000	A Ltd $000	B Ltd $000
Non-current assets	251.00	157.20	310.00
Inventories	34.00	16.00	56.00
Debtors	26.80	28.00	31.00
Cash	15.00	15.00	14.00
Investments:			15.00
Shares in A Ltd*	177.75		
Shares in B Ltd*	218.40	72.80	
	722.95	289.00	426.00
Less liabilities	35.00	52.00	62.00
	687.95	237.00	364.00
Less capital maintenance reserve	163.95	72.00	48.00
	524.00	165.00	316.00
Less paid-up capital	500.00	100.00	300.00
Retained profits	24.00	65.00	16.00

Note: *The proportionate current money's worth of the underlying net assets valued at their current cash equivalents.

dispensed with; the group notion is unnecessary for disclosing the financial affairs of the related entities either separately or collectively.

(ii) The traditional 'elimination rule' has the equal potential to exaggerate understatements and overstatements of the current monetary worth of assets traded between related entities. For example, the application of the elimination rule in the circumstances posited would have moved the amount stated in the consolidated statement of financial position for non-current assets further away from their worth at 30 June 2005 than would have been the case had the rule not been applied – were the selling price of the assets (say) $251,000, the net $9,000 eliminated from the H Ltd non-current assets (ex A Ltd) if left would have recorded the assets at $241,000, still short of their current worth, but in the right direction. At the same time, the elimination of the depreciation on those traded assets would have overstated the reported group profit. The tax effect adjustment would understate the tax expense and overstate the profit. The same is true regarding some of the amounts emerging from the trading in short-term inventories. The elimination of (say) $6,500 unrealised profit would have reduced the inventory to $76,100, well short of its current worth of $106,000. In respect

Table 17.2 H Ltd statement of financial position

	H Ltd Subsidiaries financial position		Statistical summary		
	$000	$000		$000	$000
Paid-up capital	500.00			400.00	
Capital maintenance reserve	163.95	663.95		120.00	520.00
Retained profits		24.00			81.00
Total residual equity		687.95	H Ltd	396.15	
			Other	204.85	601.00
Debentures					30.00
Trade creditors	35.00				54.00
Provision for dividends					30.00
		722.95			715.00
Non-current assets		251.00			467.20
Inventories		34.00			72.00
Debtors		26.80			59.00 (a)
Investments					15.00
Shares in A Ltd		177.75			
Shares in B Ltd*		218.40			72.80 (b)
Cash		15.00			29.00
		722.95			715.00

Notes: (a) See Figure 17.2 for a sample inter-entity indebtedness matrix (for Hooker Corporation).
(b) Held by another controlled entity, A Ltd.

to other amounts, the movement would not have been sufficiently in the correct direction. Stating assets at approximations of their current selling prices avoids those anomalies. The elimination rule is unnecessary. It matters little under the proposed system whether the transactions are sham – not at so-called 'arm's length'. Ultimately it matters little at what price goods and services are traded between the related enterprises, whether it is equal to, above or below the prices otherwise prevailing in the market. It does not matter from whom or when the physical assets are purchased. At least no later than reporting date, each of the physical assets would be restated at the evidenced prevailing market prices as verified by the auditors. It is worth noting that this is a task that the auditors are required to do for many assets at present and possibly even more so in the future, pursuant to AASB 1041 and other legislative strictures; clearly much more so than when Chambers first proposed his system in principle.

(iii) Under the proposed method, the amounts stated in the H Ltd statement for the investments held in A Ltd and B Ltd correspond with the proportionate share of the market worths of the underlying net assets of the companies in which the shares are held.

(iv) Investments in listed and unlisted companies would be stated on the same monetary basis. The expectations of the market embodied in share prices would be disclosed in a manner facilitating a comparison with the current financial state of the relevant company.

(v) The 'outside equity interest' of minority shareholders in the subsidiaries is stated on the same basis, as is that of the parent company. It is not necessary to resort to the conventional consolidation rhetoric that the interests of the outside shareholders are supplementary data prepared from the group point of view, and that the amount of the minority interest is a balancing item. The usual arguments as to whether all or only the 'group share' of 'unrealised profits and losses on intra-group transactions' should be eliminated – 'whether the outside equity interest in unrealised profits and losses is earned or incurred' is completely avoided.

(vi) The proposed method automatically takes into account the 20 per cent interest of A Ltd. in B Ltd, without resort to calculating 'indirect outside equity interests', as would be necessary in preparing the consolidated statement.

(vii) Were it desired, the data for all the related entities, or for collections of them, can be aggregated or otherwise arranged in whatever format is desired with complete mathematical propriety, for all the data are indicative of contemporary amounts of actual cash or its equivalent.

(viii) The parent company's statement of financial position continuously presents contemporary representation of the worth of the investments in the controlled entities. No additional statement is necessary. The statistical summary of the assets and liabilities of the subsidiaries is required only for the purposes of providing information of the nature, composition and current worth of their separate companies' assets and liabilities. In Australia, many of the companies deemed as 'large' would also be required to prepare separate accounts and have them audited.

(ix) The proposed statistical summary of assets and equities has the potential to provide more information regarding the individual subsidiaries and other controlled entities than consolidated financial statements, by virtue of its capacity to be arranged to present data about the controlled entities' separate assets and liabilities, or to provide aggregates and sub-aggregates as required. It is to be noted that controlled entities' investments in other entities would be accounted for on the same basis as their parent company has accounted for its investment in them.

(x) Aggregate and net inter-company (entity) indebtedness are disclosed; as are the gross and net amounts owed to and by the related companies through the products of the supporting inter-company debt matrix. Such an N × N matrix would show the amounts owed to and by the related companies to one another and by the related companies to unrelated entities. Whereas the related companies' indebtedness will net out, it would be possible to identify to whom each is indebted (essential to determine their respective solvencies), the capacity of each related company to offset mutual indebtedness with another related company, and the total indebtedness of each to both related and unrelated companies. Computer spreadsheet mechanisms make this a relatively easy task. It has been suggested to us that the matrix would become unduly messy where the number of subsidiaries is large. For example, consider Australia's News Corporation with its approximately 800 subsidiaries. There the number of inter-company claims and cross-claims would be extensive. But knowledge of those claims and the need to 'eliminate' them is already required as part of conventional consolidated accounting techniques. Under our alternative, all that is being proposed is a listing of those claims via a formal spreadsheet, thereby enabling those legally binding claims and cross-claims to become *transparent* rather than be eliminated, as at present.

(xi) With corporate liquidations, administrators already need to prepare schedules of cross-claims and others within and outside the group when preparing a statement of affairs. This has been demonstrated in Houghton *et al.*'s (1999) analysis of Australia's largest administration, involving the Hooker Corporation. The type of matrix proposed is illustrated in Figure 17.2, drawing on Houghton *et al.*'s Hooker liquidation data. Similar cross-claim data would apply in ongoing firms. A feature of the way the data are presented is the ease of identifying possible cash flow implications of the inter-company external asset/liability positions of the companies in the group. Similarly, N × N matrices could be prepared for other intra-group elements such as sales, expenses, profits and dividends.

(xii) Also, with today's technology there would be minimal trouble in having these inter-company receivables and payables updated and reported continuously to interested parties if necessary. These matrix data could even be placed on a company's website and downloaded by those who require it. Indeed, one would presume that the data in this proposed matrix must already exist for auditors to be able to do their job properly and for directors to be able to attest in an informed way to the respective solvencies of their companies.

(xiii) Market prices for listed investments would be the primary basis for statement of financial position reporting. But, either when listed or not listed, there would always be a reporting of the proportionate share of the investee's underlying net assets on the basis of their cash value or approximations to it as evidenced by their current selling prices. The proportionate share in the underlying net assets of the investee would be stated in parentheses immediately below the market price of the investment. Thus all inter-corporate investments – irrespective of whether they bestowed a controlling interest – would be accounted for on the same basis, disclosing where applicable both the market price of the shares and the proportionate underlying net assets of the investee.

Figure 17.2 Inter-entity indebtedness matrix – Hooker Corporation

Lending Company	Borrowing Company 1	2	3	4	5	6	7	8	...	26	27	Internal assets	External assets
1		24,631,496	2,787,954					7,328,032		1,916,048		109,879,061	76,337,335
2			75,321	336,704			311,857	350,017			719,440	2,609,164	25,523,512
3												0	834,262
4	1,886,487											1,886,487	1,001,833
5	67,792,306	440,846				6,937						68,240,089	22,103,584
6	6,434,972	32,092										6,467,064	1,019,142
7	3,433,477											3,433,477	3,533,127
8						6,249,135						6,249,135	270,403
9												0	25,319
10												0	6,597,296
11												0	3,345,032
12		2,343,810						13,451,000				15,795,092	2,745,765
13												0	519,351
14												6,375	28,169,567
15												0	16,334,826
16	93,207,497											93,207,497	612,840
17												2,166	10,036,065
18												12,700,551	22,821,537
19												1,043,415	1,742,448
20	41,512,071											43,365,571	38,815,223
21												0	2,387,578
22												0	1,290,313
23												0	1,928,129
24	6,806,813											6,806,813	19,377,359
25												0	895,583
26												0	976,143
27	3,244,227											3,244,227	7,690,076
Internal Liabilities	226,661,660	25,104,716	2,863,275	336,704	0	6,256,072	311,857	21,129,049		1,916,048	719,440	374,936,184	296,933,648
External Liabilities	1,644,061,448	35,231	6,438	12,246	57,552,323	762,969	468,067	35,195			891,482	1,983,623,992	

Source: F. Clarke, G. Dean and E. Houghton, 'Revitalising group accounting: Improving accountability', Australian Accounting Review, November 2002, pp. 58–72 at 69. See also p. 252.

CHAPTER 18

Fatal Attrition – Accounting's Diminished Serviceability

Piece-meal patching will not make a worm-eaten craft seaworthy; neither will piece-meal tinkerings of individuals, boards and committees make cost-based valuations trustworthy.

R.J. Chambers (1991, p. 18)

No matter from what angle corporate failure is observed, accountants and their accounting products deserve major attention – and for good reason. Without question, the financial implications of corporate failure have an impact upon the welfare of the community, irrespective of either the causes or the personal culpability on the part of major participants in the corporate's affairs.

In the aftermath of the greedy '80s the levels of criticism and litigation against accountants, auditors in particular, evidence the perceived involvement of accountants and auditors in failures and in some instances their perceived responsibility for them (Table 18.1).[1] This anxiety continues in the post-mortems following the new millennium failures, like HIH, One.Tel, Harris Scarfe and (say) Enron and WorldCom. Undoubtedly the accounting profession is extremely sensitive to its members' exposure to litigation in the aftermath of those failures. Ongoing attempts by the professional bodies to have legislation limit accountants' liability for negligence bear witness to that.[2] In Australia there are increasing calls for action as the insurance companies suffer financial difficulties after the major calamities of the September 11 World Trade Center disaster and the collapse of HIH.

So too does the public comment on behalf of those bodies about the need for closer definition and monitoring of the ethical conduct of accountants.[3] Since the late 1980s, office holders in the ICAA and ASCPA (now CPA Australia) have been quick to voice their allegiance to a more detailed ethical code. Currently this is being iterated by professional, business and government spokespersons.

Life after litigation?

Over the last two decades, accountants' liability pressures have increased as the profession has faced recurring alleged performance 'crises'.

Upon commencing his term of office, incoming 1993 President of the ASCPA was quite open on that score with the comment that by becoming involved in the 'tax scams of the '70s' and 'the entrepreneurial corporate collapses of the '80s', the profession's highly prized self-regulation was put at risk, and with it the very essence of professionalism:

> The threat of increased outside regulation of the profession is ever present ... Many members don't understand that once we lose self-regulation, we are no longer a profession; we become artisans working to a cookbook provided by others.[4]

A question we shall return to is whether this means that the profession should produce its own cookbook of procedures, to be followed come what may. If so, one must ask whither professional judgment? As noted, this type of concern applies equally to the new millennium.

Senior members of the regulatory bodies have pursued a similar line. Henry Bosch led the criticism of the unethical behaviour of many of the 1980s entrepreneurs – 'corporate cowboys' in his terms. It would seem he saw business evil at every turn while others saw none.

Bosch noted that when he first joined the NCSC, 'a few flamboyant entrepreneurs were perceived as folk heroes', and that their apparent 'dramatic financial success' received acclaim. '... Cautionary words from regulators were received with surprise and distaste.'[5] True enough. But those warnings regarding Bond, Skase, Goward and the like were generally late in coming, low-key.

The revelations at the HIH Royal Commission, the myriad dot.com Liquidators' investigations and the US inquiries into, *inter alia*, the Enron, WorldCom, Sunbeam collapses, and the spate of US 'earnings restatements' have undoubtedly rekindled the business ethics debate. Some are now equating ethics with corporate governance – *laissez faire* has almost returned.

In the public rhetoric related to accounting and auditing practices the pervading emphasis has been upon deviant, unethical behaviour. It is questionable whether all, or even the majority, of the behaviour complained of is deserving of being labelled deviant. Not so, at least insofar as it implies behaviour that always entailed an improper departure from the accounting norm. Evidence has been provided here that much of the publicly disclosed accounting by failed companies was in accord with the then established and compulsory rules. Much accounting was *creative* – but compliant. Undoubtedly, other misleading accounting practices were *feral*.

The profession has acknowledged that some behaviour of its members in those collapses was less than professional. Disciplinary actions against members occurred in the 1990s, but the process was criticised for the hearings being slow to commence and not open to the public.[6] Failures in the 1990s presaged a renewed push to revise the nature of those disciplinary proceedings.

Table 18.1 Selected negligence claims, notifications lodged with insurers and reported settlements

Plaintiffs (clients and liquidators of clients of)	Defendants	Damages claims/(result) $m
Duke Group	Ernst & Young, KPMG Peat Marwick & Ors, settled out-of-court reportedly for $35 million	$175 ($35)
Farrow Finance Company	ASC civil action against ANZ Executors Trustee Co. and the auditors, Day Neilsen Jenkins; settled out-of-court reportedly for $15 million.	$20 ($15)
Rothwells	KPG Hungerford; settled out-of-court reportedly for $16.25 million.	$40 ($16.25)
National Safety Council	Horwath and Horwath; settled out-of-court reportedly for $4 million.	$263 ($4)
Estate Mortgage unitholders	Priestley and Morris and Ors; settled out-of-court reportedly for $31 million.	$600 ($31)
Estate Mortgage Financial Services	Tyshing Price and Co.	$25
Deposit and Investment Group	KPMG Peat Marwick; settled out-of-court for undisclosed amount.	$73
Battery Group	Deloitte Ross Tohmatsu; settled out-of-court reportedly for $12 million	$132 ($12)
AWA	The initial judgment against Deloitte Ross Tohmatsu of $23.9 million was appealed and settled out-of-court reportedly for $12.4 million	$50 ($12.4)
Titan Hills	Coopers and Lybrand & Ors; settled out-of-court reportedly for $17 million	($17)
State Bank of Victoria	Day Neilsen Jenkins, Ian Johns & Ors	$900
Spedley Securities	Priestley and Morris & Ors; settled out-of-court reportedly for $22 million	$600 ($22)

Tricontinental	KPMG Peat Marwick, settled out-of-court reportedly paying the Victorian Government $136 million	$1,094 ($136)
Independent Resources	Deloitte Ross Tohmatsu	$44.5
Adelaide Steamship	Deloitte Ross Tohmatsu and former directors; appeal of auditors against the validity of ASC action was successful in April 1996 but the ASC successfully overturned the decision on appeal; settled out-of-court reportedly for $20 million.	$340 ($20)
Southern Equities (Bond Corporation Holdings)	Arthur Andersen; settled out-of-court reportedly for $110 million.	$1,000 ($110)
Colombia Tea and Coffee	Nelson Parkhill	Nominal damages
Keydata (formerly Budget Corp)	Coopers & Lybrand & Westgarth Baldick; settled out-of-court for undisclosed amount.	$17 ($17)
Linter Group	Price Waterhouse, concerns deals worth $320 million	$320
State Bank of South Australia	KPMG Peat Marwick & Price Waterhouse; settled out-of-court reportedly for $120 million.	$4,300 ($120)
Westmex	Grant Thornton; settled out-of-court for undisclosed amount.	$60

Sources: 'Clients – and liquidators of clients – sue firms for damages totalling $2 billion plus', *Chartac*, September 1991; and miscellaneous newspaper articles, including: I. Ries, 'Auditors find themselves in the hottest seat of all', *Australian Financial Review*, 10 January 1992, p. 44; M. Gill and B. Pheasant, 'Record claim against KPMG', *Australian Financial Review*, 2 June 1992 and J. Falvey, 'Spedley claim may be $750 million', *Daily Telegraph Mirror*, 10 June 1992, p. 36; 'ASC seeks $20m. damages in Farrow case', *Australian Financial Review*, 24 March 1993, p. 3; B. Pheasant, 'Auditors in danger from $2.5 billion claims', *Australian Financial Review*, 30 June 1993, pp. 1 & 6 and B. Pheasant, 'Accountants want to stop the damage', *Australian Financial Review*, 30 August 1993, p. 14. See also W. Hogan, 'Accounting Introspection', *Australian Accounting Review*, November 1994, pp. 54–64, especially Table 1.

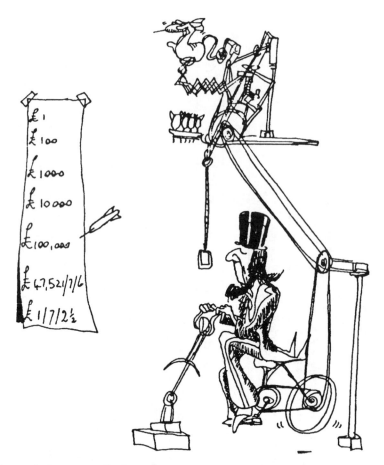

'What profit do you want?', *Company Accounting Standards*, a Report of the Accounting Standards Review Committee, 19 May 1978, p. 54. Subject to Crown copyright; reproduced with the permission of the Crown.

Commingling creative and feral accounting practices within complex corporate structures ensures that the financial outcomes are nearly impossible to unravel – a nightmare for investors, directors and auditors. The use of the nefarious 'pro forma earnings statements' by many companies in the United States and Australia in the 1990s has demonstrated that investors could equally use a dart to choose an appropriate profit figure. Unprofessional auditing, *if* it occurs, simply adds to the muddle.

Without doubt, many conventional accounting rules allowing optional treatments were, and remain, deviant with respect to common financial sense and experience. But they are compliant with the mandatory Accounting Standards. In many respects, Bosch's 1980s corporate cowboys were made the scapegoats as far as accounting is concerned. Since the collapses of HIH and One.Tel in Australia and Enron, WorldCom, and the like in the United States, commentators have targeted auditor independence as the culprit. But a considerable portion of the blame could properly be levelled at the financial information system responsible for cementing those practices into commerce in the first place. For the complaints alleged that the financials of controlled entities had been kept *off the balance sheet* at Enron, that Waste Management had reduced its *depreciation charges* on its truck fleet, that HIH's *solvency* at the 30 June 2000 reporting date was equivocal according to the published accounts, that WorldCom had incorrectly *capitalised operating expenses*, that Xerox and Enron brought forward revenues. Such allegations, for example, could all emerge through purported compliance with the Standards of the day, without any intention to deceive. Whereas the intention to deceive may be proved to be evident in some cases, it was not necessary to the outcome. It is a natural product of the *system* as it is. And that makes deceit more difficult to detect.

Nonetheless, over more than 35 years the accounting profession in Australia has been keen to sheet home the blame for accounting failure to virtually everybody outside of the accounting profession. Chapter 2 noted that its 1966 response to the spate of Australian failures during the 1960s exposed a virulent predisposition to 'tip the bucket' on whomsoever happened to be in sight. Primarily, managers were blamed for those 1960s failures. Some aspects of the quality of company accounting and disclosure came under attack in that report. But sloppy-to-bad management attracted most of the profession's invective.[7]

Auditing then received some criticism, with an emphasis on strengthening the hand of the auditor and requiring complete independence from any unwarranted pressures that might be brought to bear on the auditor by directors.[8] This independence angle has been rekindled following the HIH and Enron affairs. There were other reforms proposed throughout that period, including recognition of the need for the parent company auditor also to be the auditor of the subsidiary companies. Yet there was no suggestion of the reform types we propose here, either that the group structure be prohibited or in some ways constrained, or that consolidated accounting be dumped.

Responses to what we proposed in our first edition were mixed. One review by a barrister questioned the suggestion that the true and fair override had been relegated to a 'second order imperative';[9] another was concerned that there was proselytising;[10] another by a former regulator observed that a major thesis of the book – that compliance with Accounting Standards was a contributor to creative accounting – was a 'triumph of hope over experience'.[11] Others noted that the analyses of the complex group failures portrayed: a very dismal story of the quality of financial reporting in Australia;[12] 'a provocative account that "will fuel a healthy debate about the role and function of accountants and accounting information in the corporate arena"';[13] 'a candid insight into the administration of companies';[14] and proposed reforms to prescribed group accounting that represent an 'extreme position but one worth debating'.[15]

Back to our 'very dismal' story. It is a story witnessed by the vast experience of making observations of the kind noted as examples here. And there is no proselytising, for the legitimate role of academe is to pursue the 'Newmanite' objectives of 'professing the truth and exposing false doctrines'. The truth is that the general structure of historical cost accounting continues to come in for only limited public criticism in analyses of failures.[16]

The escapades of Christopher Skase, Alan Bond, Russell Goward, Abe Goldberg, Brian Yuill, Laurie Connell, Alan Hawkins, George Herscu and (say) John Spalvins differ little from those of the entrepreneurs of today in that the emphasis remains on the individuals – Ray Williams, Jodee Rich, Rodney Adler, Brad Cooper and co. The 'cult of the individual' was equally emphasised in the 1960s' press, when Herbie Palmer and the Catel brothers were in focus, and when the name of Stanley Korman was prominent. While they might well have deserved attention, it effectively transferred focus from how the environment of failure – the settings: the underlying framework of the accounting and auditing practices, institutional, legal and regulatory frameworks – allowed deception, unintentionally masked pending failures and exacerbated their financial outcomes of many companies. Virtually nothing has changed!

But now, as in the past, press exposure of the frailties, the mistakes, the ineptitude, the peccadilloes of the individuals, made and still make for better reading and more entertaining viewing.[17] They do nothing, however, towards rectifying the underlying problems in the system. If anything, they push solutions further from sight. The failures and their consequences sit in the wings ready to be repeated at a later date – as they were in Australia in the 1970s, in the 1980s, and now in the 2000s, with the predictable but unjustified dismay, surprise and indignation of politicians, investors, corporate regulators, accountants and auditors. A convenient but costly case of 'out of sight and out of mind', 'on-again, off-again', regulatory fervour, as successive waves of corporate failure flow in and out.

No doubt the '1966 Report' on company failures spurred on those in the profession who perceived the need to specify a more definitive set of rules for the processing of accounting data in the 'professional cookbook' fashion implied earlier. Indeed, the push for a complex set of Statements of Accounting Standards and the push for compulsory compliance with them in Australia might well be rooted home to it, and, along with it, the beginning of the Australian slide in respect of corporate regulation.

In consumer protection terms, the slide was southwards – from an emphasis on the rights of the consumers of financial information to receive serviceable data and towards promulgation of an accounting cookbook – a checklist, conducive to effecting regulation but devoid of any prospect of disclosing the wealth and financial progress of corporations. That slide in Australian accounting was noted in the 1990s, even from within the profession:

> [Accounting firm] staff ... faced with a transaction, rigorously leaf through
> the rulebooks to try and find where it fits, and do not sit back and say what
> really happened. So we have this focus on the rule book rather than the
> commercial reality.[18]

And again as the new century broke.[19]

Returning to the 1990s: 'Whilst outsiders, including the Deputy Governor of the Bank of Scotland, tell a similar story ... many accountants have failed to properly exercise judgement, are too anxious to conform and are too caught up in the technicalities of accounting standards rather than their overall objectives'.[20]

That 'is happening' when others within the profession are claiming that there is 'substance over form' in accounting for transactions, and that substantial reforms improving the system's checks and balances either have been or will shortly be implemented. Contemporary responses from corporate regulators and from the accounting profession to the failures during the 1970s, 1980s, the 1990s and now post-2000 have been generally repeat performances. The 1966 Report was a template. Whereas the rhetoric has been couched in newer terms, the fundamental message has remained the same. Bad management, the unethical behaviour and dishonesty of some entrepreneurs have been singled out as the primary causes of the *unexpected* failures. The causes implied have the familiar ring – so does the remedy – promulgation of more Accounting and Auditing Standards, now with statutory back-up to ensure compliance, became the entrenched formula for regulating the disclosure of financial information. Specification of more compulsory Standards was the 1990s' fad. It was the flavour of the decade – despite the lack of evidence that it would likely succeed, particularly so in Australia, when it had been so ineffective here and elsewhere in the past. Today's mantra is to ensure auditor independence, again with little evidence that such a move would mean the capital market necessarily will be better informed.

Henry Bosch, both during his time at the NCSC and since, has been vigorous in his pursuit of more Accounting Standards as a mechanism for the regulation of financial disclosure. Australia has conformed to the pattern elsewhere in the English-speaking world in this respect. In the United States the promulgation of Standard accounting practices proceeded initially through the operation of the American Institute of Certified Public Accountants'

Accounting Principles Board to the current outpourings of the Financial
Accounting Standards Board – with over 150 Standards published to date.
Regulation through the threat of sanction for non-compliance with the prescribed rules appears to have been spawned by the push for a formula approach
to financial disclosure – the 'cookbook approach'.

Central to that theme has been the philosophy that the greater the number
of rules, the more predictable the regulators' behaviour, the less accountants can
exercise professional judgment – the more effective the regulation. Perversely,
it reveals a fatal attrition of professional judgment – the greater the regulation,
the less reliable accounting has become.

A none too subtle twist in the post-2000 debate has been the attention given
to internal governance measures directed more to regulating individuals, than
to addressing the defects in the *system*, *per se*. That too has been not all that
different from the professional responses to the 1970s' failures. Now, as then,
the bulk of the attention is turning to measures intended to prevent or detect
perceived inappropriate behaviour by directors, managers and the like. One
reasonable inference to be drawn is the pervading perception that corporate
executives are exploiting and manipulating an otherwise basically sound system.
But, virtually all the accounting and auditing problems that have emerged
recently in both the Australian and US fallouts have had their counterparts in
the aftermaths of the earlier episodes of corporate collapses.[21]

More and tighter rules governing the behaviour of corporate managers and
directors continue as main items on the agenda. *Corporate governance*, the
1990s new-age buzz-phrase within commerce generally has gradually gained
the ascendancy. Definition of the principles of good practice in corporate
governance has entertained analysts of corporate failure even more so in the
2000s than it did in the 1990s. Individuals are to be controlled rather than the
system rectified. Scant attention is being given to accounting and auditing as
instruments of corporate regulation. Where they have received attention, it is
mainly as a side issue to the focus on the allegedly recalcitrant behaviour of
accountants and auditors. Whether to expense stock options has been addressed
more in the context of it being a potential curb on executives' pursuit of short-
term boosts to shareholder value and the linked rewards that ensue, than on the
grounds that it properly discloses the financial outcome of a stock option
scheme. It continues to be claimed that the nebulous *bad management* would
be overcome by applying the principles of corporate best *practices*. Yet few note
that accounting that produces data indicative of the actual financial outcomes
of whatever it is that the executives have done with a corporate's resources, is a
critical monitor of whatever best practice is perceived to be.

History is relived, for that analysis sits nicely with the 1991 monograph
on 'Company Failure'[22] commissioned by the ICAEW. It had declared that

failure could not be sheeted home either to inadequate audit or to accountancy in general; management, changing economic conditions, product failure and the like, all stand more accused. Our concern lies with the relative weightings given to those factors in the light of the unexpected nature of those failures, and specifically the down-playing in analyses of the role of accounting in unexpected corporate collapse.

A thrust in many institutional prescriptions has been that companies' financial data should be used to anticipate failure. If only they *were* a reliable enough indicator of failure or success.

However, the truth is that the present contents of companies' published income statements and balance sheets are not serviceable for determining their current financial positions or for discovering how they arose. That is ironic, given that the Australian Accounting Standards now label the annual financial statements *Statement of Financial Performance* and *Statement of Financial Position*. Nor are those data indicative of the critical financial characteristics of companies. If they do translate into reasonable predictions, it is simply a case of serendipity. Without knowledge of a company's present financial position and how it arose, one is badly placed to predict likely future financial positions and periodic outcomes, including failure.

One early product of the 'better corporate governance' movement was the 1992 wisdom of the Cadbury Committee in the United Kingdom, in particular its 'Code of Best Practice'. Ultimately however, the Code amounted to little more than a series of motherhood statements regarding the virtues directors must display and be seen to display, plus the recommendation for audit committees to be mandatory for all public companies. Essentially Cadbury's 'Best Practice' presumed company managers now possess less integrity, have more questionable ethics, and are more inept and more easily compromised than the community at large. Overall, the inevitable impression to be gained is that bad, dishonest or unethical conduct by managers, directors and the like are the major causes of *unexpected* corporate failure – and that the Code would set that right. At best, history reveals that as a pious hope.

No sustainable evidence has emerged to the effect that corporate managers' ethical behaviour was less acceptable than that of any other cross-section of the Australian (or UK) community: it is at a lower ebb now than it was in the past. Many instances of unscrupulous and unethical business practices in the past indicate that the current band of corporate cowboys is no worse than its predecessors.[23]

It is wrong to consider the current problems as new phenomena. Commonly suggested remedies take little heed of lessons of the past. Cadbury's *Code* and its copies are typical. Significantly, nowhere did the Code explain how the appointment of audit committees would ensure that the financial information disclosed by companies would be indicative of their wealth and progress. Curiously though, the Code specifies that directors must present:

> … a balanced and understandable assessment of the company's position'
> (para. 4.1) and the Final Cadbury Report on *The Financial Aspects of Corporate Governance* declared its support for the cardinal principle of financial reporting
> '… that the view presented should be true and fair … [aimed at] the highest level of disclosure.

Commitment to the 'true and fair' criterion by the Committee stands in stark contrast with its official professional abandonment in Australia.

Definitions of corporate governance have moved on since Cadbury's *Best Practice*, but it remains the template; Hilmer's discourse on corporate governance in his *Strictly Boardroom*, the series of 'Bosch Codes' and the general corporate governance paranoia in the financial press have the same focus as Cadbury. The ASX's *Corporate Governance Council* addresses the traditional issues. ASIC's beam on corporate governance likewise has picked up Cadbury-like threads – as has *CLERP 9*. We might expect no greater fidelity on the part of managers by virtue of the watchdog activities of Cadbury-type audit committees and greater monitoring of compliance with the approved Accounting Standards by audit supervisory boards and the like. Perversely, as a consequence, we also expect a greater incidence of creative accounting.

Corporate managers are placed in a no-man's-land, between a rock and a hard place – between the sword and the wall. The cure is likely to be worse than the complaint. In this setting the ASX's reluctance to adopt the Cadbury recipe in favour of compulsory disclosure and explanation by directors of their corporate governance measures prior to the events post-2000 was arguably on the right track. Succumbing to the pressure put on it to mandate governance measures as part of its listing rules is understandable. The talk has been long and loud by the pro-corporate governance lobbyists, but misplaced. On that score the ASX has been hijacked!

Consumerism

The analyses of the cases demonstrate how compliance with the Accounting Standards has been as likely to produce data that were not serviceable for the making of the ordinary financial assessments of the wealth and progress of companies. Yet, virtually nothing has been said of that. Perhaps the closest comment to acknowledging the role that the Accounting Standards play in creative accounting is the allusion to fewer rules (fewer Standards) that might lessen opportunities for genuine error and for deliberate manipulation.

Clearly, for the most part, corporate regulators and the spokespersons for the accountancy bodies have not seen it that way. Henry Bosch, his predecessors and successors at the NCSC, ASC and ASIC all appear to be obsessed with the idea that we need more accounting rules of the kind currently in vogue. Changes to the national companies legislation requiring compliance with the Accounting Standards, ASC and ASIC surveillance, UIG wisdom statements and consequent actions against firms and auditors for not complying with them are indicative of that 'magnificent' obsession. Everything that has occurred post-2000 reinforces that viewpoint.

Against that background the inevitable conclusion is a widespread presumption that accounting practice provides serviceable financial data. Certainly the US Treadway Commission, the UK Cadbury Committee and other proposals such as Hilmer's *Strictly Boardroom* seem to hold that view. If so, then virtually all that those inquiries into how directors ought to direct, how managers ought to manage, how audit committees ought to scrutinise audit, are not much to the point. Cadbury's 'Code of Best Practice' strongly recommended that all listed companies have audit committees. Interestingly, both One.Tel and HIH (as did Enron!) had an audit committee. The push for mandatory audit committees was a major part of the *Ramsay Report into Auditor Independence* and it has been included as an integral part of the mid-2002 proposed reforms in *CLERP 9* (limited to the Top 500 listed companies) and the August 2002 JCPAA *Report 391*.

Since an audit committee should ensure compliance with the current Accounting Standards, arguably companies and the public at large would be better off without audit committees. It is odds-on that compliant accounting will be creative. Perversely, there *is* a chance of something serviceable coming from non-compliance, subject to the rigours of the market and professional audit oversight to ensure truthful accounts are presented. Post-Enron regulators worldwide may be changing their view. Many are seeking to have directors swear that the figures in their reported accounts are 'true'. They are said to be in the best position to determine the 'true state of an entity's financial affairs'.[24] Some academic accountants might have to go back to basics as they have argued 'truth' is something that is unobtainable!

Nonetheless there is little sign of anything other than superficial changes to existing accounting practices. Essentially what is currently prescribed in the Standards is a capitalisation-of-expenditures model – historical cost accounting with the odd market price adjustments.

No compelling evidence demonstrates how more of the same variety of accounting data can improve the state of play. Analysts, for example, declared that until (and unless) Adsteam published consolidated statements, a reliable understanding of its financial position would be impossible. Precisely the opposite was more likely the case. Fiction-laden consolidated statements are the artifact *par excellence* of accounting, a proven long-standing vehicle for obfuscation. Enron provides contemporary evidence of that.

None of the contemporary observers of the present corporate state (in their public utterances, at least) indicates awareness that the long history of *unexpected* corporate collapse contradicts the view that all we need is more of the same variety of public financial information. None has explained why the financial information critical to administrators' assessments and evaluations when a company is known to be in financial distress is treated as if it were irrelevant when the company is regarded as a going concern. Nor is it explained how such perceptions of financial distress or health are formed by administrators in the first place without current selling price data.

Whereas there are examples that expose awareness of what is required, often the logic is astray.

Over a decade ago, Ernst and Young's *A Guide for the Company Director*, for example, enshrined the peculiar but pervading logic. Directors of a *failing* company, it explained, '... must have reliable and up-to-date information on the company's financial position ... liabilities scheduled by due date [and] of realisable values of assets ...'.[25] True enough. But they need that information continuously, in both good and bad times. How else can anybody, inside or outside a company, assess whether it is failing, or when it is necessary to take steps to reverse the decline? Under the Corporations Act, directors are required to possess knowledge of an entity's current and expected solvency positions – an onerous task; one in which, as we have shown, accounting, however, has a major role to play continuously. Recourse to the market resale prices of assets (marking-to-market) would appear an imperative – albeit insufficient of itself – in meeting that legal obligation. Conventional accounting certainly does not routinely and compulsorily produce information serviceable for those purposes, even on an annual basis.

It is against that background that the current groundswell of support for Australia's adoption of the International Financial Reporting Standards (IFRs) has gathered pace. Australia's Financial Reporting Council has indicated that complete compliance with the IFRs is planned for 2005. Government in its *CLERP 9*, the ASX, regulators and the accountancy bodies have endorsed the move. None has explained how it will improve accounting. Overall, the criticisms made here of the Australian Accounting Standards apply equally to the IFRs. A warped logic dictates that having companies' financial statements that are equally misleading worldwide is an improvement!

Accounting and the consumer

Accounting practice enjoys a peculiar insulation from the conventional idea in western law that consumers reasonably expect that goods and services are fit for the uses commonly made of them. Why accounting retains this exception is inexplicable. Moreover, the denial of ordinary rights enjoyed in most other settings is being institutionalised. Consider the following disclaimer in the 1995 revised Australian Auditing Standard AUS 202:

> Although the auditor's opinion enhances the credibility of the financial report, the user cannot assume that the opinion is an assurance as to the future viability of the entity nor the efficiency or effectiveness with which management has conducted the affairs of the entity.

What purpose that statement serves is a mystery. The import of the second clause appears to contradict what the first professes. An auditor's opinion regarding a company's state of affairs lacks credibility if it cannot be relied upon by those making predictions about the company's future financial viability. If it cannot be relied upon, then the financial information to which the auditor's opinion refers does not deserve the credibility attributed to it.

In that context, an auditor's opinion contrasts dramatically with the quality assurances usually given to consumers of ordinary goods and services. Whereas the products of the accounting process are possibly not goods of the kind contemplated in the usual consumer laws, those who use financial data set out in published financial statements do so with expectations reasonably identical to those who purchase the usual run of goods and services. It is reasonable that those who draw financial inferences from raw financial statement data should enjoy the expectation that they are fit and serviceable for that use. With respect to the absolute amounts set out in the financial statements, it would appear reasonable that the data may be used to inform readers regarding the nature, composition and contemporary monetary worths of both the liquid and the physical assets, and the contractual amounts of the various liabilities. A presumption of serviceability reasonably also applies to the indicators of the financial relationships to be derived.

It is unimaginable that anyone expects accounting data to be otherwise than fit to be used to calculate a variety of financial ratios held out to be indicative of the company's financial characteristics – solvency, rate of return, earnings per share, liquidity, the relative contributions of debt to equity in financing the operations, the asset backing for the equity interests, the interest cover given by the level of profits, the financial implications of the relationships between the separate and aggregative amounts of the different classes of assets, and between the different classes of liabilities. Each relates to a specified date. In this respect accounting is like every system of instrumentation. Its signals must correspond to changes in the characteristic depicted.

Drawing financial inferences from published financial data, and from the products of calculations made with them, is indisputably an everyday commercial practice. Invariably, the financial press worldwide publishes lists of financial ratios and offers comment on those relationships whenever the results of companies are announced. Invariably published financial statements prepared within the framework of procedures specified by the national Accounting Standards are the source of the data used. Unquestionably so, those absolute amounts and ratios are produced around the world. Brokers' broadsheets on companies' financial positions, progress and prospects, draw primarily from that source; as do the financial analysts and ratings agencies which specialise in tracking the financial results of companies' operations and sell their conclusions as services on a regular basis: Moody's, Dun and Bradstreet, Standard and Poor's. So do those who incorporate it on an *ad hoc* basis as part of a wider variety of financial journalism, the financial press in general. Online connection to the financial press has extended access to those uses of conventionally prepared accounting data.

Virtually every textbook on financial accounting published in the English language over the past 75 years contains sections on analytical techniques requiring such calculations to be made from data drawn from companies' published accounts. It is reasonable to presume that the endurance of those expositions in teaching materials is indicative of at least a pervading belief that the data can be used properly in that manner.

Likewise the publication of similar calculations, schedules of conventional ratios and aggregates is commonplace in the annual reports of companies in many countries. Frequently, as previously in Australia's Stock Exchange Statex service, and now in the five- to ten-year (or more) summaries published by companies, they invite inferences that comparisons are expected to be made, and that the data are serviceable for that purpose. Many distress prediction models entail similar calculations from data similarly derived. In fact, doing so is the emphasised thrust of that research.[26] Thus the use of published financial data in those ways seems to have the unqualified endorsement of the financial markets, the regulatory agencies, commercial agencies, the financial press, teachers, scholars and the community in general.

None of the Standards is set within an explicit framework of data serviceability. Whereas Australia's SAC 3 declares that the necessary qualitative characteristics of general-purpose financial statements include the data being *relevant, reliable, comparable* and *understandable*, none of the Standards explains how those criteria are met through compliance with them. Collectively, these criteria coalesce into the single serviceability criterion we have specified. But accounting quality control proceeds in a manner completely different from other systems of product control. That is curious when the professional bodies enthusiastically endorse a study of such matters as total quality control and total quality management, as part of accreditation programmes. Even more so, when accredited teaching programmes in Australia, and the professional courses and examinations in the United Kingdom and the United States, require the successful study of consumer law. Accounting students in these programmes have to understand how manufacturers are to produce goods of merchantable quality, but they are not exhorted to produce accounting data possessing the same basic quality.

The idea of serviceability enjoys unqualified public and government support, by far exceeding that of the notion of *caveat emptor*. The latter notion, so evident in the extract above from Auditing Standard AUS 202, can only serve to warn those who have the competence to assess for themselves technical and qualitative characteristics. *Caveat emptor*, however, is of no help to the inexpert. For the layperson, it is merely a warning to be wary. In every other setting it is always secondary to the general principle of serviceability. Laypersons reasonably expect professionals to protect them from having to make uninformed judgments and assessments. Evoking a *caveat-emptor*-like shield contradicts the ethos of professionalism.

Recourse to consumer law's central notion of merchantable quality (fitness for use, serviceability) is apt for accounting purposes. Users of published financial data are consumers, albeit of a particular kind. Financial data are, in a sense, economic goods.[27] In the same way that tomato sauce must be fit for its ordinary use – safe for human consumption – data from published financial statements might reasonably be expected to be fit for the uses we know are ordinarily made of them.

Consumers and consumer protection agencies concentrate on products, not the processes from which they emerge. Possibly the specification of serviceability evokes a natural selection mechanism by which a common production process emerges. If it does – then so be it. If not – does it matter? If there were a number of different ways of achieving the essential quality, it would not matter if one producer used one method and a second chose another. Accounting regulation might well benefit from adopting a similar approach.

Financial data serviceability

Features making financial data serviceable are readily identified. Primary assessment of a company's solvency (for both going concerns and distressed companies) necessitates the comparison of its immediate debt and the current money's worth of its available assets. Debt to equity ratios relate debt (actual money owing) to the money's worth of the aggregate of the shareholders' stakes in the company. Security for borrowing is assessed, *inter alia*, through the comparison made of the proposed borrowing and the money's worth of the assets pledged or available for debt cover. Asset backing, for example, is assessed by relating the number of shares issued to the difference between the amounts of the company's debt and the aggregate of its money balances and the money's worth of its physical assets.

Each of those assessments and evaluations reduces to a comparison (of one kind or another) of amounts of actual money owed, money possessed or legally obtainable, and approximations of the money's worth of physical assets. Comparable rates of return of the type specified are calculated meaningfully only as the rate of increase in the money's worth of the net assets. Again, that necessitates (*inter alia*) comparison of contemporary amounts of actual money and approximations of the money's worth of physical assets with the similar aggregates contemporary at a prior time.

That is achievable only if the accounting system is directed to produce a continuous stream of data indicative of the actual financial consequences of the transactions undertaken by a firm and of the events to which it is subjected. That will be where the central focus of accounting entails a continuous marking-to-market of its physical assets, and the recording and reporting of its monetary assets and liabilities at their contractual face amounts. That is how monetary calculation is undertaken whenever the objective is to obtain a reliable indication of financial performance over a period and of the financial position in which it has resulted.

Nobody with experience of money and monetary calculation in the real world is likely to dispute that. Virtually everybody will have experienced calculating that way in respect of their own financial affairs, business or household, when they desire useable financial information as a basis of periodic assessment and evaluation. It does not require the invention of a *special* 'conceptual framework'. To everybody who has purchased and sold, handled money, faced prices and price structures, experienced the differential impact of changing prices and price levels, such things are unexceptional, common commercial knowledge, not peculiar to accounting.[28]

Each of the financial indicators refers to commonly considered aspects of contemporary relationships between the financial features of a firm at a specified date, its financial position or changes that have occurred in that position over time. With respect to those primary, elementary and expected uses, only data indicative of actual amounts of money, or claims to money by or from the firm, or indicative of approximate money's worth of its fungible assets are serviceable. Only data of that kind are pertinent for the identification of the financially sound company, the company at financial risk and the company already in financial trouble. That many of the products from conventional accounting were not serviceable for doing that is illustrated in the above examples drawn from healthy, ongoing firms, and in the post-mortems on the failed.

That leads to the inevitable proposition: Accounting data ought to satisfy the same general serviceability criterion of quality that applies elsewhere in the consumer society – that they must be fit for the uses ordinarily, knowingly and predictably made of them. That entails abandoning those Accounting Standards not directed to marking-to-market the fungible assets, and stating other assets and liabilities at their face amounts. The fantasy of injecting financial statements with artifacts of the system – those data neither indicative of a financial state nor representative of an actual asset, liability, revenue or expense item – is avoided.

Many of the current Australian Accounting Standards and those in the IASs' package do not measure up to those criteria. They will have to be abandoned!

At the end of the day, one *General Purpose Standard* specifying the necessary achievement of the *serviceability criterion* is all that is needed. Professional accountants, like other professionals, are best equipped to determine how to achieve and maintain it.

Chasing regulatory reforms[29]

Regulatory reform has been prompted by a strange confluence of circumstances. First, because some failed companies were audited by the same firm, Andersen, for example – Enron, WorldCom, Waste Management, Sunbeam, and HIH – it has been taken as (albeit circumstantial) evidence of systemic defects in the auditing process. And because in each instance, non-audit services were also provided, a lack of auditor independence has also been presumed – and presumed to be integral to the unexpected failures. Audit reform, especially on the independence front, has been demanded. The package of reforms proposed include: a desire for better (higher quality, in the new-age), more Standards-compliant information for investors, making executives more accountable, and developing stronger, more accountable auditing systems. To this end, there have been specific calls to prohibit joint provision of audit and non-audit services, to mandate audit committees and auditor rotations, assurances that auditors are independent, and that the International Financial Reporting Standards are substituted for nationally promulgated Accounting Standards.

The tenor of those demands mimics the rhetoric surrounding like sagas in previous decades. In the United States, these include: the Penn Central and the Equity Funding affairs of the 1970s and the S&L fiascos in the 1980s and '90s; the unexpected collapses of Minsec and Cambridge Credit Corporation in Australia in the 1970s; of Bond Corporation and Adsteam in the 1980s, and of HIH, One.Tel and Ansett in the 2000s; and in the United Kingdom: collapses of Pergamon in the 1970s, the Maxwell Corporation and BCCI debacles of the 1990s.

Unease and calls for reform invariably have followed large, *unexpected* failures not long after the reporting of their financial results with clean audit reports attached. Recent revelations related to HIH and Enron have again led many to question the usefulness of audited accounting data as a sound basis for financial assessments and evaluations by investors, regulators and other interested parties. The particulars of the collapses and perceived accountability deficiencies have caused some to argue that there has been a loss of confidence in the securities market being a 'fair game'. Others have observed that accounting and auditing is in a 'state of crisis' (Volker 2001 as cited in Dean 2002). The reprises are certainly familiar.

Responses to the current (almost identical) claims against the profession, and the concomitant similar regulatory and professional reform proposals being canvassed, are essentially cosmetic. They are likely to have minimal effect in preventing the types of large unexpected collapses and associated wealth redistributions that were the catalysts for the demand for reform.

The size and continuity of the unease expressed in the financial press and from witnesses called before the numerous inquiries in the United States and Australia, following the Enron and HIH collapses, confirm that auditors are definitely under scrutiny. A US Grand Jury indictment and prosecution of Andersen LLP on 'Obstruction of justice' charges confirm that.

Where auditors are found to be dishonest, allow inducements to compromise their work, or are dilatory or incompetent, they deserve to be punished, for their default is a matter of not being professional. Incongruously, auditors can be as honest as possible, have impeccable integrity, be competent, intrepid to the hilt, but if they follow the conventional accounting rules in framing their judgment, they almost certainly will be signing off on what is mostly financial nonsense! The lynchpin of auditing has (for the most part) been left out of the discussion to date – for the necessity that accounting data are serviceable in the uses ordinarily made of them lies at the core of the audit function.

Letters in the Australian financial press, numerous editorials about HIH and Enron,[30] and the numerous expressions of unease generally over US companies' use of pro forma earnings statements to allegedly mislead[31] have highlighted concerns about auditing and accounting.

Audit failure or audit impossibility?

'Audit failure' is currently depicted as primarily a matter of a lack of auditor independence. This is contestable. The Ramsay Report on 'auditor independence', the 2002 discussion papers *CLERP 9* and JCPAA *Report 391*[32] generally confine the independence debate to the ethical and social dimensions of the auditor–client relationship. The proposed reforms ignore the constraints imposed by accounting rules upon the auditor's ability to form an 'independent opinion' on financial statements. Thus, those reforms have little likelihood of being successful.

While the auditing independence debate resurfaced in Australia soon after the HIH, One.Tel, Harris Scarfe and Ansett collapses, unwarranted parallels have been drawn between them and the US collapses. Of course, the Andersen firm is a common element in respect of some of them. But as Table 19.1 shows, SEC investigations in the United States have entailed each of the formerly 'Big Five' and the surviving 'Big Four'. Common too was the appointment of past Andersen auditors of Enron to its board and the apparent provision of non-audit services (NASs) by Andersen to their audit clients HIH and Enron. Nonetheless, it is sobering to note that there does not appear to be any statistical relationship between the provision of NASs and the form audit reports take, and we are unaware of any compelling anecdotal evidence of cases where those dual activities have been shown to have compromised the independence of the auditors. The Enron case is curious in this respect: US$27 million in NASs has been rated against US$25 million in audit fees. Perhaps it might be that the amount of the audit fees compromises the quality of non-audit advice provided.

It is argued in the United States that the NAS income is 'more valuable' than the audit fee because it has a greater potential to increase. Be that as it may, a US$25 million audit fee is no small matter. With that at stake, the existence of NASs would seem insufficient reason to cry a lack of independence – the audit fee itself is enough to have pinched Andersen, were it to have been lost. Andersen may well have been in the wrong place at the wrong time – a victim of regulatory exuberance – where in other circumstances other audit firms may well have found themselves. The point is that all the major audit firms have been having their troubles undertaking the audits of large corporates. 'Why' has not been inquired into in a reasonably Jesuitical manner. 'Audit failure' has been presumed, and all too often for the likes of Andersen, according to the regulators. But the widespread difficulties of the major audit firms indicate that the problem is not confined to one firm. In other disciplines such a commonality would evoke a search for a different answer to individual failure.

Something akin to the notion of *audit impossibility* would almost certainly come to mind.

We are assuming that auditing is still perceived to be a professional service activity and not just another business. Given this then, the matter of professionalism is paramount – whether an auditor within the current accounting/audit structure can have an 'independent frame of mind' in forming an opinion regarding the 'truth and fairness' of the financial statements, on whether those statements are truly indicative of the financial performance and financial position of the company. Here, auditors are faced with a no-win situation, required as they are to form their opinion on whether the Statement of Financial Performance and the Statement of Financial Position are 'true and fair' indicators of the company's financial performance over the stipulated period and its financial position at the stipulated date, conditioned by a *default recourse* to (so the pervading belief seems to be) whether the company has complied with the Accounting Standards, Australia's GAAP. Yet, a company's compliance with the Standards virtually ensures that the income statement will not show its actual financial performance, or the balance sheet its actual financial position in any meaningful, serviceable way. In the present framework of inevitable accounting failure, audit impossibility is the equally inevitable outcome!

As noted in Chapter 15, HIH's published financials at 30 June 2000 brought to account nearly $1 billion dollars of Future Income Tax Benefits, goodwill and various capitalised expenditure, all potentially in accord with the prevailing Standards. Those balances are of highly contestable relevance to any assessment of the company's solvency at the time or of its overall financial position. That scenario is not unique to HIH. It has been the story in respect of so many of the other companies discussed in this volume that have collapsed *unexpectedly* – their financial statements, though primarily in accord with the prescribed accounting rules, conventions and Standards of their time, have failed to provide reliable indications of the drift in their wealth and financial progress. Nor is it unique to companies that have failed. It is endemic of the form and content of the published financial statements of all companies complying with the approved, compulsory Accounting Standards.

On numerous occasions, attention has been drawn to how the artifacts of conventional accounting prevent financial statements from disclosing dated commercial realities, while making auditors substantially dependent upon the preparers of accounts for the dubious financial information reported in them.[33] For example, it is worth asking what is the financial significance of accounting artifacts such as tax-effect balances, the tax-effect calculation of income tax expense charged against revenues to quantify financial performance, the capitalised costs, a variety of intangibles and goodwill booked as assets?, amounts for physical assets not marked-to-market?, amortising historical costs?, applying the 'accrual principle' on a temporal basis?, recognising only 'realised gains', but both realised and unrealised losses?, preparing consolidated financial statements?, and the like?

Since the UK Companies Act of 1844, company directors have been charged with the responsibility of preparing financial reports, and auditors with the duty to authenticate the contents of them. The perception that company directors and officers, more familiar with company affairs than auditors could possibly be, might influence the opinions formed by auditors provoked the notion that auditors should be free of non-trivial commercial dealings with clients and their officers and free of family ties with them. The recommendations of the Australian Federal government-initiated Ramsay Report thus draws upon long-standing thought. Those freedoms were to be the guarantors of the reliability of the financial accounts – the substance of what is now implied by the notion of audit independence.

With the exception of cash, receivables and payables, the idea of authenticating the contents of periodical accounts by recourse to independent evidence has been submerged in relation to physical assets. For the most part, external evidence has been replaced by professional prescription. The manner in which transaction data are to be processed and financial statements prepared are prescribed by the Standards, without considering whether the data that emerge are generally serviceable for the purposes routinely made of them – determining the wealth and progress of the companies to which they relate and for deriving indicators of their salient financial characteristics.

That the compulsory accounting infelicities noted above exist equally in the accounts in those companies that have not collapsed as in those that have, undermines the objective of corporate regulation. The evidence is that compliance with the Accounting Standards is a pervading cause of misleading, creative, accounting data. On that count, the financials of most of the companies that have not failed are frequently as unreliable as those that have. Auditors are caught in accounting's 'GAAP trap'. They are denied the opportunity to exercise a 'mental attitude' when forming an opinion that is 'independent' of those who prepare financial statements.

Generally, auditors acting in accord with the Accounting and Auditing Standards are not required to have recourse to commercial evidence outside of the reporting entity when forming an opinion on the accounts. In a most important respect, by no fault of their making, auditors are 'dependent': dependent on the prescriptions in the Standards, dependent on the mores of tradition, dependent on the folklore of accounting and auditing practice that fails to meet the qualitative tests applied in respect of all other goods and services. This is not because of malpractice on the part of auditors, but by virtue of the demonstrably defective (in terms of serviceability) accounting and reporting system in which auditing functions.

Ramsay's Auditing Independence Supervisory Board and mandatory audit committee and auditor rotation recommendations (and similar reform proposals locally in *CLERP 9*, internationally by IFAC and in the United States in *Sarbanes-Oxley Act* response to the Enron collapse) address arguably more the 'independent status' of auditors than their 'independence of mind'. Unlike the law, where the independence of judicial opinion is buttressed by the laws of evidence, the independence of auditors' judgments has no corresponding safeguard. Unless and until auditors are required to obtain commercial evidence of financial facts outside the reporting entity, the independence debate is likely, as in the past decades, to continue to rage without satisfactory resolution.

In the absence of full mark-to-market accounting that has external commercial referents, auditors shall continue to be at the behest of their clients' financial calculations – a situation in which 'independence of mind' can neither exist nor be shown to exist. There is little likelihood that the recycled ideas being proposed will mitigate unexpected corporate collapses and their associated fallout.

Reliable financial statements are the very objects of the audit independence concept. Yet, compulsory compliance with the present suite of Accounting Standards presents as the greatest inhibition to auditors achieving independence. That constraint ensures that 'surprise' continues to be a prevailing characteristic of corporate failures, and that auditors will continue to attract poorly zeroed flak.

Ethos Abandoned – Vision Lost: Accounting at the Professional Crossroads?

We should speak ... of the immorality of accounting; for it has been the quirks of accounting that have provided many of the opportunities for misdemeanours of ... corporate officers.

R.J. Chambers, (1991, pp. 16–17)

Talking ethics became a 1990s growth industry. This was not surprising, for at that time the accounting profession sought also to allege a decline in moral standards amongst corporate officers as a major factor contributing to *unexpected* corporate collapse. Regulators of corporate activity, the financial press and politicians also were quick to jump on the ethics bandwagon. No doubt they thought that this would put an end to the 'creative accounting-cum-earnings management' type problems. Clearly, it has not.

Immediate post-1980s headlines in the financial press were representative of the initial ethics push: 'Ethics becoming the buzzword of the '90s',[1] 'Call for higher business ethics',[2] 'Ethics rise in the West',[3] 'Corporate ethics come under the microscope',[4] 'Accounting education in "chronic neglect"',[5] and 'Big business elders crusade for higher ethics';[6] as were subsequent accounts: 'Declining ethics ... bad company',[7] 'Profession begins to get serious about its ethics',[8] 'Society needs dose of ethics to purge its "moral chaos"',[9] 'Phillips bows out with call for code of ethics',[10] 'Another counselling centre for ethically troubled accountants',[11] 'Ethics is a tricky business',[12] 'The selling of ethics',[13] and 'Where does the buck stop?'.[14]

One could well ask, where indeed?

There was more of the same in the post-2000 post-mortems. This time, re-jigging the corporate governance regime has been the major focus. It was argued that what was needed was greater moral behaviour by officers and a better system to monitor it. Corporate morality is a cultural attribute to be nurtured. Accordingly, there has continued to be a hankering for detailed rules to force the preferred governance measures.

It is no surprise that in that climate a wider framework than an appeal to the better nature of corporate officers has been invoked. The original appeal for more ethical behaviour has been subsumed into an expanded notion of corporate governance. In turn, the original voluntary nature of corporate governance, its self-imposed regime of checks and balances, has been transformed into an additional layer of rules and prescriptions with which company officers have to comply. In the United States the *Sarbanes-Oxley Act* of 30 June 2002 has spelled out how US corporations are to be governed. These rules include mandating the introduction of an audit committee for all listed companies and further requiring that only non-executive directors are on those committees. The audit committee shall have oversight of appointment and compensation of the company's auditor and help establish procedures to deal with accounting and auditing issues that surface, even from whistle-blowing employees. In Australia the ASX has buckled under the weight of the push by the regulators, the government, and the popular financial press to establish an ASX Corporate Governance Council that has specified that the top 500 listed companies must have an audit committee comprising a majority of independent (non-executive) directors. To that end, ASIC chief David Knott has explained that corporate governance in its new guise essentially has two legs:

1   the mechanisms by which corporations are directed and controlled; and
2   the mechanisms by which those who direct and control a corporation are supervised.[15]

The original issue of corporate and professional ethics might have been perceived as a relatively simple matter to grasp. The accountants' quest for professional recognition should have pointed them immediately towards the social orientation – a primary duty to the public – universally accepted to be a primary characteristic of the professional.[16] Or so one might imagine. Ever since the specification of accounting provisions in the *UK Companies Act 1844*, the explicit legislative theme has been that published financial information in the form of a company balance sheet and subsequently the income statement were to be *full and fair* representations of the company's financial state of affairs and changes therein.

Truthful accounts were deemed to be a *quid pro quo* of incorporation. The obligation to provide them might be seen to have the original nature of the corporate governance mechanism. For whatever corporate managers, directors, accountants and auditors do, and no matter how they do it, true and fair financial statements were to disclose the financial consequences from which the behaviour of those officials, their competence or incompetence, honesty or dishonesty, could be gleaned, evaluated and acted upon.

Unquestionably, the ethos of corporate accounting was that those interested in a company's financial affairs were to be accurately informed through the annual financial statements being made public. Beyond question, that was the explicit charge emerging from the Gladstone Committee of Enquiry which preceded the 1844 Act and followed a series of major joint stock company collapses.

Over time, the 'full and fair' phrase has undergone minor changes – for example, *full and correct, true and correct* in the *NSW Companies Act 1936*, *true and fair* in the *UK Companies Act 1948* and Australia's *Uniform Companies Acts 1961*, and similar phrases used elsewhere, such as *fairly presents*. But there has never been compelling argument that the original ethos was no longer the pervading essence, despite lengthy debate in the literature as to precisely what the phrases meant; whether for example, the words should be read separately or as one.[17] Accordingly, there have been countless changes in recommended accounting practices since the 1960s, then promulgation of prescribed Accounting Standards, changes in the Standards-setting mechanism,[18] successive revisions of Australian company laws up to 1992, and now calls for more changes of a similar genre post-2000. But the overriding ethos has, or should always have, been that a company's published accounting data show a *true and fair* view of its state of affairs at a stipulated date and its financial performance in the period prior to that date.

Camouflage the facts!

Typically, few are letting the facts get in the way. Consideration of ethics by the profession has been a whirlwind, faddish movement which has diverted attention away from accounting's core activities. Now it is corporate governance talk that clouds the issues.

A matter of ethics

Nobody appears to have spelled out on behalf of the accounting profession the form of ethical behaviour to be taken into the corporate arena. It has become something which everybody is expected to understand, a code to which everybody (except the offenders) automatically and voluntarily subscribes. Hence, the ethics push has proved to be a red herring, a diversion. Sceptically, one commentator has claimed in respect of the US experience that it is a 'defensive strategy necessary to assuage public fears that a State-granted trade monopoly and self governance will not be abused in favour of a profession's members … a shield behind which various forms of behaviour can be "tolerated"'.[19] The corporate governance push (incorporating ethics) will prove to be much the same.

In the western world, where the tenets of market-driven commercial activity are embraced, it is less than clear what *is* ethical commercial behaviour and what is not. With a set of secular laws in place and voluntary compliance with the principles of the underlying Judeo-Christian framework, staying within the law and being constrained financially by the market are the final determinants of the manner in which western commerce proceeds. Consider Professor David Fischel's attack on 'greed bashing' and the 'greed is good' stance forming the basis of his support for the actions of the embattled Michael Milken, the 1980s' 'junk-bond king'.[20]

Motherhood statements have characterised the ethics push. Now they chacterise the talk and the specification of the soft end of corporate governance. Talk of corporate responsibility to protect the environment, responsibility to warn customers of limits on the serviceability of products, obligations to provide community services, contributions to charities, and the like, are rather empty platitudes, without legal force or the force (sometimes) of commonsense to back them up. It should be noted that Enron was seeking myriad ways of improving its environmental image.

It is interesting to note, when it suits, how the personification of corporate activity sheeted home the blame for dubious corporate activity to the legal entity itself, not to its human agents – its directors, managers, employees, accountants and auditors – and the system in which they function.[21] Yet, surely only the human agents have conceived, implemented and followed through the actions complained of; only they made the choices between alternative proposals; only they directed the manner in which the corporate vehicle interacts with other corporations and real individuals within the community. It surely is contestable whether corporate officers are necessarily acting in the best interests of their corporation if its resources are diverted from the market-driven financial objectives. In this regard the revelations within the HIHRC of the philanthropic actions of Ray Williams at HIH have raised the issue again.

In contrast, the new-age corporate governance push is displacing the focus on self-imposed ethical behaviour with the layer of structural governance rules, but, as with its ethics predecessor, without a system of accounting that will reveal the actual financial consequences of their efficacy. Cause and effect have been a preoccupation in the regulators' analyses of corporate collapses. Although cause and effect is a hotly disputed relationship in the discipline of history, the superficial histories accorded many corporate collapses embrace a rather strong willingness by observers to jump to simplistic explanations. Corporate regulators in Australia – ASIC (and, before it, its predecessors the NCSC and the ASC), APRA, and the accounting profession previously – have been quick to sheet home many of the problems of declining ethical behaviour by managers and financiers,[22] and put their money on specific governance rules that dictate the behaviour of auditors, directors, company boards, audit committees, and corporate executives in general.

Of course, directors and accountants who have departed from the prescribed Accounting Standards have been, and continue to be, targeted as deviants engaging in creative accounting. But, as we have argued above, some may have been precisely the opposite. The evidence reveals creative accounting arising as likely from complying with those Standards as deviating from them.

Whether the moral behaviour of corporate officers has declined is contestable.[23] There is good reason to support that it has not. In the distant past,
as in the 1980s, 1990s and now, the practices of leading business people
and accountants have been the subject of criminal cases, civil cases and
professional disciplinary cases.[24]

Distinguishing business ethics as a class of behaviour of its own is a
curious fad of the commentators on corporate failure. Business activity is really
only one of many facets of human endeavour. No good reason exists why
business ought to be different from how other human relations proceed with
respect to the relations of one participant to another. A delineation of business
ethics from other human behaviour has skewed the debate from the real issue
deserving attention – the features of the general commercial and financial
framework in which corporate fraud and *unexpected* failures have occurred.
Concentrating on the financial shenanigans of a few individuals who either have
set out or, by dint of unfortunate temporary financial circumstances, were
induced to deceive has little to commend it. It has been a fertile ground,
producing many 1990s reports (codes), including, in Australia, several editions
of Bosch's *Corporate Procedures and Conduct*, the IFSA's (formerly AIMA)
1997 *Corporate Governance: A Guide for Corporate Managers and Corporations*; in the United Kingdom, Cadbury's *Code of Corporate Governance*;
numerous European codes, and in the United States, the American Law
Institute's *Principles of Corporate Governance: Analysis and Recommendations*, the Ramsay auditor independence enquiry, and the JCPAA enquiry into
the independence of registered company auditors. Missing has been an
exhaustive discussion of the framework within which, and the processes by
which, a commercial society may proceed about its business in an orderly,
reasonably well-informed manner, fairly and equitably. Of course, one is in
trouble immediately by making such comments. 'Reasonably well-informed',
'fairly' and 'equitably' are open to definition, and virtually every definition will
attract complaint and dispute.

There can be no doubt that the behaviour of some entrepreneurs of failed
1980s enterprises and their counterparts subsequently was less than a fulfil-
ment of their fiduciary responsibilities. Descriptions of the collapses and the
observations of the judiciary (for example, regarding Estate Mortgage, Spedley
and Hooker), and the recommended laying of charges by the DPP for ASC
(at Qintex, Rothwells, Interwest, Linter, Duke, Bond, Westmex, Budget and
Independent Resources) in the 1980s, and in respect of judicial actions regarding HIH and Harris Scarfe in the 2000s, have pointed to questionable action
and inaction of some managers, directors, accountants and auditors, at least
morally, and in other cases legally, insofar as they affected the fortunes
of investors.

But then, what of those investors? What of the shareholders, noteholders, creditors and particularly the financial institutions who stumped up so much of the financial wherewithal to allow projects, schemes and the speculation (especially in property) to proceed? In the post-2000 wash-up much attention is being given to the inadequacy of the press as vigilant monitors and the conflicts of interest that allegedly influenced actions of many financial analysts with ties (albeit supposedly protected by Chinese walls) with mutual fund investments.[25] What might be said of their motives for investing in the prospective high-return ventures? Managers and directors whose behaviour is now under the microscope, those deemed 'corporate cowboys' of the 1980s and beyond, might well be said to have been buoyed along on the encouragement of the investors who supported their ventures, who were happy to hunt with the pack in the pursuit of high returns. It is but a short step from that scenario to a proposition that the investors generally were quite content with the *modus operandi*, so long as they did not have to share the blame if it came unstuck. It is instructive to note that initially few were publicly vocal in their questioning of the entrepreneurial push. Just the opposite: it was almost universally applauded,[26] as were those who were driving it. They were fêted nationally and internationally, seemingly never short of friends and admirers, many in high places.

We have suggested that the behaviour of some Australian entrepreneurs in the 1980s and beyond was no worse than that of their counterparts in previous decades. The history of corporate failure is replete with instances of scallywags and con-men, cheats, swindlers and crooks, who misled investors. Many were referred to earlier.

Predictably the 1990s exposed its own high-rollers, for example, Leeson (Baring's derivatives trader), Igucha (Daiwa's bond trader), Benson (Metallgesellschaft's oil futures trader), Hamanaka (Sumitomo's copper trader).[27] Post-2000 enquiries into the 'corporate scandals' in the US and the collapses in Australia invite the inference that others may soon qualify for admission to that list.

In contrast, it might be argued, in mitigation of the questionable deeds of some Australian entrepreneurs over the last three decades, that they were spurred on by an investing public besotted by the support of corporate high-rollers, brokers, analysts and even governments, all right behind them, supportive and applauding their ventures. And, we might presume, even lauding their performance.

A contentious view is that it would not have mattered too much what the entrepreneurs' intentions were, for if they had complied with the official Accounting Standards their financial reports were bound to be *potentially* misleading. While we do not suggest there was any deceit and evil intent, this mattered little insofar as investors were nonetheless fed misleading financial signals about the financial wealth and progress of public entities. Fraudulent behaviour simply exacerbates such a situation. Misleading information was going to appear anyway.

Perhaps the personal ethics of the main public players in Australia's corporate collapses ought not to be on trial, or at least on trial as much as they are, and in particular not so insofar as accounting is an issue. Hugh McKay succinctly noted a theme we have pursued here, that '[t]he exploitation of morality is one of the most corrosive of contradictions'.[28] Media attention on the individuals, our 'cult of the individual', has skewed public attention from the whales and towards the minnows to capture the human-interest angle.[29] Such attention is short-lived. Those individuals will leave the scene anyway, to be replaced by others – inevitably, unless the circumstances in which they operated are changed to prevent it.

Yet, most of the corporate governance mechanisms emerging in the brouhaha following the latest round of large collapses are, in effect, measures to control individuals' wrongdoings. Individuals, rather than the system, remain on trial.

What ought to be under close scrutiny is the loose regulatory framework in which commerce and industry proceeds and is supposed to be accountable. The overemphasis on the individual will be enduring unless deliberate action is taken to alter it.

True and fair: fare-thee-well?

Neither accountants nor corporate managers should have had any doubts as to their overriding ethos. The *true and fair* override is consistent with a commonly held view embodied in this dictum:

> To be effective as a stimulus to ethical thought and behaviour, a code of ethics should set out principles, ideals, virtues and values. What it should not do is prescribe behaviour through a set of rules and regulations.[30]

Under the *true and fair* ethos, ethical behaviour by accountants necessitated that they produce financial data indicative of the financial characteristics they are held out to represent. Few professional groups have as explicit an ethical charge presented to them as that, and few have had it enshrined continuously (for nearly 160 years) in legislation as widely used as the company laws. One might have expected accountants and corporate managers to have jealously guarded that edict.

Just the opposite appears to have occurred. Many have abandoned it.[31] Only recently, apparently, is it being considered for a revival – but only by those seen by some to be the mavericks and mavens of the profession.

Described by one regulator as an 'accounting anachronism', the 'true and fair' criterion was replaced in the early 1990s with industry and professionally developed codes and rules (the Standards) to be the dictates of practice. One accounting textbook quickly and erroneously referred to 'true and fair' as being carried forward in legislation 'as something of a museum piece'.[32]

Without vehement objection by the accounting profession to its most explicit ethical peg being thus demoted, the *true and fair* override clause is taken to be a second order imperative, thereby enforcing a stricter compliance with the profession's Accounting Standards. If directors or auditors are of the view that the published data are not true and fair, they are to report to that effect, not in the 'accounts proper', but in the *Notes to the Accounts*. Not surprisingly, some 'maverick' practitioners and corporate officers reacted quickly and strongly. Two good early examples in the 1990s were the actions of the directors of Westfield Holdings and the QBE and NRMA Insurance groups. The latter, having been refused court exemption from compliance with the Standard covering Accounting for General Insurance Business (AASB 1023), reported its 1992 results under two heads – as per the Accounting Standards, and according to the Directors' Preferred Method of Accounting.[33] The directors at Westfield exercised their judgment to satisfy their true and fair Corporations Law (as it was then) obligations when they 'derecognised' management agreements as an asset – a sensible move, we would argue. However, their action did not accord with Australian Accounting Standards. Complicating matters even further, it seemed that it would have been in accord with existing International Accounting Standards. Life for directors was certainly not meant to be easy.

It is surprising that the accounting profession generally has traded such a unique ethical benchmark for the misguided safe-harbour afforded by compliance with its Standards. Though the trade fits neatly into the concurrent attempts by accountants to *limit* liability arising from their professional work.[34]

Interestingly, following the post-2000 collapses there have been indications of unease with the way the true and fair override was seen by some to have been demoted. Against the failure, arguably, of the financials of HIH, One.Tel and Harris Scarfe to indicate the full extent of those companies' financial difficulties until almost immediately prior to announcement of their collapse, and the continued adjustments for *one-offs*, *special* items, *unusual* items, *non-recurring* items by those that have not failed, the efficacy of the current dictum in *accord with the Accounting Standards* cannot be considered a success.

Some senior Australian practitioners have, indeed, openly declared that true and fair ought to be the primary criterion (see Chapter 2), perhaps the only criterion. Submissions to and evidence before the Joint Committee of Public

Accounts and Audit inquiring into the *independence of registered company auditors*, and also to the HIH Royal Commission, have brought forth strong 'true and fair' support. There has also been the reactionary plea for the retention of the technical interpretation. Gradually, commonsense may be returning to the framework of commerce.

Limiting liability – if the cap fits, wear it!

There should be little doubt that the level of professional indemnity insurance taken out by corporate directors and auditors is the primary factor limiting the extent to which damages for negligence might be extracted through litigation. Those individuals' personal wealths are unlikely to amount relatively to much. Divesting of property ownership is expected to mitigate exposure to personal loss. In the wake of past litigation, and with the prospect of more to come, it is to be expected that insurance cover will be increased and premiums will continue to rise.[35] Accountants in general, and auditors in particular, have found the insurance slug unpalatable. Their responses, while predictable, are somewhat questionable. As professionals, they claim sizeable fees for their services, but appear unwilling to accept the relationship between the level of fees and the risk for which it compensates.[36] As business people the push by accountants is understandable – perhaps herein lies the problem – are accountants moving away from their professional roots?

While it might be claimed that fees have increased to meet the high insurance premiums and have been passed on to clients, it is far from clear that fees were correspondingly lower before the spate of litigation or the surge in indemnity premiums. The same is true of company CEOs, directors and valuers: insurance premiums are high, but then so are directors' and valuers' fees.[37] Many seem increasingly to want to have their cake and eat it too.

To that end, following similar moves overseas, accountants in Australia have pursued having financial liability for the consequences of their professional services limited by statute. A statutory cap on their liability arising through actions under the Corporations Law was sought.[38] Such a proposal has a history of approximately 70 years.[39] The anguish felt by accountants and auditors could only have been exacerbated by the post-2000 events. A document (*Professional Liability in Relation to Corporations Law Matters*), prepared in June 1993 (updated in March 1996) by the Working Party of the Ministerial Council for Corporations, canvassed the professional bodies' alternative mechanisms to statutory capping, *inter alia*: combining self-regulation and auditor rotation, placing a limit on the useful life of financial accounts, permitting accountants to incorporate with consequential limited liability, and permitting companies to pay directors' indemnity premiums so as to split the claims on auditors by having directors well insured too.[40] While the WA and NSW legislation (reinforced by NSW's tort legislation in 2002) sought to restrict liability, accounting firms are not satisfied. There are concerns that, without national tort legislation, loopholes will persist. Also, due to several claims against auditors during the 1990s under the Federal Trade Practices Legislation (and similar Fair Trading State Acts) there is still the perception that users of accounts have the opportunity to seek damages of an unlimited amount.

Activity is hotting up in this area. At the federal government level, CLERP 9 appears to have indicated the national government's rejection of the idea of extending the WA and NSW government caps on professionals' liability. But other ongoing federal government inquiries may see it differently.[41] As this volume goes to press there is speculation that there may be legislation introduced in all Australian states to cap liability for negligence.

Incorporation by professionals runs counter to the exercise of individual judgment, the very hallmark of professional behaviour – that which distinguishes the professional from the artisan. Nonetheless, it looms as a likely outcome in the wake of its endorsement in *CLERP 9*, with recommendations that audit firms be permitted to incorporate and that proportional liability be instituted. Nonetheless, it seems that the legislative intention is to *lift the veil* in the event of negligence.

Proposals for proportionate liability, ensuring directors with sufficient insurance cover would share the damages with accountants, are reasonable, provided the objective is to increase the recovery of financial losses by the aggrieved. But they may be seen to be less than honourable if undertaken as an alternative to rectifying a primary cause for the actions in the first place. It is difficult to imagine how accountants, directors or valuers can gain *public respect* – maintain their professional status – by liability limiting.

All proposals to limit auditors' liability relieve them from exposure to having aggrieved investors and creditors dip into auditors' 'pockets' potentially deepened by by indemnity insurance. However, they do nothing to prevent the potential for financials being misleading.

It is even more difficult to understand how such actions can remedy unethical behaviour. Public opinion may view them as adding to it. Directors and valuers cannot expect to collect sizeable fees and be perceived to be not fulfilling their fiduciary obligations in return. Accountants and auditors cannot expect to collect large fees while being perceived as failing to deliver quality products with impunity. It was suggested previously, perhaps unkindly, that those who are finding it too hot in the kitchen ought to get out.[42] Notwithstanding directors' and accountants' desires, neither can enjoy their commercial status, receive their financial rewards, without accepting the risks.

Technical subservience: professionalism lost?

Attacks on the professionalism of auditors and accountants, following corporate collapses commonplace pre-2000, have become even more so post-2000. Whereas Australians are said not to be litigious by nature, they have found it in their water in recent times to launch numerous negligence (now often class action) suits against members of the accounting profession and corporate officers. Avowed litigants (presumably by nature) in the United States no doubt have shown the way and have been good teachers. But the locals have been willing students. Claims in the United States have generally dwarfed those in Australia and the United Kingdom in the past. In the United States, for example, in 1991 the seventh-largest accounting firm, Laventhal & Howarth, was placed in bankruptcy due to the settlement of litigation claims.[43] Claims against auditors, catalogued in Table 18.1, are also of alarming proportions. Indeed, it is no wonder Australia has been ranked number two in the world after the United States in the litigation-against-auditors stakes.[44]

Notable were the post-2000 reported out-of-court settlements related to the Bond Corporation and Adsteam imbroglios. These came nearly ten years after those companies were placed in administration. At Bond, Andersen's reportedly agreed to a $110 million settlement. At Adsteam, the amount was reported to be $20 million, shared equally by the auditors and the directors.[45] In the latter, of particular significance were the terms of the settlement in which the accounting firm entered, *inter alia*, a covenant with ASIC to ensure that its clients in the future complied with the Accounting Standards. Thus, in a perverse twist to auditors' woes, arguably a major contributor to them had tenure bestowed upon it.

A common thread in the reporting of those claims is the theme that those auditors may have acted unprofessionally, that they may have been negligent in carrying out their audits, or that their ethics may have declined. In certain cases this *may* have been so and equally possible that it was not.[46] Explanations of what auditors generally were expected to do that they failed to do, how they were expected to behave differently, are curious omissions in most of that reportage. Actually, there are contestable explanations within the framework of accounting and auditing rules with which accountants have to comply. Exposure to litigation is inherent in the former and risk to their professional status in the latter. That is a tragic outcome for a professional group. They are on a hiding-to-nothing from the start – a 'mission impossible'.

Nowhere has that been more pronounced than with the demise of the Andersen firm following its involvement in the Enron affair, the document shredding, and the firm's conviction for interfering with the administration of justice in the United States. Andersen's previous run-ins with the SEC over Sunbeam, and Waste Management, Global Crossing, Arizona Baptist Foundation and then in the WorldCom matter, set the firm up as the obvious target to be made an example of. With unfortunate timing, Andersen's con-current trouble in Australia with the HIH collapse, was possibly as much a rubbing off from its US troubles, a case of guilt by association.

The risk is that the Andersens' blood-letting will obscure the plight of auditors generally. Few commentators have bothered to note, as Table 19.1 shows, that the remaining Big Four in the US have featured in the major US corporate falls from grace too. Data in Table 18.1 revealed a similar spread of litigation against the larger audit firms in Australia in the 1990s.

It has been implied that Andersen was a sacrifice to assuage the USA's Capitol Hill.[47] In Australia, the firm's disappearance from the auditing business may well have served a similar purpose. But, nothing likely to improve the effectiveness of auditing has emerged. Proposed remedies continue to pursue tired red herrings – the fact that the problems besieging auditors are accounting problems remains out of focus.

Two matters are to be noted from the data in Tables 18.1 and 19.1. First, only the top-flight audit firms have the experience and expertise to undertake the audit of the major corporates of the kind whose collapse hits the headlines. Second, that the top-flight firms are exposed in this fashion is redolent of the inherent hazard endemic of the systemic defects in accounting to which they are shackled. Auditors continue to be in a no-win situation. The count is over before they enter the ring.

Curiously, no claims with respect to relying on the Accounting Standards have arisen in the litigation surrounding corporate collapse. Though they may

Table 19.1 Major US accounting investigations/lawsuits (as of June 2002)

Company	Auditor
Adelphia	Deloitte & Touche
Computer Associates	Ernst & Young
Enron	Arthur Andersen
Global Crossing	Arthur Andersen
MicroStrategy	PricewaterhouseCoopers
PeopleSoft	Ernst & Young
PNC Financial Services	Ernst & Young
Qwest	Arthur Andersen
Waste Management	Arthur Andersen
Worldcom	Arthur Andersen
Xerox	KPMG

Source: BusinessWeek, June 10, 2002, pp. 42–3.

well eventuate within that setting were the outcomes of compliance we have detailed, to be noted.

If this comes to pass, argument as to whether compliance with professional rules is a strong defence against negligence claims will be riveting stuff – *déjà vu* of the events surrounding the 1931 UK Royal Mail case, but with the benefit of over 70 years of UK case studies to draw upon. Or in the US jurisdiction, over 30 years since the rulings in the Continental Vending and Bar Chris cases in the 1960s.

Such an outcome could further damage accountants' professional status considerably. Auditors may well be as diligent as possible within the framework in which they are forced to work, but incur possible exposure to litigation; damned for certain if they do not comply it seems, and, arguably, to be damned some day if they do.

Some of the blame for that situation must be borne by the auditors themselves. Specification of Standards within which they are to work has been embraced by many as a kind of safe-harbour against litigation.[48] In this regard, some auditors may have been willing travellers with the regulators, who have found having sets of rules as convenient benchmarks against which to test corporate reporting performance. Neither can have it both ways. Auditors and accountants need to distance themselves from the Standards as quickly as possible. In the current setting perhaps flooding the 'Notes' with the data they consider to reflect a 'true and fair view' might be a way to proceed.

Likewise for the regulatory watchdogs. It is not beyond the realms of possibility that their enforcement of compliance with the Accounting and Auditing Standards currently in force could, at some time in the future, be viewed with disapproval on their part. In analyses of the HIH debacle the actions of ASIC and APRA are being scrutinised closely. If watchdogs do not protect the community at large, as they are expected to, then it is commonsense for their performances to be questioned.

So, too, on those grounds, may the performance of the Accounting Standards-setters be assessed. For, were it to be realised how inadequate the Standards are for producing serviceable accounting data, then the work of those who devised them may well attract more attention from the financial victims of corporate failures than the directors, managers, accountants or auditors.

The events post-2000, both here and in the United States, have justified the warning issued in the 1997 edition[49] that the current state of accounting was a time bomb likely to damage both practitioners and regulators. Yet the regulators and those drafting the Accounting Standards and the Corporations Act continue to go down the same seemingly potentially hazardous path – more Standards and regulations of the kind that we have demonstrated in this volume to have failed in the past – as *black-letter* as ever, though now being heralded as a *principles-based* regime.

Professional accountancy bodies in Australia, as elsewhere before them, have spent considerable time and fortune over the past decades massaging a public image of their not-to-be-denied professional status. The 1990s possibly marked a discontinuity. Trouble is, the professional bodies appear to believe their own advertising – the product so needing an overhaul remains virtually unchanged. Centres of Excellence are under CPA Australia patronage – including financial accounting, management accounting, public sector accounting, treasury groups. It is credentialism at its extreme. Existing practices have thus extended the appearance of having the underpinning force of a body of theory. Arguably, these centres have further entrenched the accounting and reporting status quo, shown over four decades in the Inspectors' and other official inquiries into corporate failures, and reportage in the financial press, to have fallen far short of the *true and fair* ethos.

Sociologist Bernard Barber identified the features of emerging or maturing professions – middle ranking in respect of generalised knowledge and community orientation, heterogeneous membership, the struggle to enforce its own rules of conduct and ethics.[50] Accountancy would seem to fit those characteristics well. Conformity to that pattern sends an important message to the commercial world regarding the efficacy of accounting products to be used for the assessment and evaluation of the financial health, the wealth and the progress of companies – they are technically very crude.

Few groups act with as much faith in the power of their own rhetoric. Attempts to talk away the supposed *gap* between what accountants and auditors do and what they are expected to be doing by the public at large is apposite. We are told what accountants do and how they do it is not questionable, it is more the case that everybody other than members of the profession and regulators has unreasonable, misguided expectations – there is an *expectation gap*[51] – a gap, that is, between what the consumers unreasonably expect from accounting and auditing and what they get.

That is true enough. One would think a better way of fixing the image would be to improve the product, improve what the consumers get, or at least argue it is not a hazard – as the tobacco lobby did. What is inexplicable is the promotion of the idea that the way to repair the damaged image of accounting and auditing is to have consumers understand that accounting data are not serviceable, that statements of financial performance and financial position are limited in their usefulness, and fairness – do not disclose a company's performance or position, wealth and progress, and whereas they are to be declared *true and fair*, they really are inaccurate and misleading. That is, to explain that there is not so much an expectation gap as what amounts to a *credibility gap*. That is tantamount to the tobacco lobby agreeing that smoking is dangerous and that smokers merely have false expectations – set them right and the danger will be gone. Possibly there is a message from the anti-smoking movement – perhaps the way forward for accounting reform is to have statements of financial performance and statements of financial position labelled *financial hazards*.

Accounting at the professional crossroads

Corporate accounting is 'in crisis'.[52] It is in a chaotic state as the evidence in this volume demonstrates.[53] Further testimony to this state are the 1990s' settlements of claims against audit firms, including one of over $135 million (Tricontinental), $120 million related to the State Bank of South Australia, and the reported 2002 $110 million out-of-court settlement of the nearly $1 billion dollar damages claim by the liquidator of Bond Corporation lodged many years earlier. The Bond claim alleged breach of duties and failure to warn the company of its impending demise. Further, there are other litigation claims pending against auditors.

Whereas the outcome of the HIHRC inquiry is yet to emerge, evidence before it and the ASIC investigation into One.Tel has revealed the flimsy foundation of many accounting practices. More importantly, they have revealed the ease with which the myriad Standards and rules of accounting practice are circumvented. And, as shown in Chapters 2 and 17 in particular, primarily because they are divorced from the financial (and legal) reality of the trans-actions to which they relate.

From the published financial statements it remains impossible (unless by chance) to assess the wealth and progress of a company, virtually impossible to calculate reliable indicators of solvency, rate of return, asset backing, gearing and the like, from the data in published financial statements prepared in com-pliance with the Accounting Standards. Published financial statements contain data which are mere artifacts of the processing rules imposed upon accountants through the compulsory imposition of Accounting Standards, some of which lead to data being pure fiction. The latter are not merely unrepresentative of what they describe – they have nothing to describe – they have no referent in the real world. The discussion on creative accounting in Chapter 2 and the instances of *creative* and *feral* accounting described in Chapters 3–17 through the 1960s to the 2000s demonstrate the continuing unserviceable state of accounting information. Is it any wonder that there is a crisis?

That evidence leads to an almost inevitable proposition: notwithstand-ing the best of intentions and the highest integrity, compliance with many

Accounting Standards will almost certainly lead to creative (misleading) accounting; deliberate deviation from historical-cost based, fiction-laden Standards is necessary to produce serviceable (truly meaningful) financial information. All of which begs further questions: Whither regulation? whither quality? whither professionalism?

There needs to be compelling evidence produced by the professional bodies or the corporate regulators to support the idea that the quality of accounting data and financial reporting can be guaranteed through mandating compliance with prescribed practices. It is reasonable to presume that the regulation is intended to protect the users of the data in company accounts from financial peril, rather than expose them to it. It is inexplicable why, in the face of evidence such as produced in this volume, the accounting data emerging from the existing regulated process fail to inform and hence protect the regulators' push for more of the same.

In a reasonably well-ordered society, one would expect, indeed demand, regulation be directed to achieving quality, reliability, fitness for use – serviceability of the product rather than mere standardisation of the processing rules. That standardisation is a virtue *per se* but is a contestable proposition at the best of times. Yet, as demonstrated here, the accounting profession appears to have led the field in the pursuit of standardisation divorced from the pursuit of serviceability. Latest moves for the adoption of the IFRSs indicate the malaise is universal. Accountants would do much better for themselves were they to adopt the current vogue and have mission statements and the like prescribed by their professional bodies with the view towards producing serviceable data in financial statements. As it is, they have 'mission impossible' forced upon them.

Apparently, compliance with prescribed processes (the Accounting Standards) is assumed to be an effective regulatory mechanism. Missing is the link between the prescribed practices and the quality of the end product. So, whereas there is regulation of process, the quality of the end product is not assured. Not one of the Accounting Standards, nor the omnibus Statement of Accounting Concepts No. 4 (SAC 4),[54] specifies *a* common, necessary, general quality characteristic which the emerging data are to possess, singly or in combination. This is at a time when quality, quality of outcomes in particular, is the general desiderata virtually everywhere. The notion of quality is somewhat like the Holy Spirit; except that whereas the Holy Spirit is everywhere, quality is the characteristic pursued everywhere – except (it seems) in accounting!

With some justification, we might also question whether compulsory compliance with prescribed processing standards is compatible with the notion of a profession. Professional activity is differentiated from that of the artisan. Artisans ply their craft according to hands-on experience, use regular and proven technology known to all in the craft without necessarily understanding why it is used, methods handed down from artisan to artisan. Their knowledge and skill, though considerable, is a common matter, rarely idiosyncratic. By contrast, the distinguishing feature of a professional is the exercise of the accumulated skill and wisdom, the out-of-the-ordinary, extraordinary expertise applied equally to both the ordinary and out-of-the-ordinary, the extraordinary circumstances. Professionals and their professions are distinguished from others by the exercise of the *differentia specifica* of their practices that set them apart from the rest of the community. That entails recognition of a social obligation, to apply one's skill and wisdom for the general benefit – requiring independent judgment as to how best to proceed.

Specifying compulsory rules (Standards) for processing accounting data, without also specifying necessary end qualities or characteristics to be achieved, poses a serious threat to accountants' claims to professional status. So does the pursuit of limited liability for the consequences for their actions. That leads to other propositions: compulsory compliance with Accounting Standards which concentrate on processes not outcomes is not necessarily conducive to producing serviceable financial data; and in any event, compulsory compliance with the prescribed processing Standards is incompatible with professional activity.

Conventional accounting practices complying with the prescribed Standards have been shown here to have contributed to masking impending failure, exacerbated losses to creditors and shareholders and provided regulators with a recurring dilemma.

Regulators of corporate activity have not heeded the lessons of history – the wailing, gnashing of teeth and the rhetoric of indignation at the sequential episodes of corporate failure have been recurrent, but ineffective, responses.

Though WorldCom's capitalisation of operating expenditures, Waste Management's lengthening of its truck fleet's assets' lives to decrease amortisation charges, Enron's and Xerox's front-end loading of revenues hit the headlines, few noted them repeat performances. It is surprising that the financial press failed to note that the accounting conventions that WorldCom, Waste Management, Enron and Xerox stretched almost certainly have induced errors in the accounts of every company that complies with them. The conventional accounting system is essentially an expenditure capitalisation system – expenditures are capitalised and gradually 'leeched' into the income statement as an everyday application of the accrual and matching system.

All that WorldCom did was overstep the mark according to the regulators. However, the *system* would not only have endorsed, but also demanded, a less extreme application of the rule. Arguably the accrual and matching rules are defective. Waste Management appears to have exploited the *rule* that depreciation is 'the allocation of a cost of an asset over its useful life'. In earlier decades US airlines 'manipulated' their profits using the Waste Management device of lengthening the 'expected lives' in conventional accounting's depreciation algorithm. But, of course, to everyone other than accountants, depreciation is not an 'allocation of cost', it is the 'decrease in price'. So Waste Management followed a defective accounting rule too, albeit in a manner that produced a result favourable for it. Enron's and Xerox's front-end loading, too, can be seen to be a product of the matching rule. It differs little in style from H.G. Palmer's accounting for hire-purchase profits. But the matching rule, applied as it is on a temporal basis in conventional accounting, invariably induces error and invites manipulation. Accruing revenues and expenses to match with presumed future expenses and revenues, almost ensures errors – even if not on Enron's or Xerox's scale.

It is not difficult to imagine that somewhere, somehow, some day, an alert judge will question the serviceability of conventional accounting data. A 1996 NSW Supreme Court judgment by McLelland CJ suggests it is nigh – he described the untangling of one Standard prescription on goodwill as 'almost a metaphysical problem'.[55] Against financial commonsense, arguably the financial nonsense promoted in the Accounting Standards will be nigh impossible to defend.

Postscript: de-regulation, serviceability, professionalism

Our case for reform outlined in Chapters 16–18 and in this chapter pursues the less detailed regulation of processes, but the more effective regulation of outcomes. Accounting Standards of the kind generally in force are conducive neither to producing serviceable accounting information nor to ensuring true professional endeavour. Regulation through the compulsory compliance with Standard processes and formats has not improved the quality of accounting data. There is no evidence even that it has achieved the comparability which is claimed as its virtue. Indeed, there is disturbing evidence to the contrary.

Notwithstanding continuing pleas by spokespersons of the profession to continue to improve the quality of accounting, the road being followed is *more* of the same – increased compliance, now in respect not only of national but also of International Financial Reporting Standards.

One would have thought it obvious that the present regulatory framework has failed to achieve the overall quality of accounting data, let alone improve it. The only regulatory defence for compulsory Accounting Standards is that they would improve the serviceability of accounting information. One would pursue that line with the expectation that the more Standards, the less the complaint and criticism of accounting from consumers, the fewer the instances of creative accounting. We have more prescribed procedures now than at any time in our history, nationally and internationally. One would have thought that there would be evidence of a decline in the dissatisfaction with the data accountants are producing – evidence of less creative accounting. The opposite has occurred (nationally and internationally).

Against that background it is most curious that ASIC continues its resolve to enforce compliance with the Accounting Standards. In 1997 the similar resolve of the (then) ASC was observed – the ASC was *determined* to '... enforce the rules and apply them strictly as worded', even, it seemed, if '[t]he ASC might say privately what you have to do does not make sense ...'. Whether it makes sense, according to the ASC, 'is not the issue'.[56] To the contrary, it *was* the issue then, and is even more so now – post-HIH, post-One.Tel, post-Harris Scarfe, post-Enron, post-WorldCom, and the rest. Whereas five years ago the ASC passed up the opportunity to be a public voice on consumer protection in respect to financial information, the ASIC now has the responsibility to do so. But, rather than acknowledge the inherent defects in the system, the ASIC has launched into a campaign to enforce compliance with the Accounting Standards. The present large *unexpected* failures have continued the flow of evidence that conventional accounting as it is enshrined in the Accounting Standards is inherently defective. That most of those Standards conform to the current IASs (and possible IFRSs) suggests that they are equally defective. Thus, it looks as if financial nonsense will continue to be protected in the safe-harbour of the Accounting Standards as we move into the new International Financial Reporting Standards regime.

Those *unexpected* corporate collapses reviewed in this volume have exposed gross anomalies and continuing generic defects of existing accounting practice. They ensure that variations on the types of comments made by Lawson 100 years ago:

This *system* is a process or a device for the incubation of wealth from the people's savings in the banks, trust, and insurance companies, and the public funds. Through its workings ... there has grown up in this country a set of colossal corporations in which unmeasured success and continued immunity from punishment have bred an insolent disregard of law, of common morality, and of public and private right, together with a grim determination to hold on to, at all hazards, the great possessions they have gulped or captured.[57]

will be repeated in another 100 years – and perhaps every decade between now and then!

Financial information as a serviceable product and accountancy as a professional endeavour are undeniably at the crossroads! We conclude by reiterating that without change, users will continue to lament that 'corporate accounting does not do violence to the truth occasionally, and trivially, but comprehensively, systematically, and universally, annually and perennially'.[58]

Notes

1 Chaos in the Counting-house

1 The opening to first edition of this book read: 'It was the best of days, yet the worst of days! On 12 October 1989 the 7.40 am train pulled out of Wahroonga station, on its way to the city. It was like every other workday. Those who had stood on the station in Sydney's executive belt, sheltering under its neatly clipped trees to avoid the morning sun, attaché-case in hand, squash racquet under arm, now slipped into seats in a mock orderly fashion. Getting a seat at that time of the day is always a lottery. But they knew it would be unbecoming for the upwardly mobile – male and female – the *yuppies, dinks, snags* and the like – to appear anxious about such a small matter. It would not be the sort of stuff that the upwardly mobile are made of, not the sort of thing you would expect to see a *Bond*, a *Skase*, a *Herscu*, a *Brierley*, a *Goward*, an *Elliott* or a *Spalvins* do in similar circumstances ... But that morning there was a difference ... Sydney's up-and-coming business glitterati gasped.'

2 Anon, 'World's biggest bust near', *The Australian*, 13–14 July 2002, p. 30.

3 P. Barry, 'Spurned Skase heirs dob in Pixie', *Sydney Morning Herald*, 23 October 2002, p. 1.

4 This emphasis is ably captured in Adam Shard's story on Rodney Adler, 'When I was a boy', and Andrew Cornell's 'The ghosts of Christmases past', pp. 14–20 and 22–30 respectively, *Australian Financial Review Magazine*, Summer 2002.

5 Anon, 'Big-Four might pull out of auditing', *Sydney Morning Herald*, 30 December 2002, p. 13.

6 R.J. Chambers, 'The poverty of accounting discourse', *Abacus*, September, 1999; J. Kay and B. Carsberg, 'Stiffening auditors' backbones: John Kay and Bryan Carsberg call for a body to scrutinise audit work and return an ethos of public duty', *Financial Times*, 2 April, 2002, p. 17; W. Schuetze, 'A memo to national and international accounting and auditing standard setters and securities regulators', *RJ Chambers Research Lecture*, 27 November, 2001; Anon, '"System is broken": world needs tougher rules of accounting', *Sydney Morning Herald*, 4 February, 2002, p. 32.

7 Further examples are provided in Z. Rezaee, *Financial Statement Fraud: Prevention and detection*, John Wiley, 2002; and H. Schilit, *Financial Shenanigans: How to detect accounting gimmicks and fraud in financial reports*, 2nd edn, (New York: McGraw Hill, 2002).

8 It is interesting that a 2002 PhD study by D.H. Holland reveals that a majority of Australian listed companies engage in 'earnings management' – as reported in

F. Buffini, 'Companies juggle earnings', *Australian Financial Review*, 26 July 2002, p. 14. This is discussed further in Chapter 2. ASIC *Media Release 02/460* details the results of its surveillance project – in sum the release noted 'there is no reason to believe that the type of accounting abuses identified in the United States pose a material risk in Australia'.

9 Consider, for example, Krasnoff's *Bob Ansett: The Meaning of Success* (1999). In the US Dunlap was fined $0.9 million and was party to US$15 million, action that is ongoing.

10 This aspect is discussed in detail in F. Clarke and G. Dean, 'Distressed businesses – predicting failure', pp. 147–84 in *Collapse Incorporated*, CCH, 2001.

11 D. Light, *et al.*, 'The secret society which sank Australia', *The Sydney Morning Herald*, 28 July 1990, p. 63. The term 'high-fliers' draws more on the personalities (Bond, Skase, Hawkins, *inter alia*) heading the companies than particulars of the companies.

12 T. Sykes, *Bold Riders*, (Sydney: Allen & Unwin, 1994), p. 571.

13 A. Main, 'All aboard Ray's HIH gravy train', *Australian Financial Review*, 8 August 2002, p. 14 details the list of alleged 'financial profligacies' noted by Wayne Martin QC, Counsel assisting the Commission – a role he described later as representing the view of the public.

14 H.Y. Izan, 'Corporate distress in Australia', *Journal of Banking and Finance*, June (1984), pp. 303–20.

15 A.E. Hussey, *Shareholder and General Public Protection in Limited Liability Enterprises from 1856 to 1969* (Unpublished MEc Thesis, The University of Sydney, 1971).

16 Dun and Bradstreet Corporation, *The Business Failure Record* (New York: Dun and Bradstreet Corporation, miscellaneous issues). Also E.I. Altman, *Corporate Financial Distress* (New York: Wiley, 1983), p. 32.

17 A. Fabro, 'Insolvencies up as business feels the GST pinch', *Australian Financial Review*, 22 May 2001, p. 3.

18 T. Sykes, *Two Centuries of Panic: A history of corporate collapses in Australia* (Sydney: Allen and Unwin, 1988), p. 548.

19 Anon, The *Institutional Investor*, November 1989, p. 127; Anon, 'Alan and his mates: Lessons from the drawn-out collapse of the Bond businesses', *The Economist*, 13 January 1990, pp. 14–15; *The Financial Times*, 5 January 1990, p. 19; P. Howard, 'Auditors in clash over standards', *Financial Forum*, August 1994, pp. 1–2. These and similar laments by H. Bosch, *The Workings of a Watchdog* (Melbourne, William Heinemann, 1990), prompted responses by spokespersons of the profession, viz, W. McGregor and J. Paul, 'Corporate collapses: Who's to blame?', *Charter*, September (1990), pp. 8–10, 13; W. McGregor, 'True and fair view – an accounting anachronism', *Company and Securities Law Journal*, December (1991), pp. 414–18. The 2000s' impact on the market through erosion of trust in the 'system' is noted throughout this volume.

20 S. Cronje *et al.*, *Lonrho: A Portrait of a Multinational* (London: Penguin, 1976), pp. 136 and 141 respectively.

21 C. Brooks, *The Royal Mail Case* (Toronto: Canada Law Book Co., 1933) (reprinted New York, Arno Press, 1980), p. xiii summarises the RMSP Co. saga; and our Chapter 16.

22 Anon, 'Finding the facts', *Sydney Morning Herald*, 25 November 1965.

23 Sykes, *Two Centuries of Panic*, p. 424; and our Chapter 7.

24 C. Ryan, 'Going for broke', *The Sydney Morning Herald*, 20 May 1989, pp. 75 and 78 at 75.

25 J. Gilmour quoted in S. Fitzgerald and C. Jones, 'Accountants come under fire', *The Sun-Herald*, 23 September 1990, pp. 12–13 at 12.

26 T. McCrann, 'Westpac takes its medicine', *The Daily Telegraph Mirror*, 21 May 1992, pp. 27–8 at 27.

27 M. Walsh, 'Lending binge was institutional hubris', *The Sydney Morning Herald*, 21 May 1992, p. 29.

28 K Murphy and T. Walker, 'Costello: audit crisis of confidence', *Australian Financial Review*, 8 February 2002.

29 F. Buffini, 'Hunt for potential disasters', *Australian Financial Review*, 4 April 2002, p. 42.

30 F. Buffini, 'Accountants call for radical audit shake up', *Australian Financial Review*, 19 April 2002.

31 P. Ritcher, 'US crisis of confidence: Why the US dollar is falling', *Australian Financial Review*, 4–5 May, 2002, *Perspective*, p. 26.

32 D. Leonhardt, 'Profit errors paid off for US executives', *International Herald Tribune*, 8 April 2002, p. 11.

33 N. Byrnes and D. Henry, 'Confused about earnings?', *BusinessWeek*, 26 November 2001, p. 77.

34 M. Vickers and M. McNamee, 'The betrayed investor', *BusinessWeek*, 25 February 2002, pp. 54–8.

35 N. Byrnes and M. McNamee, 'Accounting in crisis', *BusinessWeek*, 28 January 2002, pp. 50–4.

36 B. Pheasant, 'Auditors in danger from $2.5bn claims', *Australian Financial Review*, 30 June 1993, pp. 1 and 6 at 6. The phrase 'in crisis' was used in a document submitted in May 1993 by the joint task force of the two major accounting bodies, The ICAA and The ASCPA, to a federal government working party on professional liability. Following Enron's collapse and the fallout associated with the Andersen audit, former Federal Reserve Chairman Paul Volcker described the accounting and auditing profession as 'in crisis' (*Newsweek*, 26 November 2001, p. 77); *BusinessWeek* labelled a special report on Enron, 'Accounting in crisis', (28 January 2002, pp. 50–4).

37 ASCPA and ICAA, *A Research Study on Financial Reporting and Auditing – Bridging the Expectations Gap* (Sydney and Melbourne: ASCPA and ICAA, 1993).

38 W.P. Schuetze, 'What is an asset?', *Accounting Horizons*, September (1993).

39 D. Greatorex *et al.*, *Corporate Collapses: Lessons for the future* (Sydney: ICAA, 1994).

40 See for example, K. Walters and J. Stensholt, 'The purification process: the business and accounting sectors are confident they will be allowed to continue to regulate themselves', *Business Review Weekly*, August 29–September 4, 2002, pp. 78–80.

41 The recent exposure given to Brad Cooper of HIH fame is an exemplar – for example: C. Ryan, 'Brad Cooper's magic beggars belief', *Australian Financial Review*, July 27–28, 2002, p. 9; J. Hewett and M. Saville, 'The golden touch', *Sydney Morning Herald*, 27 July 2002, p. 27. Adele Ferguson's account of the HIHRC's

activities concludes "The HIHRC has spent too much money on peripheral issues … takes delight in picking on and character-assassinating individuals", 'The HIH Royal Commission', *BRW* 12–18 December, 2002 pp. 48–57.

42 D. Miller, *The Icarus Paradox: How exceptional companies bring about their own downfall* (New York: Harper Business, 1990), p. 2.

43 As suggested by Mark Burrows on Andrew Olle's 2BL (ABC Radio) morning programme, 8 April 1992.

44 Bosch, *Workings of a Watchdog*, pp. 123–4.

45 Anon, 'Bean-counters fight back', *The Economist*, 14 December 1991, pp. 79–80. Also P. Sikka *et al.*, 'Guardians of knowledge and the public interest: Evidence and issues in the UK accountancy profession', *Accounting, Auditing and Accountability Journal*, Vol. 2 No. 2 (1989), pp. 47–71; R.A. Chandler, ' "Guardians of knowledge and public interest": A reply', *Accounting, Auditing and Accountability Journal*, Vol. 4 No. 4 (1991), pp. 5–13; F. Mitchell *et al.*, 'Accounting for change: Proposals for reform of audit and accounting', *Fabian Discussion Paper*, Number 7, 1991; and P. Sikka *et al.*, ' "Guardians of knowledge and public interest": A reply to our critics', *Accounting, Auditing and Accountability Journal*, Vol. 4 No. 4 (1991), pp. 14–22.

46 T. McCarroll, 'Who's counting', *Time*, 13 April 1992, pp. 48–50 at 49. See also W. Sternberg, 'Cooked books', *The Atlantic Monthly* (January 1992), pp. 20–22, 24, 26, 35 and 38.

47 Public Oversight Board, *Issues Confronting the Accounting Profession: A Special Report by the Public Oversight Board of the SEC Practice Section* (Stamford, CT: AICPA, (5 March 1993), emphasis added.

48 Respectively: C. Ryan, 'Auditors are being called to account', *Sydney Morning Herald*, 29 April 1989, pp. 41 and 48; Anon, 'The accounts are a joke', *Sydney Morning Herald*, 29 May 1989; T. Sykes, 'Audit served no useful purpose', *Australian Business*, 12 September 1990, p. 6; R. Walker, 'What makes an audit "true and fair"?', *Business Review Weekly*, 11 January 1991, p. 61; T. Kaye, 'Uproar on accounting proposals', *Australian Financial Review*, 29 March 1993, pp. 1 and 35; B. Pheasant, 'Auditors in danger from $2.5 bn claims', *Australian Financial Review*, 30 June 1993, pp. 1 and 6; B. Pheasant, 'Accountants want to stop the damage', *Australian Financial Review*, 12 August 1993, p. 14.

49 W.P. Birkett and R.G. Walker, 'Response of the Australian accounting profession to company failure in the 1960s', *Abacus*, Vol. 7 No. 2 (1971), pp. 97–136. And, for example, in the 1970s, 'Cambridge fall calls joint accounting into question', *Australian Financial Review*, 19 January 1976; 'The need for a new spirit of realism in accounting', *Australian Financial Review*, 5 April 1979; 'What in hell's name happened?', *Australian Financial Review*, 14 February 1979. Reference to *déjà vu* was discussed in F.L. Clarke and G.W. Dean, 'Chaos in the counting house: Accounting under scrutiny', *Australian Journal of Corporate Law*, Vol. 2 No. 2 (1992), pp. 177–201; and again in R.G. Walker, 'A feeling of *déjà vu*: Controversies in accounting and auditing regulation in Australia', *Critical Perspectives in Accounting*, Vol. 4 (1993), pp. 97–109.

50 See, *inter alia*, B. Pheasant, 'Ripples on the corporate front', *Australian Financial Review*, 11 March 1992. 'Fuzzy law' is discussed in J.M. Green, 'Rogues – how to keep them out of the boardroom', *Company and Securities Law Journal*, December 1990, pp. 414–19; ' "Fuzzy Law" – a better way to stop "snouts in the trough" ', *Company and Securities Law Journal*, June 1991, pp. 144–57; 'A fair go

for fuzzy law', *Parliamentary Joint Committee on Corporations and Securities Conference*, March 1992; and D. Forman, 'A fuzzy route to greater clarity?', *Business Review Weekly*, 9 July 1993, pp. 34–5.

51 W. McGregor, 'True and fair view – an accounting anachronism', *The Australian Accountant* (February 1992), pp. 68–71; W. McGregor, 'The conceptual framework for general purpose financial reporting', *The Australian Accountant*, December 1990, pp. 68–74; D. Waller, 'Time to get rid of true and fair?', *The Accountants' Magazine*, December 1990, p. 53; and say, A. Kohler, 'Tony Hartnell throws a spanner into the works', *Australian Financial Review*, 28 March 1991, p. 56.

52 These views are expressed in respective submissions to the Joint Committee on Public Accounts and Audit, 'Review of Independent Auditors', 2002 (www.aph.gov.au – follow links). Also see A. Kohler, 'Business regulation is back … big time', *Australian Financial Review*, 27–28 July 2002, pp. 21 and 23.

53 *Interim Report … into the Affairs of Reid Murray Holdings Limited and Certain of its Subsidiaries* (Victorian Govt Printer, 1963), p. 10.

54 Finance editor, 'Learning the hard way: The Reid Murray Lesson', *The Sun*, 4 December 1963.

55 Committee of General Council of the Australian Society of Accountants, *Accounting Principles and Practices Discussed in Reports on Company Failures* (Melbourne: ASA, 1966).

56 Consider also: UK Combined Code (following Cadbury, 1992), Belgium's Cardon Report, France's Vernon Report, Netherlands' Peters Report, the 1999 OECD report. Discussion of these appears in R. Prickett, 'The state of independents', *Financial Management*, July/August, 2002, p. 11.

57 L. Cunningham, 'Sharing Accounting's Burden: Business lawyers in Enron's Dark Shadows', *Unpublished Working Paper*, April 2002; http://ssrn.com/abstract_id =307978.

58 Cases are described in E. Woolf, *Auditing Today* (London: ICAEW, 1981); and in R. Beckman, *Crashes: Why they happen – what to do*, London: Gratton, 1990.

59 See Chapter 2 references for cases referred to in this paragraph.

60 J. Ewing and D. Fairlamb, 'The fall of Leo Kirch: All the media baron's connections might not save him now', *BusinessWeek*, 11 March 2002, pp. 30–2.

61 We note his rejection of our observations in a book review of our first edition, *Companies and Securities Law Journal*, 9 September (1997), but we stick to our claim.

2 Creative Accounting – *Mind The GAAP*

1 B. Sidhu describes professional developments in Australia and overseas in 'The new "deferred tax": a comment on AARF Discussion Paper 22 "Accounting for Income Tax"', *Australian Accounting Review*, (March 1996), pp. 37–49, while earlier, F. Clarke, 'Deferred tax: hocus pocus', *Accountancy*, August (1977) discussed the unserviceability of tax effect accounting.

2 T. Boreham, 'Regulator takes a new look at abnormal items', *Business Review Weekly*, 25 September 1995, pp. 96–7.

3 *ibid*.

4 R.J. Chambers, 'Financial information and the securities market', *Abacus*, Vol. 1 No. 1 (1965), pp. 3–30 at 16. A leading American practitioner, Leonard Spacek, held a similar view in the 1960s.

5 R. Craig and F.L. Clarke, 'Phases in Australian Accounting Standards setting: Control, capture, co-existence and co-ercion', *Australian Journal of Corporate Law*, Vol. 3: 1 (1993), pp. 50–66 at 60.

6 Chanticleer 1977a, 'Accountants dream of the BHP statement of profitability', *Australian Financial Review*, 25 July 1977 (as cited in J.J. Staunton, 'Widows, orphans and lessons for accounting', *Management Forum*, (June 1978), pp. 134–9 at 134). R.J. Chambers, *Securities and Obscurities* (1973), describes many such instances worldwide.

7 Chanticleer 1977b, *Australian Financial Review*, 25 July 1977 (as cited in Staunton, *ibid.*).

8 Bosch, *Workings of a Watchdog*, p. 121.

9 Staunton, 'Widows, orphans and lessons for accounting', provides some instances of this international characteristic, as does Bosch, *ibid.*, p. 121; and accounting academics, Chambers, Briloff, Spacek and Mattessich.

10 A. Briloff, 'Revisiting unaccountable accounting revisited', *Critical Perspectives in Accounting*, Vol. 4 No. 4 (1993), pp. 310–35.

11 Synonyms used include *cooking the books* and *window-dressing*. Similar observations appeared in Australia and overseas in the late 1980s, even prior to the October 1987 share market crash: H. Killen, 'A correction for creative accountants', *Australian Financial Review*, 15 May 1987, p. 10; and Anon, 'Amateur accountants: Britain's Accounting Standards Committee is under-financed, under-staffed and under-powered', *The Economist*, 11 April 1987, pp. 14 and 16. A commentary on creative accounting in Britain in the 1980s appeared in D. Tweedie and G. Whittington, 'Financial reporting: Current problems and their implications for systematic reform', *Accounting and Business Research*, Winter (1990), pp. 87–100. See also footnotes 24–35, Chapter 2.

12 G. Breton and R.J. Taffler, 'Creative accounting and investment analyst response', *Accounting and Business Research*, Spring (1995), pp. 81–92.

13 J. Argenti, *Corporate Collapse* (Maidenhead: McGraw Hill, 1976), pp. 141–2.

14 References to authors cited and others in date order: W.Z. Ripley, *Main Street and Wall Street* (New York: Little Brown and Company, 1927; reproduced Kansas: Scholars Book Co., 1974); A.A Berle Jr and G.C. Means, *The Modern Corporation and Private Property* (New York: MacMillan, 1932); A. Andersen, 'Present-day problems affecting the presentation and interpretation of financial statements', *Journal of Accountancy*, November (1935), pp. 330–44; C. Blough, 'Some accounting problems of the Securities and Exchange Commission', *The New York Certified Public Accountant*, April (1937); Twentieth Century Fund, *Abuse on Wall Street: Conflicts of interest in the securities markets* (Westport, Connecticut: Quorum Books, 1937; 1980); and A. Barr, 'Accounting and the SEC', in A. Barr, *Written Contributions of Selected Accounting Practitioners, Volume 3*, Alabama (1959); A. Briloff, *Unaccountable Accounting* (New York: Wiley, 1972), *More Debits Than Credits* (New York: Harper & Row, 1976) and *Truth About Corporate Accounting* (New York: Wiley: 1981), E Stamp and C. Marley, *Accounting Principles and the City Code: The case for reform* (Altrincham: Butterworths, 1970); R.J. Chambers, 'Financial information and the securities market', *Abacus* (September 1965), pp. 3–30 and *Securities and Obscurities* (New York: Gower Press, 1973) reproduced as *Accounting in Disarray* (New York: Garland Publishing Inc., 1986).

15 M. Stevens, *The Accounting Wars* (New York: Collier Books, 1986); I. Griffiths, *Creative Accounting: How to make your profits what you want them to be* (London: Allen and Unwin, 1986); M. Jameson, *A Practical Guide to Creative Accounting* (London: Kogan Page, 1988); D. Tweedie and G. Whittington, 'Financial reporting: Current problems and their implications for systematic reform', *Accounting and Business Research*, Winter (1990), pp. 87–100; I. Kellogg and L.B. Kellogg, *Fraud, Window Dressing and Negligence in Financial Statements* (New York: McGraw Hill, 1991), T. Smith, *Accounting for Growth: Stripping the camouflage from company accounts* (London: Century Business, 1992), H.M. Schilit, *Financial Shenanigans: How to detect accounting gimmicks and fraud in financial reports* (New York: McGraw Hill, 1993; 2nd edn, 2002) and C.W. Murford and E. Cominsky, *The Financial Numbers Game: Detecting creative accounting practices* (New York: Wiley, 2002).

16 Jameson, *ibid.*, p. 20.

17 *ibid.*, p. 20.

18 Griffiths, *Creative Accounting*, p. 5, emphasis added.

19 *ibid.* 'Foozle' was used by H. Russell, *Foozles and Fraud* (Altamone Springs, Florida: Institute of Internal Auditors, 1978) to designate the action of a manager portraying a company in the best light, bordering on that fine line between what is regarded as legal and illegal.

20 R.G. Walker, 'Ten (legal) ways to cook your books', *Business Review Weekly*, 2 June 1989, pp. 50–3, 55.

21 Bosch, *Workings of a Watchdog*, p. 29.

22 Bosch, *ibid.*

23 Bosch, *ibid.*

24 Bosch, *ibid.*, p. 123.

25 The significance of this standard was discussed by J. Trowell, 'Asset valuation: Recoverable amount and measurement error', *The Australian Accounting Review*, November (1992), pp. 27–33. The actual variety of methods used is discussed in R. Begum and B. West, 'Non-current asset valuation: An Australian survey', *Charter* (February 1996), pp. 49–51. Subsequent authors like Walker and Walker (2000), have queried the mathematical propriety that expected cash flows can be added without discounting to arrive at a recoverable amount figure. Others have queried the process *per se.*

26 For illustrations of some revenue increasing and expense decreasing methods used in the recent sagas refer to Z. Rezaee, *Financial Statement Fraud: Prevention and Detection*, Wiley, 2002, especially Exhibit 3.1.

27 For example, Raptis – $71 million off property values; Equitylink's $2.1 million pre-tax operating profit dipped when $40 million was written off 'management rights'; In 1991–92 Fay, Richwite and Co's pre-tax bank operating profits of $NZ44.5 million was more than offset by the NZ$122.5 million goodwill on acquisition write-off; IEL's pre-tax operating profit (after interest) of $92 million was reversed by an abnormal loss of $482 million; and CRA reported an after-tax operating profit of $350 million, only to have it reduced by extraordinary write-offs of $384 million – primarily relating to its Bougainville copper mine – resulting in a net loss of $34 million!

28 M. Stevens, 'Winners in the race for recovery', *Business Review Weekly*, 23 April 1993, pp. 64–71 at 67. Consider also that included in the 20 'Biggest "abnormal

losses" for that half year were NAB with $126.6 million, Adsteam $107.81 million, Westpac $84.7 million, David Jones $73.74 million ... TNT $45.89 million ... News Corp $37.25 ... ANZ $23.80 million down to Premier Investments with $18.51 million'.

29 See T. Blue, 'Now it's open season on directors', *Australian Business*, 3 July 1991, pp. 54–5.

30 S. Ellis, 'Westpac hits $2.2 bn brick wall', *Sydney Morning Herald*, 21 May 1992, p. 29 (emphasis added). Several finance studies have examined whether the share market can forecast the declining fortunes of companies, notwithstanding the picture painted in the reported accounts. A summary appears in: R.H.A. El Hennawy and R.C. Morris, 'Market anticipation of corporate failure in the UK', *Journal of Business Finance and Accounting*, Vol. 10, No. 3 (1983), pp. 359–72. Also articles have examined whether audit qualifications act as a signal or red flag to failure (W. Hopwood *et al.*, 'A test of the incremental explanatory power of opinions qualified for consistency and uncertainty', *The Accounting Review*, January (1989), pp. 28–48).

31 Data from the 1990s is revealing. During the 1991 and 1992 financial years, 100 companies from the top 500 listed on the ASX reported $1.9 billion and $1.05 billion respectively as catch-up adjustments – corrections to previous calculations in the compulsory depreciation simulations.

32 In 1991 tax effect accounting by those companies in f/n 31 alone produced balance sheet balances aggregating $12 billion in 1991 and $12.2 billion in 1992 – all potential adjustments to be made in subsequent years.

33 B. Jamieson, *Accounting Jungle* (Sydney: Business Review Weekly Publications, 1995).

34 Neil Chenoweth, 'The great profit recovery', *Australian Financial Review*, 11 September 1995, pp. 1 and 24.

35 Other 1995 abnormal write-offs included Westfield Holdings ($275 million), Ampol Exploration ($224 million), Pacific Dunlop ($157 million) and Coles Myer ($112 million), causing one journalist to muse whether those companies' managers had been 'realistic in capitalising items in the past because the write-downs have not been in response to any sudden and unforeseeable changes in circumstances' (see T. Boreham, 'Regulator takes a new look at abnormal items').

36 T. Kaye, *Sydney Morning Herald*, 29 June 1996, p. 79.

37 Trowell, 'Asset valuation'.

38 L. Fox, *Enron: The Rise and Fall* (John Wiley & Sons, Inc., Hoboken, New Jersey, 2003), pp. 40–2, 127–8.

39 F.L. Clarke and G.W. Dean, 'Company officers at risk', *Company Secretary*, February (1995), pp. 13–16. This aspect is discussed in depth in the submissions of M. Liebler and F. Clarke, G. Dean and P. Wolnizer to the 2002 Joint Committee on Public accounts and Audit, 'Review of Independent Auditors' (www.aph.gov.au).

40 It is unclear in some cases exactly what revaluation basis was relied upon by directors. With the 1992 Westpac revaluation it is clear. In releasing the results it was stated that the property and loan-related asset write-downs were to bring them in line with the *amount realisable from a willing buyer to a willing seller* allowing up to two years for settlement.

41 R.G. Walker, 'ASC must tackle misleading valuations', *New Accountant*, 23 January 1992, p. 9. The revaluation in May 1992 by Westpac of its property portfolio provides further support for this claim.

3 The Corporate 1960s: Dubious Credit and Tangled Webs

1 Consider, *inter alia*, B. Barlev and R. Haddad, 'Fair value accounting and the management of the firm', *Critical Perspectives on Accounting*, forthcoming 2003, who note that there are signs the move is beginning because of the continuing concerns over the relevance of the data currently reported.

2 Birkett and Walker, 'Response of the Australian accountancy profession to company failure in the 1960s', p. 104.

3 *ibid.*, p. 108.

4 *ibid.*

5 See Argenti, *Corporate Collapse*; S. Holmes and D. Nicholls, *Small Business and Accounting* (Sydney: Allen & Unwin, 1990); Miller, *The Icarus Paradox*; and S. Makridakis, 'What can we learn from corporate failure?', *Long Range Planning*, August (1991), pp. 115–26. In Australia, recently, the same claim was made in the Greatorex *et al.* study.

6 Similarly, McGregor and Paul, 'Corporate collapse'; McGregor, 'True and fair view'; C. Cohn, 'Brian Waldron – new ASCPA National President', *The Australian Accountant*, May (1991), pp. 20–2; and C. Pratten, *Company Failure* (London: ICAEW, 1991). All suggest that accounting was not a major contributing factor in 1980s' company collapses in Australia and the UK, respectively. In the 1970s' *Cambridge Credit Corporation* case the defendants also adopted this line of reasoning, suggesting that 'bad management' and 'economic circumstances' were the primary cause of failure. An *Australian Financial Review* editorial speculated that in the pending (1990s) court cases involving auditors of 1980s corporate collapses, defence counsel will be adopting similar pleading. It is sceptical of the likely success of this approach ('Auditors v. 1980s' excesses', 27 May 1992, p. 18). Several letters to the editor were generated, viz. G.H. Bennett, 'Auditors check prepared books', *Australian Financial Review*, 3 June 1992, p. 16; D. Smithers, 'Urgent need for national laws to protect auditors', *Australian Financial Review*, 5 June 1992, p. 16; M. Macleod, 'Takes two to do the audit tango', *Australian Financial Review*, 12 June 1992, p. 18; and A. Roff, 'Ensuring auditors stay independent', *Australian Financial Review*, 17 June 1992, p. 15.

7 Australian Bankers Association, *Corporate Failures* (1990) and R.J. Chambers, 'Accounting and corporate morality – the ethical cringe', *Australian Journal of Corporate Law*, Vol. 1 No. 1 (1991), pp. 9–21.

8 General Council of the Australian Society of Accountants, *Accounting Principles and Practices Discussed in Reports on Company Failures*, pp. 6–8. The UK accounting profession commissioned a similar inquiry 25 years later (Pratten, *Company Failure*) following the flurry of the high-profile corporate collapses and what the profession perceived to be the ill-informed comment they had drawn.

9 *ibid.*, p. 7.

10 Chambers, 'Accounting and corporate morality – the ethical cringe', p. 18.

4 Reid Murray: The Archetypal Failure

* The Reid Murray case draws on the official reports of the inspectors appointed by the Victorian government: B.J. Shaw, *Final Report of an Investigation ... into the Affairs of Reid Murray Holdings Limited* (Melbourne: Victorian Government Printer, 1966). B.L. Murray and B.J. Shaw, *Interim Report of an Investigation ... into the Affairs of Reid Murray Holdings Limited* (Melbourne: Victorian

Government Printer, December 1963), B.L. Murray and B.J. Shaw, *Interim Report of an Investigation … into the Affairs of Reid Murray Holdings Limited* (Melbourne: Victorian Government Printer, March 1965); *Interim Report of an Investigation … into the Affairs of Reid Murray Holdings Limited* (Perth: WA Government Printer, 1963); and University of Sydney class notes prepared by the late Ray Chambers, expert witness in litigation following the collapse of the Reid Murray group.

1 P. H. Karmel and M. Brunt, *The Structure of the Australian Economy* (Melbourne: Cheshire, 1963).

2 Shaw, *Final Report … into Reid Murray*, pp. 70–1.

3 *ibid.*, p. 63.

4 M. Kidman, 'Acacia to pursue Solpac takeover', *Sydney Morning Herald*, 13 April 1996, p. 84.

5 Murray and Shaw, *First Interim Report … into Reid Murray*, pp. 40–3.

6 *ibid.*, p. 95.

7 The price illustrated is the last sale for every other month as disclosed in the *Sydney Stock Exchange Gazette*.

8 Murray and Shaw, *First Interim Report … into Reid Murray*, p. 107, emphasis added.

9 Refer to submissions of M. Liebler and F. Clarke, G. Dean and P. Wolnizer to the 2002 Joint Committee on Public accounts and Audit, 'Review of Independent Auditors' (www.aph.gov.au).

10 Chapter 8 demonstrates that a similar series of events and current asset reporting occurred at Cambridge Credit Corporation only a decade later.

11 Murray and Shaw, *First Interim Report … into Reid Murray*, p. 109.

12 *ibid.*

13 As cited in Sykes, *Two Centuries of Panic*, p. 323.

14 *ibid.*, p. 298.

15 *ibid.*, p. 303.

16 Shaw, *Final Report … into Reid Murray*, p. 93.

17 Murray and Shaw, *Interim Report … into Reid Murray*, p. 92, emphasis added.

18 Sykes, *Two Centuries of Panic*, p. 327.

19 Stanhill changed its name to Banyule Australia Pty Ltd during 1963. It was the antecedent of an incestuous web of companies forming the Stanhill and Factors Groups, some of which would be public and some private. Many investors in the public companies would see much of their money disappear into the private ones owned by the Korman family.

20 A fuller version of the Korman saga appears in *Corporate Collapse* (1997, pp. 55–68), Chapter 5, 'Stanhill: Private and public corporate "Games"'.

21 P. Murphy, *Third and Final Report of an Investigation … into the Affairs of Stanhill Development Finance Limited …* (Victorian Government Printer, November 1967), p. 149.

22 *ibid.*, p. 169.

5 H.G. Palmer: 'Gilt' by Association

* This chapter is based on F.L. Clarke, University of Sydney BEc Honours major essay, 1969, and H.G. Palmer, *1965 Statement of Affairs*.

1 T. Fitzgerald, 'H.G. Palmer: The outlook now', *Sydney Morning Herald*, 14 December 1965, p. 18.

2 Other business people referred to in this collection having a similar indenture period were O'Grady (Reid Murray) and Stanley Korman (Stanhill group).

3 Anon, 'Prospectuses ... should be true and accurate', *Australian Financial Review*, 5 June 1969, pp. 4 and 6 at 4.

4 Sykes, *Two Centuries of Panic*, p. 371: 'Both groups were started by individuals during the Depression; both blossomed in the 1950s; both remained under executive control of their founders. More importantly, both were really financiers rather than retailers. But, whereas Reid Murray diversified widely, Palmer stayed ... a financier of retail sales.'

5 Anon, '"Bolt from the blue" bid by M.L.C. for Palmer', *Australian Financial Review*, 9 April 1963, p. 3.

6 *ibid.*

7 Anon, 'H.G. Palmer sets records', *Australian Financial Review*, 23 April 1964, p. 20.

8 Anon, 'A matter of gearing', *Australian Financial Review*, 21 March 1963, p. 20.

9 Anon, '"Bolt from the blue"', p. 3.

10 Sykes, *Two Centuries of Panic*, p. 372.

11 R.R. Hirst and R.H. Wallace (eds), *Studies in the Australian Capital Market* (Melbourne: Cheshire, 1964), pp. 414–23 noted that only after the early 1950s were debentures and other forms of long-term debt issued commonly by publicly listed companies. By 1954/55, £27.6 million was raised, increasing to over £200 million by 1959/60 (p. 408).

12 *ibid.*, p. 409. Other critics included R. Chambers, 'Information and the securities market'.

13 Anon, 'H.G. Palmer shareholders on clover', *Daily Telegraph*, 31 August 1958.

14 Anon, *Australian Financial Review*, 5 October 1961.

15 Anon, 'Palmer progress', *Daily Telegraph*, 8 April 1962, emphasis added.

16 These scandals are summarised in Bloomberg, 'Mr Copper: From high-roller to has been', *Sydney Morning Herald*, 15 February 1996, p. 88.

17 Report of evidence before S.M. Scarlett, 7 July 1966, cited in *Sydney Morning Herald*, 8 July 1966, pp. 7 and 8. Anon, 'H.G. Palmer case – witness tells of 1964 forecast: Bad debt situation "must show up"', *Sydney Morning Herald*, 8 July 1966.

18 Sykes, *Two Centuries of Panic*, p. 375.

19 Anon, 'Palmers a good buy', *Australian Financial Review*, 7 August 1964, p. 18.

20 Brooks, Royal Mail Case, p. 210; and our Chapter 16.

21 Anon, 'H.G. Palmer, gets 4 years ... auditor 3 years – Prospectuses should be true and accurate', *Australian Financial Review*, 5 June 1969, pp. 4 and 6 at 4.

6 Going for Broke in the 1970s

1 Accounting Standards Review Committee Report, Chairman R.J. Chambers, *Accounting Standards* (Sydney: NSW Government Printer, 1978), and covering letter with the report.

2 Current work on archiving the *Chambers Collection* of over 30,000 pieces of correspondence from 1947 to 1999, including many related to the formation of, and limited response to, this report is being undertaken by the University of Sydney Fisher Library. Its completion will assist historians in pursuing this matter further.

3 L. Wood, 'Corporate tax-rate cut to play havoc with results', *Australian Financial Review*, 10 June 1993, p. 23.

4 D. Janetzki, *The Gollins Years* (Brisbane: Privately published, 1989).

7 Minsec: Decline of a Share Trader

* Analysis is based on University of Sydney Department of Accounting course notes prepared by I. Eddie with assistance from G. Dean, and from *Inspectors' Report, Investigating the Affairs of Mineral Securities Ltd. ...,* Vols 1–3 (NSW Parliament, 3 March 1977); *Report of the Senate Select Committee on Securities and Exchange, Australian Securities Markets and Their Regulation*, Vol. 1 (Commonwealth Parliament, 1974; *Rae Report*); T. Sykes, *The Money Miners: Australia's Mining Boom 1969–1970* (Sydney: Wildcat Press, 1978); J. Byrne, 'The Minsec Affair: Parts 1–6', *The Australian*, 23–28 April 1973; G. Souter, 'The rise and fall of the House of Minsec: Parts 1, 2 & 3', *Sydney Morning Herald*, 20, 22 and 23 February 1971; W. Horrigan and C.R. Weston, 'Australian money markets: The aftermath of Minsec', *The Banker*, January 1977, pp. 43–7; and Sykes, *Two Centuries of Panic*.

1 G. Souter, *ibid.*, Part 2, p. 7.

2 Miller, *The Icarus Paradox*.

3 *Rae Report*, p. 14.1.

4 *Inspectors' Report*, Vol. 1, p. 10.

5 *ibid.*

6 *Rae Report*, p. 14.15.

7 S. Salsbury and K. Sweeney, *The Bull, the Bear & the Kangaroo: The history of the Sydney Stock Exchange* (Sydney: Allen & Unwin, 1988), pp. 350–4.

8 AARF ED 59, 'Accounting for Financial Instruments' (1993) broke from the tradition of not requiring stocks to be marked-to-market; however, its purview was limited to financial instruments of banks and financial institutions.

9 *Rae Report*, p. 14.42.

10 *Inspectors' Report*, Vol. 1, p. 18. There are similarities with the disclosure/non-disclosure of items revealed at the Royal Mail trial some 40 years earlier in the UK (see Chapter 16).

11 Clarke and Dean, 'Chaos in the counting-house'.

12 *Inspectors' Report*, Vol. 1, p. 167.

13 Back-to-back loans were a common practice in the affairs of 1980s corporate failures. They were referred to in analyses of one of those collapses, Bond Corporation, as 'BBs' or 'Brigitte Bardots'. Rod Johnson, 'Back-to-Back Loans: A fraud in transition', *Australian Accounting Review*, Vol 10 No 3, 2000, pp. 62–72 discusses this in detail.

14 *Rae Report*, p. 14.75.

15 *ibid.* Back-to-back loans figured prominently in C. Raw's account in *Money-changers* of Robert Calvi's 1970s fraud involving Banco Ambrosiano, the Vatican's IOR and entities connected with both (see R. Johnson, 'Back-to-Back Loans').

16 R. Johnson, 'Back-to-Back Loans' discusses those back-to-back loans in detail.

17 *Inspectors' Report*, Vol. 1, p. 50.

18 *Rae Report*, p. 14.123.

19 *Inspectors' Report*, Vol. 1, p. 72.

20 Complicating this saga is whether the market was being made by the dealings of the Minsec group of companies.

21 *Rae Report*, p. 14.63.

22 *ibid.*, p. 14.67.

23 *ibid.*, p. 14.74.
24 *Inspectors' Report*, pp. 199–200.
25 Announcement to Sydney Stock Exchange, 3 February 1971.
26 Sykes, *Two Centuries of Panic*, pp. 424–5.
27 This rescue operation is described in Reid, *The Secondary Banking Crisis*.
28 *R v. M* [1980] 2 NSWLR 195 (January 1981)
29 *ibid.*

8 Cambridge Credit: Other People's Money

* Analysis is based on G. Dean, 'Accounting for real estate development: Cambridge
   Credit Corporation case study', pp. 140–72 in R.T.M. Whipple (ed.), *Accounting
   for Property Development* (Sydney: The Law Book Co. Ltd, 1985); *Report of
   Inspectors, First Interim Report by the Corporate Affairs Commission into the
   Affairs of Cambridge Credit Corporation Limited and Related Corporations* Vol. 1
   (Sydney: NSW Government Printer, No. 222, 25 August 1977; *Inspectors' 1st
   Report*); and *Report of Inspectors, Second Interim Report by the Corporate Affairs
   Commission into the Affairs of Cambridge Credit Corporation Limited and Related
   Corporations* Vol. 2 (Sydney: NSW Government Printer, No. 23, 13 September
   1979; *Inspectors' 2nd Report*).
1 See *Sydney Stock Exchange Investment Service*, C29 (1963), p. 6.
2 Graphical illustrations of the complexity of the group structure are provided by the
   Inspectors. See *Inspectors' 1st Report*, pp. 286–7 and *2nd Report*, p. 290.
3 *Inspectors' 1st Report*, p. 22.
4 *ibid.*, p. 23.
5 *ibid.*, p. 24. Unearthing this penchant for 'a one-man show' operation is a recurring
   feature of investigations following collapses of large public companies.
6 *Inspectors' 2nd Report*, pp. 21–2.
7 Further details are provided below and in the *Inspectors' 2nd Report*, pp. 59–63.
8 *Inspectors' 1st Report*, para. 2.148 (specific examples of this channelling of losses
   appear at paras 2.96 ff.).
9 *Inspectors' 2nd Report*, p. 29.
10 *ibid.*, p. 281.
11 *ibid.*, p. 29.
12 *ibid.*, 'Conclusions', pp. 277–83; specifically, paras 6.35–7 and Appendix III.
13 *ibid.*, pp. 51–2, emphasis added.
14 *ibid.*, p. 52.
15 *Inspectors' 1st Report*, p. 65.
16 Securities and Exchange Commission (1965): *Accounting Series Release No. 95*,
   USA.
17 Securities and Exchange Commission (1975): *Accounting Series Release No. 173*,
   USA.
18 *Inspectors' 1st Report*, pp. 65 ff.
19 *ibid.*, p. 52; para. 4.8 at p. 168; para. 8.199 at p. 278 and *Inspectors' 2nd Report*,
   pp. 272–3. Reliance on substance over form has been promoted by accountants in
   Australia, the United States and the United Kingdom – see *APB, Opinion No. 4*
   (1970); in the UK ICAEW *Technical Release*, TR 603, 'Window dressing and
   substance v. form' (1985); and in S.J. Martens and J. McEnroe, 'Substance over
   form in auditing and the auditor's position of public trust', *Critical Perspectives in*

Accounting, December (1992), pp. 389–401 and Chambers, *Accounting Thesaurus* (1996).

20 *Inspectors' 2nd Report*, pp. 38–9, 148–50 and 269–70.
21 See *Cambridge Credit Corporation Ltd v. Hutcheson and Ors* (1983) 8 ACLR 123 at 133–158 and *Inspectors' 2nd Report*, pp. 151–247.
22 8 ACLR 123 at 162.
23 *Inspectors' 2nd Report*, p. 43.
24 Anon, 'Auditors not liable for damages', *Sydney Morning Herald*, 17 September 1983, p. 7.
25 *Inspectors' 2nd Report*, p. 20, para. 2.3, emphasis added.
26 *ibid.*, pp. 251–2 and 278.
27 *ibid.*, p. 251.
28 In 1973, for the first time in ten years, the total borrowings due exceeded by $30 million the total receivables due. Interestingly, even then management was able to report the two-year cover at around 1.03.
29 *Inspectors' 2nd Report*, p. 16.
30 *ibid.*, p. 17.
31 *ibid.*, p. 277, para. 6.4 and Table 9.4 in this book.
32 Sykes, *Two Centuries of Panic*, p. 466, is critical of the delay in criminal proceedings against Cambridge's directors, Hutcheson, Whitbread, Davis-Raiss and its auditor, Purcell: as is Bosch, *The Workings of a Watchdog*.
33 Details are provided in the 1994–95 ASC *Annual Report*, pp. 32–41.
34 *Cambridge Credit Corporation Ltd v. Hutcheson and Ors* (1985); unreported Supreme Court of NSW, No. 3462 of 1977, 25 March 1985, pp. 68–9, emphasis added.

9 Uncoordinated Financial Strategies at Associated Securities Ltd

* This chapter draws on F.L. Clarke and G.W. Dean, 'Uncoordinated financial strategies: The experience of ASL', in R.J. Jüttner and T. Valentine (eds), *The Economics and Management of Financial Institutions* (Melbourne: Longman Cheshire, 1987), pp. 437–53; and from a more detailed post-mortem of the collapse of ASL by G.W. Dean and F.L. Clarke, Working Paper, 'Anatomy of a Failure: A Methodological Experience – The Case of ASL', Centre for Studies in Money, Banking and Finance, Macquarie University, July 1983 (hereafter Working Paper).
1 R. Meadley, 'What in hell's name happened?', *Australian Financial Review*, 14 February 1979, p. 4.
2 This was a common reaction of investors and creditors immediately after the announced collapses at H.G. Palmer, Reid Murray, Minsec and Cambridge Credit Corporation, to name a few of the early examples. 'Auditors called to account' and 'Auditors under scrutiny', for example, heralded the collapse of HIH and of One.Tel.
3 R. Gottliebsen *et al.*, 'The inside drama of a $300 million crash: The ASL story', *The National Times*, 10 March 1979, pp. 22–5 and 27 at 22.
4 Trends in finance company borrowings (1945–63) are outlined in R.R. Hirst and R.H. Wallace, *Studies in the Australian Capital Market* (Melbourne: F.W. Cheshire, 1964), pp. 154–9. Trends for the 1960s and 1970s are provided in the Australian Finance Conference (AFC) members' submission to the Australian Financial System of Inquiry (1979); and M.T. Skully, *Working Paper*, 'Finance Companies in

Australia: An Examination of Their Development, Operation and Future', Centre for Studies in Money, Banking and Finance, Macquarie University, February 1983.

5 Gottliebsen *et al.*, 'The ASL story', p. 22.

6 *ibid.*, p. 23.

7 M.T. Daly, *Sydney Boom or Bust: The city and its property market 1850–1981* (Sydney: Allen & Unwin, 1982), pp. 91–2. For further details of ASL's land operations, see Dean and Clarke, 'Uncoordinated financial strategies: The experience of ASL', p. 13.

8 Gottliebsen *et al.*, 'The ASL story', p. 23.

9 A phrase coined by the *Australian Financial Review* when Sir Reginald Ansett, Sir Henry Bolte and Sir Cecil Looker, along with the other directors of Ansett, made the decision to stop further injections of Ansett money to prop up ASL.

10 Comprising finance to developers for the acquisition and development of raw land into residential blocks and, to builders, investors and owner-occupiers for housing construction.

11 Australian Finance Conference – Member companies of the AFC (including ASL) account for more than 85 per cent of the total assets of all finance companies and general financiers. For further details, see P.J. Barker and P.J. Mair, 'Finance companies', *Reserve Bank of Australia Bulletin*, August 1982, p. 76, where there is further evidence of finance companies' increasing investment in leasing.

12 For illustrations of the share market's response to ASL operations from January 1971 to February 1979, see Dean and Clarke, *Working Paper*, especially Appendices II and III. Sykes, *Two Centuries of Panic*, p. 493 notes that in October 1973 'the first whisper went around that all was not well at ASL and the share price was marked down from $1.80 to $1.30'. It was on a downhill slide thereafter until the collapse in 1978.

13 Daly, *Sydney, Boom or Bust*, p. 103. Contrary to the suggestion by Sykes, *Two Centuries of Panic*, p. 494, the Royal Bank of Scotland, with its less than 30 per cent capital in ASL, was 'never perceived as [ASL's big brother] and it was not'. These support actions and continuing investment in ASL by the bank provided some form of assurance to the market.

14 Daly, *ibid.*, p. 74.

15 Evidence supporting this proposition is found in Daly, *ibid.*, pp. 71–82, and Baker and Mair, 'Finance companies', pp. 75–83.

16 For details refer to Daly, *Sydney, Boom or Bust*, Table 3.6 at pp. 80–1; Reid, *The Secondary Banking Crisis, 1973–75*; and R.A. Schotland, 'Real estate investment trusts', in *Twentieth Century Fund, Abuse on Wall Street: Conflicts of interest in the securities markets* (Westport, CT: Quorum Books, 1980), pp. 158–223.

17 Daly, *Sydney, Boom or Bust*, p. 73.

18 Gottliebsen *et al.*, 'The ASL story', p. 22.

19 Daly, *Sydney, Boom or Bust*, p. 73.

20 *ibid.*

21 W. Guttmann and P. Meehan, *The Great Inflation* (London: Saxon House, 1975), pp. 14–17; and G. Dean, F. Clarke and F. Graves, *Replacement Costs and Accounting Reform in Post-World War I Germany* (New York: Garland, 1990).

22 C. Bresciani-Turroni, *The Economics of Inflation* (London: Allen & Unwin, 1937), p. 28.

23 *ibid.*

24 Guttmann and Meehan, *The Great Inflation*.
25 Reported in *The National Times*, July 1978.
26 Sykes, *Two Centuries of Panic*, p. 498
27 The belief of the ASL's directors in the advantages of having the Royal Bank of Scotland as an investor are impregnated on the minds of the reader of any ASL annual report for the years 1960–76.
28 F.L. Clarke *et al.*, 'Testing failure trajectories – European/Non-European contrast', 17th European Accounting Association Annual Congress, Venice, 1994; G. Dean and F. Clarke, 'Distressed businesses – predicting failure', pp. 147–84 of *Collapse Incorporated*, (CCH, 2001).

10 The 1980s: Decade of the Deal?
1 J. McManamy, *The Dreamtime Casino* (Melbourne: Schwartz and Wilkinson, 1990).
2 P. Barry, *The Rise and Fall of Alan Bond*, p. 286.
3 J. Green, '"Fuzzy law" – a better way to "stop snouts in the trough"?', *Company and Securities Law Journal*, June (1991), pp. 145 and 149, emphasis added.
4 Other criteria include relevance, materiality, consistency and prudence. All require directors', accountants' and auditors' judgments.
5 Refer to R.J. Chambers, 'Conventions, doctrines and common sense', *The Accountants' Journal*, February 1964, pp. 182–7.
6 R.W. Gotterson, *Report of a Special Investigation into the Affairs of Ariadne Australia Limited & Ors* (Sydney: NSW Government Printer, 1989).
7 T. Sykes, editorial, *Australian Business*, 12 September 1990, p. 6.
8 Public Oversight Board Report, 'Issues Confronting the Accounting Profession'.
9 Reported view of former KPMG Peat Marwick partner, Stuart Grant, upon his appointment to the ASC as Executive Director Accounting Policy in 1993, cited in B. Pheasant, '"True and fair" change seen as backward step', *Australian Financial Review*, 16 November 1992, p. 18.

11 Adsteam on the Rocks
1 Respectively A. Kohler, 'Adsteam a humiliation for the accounting profession', *Australian Financial Review*, 2 April 1991, pp. 1 and 52, and G. Burge, 'Adsteam's $4.49 billion loss is biggest ever', *Sydney Morning Herald*, 1 October 1991, p. 25.
2 M. Stenberg, 'DJs will not go cheap, says Adsteam', *Sydney Morning Herald*, 20 November 1993, p. 41.
3 M. Meagher and F. Chong, 'One-man bands?: How their companies would fare without them', *Business Review Weekly*, 20 February 1987, pp. 44–5, 47–8, 51, 53, 55–6, 59 and 63 at 59.
4 P. Rennie, 'Charting a course for Adsteam', *Business Review Weekly*, 26 August 1988, p. 125.
5 *In the Matter of The Adelaide Steamship Company Limited v. James Gunars Spalvins and Ors*, No. SG3036 of 1994 in the Federal Court of Australia, SA District Registry, General Division, December 1994. See also J. Parker, 'ASC appeals in ASC case', *Sydney Morning Herald*, 6 May 1996, p. 35. There were several appeals by both parties – the matter was settled out-of-court in November 2000 – see footnote 19 below.
6 T. Sykes, 'Adsteam unmasked', *Australian Business*, 19 April 1989, pp. 16–19.

7 R. Gottliebsen, 'Spalvins, the quiet acquirer', *Business Review Weekly*, 28 April 1989, pp. 20–5.

8 M. Peers, 'Intricacies cloud Adsteam's losses', *Australian Financial Review*, 13 February 1990, p. 16.

9 P. Rennie, 'What's the problem? Spalvins wonders', *Business Review Weekly*, 16 February 1990, pp. 29–30.

10 R. Gottliebsen, 'Spalvins' fatal flaw', *Business Review Weekly*, 3 May 1991, pp. 40–51.

11 M. Peers, 'Adsteam loses another 36c as panic spreads', *Australian Financial Review*, 20 September 1990, pp. 1 and 8 at 8.

12 A. Kohler, 'Now it's full steam ahead into retailing for Spalvins', *Australian Financial Review*, 31 October 1990, p. 68.

13 Rennie, 'What's the problem?', p. 30.

14 T. Sykes, 'Adsteam accounting made clear', *The Bulletin*, 14 April 1992, p. 93.

15 Anon, 'Accountancy Hotline: Spalvins judgement', *Business Review Weekly*, 1 June 1990, p. 110.

16 McIlwraith, 'John Spalvins out of steam', *Australian Financial Review*, 5 July 1991, pp. 27 and 29 at 29.

17 Sykes, *Bold Riders*, p. 435, emphasis added.

18 J. Parker, 'Taking Adsteam apart', *Australian Business*, 25 July 1990, pp. 16–19.

19 ASIC *Media Release 00/452*, 'Adsteam settlement: history of proceedings and joint public statement', 2 November, 2000.

12 Bond Corporation Holdings Ltd (Group): Entrepreneurial Rise and Fall

* Assistance by M. Tan in preparing the acquisition and divestment details of the Bond group of companies is gratefully acknowledged. Sources are cited throughout the text, including the publicly disclosed extracts from the ASC's *Sulman Report* presented in early 1992 but not publicly released; P. Barry, *The Rise and Fall of Alan Bond*; T. Maher, *Bond* (Melbourne: William Heinemann, 1990); the *SSE Investment Review Service*; and articles by M. Maiden, 'Bond's triumphs and troubles', *Australian Financial Review*, 4 December 1989, pp. 19, 20, 69, 70, T. Sykes, 'The case against Bond', *The Bulletin*, 25 February, 1992, pp. 26–9 and R. Gottliebsen, T. Treadgold and J. Kavanagh, 'Trapped in the web of WA Inc', *Business Review Weekly*, 8 September 1989, pp. 20–4. Alan Bond was convicted of fraud involving the purchase of *La Promenade*. Another investigation by the ASC into transactions around the time of the Bell Resources '$1.2 billion deposit' resulted in Alan Bond (together with two other BCH directors, Messrs Oates and Mitchell) being charged with fraud in January 1995. Extradition attempts to get Oates to face trial are continuing as this second edition goes to press.

1 J. McGlue, 'Final nail driven into Bond Corp', *Sydney Morning Herald*, 24 December 1993, p. 13.

2 Barry, *The Rise and Fall of Alan Bond*.

3 J. McGlue, 'Bond Corp auditor sued', *Sydney Morning Herald*, 11 April 1996, p. 25. Events post-1996 are covered in the following press accounts: AAP, 'Bond liquidators suing Arthur Andersen for $1bn', *Sydney Morning Herald*, 22 November, 2001, p. 28; L. Taylor, 'Alan Bond's back under full sailing', *Australian Financial Review*, 11/12 August 2001; M. Drummond, 'I am not guilty says unrepentant Bond', *Australian Financial Review Weekend*, 28 December 2001 – 1 January 2002, p. 4.

4 Miller, *The Icarus Paradox.*

5 As suggested by Mark Burrows on ABC broadcaster Andrew Olle's 2BL morning programme on 8 April 1992.

6 Interestingly, troubled assets seem attracted to troubled companies. Land held by the Korman and Reid Murray groups was found in the asset portfolios of troubled companies in the 1970s and 1980s, including Cambridge Credit and Tricontinental and Bond's purchase of Robe's shares. FAI Insurances would buy New York's St Moritz Hotel from Bond Corporation in the mid-1990s.

7 Barry, *The Rise and Fall of Alan Bond*, pp. 70–80.

8 Maiden, 'Bond's triumphs', p. 19.

9 Consortium members (respective interests) were Bond Corporation (50 per cent), Dallhold (10 per cent), Endeavour Resources (30 per cent), Amalgamated (5 per cent) and Leighton Mining N.L. (5 per cent).

10 A. Cromie, 'Bond keeps it in the family', *Business Review Weekly*, 2 July 1993, pp. 40–7 at 41. Other transactions discussed formed the basis of an ABC 'Four Corners' programme (26 July 1993) detailing aspects of Alan Bond's bankruptcy.

11 Barry, *The Rise and Fall of Alan Bond*, pp. 193–208.

12 Sotheby's, who sold the *Irises* painting, provided the majority of finance for the purchase of *Irises*. With this painting Alan Bond was described as one of the 75 biggest art collectors of the 1980s. The collection was acquired through a web of dealings between BCH group companies and Dallhold Investments. Clearly, 'there is nothing new under the sun', as further evidenced by the liquidation of the Bond Corporation empire's burgeoning Impressionist art collection. This had parallels with the 1941 'sale of the century' of William Randolph Hearst's collection, including Van Dyck's *Queen Henrietta Maria.*

13 *The Queen v. Alan Bond* (1997), p. 18.

14 Gottliebsen *et al.*, 'Trapped in the web of WA Inc', p. 21.

15 *ibid.*, pp. 21–2.

16 *ibid.*, p. 22.

17 A. Nolan, 'The position of unsecured creditors of corporate groups: Towards a group responsibility solution which gives fairness and equity a role', *Company and Securities Law Journal*, December (1993), pp. 461 ff. at 468.

18 This was achieved by way of a 93-page document, 'The Bond Group of Companies: A Financial Analysis by Lonrho plc', November 1988.

19 M. Stevens, T. Treadgold, N. Way and D. Uren, 'Bond Corp all at sea', *Business Review Weekly*, 12 January 1990, pp. 16–19. Financial journalist A. Cromie notes, 'Beckwith, Oates and Mitchell were Bond's key men. The value placed on them was shown in 1987': A. Cromie, 'Bond's men rise from the ashes', *Business Review Weekly*, 17 September 1993, pp. 62–8 at 63.

20 As reported in G. Haigh, 'UK judge chides Bond over lack of Bell records', *Sydney Morning Herald*, 22 July 1989, p. 41, and Anon, 'Bond tells jury of problems with memory', *Sydney Morning Herald*, 6 August 1996, p. 4.

21 Reported in Shaplen, *Kreuger: Genius and Swindler.*

22 For example, in the Lonrho document all debt in BCH was aggregated into one figure, including debt of a non-recourse nature.

23 Nolan, 'Towards group responsibility', p. 489.

24 *Annual Report*, 'Chairman's Report', p. 2.

25 See Barry, *The Rise and Fall of Alan Bond*, and H. Armstrong and D. Goss, *The Rise and Fall of a Merchant Bank* (Melbourne: Melbourne University Press, 1995).

26 An insight is provided in R. Gottliebsen and M. Stevens, 'Why the banks lent Bond $7 billion', *Business Review Weekly*, 8 December 1989, pp. 24–6 and 29.

27 M. Stevens, D. Uren and J. Kavanagh, 'Bond's biggest creditors', *Business Review Weekly*, 7 July 1990, pp. 20–2 and 26, and T. Sykes and T. Blue, 'The bankers behind Bond', *Australian Business*, 13 September 1989, p. 19.

28 M. Meagher and F. Chong, 'One-man bands? How their companies would fare without them', *Business Review Weekly*, 20 February 1987, pp. 44–5, 47–8, 51, 53, 55–6 and 59 at 45.

29 P. Rennie, 'Bond sails through the crash', *Business Review Weekly*, 11 December 1987, p. 141.

30 R.G. Walker, 'Brought to account: Normal items? Extraordinary!', *Australian Business*, 10 February 1988, pp. 95–6 at 96.

31 R.G. Walker, 'Window-dressing at Bond Corp', *Australian Business*, 24 February 1988, pp. 77–8 at 77.

32 BCH, *Annual Report* (1986/87), p. 86, note 10.

33 *ibid.*, p. 114, note 29(i).

34 Walker, 'Window-dressing', p. 78.

35 BCH, *Annual Report* (1986/87), p. 87, note 10.

36 *ibid.*

37 B. Dunstan, 'Eagle eye on company accounts', *Australian Financial Review*, 7 March 1988, pp. 75–6.

38 Walker, 'Window-dressing', p. 77.

39 *ibid.*, pp. 77–8.

40 M. Stevens, 'London waits for Bond's response', *Business Review Weekly*, 9 December 1988, pp. 39–40 at 39.

41 T. Sykes, 'Inside the Bond accounts', *Australian Business*, 19 October 1988, pp. 36 and 38 at 38.

42 T. Sykes and T. Blue, 'Bond's big sell-off', *Australian Business*, 13 September 1989, pp. 18–20 at 20. Those transactions are also discussed in R.G. Walker, 'A feeling of *déjà vu*: Considerations of accounting and auditing regulation in Australia', *Critical Perspectives on Accounting* 4 (1993), pp. 97–109 at 102–3; Maher, *Bond*, pp. 281–4; and Barry, *Rise and Fall of Alan Bond*, pp. 243–8.

43 Barry, *The Rise and Fall of Alan Bond*, p. 261.

44 T. Sykes, 'The end of Bond Corp?', *Australian Business*, 10 May 1989, pp. 16–18 and 20 at 16.

45 J. Wainwright, *Sunday Telegraph*, 22 October 1989, p. 23.

13 Westmex Ltd: The Security Façade of Cross Guarantees

1 Y. van Dongen, *Brierley: The man behind the corporate legend* (Auckland: Viking/Penguin Books, 1990), p. 177.

2 *ibid.*, pp. 233 ff.

3 A 'closed group' usually comprises a parent company and one or more of its wholly-owned subsidiaries agreeing to be bound by a deed of cross guarantee formally approved by a regulatory body (first the NCSC, the ASC and now the ASIC). Refer

J. Hill, 'Cross guarantees and corporate groups', *Company and Securities Law Journal*, 10 (1992), pp. 312–17; J. Hill, 'Corporate groups, creditor protection and cross guarantees: Australian perspectives', *Canadian Business Law Journal* (April 1995); and G. Dean, F. Clarke and E. Houghton, 'Cross guarantees and the negative pledges: A preliminary analysis', *Australian Accounting Review* (May 1995), pp. 48–63; G. Dean, F. Clarke and E. Houghton, 'Corporate restructuring, creditors' rights, cross guarantees and group behaviour', *Company and Securities Law Journal*, 17 No 2, (1999), pp. 85–102.

4 Figure 13.1 depicts only 21 companies – the other 15 companies within the 'closed group' were shelf companies with zero assets and liabilities.

5 Westmex, *Annual Report*, Chairman's Report, 1988/89, pp. 4–16 at 4.

6 For a listing of those fads since the end of World War II, refer M. McGill, *American Business and the Quick Fix* (New York: Henry Holt and Company, 1988), F. Hilmer and L. Donaldson, *Management Redeemed* (Sydney: Simon & Schuster, 1996), J. Micklethwait and A. Wooldridge, *The Witch Doctors: What the management gurus are saying, why it matters and how to make sense of it* (London: Mandarin, 1997), and J. Collins, *Good to Great: Why some companies make the leap and others don't* (Sydney: Random House, 2001).

7 *ibid.*

8 Westmex, *Annual Report*, 1988, p. 6, emphasis added.

9 P. Rennie, 'Goward continues to impress', *Business Review Weekly*, 3 February 1989, pp. 91 and 92 at 91.

10 C. Chapel, 'Since Black Tuesday, cash is kingmaker', *Business Review Weekly*, 13 May 1988, p. 89.

11 P. Rennie, 'Goward continues to impress', p. 91.

12 R. Baker, 'Westmex: Acorn award – outstanding new entrant', *Australian Business*, 5 April 1989, pp. 62–3 at 62.

13 Henry Bosch, as cited in B. Hills, 'Sex, lies & ticker tape', *Sydney Morning Herald*, 28 September 1991, p. 39. See also T. Blue, 'When to blow the whistle', *Australian Business*, 21 August 1991, pp. 61–2.

14 Reported in Hills, *ibid.*

15 C. Wood, 'Plan for open disciplinary hearings on auditors', *Business Review Weekly*, 1 July 1996, pp. 78–9.

16 M. West, 'BT sues auditors for $60 million', *Sydney Morning Herald*, 31 January 1996.

17 Hills, 'Sex, lies & ticker tape', p. 39.

18 Details of companies taking advantage of the accounting and audit relief provisions are given in Clarke, Dean and Houghton, 'Cross guarantees'.

19 An analysis of the potential distortions that may arise in such compromise proposals was detailed in E. Houghton, G. Dean and P. Luckett, 'Insolvent corporate groups with cross guarantees: A forensic-LP case study in liquidation', *Journal of the Operational Research Society*, May 1999, pp. 480–96.

20 (1991) 9 ACLC 1483. This case was not contested. J.N. Taylor Holdings Ltd was a BCH satellite acquired late in 1988 and placed in liquidation in 1990.

21 Uncertainty was not wholly alleviated by the 1992 judgment of McLelland J in the NSW Supreme Court case, *Westmex Operations Pty Ltd (In liq.) v. Westmex Ltd (In liq.) & Ors* (1992) 10 ACLC 1179 and its confirmation by the 1993 NSW Supreme Court of Appeal in *Westmex Operations Pty Ltd (In liq.) v. Westmex Ltd (In liq.)*

& Ors. This issue is explored elsewhere and in the next chapter. See G.W. Dean, P.F. Luckett and E. Houghton, 'Notional calculations in liquidations revisited: The case of the ASC class order cross guarantees', *Company and Securities Law Journal*, August 1993, pp. 204–26; 'Case Note: *Westmex Operations Pty Ltd (In liq.) v. Westmex Ltd (In liq.) & Ors'*, *Company and Securities Law Journal*, December (1993), pp. 448–51; and in P. Luckett, G. Dean and E. Houghton, 'Cross debts and group liquidations: A cross claim liquidation model', *Pacific Accounting Review*, December (1995), pp. 73–102; G. Dean, F. Clarke and E. Houghton, 'Corporate restructuring, creditors' rights, cross guarantees and group behaviour', *Company and Securities Law Journal*, 17 No 2, (1999), pp. 85–102; and E. Houghton, G. Dean and P. Luckett, 'Insolvent corporate groups with cross guarantees: A forensic-LP case study in liquidation', *Journal of the Operational Research Society*, May 1999, pp. 480–96.

14 2000 and Beyond: Crisis in Accounting and Audit

1 Respectively: Federal Reserve Chairman, Dr Alan Greenspan (attributed to a speech at The American Enterprise Institute, 5 December, 1996) and internationally acclaimed economist, John Kenneth Galbraith extracted from *The Great Crash* (1929, p. 152).
2 Anon, 'The incredibly shrinking stock market', 21 July 2002, *New York Times, Week in Review*, http://www.nytimes.com/2002/07/21/weekinreview/20020721 _MARKET_GRAPHIC.html.
3 J. Cassidy, *Dot.con* (2002).
4 For specifics refer to J. Cassidy, *Dot.con* (2002, especially Table 1, p. 293).
5 J. Spinner, 'Sullied accounting firms regaining political clout', *Washington Post*, 12 May 2002, p. A01.
6 Former Federal Reserve Bank Chairman, Volcker, as cited in 'Confused about earnings?', *BusinessWeek*, 26 November, 2001.
7 A. Hepworth, 'Judges face busy time as watchdogs pounce', *Australian Financial Review*, 11 January 2002, pp. 8 and 9.
8 *JCPAA Report 391*, p. xvii, 'Terms of Reference'.
9 R Chambers, *Securities and Obscurities*, 1973; Clarke *et al.*, *Corporate Collapse*, 1997; F. Clarke, G. Dean and P. Wolnizer, 'Auditor independence reforms – *déjà vu*', *Abacus*, June, 2002.
10 R. Chatov, *Corporate Financial Reporting*, Free Press, 1975.
11 *JCPAA Report 391*, p. iii.

15 HIH – Unfettered Hubris

1 Frank Clarke and Graeme Dean, 'Corporate collapses analysed', pp. 71–98 *Collapse Incorporated*, CCH 2001.
2 Since the formation of the HIHRC was announced the media has had a field day in exploring the lives of many individuals associated with HIH – such as Ray Williams, Rodney Adler and Brad Cooper. A. Shand's profile on Rodney Adler, 'When I was a boy – from schoolhouse to courthouse', *Australian Financial Review Magazine*, Summer 2002 edition, pp. 16–20 is an apt example.
3 Justice Owen's brief is to inquire 'into the reasons for, and the circumstances surrounding the failure of HIH – specifically, whether any HIH directors or other staff contributed to its failure or failed to make "desirable disclosures" of its

financial position'. As this volume goes to press the 18 month Commission had completed its hearings – an estimated $40 million had been spent calling more than 150 witnesses, resulting in over a million pages of evidence; counsel assisting the Commission provided over 2000 pages of submissions in their summing up.

4 See Andrew White, 'Flow-on effects of recent collapses', pp. 41–70; J. Canning and Andrew Wheeler, 'Venture capital – investment repercussions', pp. 129–46 in *Collapse Incorporated*, CCH 2001.

5 See, for example, *Australian Financial Review*, 14 November 2002 for discussion of suits lodged by the HIH's Administrator against APRA, its directors and its auditor.

6 M. Westfield, 'Howard wants the truth to take its time – HIH Royal Commission', *The Australian*, (19 June 2001), p. 4.

7 Of particular interest here is APRA's revelation to the HIHRC that it was severely under-resourced, as confirmed in evidence of international prudential regulation expert John Palmer, who had been commissioned by APRA to investigate its practices.

8 E. Sexton, 'Liquidator sues HIH auditor [and others]', *Sydney Morning Herald*, 15 November 2002, p. 23.

9 See footnote 2 above.

10 Elisabeth Sexton, 'Liquidator sues HIH auditor [and others]', *Sydney Morning Herald*, 15 November 2002, p. 23.

11 See, for example, T. Sykes, 'Resurrected report [1995 Ernst and Young due diligence report] raises doubts about HIH's insolvency', *Australian Financial Review*, 22–23 June, 2002, p. 12. See also B. Zenwirth, 'HIH falls short on technicals', *Australian Financial Review*, Letter, 9 December 2002, p. 50 and a reported summary of his address at a HIH public hearing day by A. Main, 'The geometry of HIH's problems', *Australian Financial Review*, 11–14 December, 2002, p. 8.

12 This decision is being appealed. ASIC also has laid criminal charges against Rodney Adler in relation to the HIH/Pacific Eagles Equities transactions.

13 C. Sutton, 'Adler tries to walk tall: former high-flyer brushes aside queries about possible stint in jail', *The Sun-Herald*, 17 November, 2002, p. 9.

14 ABC documentary, 'Odds on to fail?', May 2002 detailed the financial significance of this warning. The HIHRC revelations confirmed this.

15 This subsection draws heavily on material first published in the *Sydney Morning Herald* Opinion piece, 'HIH will leave crucial questions unanswered', 22 June 2001, p. 14 co-authored by Robert Walker, Frank Clarke and Graeme Dean.

16 Ray Chambers, 1973b, p. 166.

17 Nearly 40 years ago Chambers ('Conventions: Doctrines and common sense', *The Accountants' Journal*, February, 1964, pp. 182–7) resiled against the folly of relying on these doctrines and conventions as the basis of conventional accounting. Being nothing more than fiats they should be rejected if they defy financial commonsense.

18 A. Main and A. Fabro, 'HIH liquidator takes aim at regulator, Andersen', *Australian Financial Review*, 14 November 2002, pp. 1 and 6.

19 Officers of the HIH Royal Commission, Background Paper No. 15, 'The Assessment of the Insolvency of a general insurance company', October 2002. Background papers 13 and 14 are also pertinent to this discussion. Another report prepared for the Commission by former Canadian regulator John Palmer concluded that APRA had not pursued fully whether FAI and HIH were solvent entities. He suggested this was due to lack of skilled staff and under-resourcing.

20 See footnote 9 above.

21 Anon, 'A tragedy of APRA errors', *Australian Financial Review*, 13 November, 2002, p. 62. Another report by Ernst and Young which was commissioned by Westpac is reported to have had some delays in its reading (A. Main 'APRA officers delayed reading critical HIH report', *Australian Financial Review*, 7 November, 2002, p. 12).

22 Tom Ravlic, 'Deal expected to put pressure on auditors', *The Age*, 16 November 2000.

23 This point was elaborated on in submissions to the JCPAA inquiry into *Auditor Independence* (2002) by Clarke, Dean and Wolnizer (2002) and R. Walker (2002) at www.aph.gov.au.

16 Groupthink: Byzantine Structures

* This chapter draws on: Clarke and Dean, 'Law and accounting: The separate legal entity principle and consolidation accounting', *Australian Business Law Review* August 1993, pp. 246–69, Clarke and Dean, 'Chaos in the counting-house: Accounting under scrutiny', *Australian Journal of Corporate Law*, and Dean, Luckett, Houghton, 'Notional calculations in liquidations revisited' and Dean, Clarke and Houghton, 'Revitalising the corporation – improving group accountability', *The Australian Accounting Review*, November 2002, pp. 58–72.

1 I. Ramsay and G. Stapledon, *Corporate Groups in Australia*, 1998.

2 (1991) 3 ACSR 531 at 540.

3 M.A. Eisenberg, 'Corporate groups', p. 4. See also A. Nolan, 'The position of unsecured creditors of corporate groups: Towards a group responsibility solution which gives fairness and equity a role', *Company and Security Law Journal*, December 1993, pp. 461–502, and J.M. Landers, 'A unified approach to parent, subsidiary and affiliate questions in bankruptcy', *The University of Chicago Law Review*, 42(4), 1975, pp. 589–652.

4 *ibid.*, emphasis added.

5 A. McGee, 'The true and fair view debate: A study in the legal regulation of accounting', *Modern Law Review*, Vol. 54 (1991), 769, at 874.

6 Details appear in R. Johnson, *Australian Accounting Review*, 2000.

7 Figure 4.3 on p. 69 illustrates the nature of the 1960s Korman round-robin – a brief description of it appears also in Clarke and Dean, 'Law and accounting'.

8 R. Baxt, 'Tensions between commercial reality and legal principle – Should the concept of the corporate entity be re-examined?', *The Australian Law Journal*, 65 (1991a), pp. 352–3; R. Baxt, 'The need to review the rule in Salomon's case as it applies to groups of companies', *Company and Securities Law Journal*, 9, (1991b), pp. 185–7. See also J. Hill, 'Corporate groups, creditor protection and cross guarantees: Australian perspectives', *The Canadian Business Law Journal* (February 1995), pp. 321–56; J. Farrar, 'Legal issues involving corporate groups', (1998) 16, *Company and Securities Law Journal*, 184, 184; and L. Griggs, 'A note on the application of enterprise theory to the problem of Phoenix companies', (1998) *2 Mac LR* 53, 63.

9 J. Green succinctly describes the four major types of 1980s corporate abuses: '(i) "skimming" or "value shifting" ...; (ii) "toys for the boys" ...; (iii) "window dressing" ... (iv) "market rigging/insider trading" ...' ('"Fuzzy law" – a better way to stop "snouts in the trough"', *Company and Securities Law Journal* 9, 3 (1991), 144 at 149.

10 Brooks, *The Royal Mail Case*, p. xv. Consider also A.A. Berle, 'The theory of enterprise entity', *Columbia Law Review*, 47 (1947), p. 343; 'Subsidiary corporations and credit manipulation', *Harvard Law Review*, 41 (1941), p. 874 and the summary article by Landers, 'Unified Approach'.

11 A hypothetical disentanglement of that complex that incorporated the financial effects of the cross guarantees was undertaken in E. Houghton, G. Dean and P. Luckett, 'Insolvent corporate groups with cross guarantees: A forensic-LP case study in liquidation', *Journal of the Operational Research Society*, May 1999, pp. 480–96.

12 K. Brice, 'Linter battle delayed as judge grants time for settlement talks', *Australian Financial Review*, 28 March 1996, p. 4.

13 P. Blumberg, *The Law of Corporate Groups* (New York: Little Brown and Co., 1983); H. Collins, 'Ascription of legal responsibility to groups in complex patterns of economic integration', *Modern Law Review*, (1990) 53, p. 731; and G. Teubner, 'Unitas multiplex: Corporate governance in group enterprises' in D. Sugarman and G. Teubner (eds), *Regulating Corporate Groups in Europe* (Nomos 1990); M. Pittard and R. McCallum, 'Superannuation funds, interlocking corporations and industrial disputes', *Australian Business Law Review*, 21 (1993), pp. 71 at 74; B. Fisse and J. Braithwaite, *Corporations, Crime and Accountability* (Cambridge University Press, 1993); R. Baxt and T. Lane, 'Developments in relation to corporate groups and responsibilities of directors — Some insights and new directions', *Company and Securities Law Journal*, November 1998, pp. 628–53; J. Farrar, 'Legal Issues involving corporate groups', *Company and Securities Law Journal*, Vol. 16 (1998) 184; CASAC, *Corporate Groups Final Report* (2000); L. Griggs, 'A note on the application of enterprise theory to the problem of phoenix companies' (1998) 2 *Mac LR* 53, 63.

14 L.C.B. Gower, *Gower's Principles of Modern Company Law*, 3rd edn, (London: Law Book Co., 1969), p. 216; see also 4th edn, (1979), p. 137.

15 Lord Denning, M.R., *Littlewoods Mail Order Stores Ltd v. I.R.C.* 1 WLR, [1969], p. 1254.

16 Baxt (1991a), 'Tensions', p. 352.

17 Hill, 'Corporate groups'.

18 R. Baxt, and T. Lane (1998), 'Developments in relation to corporate groups and responsibilities of directors – some insights and new directions'.

19 Baxt (1991a), 'Tensions', 352. However, 'in *Industrial Equity Ltd v Blackburn* (1977) 137 CLR 567 the High Court of Australia confirmed the need to preserve, as a matter of law, a rigid demarcation between wholly-owned subsidiaries in the same group of companies as well as their holding company', *obiter* in Supreme Court of New South Wales in *Qintex Australia Finance Ltd v. Schroders Australia Ltd* (1991) 3 ACSR 267 at 268–9, and 9 ACLC 109 at 110.

20 Supreme Court of New South Wales in *Qintex Australia Finance Ltd v. Schroders Australia Ltd* (1991) 3 ACSR 267 at 268–9, and 9 ACLC 109 at 110.

21 *Briggs v. James Hardie and Co. Pty Ltd* (1989) 16 NSWLR, 549 at 577.

22 *Re Southward and Co. Ltd* [1979] 1 WLR 1198 at 1208. Other instances are noted in Gower, (1979), *ibid.* under the subsection 'Associated companies', pp. 128–33. *The Report of the UK Review Committee on Insolvency Law and Practice* (Cork Report) in 1982 at Chapter 51, pp. 434–44.

23 Hadden, 'Regulation of corporate groups'.

24 These issues are discussed in J. Farrar, 'Insolvency and corporate groups', *Corporate Groups and Corporate Management: Recent Developments and Reform Proposals*, University of Sydney Faculty of Law Continuing Legal Education Conference, March 1992; and in Hadden, 'Regulation of corporate groups', and in Nolan, 'Towards group responsibility'.

25 The HIH Royal Commission prepared a discussion paper on the issue of solvency as it related to the particulars of HIH.

26 J. Loftus and M. Miller, *Reporting on Solvency and Cash Condition*, Accounting Theory Monograph, 11, (Melbourne: AARF, 2000) consider the accounting issues related to solvency assessments.

27 *ASC Digest, Update 41*, 'Report on the Public Hearing on Accounts and Audit Relief for Wholly-owned Subsidiaries' (1991), para. 31.

28 Bosch, *Workings of a Watchdog*, pp. 54 and 68. Some of the claims raised by Bosch are addressed in Clarke and Dean (1992, 1993) and Dean, Luckett, Houghton, listed in footnote *, Chapter 16.

29 *ASC Digest, Update 41*, 'Report on the Public Hearing on Accounts and Audit Relief for Wholly-owned Subsidiaries', (1991), para. 31.

30 B. Pheasant, 'ASC request on accounts queried', *Australian Financial Review*, 20 August 1993, p. 26. The ASX and the ASC were unsatisfied with Washington H. Soul Pattinson's (WHSP) initial refusal to consolidate into the parent company's accounts its 49.8 per cent share of Brickworks Ltd. The ASX eventually accepted Pattinson's compromise to provide as a separate note in its accounts for the year ended 30 June 1993 a set of consolidated accounts including Brickworks Ltd. (See E. Mychasuk, 'Regulators battle over Soul accounts', *Sydney Morning Herald*, 11 June 1993, p. 23.) As from 31 July 1993, directors of WHSP agreed to a further request from the ASC to consolidate Brickworks into the accounts of WHSP even though in their opinion this would not 'provide a true and fair view'.

31 G. Garnsey, *Holding Companies and their Published Accounts*, London, Gee and Co. (1923); reproduced as *Holding Companies and their Published Accounts: Limitations of a Balance Sheet* (New York: Garland Publishing Inc., 1982). Garnsey put forward several alternatives to account for groups: separate publication of subsidiaries' balance sheets; publication of consolidated balance sheets embracing both holding companies and their subsidiaries.

32 D.W. Locascio, 'The dilemma of the double derivative suit', *Northwestern University Law Review*, 83, 3 (1989), 729 at 757.

33 Dean, Clarke and Houghton provide a detailed analysis of the *September Transactions* in 'Corporate restructuring, creditors' rights, cross guarantees and group behaviour', *Company and Securities Law Journal*, March 1999, pp. 85–102.

34 Baxt and Lane (1998), *ibid.*, p. 653.

35 I. Verrender, 'An employment tactic to stymie the unions', *Sydney Morning Herald*, 10 April 1998, p. 5.

36 'Groupthink' in ensuring firm-specific asset security to the 'group's' bank financiers is implied in Note 13 of the 1997 Annual Report of Lang Corporation. It states that Non-Current Bank Loans of approximately $228 million were 'secured by way of mortgages and fixed floating charges, real property mortgages and equitable mortgage over the assets of various *entities within the economic entity*'. (p. 25, emphasis added).

37 Peter Fusaro & Ross M. Miller, *What Went Wrong at Enron* (John Wiley & Sons, Inc., Hoboken, New Jersey, 2002), pp. 34–5.

38 Loren Fox, *Enron: The rise and fall* (John Wiley & Sons. Inc., 2003 Hoboken, New Jersey), pp. 40–2; 127–8.

39 P. Barry, *Rich Kids* (Sydney: Bantam, 2002).

40 Anon, 'Collapse shows limits of competition policy', *Australian Financial Review*, 15 September 2001, p. 19.

41 Extract from *ASIC Media Release* 02/69, 'ASIC'S Ansett investigation focuses on financial disclosures by Air New Zealand Limited', March 2002.

17 Groupthink – Group Therapy: Consolidation Accounting

*   This chapter draws on: Clarke and Dean, 'Law and accounting: The separate legal entity principle and consolidation accounting', *Australian Business Law Review*, August 1993, pp. 246–69, Clarke and Dean, 'Chaos in the counting house: Accounting under scrutiny', *Australian Journal of Corporate Law*, Dean, Luckett and Houghton, 'Notional calculations in liquidations revisited' and Clarke, Dean and Houghton, 'Revitalising group accounting ...'.

1   Hadden, 'Regulating corporate groups', p. 72.

2   J. Hill, 'Cross guarantees and corporate groups', *Company and Securities Law Journal* (October 1992), 312 at 317 lists some critics.

3   Gower, *Modern Company Law*, pp. 118–19 (emphasis added).

4   *Littlewoods Mail Order Stores Ltd v. I.R.C.* 1 WLR [1969], 1254.

5   *D.H.N. Ltd v. Tower Hamlets* [1976] 1 WLR, 852, emphasis added.

6   *Industrial Equity Ltd v. Blackburn* (1977), 137 CLR, 567.

7   ASC Media Release 91/64, Issues Paper 29, *Public Hearing: Accounting Relief for Wholly-Owned Subsidiaries*, para. 3 fn. 4.

8   S. Jemison, 'Why not sack Clark, SBSA director asked', *Australian Financial Review*, 22 May 1992, p. 55. Details of the complexity of these off-balance sheet operations were revealed in T. Maher, 'Why the State Bank went south', *Australian Business*, 20 February 1991, pp. 12–16. S. Jemison, 'Counsel turn up the heat as ex-director gives evidence', *Australian Financial Review*, 25 May 1992, p. 48.

9   Mason J in *Industrial Equity Ltd v. Blackburn* (1977), 137 CLR, 567.

10 This is reinforced by the financial imbroglios in 'closed group' liquidations where attempts to administer regulatory-approved class cross guarantees has proven nigh impossible. It would seem in respect of 'liquidated' and 'going concerns' a 'state of affairs' presupposes a 'legal' form.

11 R.G. Walker, *Consolidated Statements: A history and analysis* (New York: Arno Press, 1978) documents the numerous functions of consolidated Statements. A condensed version appears in R.G. Walker, 'An evaluation of the information conveyed by consolidated statements', *Abacus* (December 1976), pp. 77–115.

12 Hadden, 'Regulating corporate groups', p. 72.

13 Walker, *Consolidated Statements*, p. 277, emphasis added.

14 First put succinctly in Chambers, *Securities and Obscurities*, pp. 225–8, reproduced as *Accounting in Disarray*, and summarised in the 1978 report to the NSW Attorney General, *Accounting Standards* at pp. 123–36.

15 A somewhat similar, radical move – prohibiting the operation of holding companies across State borders – occurred in the United States following the abuses perpetrated by virtue of complex group structures such as Ivar Kreuger's international match labyrinth and utility company group structures operating sub/sub holding companies

across state boundaries. Many congressmen at the US Congressional Hearings before the Senate Committee on Banking and Practice into the 1920s holding company abuses expressed concerns about complex group structures – some of which are reproduced in Clarke and Dean, 'Chaos in the counting house', (1992). J. Farrar, 'The regulation of corporate groups', *Company and Securities Law Journal* (August 1998) acknowledges that while this is an extreme option, it is clearly worth debating.

16 Refer to the Maxwell Reports, 2000.

17 See Rogers J. Suggestions in several Qintex decisions in the late 1980s.

18 For details of pre-1980 company failures in Australia see Sykes, *Two Centuries of Panic*, while more recent controversial consolidation accounting practices are revealed in R.G. Walker, 'Off-balance sheet financing', *UNSW Law Journal*, 1992 Vol. 15(1), pp. 196–213, Hadden, 'Regulating corporate groups' and Sykes, *The Bold Riders*.

19 Chambers, *Securities and Obscurities*, p. 225.

20 *Spedley Securities Limited (in Liquidation) v Greater Pacific Investments Pty Limited (in Liquidation) and Ors, 50177 of 1991: The October Transactions*, p. 10.

21 B. Pheasant, 'Goldberg trust held Brick and Pipe stake', *Australian Financial Review*, 12 February 1992, p. 23.

22 B. Pheasant, 'Backdating gave Goldberg $160 million', *Australian Financial Review*, 14 February 1992, p. 19; and the judgment in the Victorian Supreme Court by Southwell J, *Linter Group Limited v. A. Goldberg and Zev Furst and Anors*, No. 2195 of 1990, 4 May 1992; and B. Pheasant, 'Former Goldberg accountant tells of "warehousing"', *Australian Financial Review*, 30 August 1993, p. 4. The latter recounts another deal with the potential to benefit private companies controlled by Goldberg at the expense of the shareholders of public companies. For details of the Rothwells' transactions see, McCusker Report, *Report of the Inspector on a Special Investigation into Rothwells Limited Pursuant to Companies Code (W.A.), Part VII – Part 1*, W.A. Government Printer, 1989; for details of the Spedley Holdings' round robin see J. Manson and T. Sykes, 'Lucky Brian', *Australian Business*, 16 May 1990, pp. 16–19; for the particulars involving Unity Corporation and the private company, Carter Holdings Pty Limited see C. Fox, 'Carter "siphoned off" $17 million, hearing told', *Australian Financial Review*, 4 February 1992, p. 17.

23 Walker, 'Off balance sheet financing', and 'A feeling of *déjà vu*'.

24 This approach draws upon a proposal made by R.J. Chambers in 1973. It was first privately illustrated through a worked example by one of the current authors, as part of MBA lecture material at the University of Sydney in 1976. What follows is our interpretation of Chambers' method, given the advent of computer technology.

25 A reviewer of the earlier edition of this book complained that no illustration was given of the alternative we described. Recent events have indicated that if the parent/subsidiary structure is not to be dispensed with, and all the signs are that the impediments remain as strong as ever, a reconstruction of the accounting for intercorporate investments and investments in other entities is long overdue. Accordingly, we provide an illustration of our mechanism in the Appendix to this chapter and a comparison between it and the metrics of conventional consolidation procedures.

26 Hadden, 'Regulating corporate groups', p. 72. Importantly, each public company within a corporate group is required to prepare a separate Annual Report to be lodged with the ASC.

18 Fatal Attrition – Accounting's Diminished Serviceability

1 For example, comments attributed to national audit partner of Coopers and Lybrand, Bob Lynn, in P. Howard, 'Auditors in clash over Standards', *Financial Forum*, August 1994, p. 1.

2 D. Hrisak and M. Dobbie, 'US Big Six limits partner liability', *Financial Forum*, December 1994, p. 7. The debate continued throughout the 1990s and into the new millennium. The United Nations held a forum in the mid-1990s on the issue – see United Nations Conference on Trade and Development, Responsibilities and Liabilities of Auditors – *Proceedings of a Forum* (New York and Geneva: United Nations, 1996). From the 1990s to the present, Australia's various governments, federal and state, have grappled with how best to handle the increases in negligence payouts. A summary discussion of the issues appears in the August 2002 *JCPAA Report* 391 (especially pp. 114–21).

3 M. Dobbie, 'Doomed to repeat mistakes?', *Financial Forum*, December 1994, p. 7.

4 Report of an interview by A. Ivanov, 'Introducing Graham Paton', *Australian Accountant*, April 1993, pp. 22–4 at 23.

5 Bosch, *Workings of a Watchdog*, p. 24. A similar line courses through the analysis of P. Brokensha, *Corporate Ethics: A guide for Australian managers* (Adelaide: Social Science Press, 1993).

6 Wood, 'Plan for open disciplinary hearing on auditors'.

7 General Council, Australian Society of Accountants, *Accounting Principles and Practices Discussed in Reports on Company Failures*, p. 7.

8 *ibid.*, p. 37.

9 M. Robson, book review, *Company and Securities Law Journal*, August 1997, pp. 303–4.

10 I. Langfield-Smith, book review, 1999.

11 H. Bosch, book review, *Company and Securities Law Journal*, September 1997, p. 388.

12 A. Barton, book review, 'A very dismal story', *Australian Accounting Review*, 1998.

13 J. Routledge, book review, *Insolvency Journal*, September, 1997, pp. 142–3.

14 G. Gould, book review, *Accounting, Finance and Business History*, vol 8:3, 1998, pp. 390–2.

15 J. Farrar, 'The regulation of corporate groups', *Company and Securities Law Journal*, 1998.

16 *Footnote 7*, p. 38.

17 A radio presenter announced to the audience that HIH Royal Commission Hearings would be returning to the less exciting accounting matters – it had been preoccupied for days with the Adler–Cooper claim and counter claim over related party transactions – much more interesting to the listeners!

18 B. Pheasant, '"True and fair" change seen as backward step', *Australian Financial Review*, 16 November 1992, p. 18.

19 Australia's Treasurer and the Prime Minister have repeatedly contrasted Australia's regulatory system as being *principles* rather than *black-letter* based. This is discussed later.

20 Cited in B. Madden, 'Change or shut up', *New Accountant*, November 1994, p. 1.

21 See instances in this volume and L. Cunningham, 'Sharing Accounting's Burden: Business lawyers in Enron's Dark Shadows', Unpublished Working Paper, April 2002; http://ssrn.com/abstract_id=307978.

22 Pratten, *Corporate Failure*.

23 Green, 'Keeping snouts out of the trough', 145; and Cunningham (2002).

24 Attributed to Australia's Treasurer Peter Costello, when introducing a new bill to crack down on directors' largesse – to seek to placate the public concern over some practices of directors.

25 Ernst & Young, *A Guide for the Company Director*, Australia (1990).

26 Criticism of the use of conventional accounting data in those distress prediction studies is contained in Clarke and Dean, 'Distressed business – predicting failure' (CCH, 2001). See also M. Lawson, 'There is also something very fishy behind a collapse', Special Report – Investor Education, *Australian Financial Review*, 17 October 2002, p. 4.

27 The information economics literature is replete with references to accounting being an economic good.

28 This point is well made in R. Chambers, 'Ends, ways and means', *Abacus*, September 1996, pp. 119–32.

29 This subsection draws extensively from the June 2002 editorial in *Abacus*, 'Auditor independence reforms – recycled ideas', pp. i–iv by G. Dean, F. Clarke and P. Wolnizer.

30 See for example: K. Brown, 'The rough side of smoothing', *Australian Financial Review*, 7 February 2002; A. Kohler, 'Horrible numbers', *Australian Financial Review*, 4 February 2002; editorial, 'Taking stock of auditors', *Australian Financial Review*, 29 January 2002; A. Ferguson, 'The culprits in corporate collapses', *Business Review Weekly*, 12 December 2001; and Jaworski, 'Accounting is the critical issue', *Australian Financial Review*, Letters, 8 February 2002.

31 G. Dean, editorial, *Abacus*, February, 2002, pp. ii–iv.

32 A. Ramsay, *Report into Auditor Independence*, AGPS, November 2001.

33 Clarke *et al.*, 1993, Dean, Clarke and Wolnizer (2002) submission to the 2002 JPCAA inquiry into audit independence and related evidence (www.aph.committees); the Dean, Clarke and Wolnizer submission to the HIH Royal Commission (www.hihroyalcom.gov.au).

19 Ethos Abandoned – Vision Lost: Accounting at the Professional Crossroads?

1 C. Fox, 'Ethics becoming the buzzword of the '90s', *Australian Financial Review*, 12 June 1990, p. 44.

2 A. Boyd, 'Call for higher business ethics', *Australian Financial Review*, 24 May 1990, p. 4.

3 Anon, 'Ethics rise in the West', *The Bulletin*, 5 June 1990, p. 22.

4 J. Hurst, 'Corporate ethics come under the microscope', *Australian Financial Review*, 29 January 1990, p. 3.

5 S. Lewis, 'Accounting education in "chronic neglect"', *Australian Financial Review*, 5 July 1990, p. 10.

6 T. Stephens, 'Big business elders crusade for higher ethics', *Sydney Morning Herald*, 26 May 1990, p. 6.

7 J. Collins, 'Declining ethics … bad company', *The Australian*, 10 July 1990, p. 13.

8 M. Lyons, 'Profession begins to get serious about its ethics', *Business Review Weekly*, 21 February 1992, pp. 73 and 75.

9 T. Forester, 'Society needs dose of ethics to purge its "moral chaos"', *The Australian*, 14 May 1991, p. 46.

10 T. Kaye, 'Phillips bows out with call for code of ethics', *Australian Financial Review*, 3 April 1992, p. 61.

11 M. Lawson, 'Another counselling centre for ethically troubled accountants', *Australian Financial Review*, 27 March 1992, p. 3.

12 H. Mackay, 'Ethics is a tricky business', *Australian Financial Review*, 23 March 1993, p. 15.

13 M. Niemarck, 'The selling of ethics', Special issue on ethics, politics and academic accounting, *Accounting, Auditing and Accountability Journal*, Vol. 8 No. 3, 1995, pp. 81–96. See also J.A. Gaa, *The Ethical Foundations of Public Accounting* (Vancouver, B.C.: Canadian Certified General Accountants Research Foundation, 1993).

14 K. Edwards, 'Where does the buck stop?', *Time*, 19 April 1993, pp. 24–9.

15 A. Knott, Monash Research Lecture, 17 July 2002.

16 R. Roslender, *Sociological Perspectives on Modern Accountancy* (1992), *op. cit.*

17 Two articles by R. Chambers and P. Wolnizer, 'A true and fair view of financial position', *Company and Securities Law Journal*, December 1990, pp. 353–68 and 'A true and fair view of financial proposals and results: The historical background', *Accounting, Business and Financial History*, March 1991, pp. 197–213, provide detailed references to many others contained in a recent anthology by R.H. Parker, P. Wolnizer and C. Nobes, *Readings in True and Fair* (New York: Garland, 1996). See also M. Liebler's submission, 2002 JCPAA *Review of Independent Auditing by Registered Company Auditors*.

18 Clarke and Craig, 'Phases in accounting standards'.

19 A. Lovell, 'Moral reasoning and moral atmosphere in the domain of accounting', Special issue on ethics, politics and academic accounting, *Accounting, Auditing and Accountability Journal*, Vol. 8 No. 3, 1995, pp. 60–80.

20 D. Fischel, *Payback: The conspiracy to destroy Michael Milken* (New York, Harper Business, 1995).

21 Graphically illustrating this was the 1950s mercury poisoning at Minamata by the Japanese chemical company, Chisso. For decades, victims seeking compensation were fighting an amorphous corporate giant. It was *as if* humans had played no role in the poisoning of the sea around *Minamata* (see W.E. Smith and A.M. Smith, *Minamata* (New York: Holt, Rinehart & Winston, 1975). In Australia this issue was considered by senior federal and state law officers, resulting in a proposed new legal code, avoiding the need to prove criminal intent, but to 'jail dirty incorporates' (Rowly Spiers, 'New law to jail dirty corporates', *Australian Financial Review*, 16 September 1992, p. 3). Legal commentators, Fisse and Braithwaite summarise the individualism v. corporate criminality perspectives discussed in legal and cognate disciplines (*Corporations, Crime and Accountability*, especially Chapters 2 and 3).

22 For example, Bosch, *The Workings of a Watchdog*, pp. 24–39.

23 A similar view was put by R. Tomasic and S. Bottomley, *Directing the Top 500: Corporate governance and accountability in Australian companies* (Sydney: Allen & Unwin, 1993). Consider also the headline covering the arrest of a leading 1970s US corporate cowboy, 'Robert Vesco ... a man who makes Christopher Skase look like Mother Theresa' in Marcus Casey, 'Wall Street swindler's pals finally desert him', *Sunday Telegraph*, 18 June 1995, p. 131, and more recently the observations of Dr Alan Greenspan as reported in an edited text of his US Senate Committee Address, 17 July, 2002, 'Greed is a false god', *The Australian*, 18 July 2002, p. 28.

24 The first edition provides some 1980s and 1990s instances. The actions against corporate officers in say the One.Tel and Harris Scarfe cases in Australia, as well as current charges against leading US business executives in several companies, are further evidence supporting our claim of more of the same.

25 P. Williams, 'In the shadow of Enron: The collapse of Enron and other giants has cast a cloud over Wall Street's best-known finance houses', *Australian Financial Review*, 17–18 August, 2002, p. 25.

26 Notable exceptions in the 1980s included financial consultants such as M. Burrows and A. Donnelly, regulators like Bosch and certain journalists noted in the accounts of failure in this book.

27 Bloomberg, 'From high-roller to has-been'.

28 Mackay, 'Ethics is a tricky business'.

29 K. Edwards, 'Where does the buck stop?', *Time*, 19 April 1993, pp. 24–9.

30 Mackay, 'Ethics is a tricky business'.

31 Such an impression is obtained from examining written submissions (and Hearings *Transcripts*) to the 2002 JCPAA *Report 391* into Audit Independence. Especially apposite are the observations cited by solicitor, Mark Liebler.

32 P. Jubb and S. Haswell, *Company Accounting* (Melbourne: Nelson, 1993), p. 163.

33 QBE Insurance Group *Annual Report* 1992.

34 As an aside, action in the 1990s by the Director of Public Prosecutions resulted in charges being laid (mostly under provisions of the old Companies Code) 'against several company officers for breaches of the "true and fair view" provisions'. (Walker, 'A feeling of *deja vu*', p. 107).

35 Reports in 1993 and 1994 indicated premiums rose by 15 per cent each year, following a 20 per cent rise in 1992 – S. Clafton, 'Professional bodies review call for liability limits', *Business Review Weekly*, 1 April 1996, pp. 68–9. Post-2000 premiums continue to rise.

36 This view is implicit in an interview by S. Harrison of ASC Chairman, Alan Cameron in the April 1993 issue of *Charter*, 'Civil or criminal remedies and the ASC', pp. 10–12.

37 J. Este, 'Interchase claim worsens valuers' indemnity problem', *The Australian*, 2 July 1995, p. 3.

38 The cap in the NSW Act is set at an amount or at a multiple of fees. Professional bodies must seek permission for the cap by applying to Professional Standards Council. In the UK the DTI sought to limit auditors' liability through changes to the companies laws. It suggested that regulations would be made under s. 310(4) of the Companies Act 1985 (Anon, 'DTI acts on auditors' liability', *Accountancy*, April 1993, p. 13). Such UK proposals have not brought any significant change.

39 C. Napier, 'The antecedents of unlimited liability in the United Kingdom: a study of corporate governance', paper 19th EAA Congress, Bergen May 1996, published in *Accounting, Business and Financial History*, 1999.

40 These and other proposals are listed in Working Party of the Ministerial Council for Corporations, *Professional Liability in Relation to Corporations Law Matters*, June 1993, especially pp. 10–35.

41 C. Merritt, 'Senate Report on Indemnity Unveiled', *Australian Financial Review*, 22 October, 2002, p. 6.

42 M.C. Wells, reported comment in proceedings of *Crime and the Professions – The Accountancy Profession*, Institute of Criminology Seminar, 18 September 1985.

43 For an account of this bankruptcy see C.W. Wootton and S.D. Tonge, 'Where do clients go when an accounting firm goes bankrupt? The case of Laventhal & Howarth', *Abacus*, September 1993, pp. 149–59.

44 M. Lawson, 'Accountants "top for claims"', *Australian Financial Review*, 2 August 1993, p. 3.

45 *ASIC Media Release, 00/452*, 2 November 2000.

46 This is often difficult to deduce as out-of-court settlements preclude the consideration of the technical and professional issues involved. This aspect is discussed in R. Johnson, 'Out-of-court settlements', *Unpublished working paper*, 2002.

47 J. Spinner, 'Sullied accounting firms requiring political clout', *Washington Post*, Business, 13 May 2002.

48 This has long been accepted. See M. Moonitz, 'Accounting principles – how are they developed?' in R. Sterling (ed), *Institutional Issues in Public Accounting*, (1974), Kansas, Scholars Book Co., (1976), pp. 143–71.

49 In the first edition we suggested that the Crown, professional accountancy bodies, legal drafters and the Standards-setters might be sitting on a time bomb!

50 B. Barber, 'Some problems in the sociology of the professions', *Daedalus*, Fall, 1963, pp. 669–88. (An issue devoted to discussing the professions.)

51 See the professional booklet, International Federation of Accountants, *Understanding Financial Statement Audits*, Melbourne, AARF (1990); also the ICAA/ASCPA *Expectations Gap* studies (1993 and 1996) and the JCPAA *Report 391, Review of Independent Auditing by Registered Company Auditors*, August 2002.

52 B. Pheasant, 'Auditors in danger from $2.5 bn claims', *Australian Financial Review*, 30 June 1993, pp. 1 and 6 at 6. Post-2000, especially in the US setting, former chairman of the US federal Reserve, Paul Volcker was reported to observe that 'accounting and auditing is in crisis' (N. Byrnes and D. Henry, 'Confused about earnings?', *BusinessWeek*, 26 November, 2001).

53 This crisis has been long recognised (see Chambers, *Securities and Obscurities*, and Briloff (1970, 1976 and 1981)). This label was used in the December 1993 AICPA/ASCPA monograph, *A Research Study on Financial Reporting and Auditing – Bridging the Expectations Gap, op. cit.*, and in a 1994 Ernst and Young Foundation monograph, *Measurement Research in Financial Accounting*, reporting the Workshop proceedings, 30 September to 1 October 1993. The workshop had discussed the 'crisis in accounting research' claimed in an unpublished pamphlet by six leading US academic researchers – further details see R. Mattessich, *Critique of Accounting* (Westport CT: Quorum Books, 1995).

54 M. Dobbie, 'ASB wants SACs to be mandatory', *Financial Forum*, August 1993, p. 1. SAC 4, which was put on hold in 1994 after vehement opposition from practitioners and their clients, was intended to prescribe the concepts to underpin accounting practices. It was re-released in 1995 but this time its application was voluntary.

55 As reported by K. Brice, 'Judgement reserved on the Acacia Part A', *Australian Financial Review*, 27 March 1996, p. 28.

56 T. Boreham, 'Mockers of rules better beware of the watchdog', *Business Review Weekly*, 19 March 1993, pp. 92–3.

57 M. Lawson, *Frenzied Finance – The crime of the amalgamated*, 1905.

58 Chambers, 'Accounting and corporate morality – the ethical cringe', p. 17.

Bibliography

Accounting Standards Review Committee, *Company Accounting Standards*, under chairmanship of R.J. Chambers (Sydney: NSW Government Printer, 1978).

Altman, E.I., *Corporate Bankruptcy in America* (Lexington, Mass.: Heath Lexington Books, 1971).

Altman, E.I., *Corporate Financial Distress: A complete guide to predicting, avoiding and dealing with bankruptcy* (New York: John Wiley & Sons Inc., 1983; 2nd edn, 1993).

Altman, E.I., *Bankruptcy, Credit Risk, and High Yield Junk Bonds*, Blackwell Publishers (Malden, Mass.: USA and Oxford: UK, 2002)

American Law Institute (ALI), *Principles of Corporate Governance, Analysis and Recommendations* (New York: ALI, 1992).

Argenti, J., *Corporate Collapse: The causes and symptoms* (London: McGraw-Hill, 1976).

Argenti, J., *Predicting Company Failure*, Accountants' Digest No. 93 (London: ICAEW, 1985).

Armstrong, H. and Gross, D., *Tricontinental: The rise and fall of a merchant bank: The first full account of one of the biggest disasters in Australian banking* (Melbourne: Melbourne University Press, 1995).

Australian Bankers Association, *Corporate Failures* (Sydney: ABA, 1990).

Australian Society of Accountants, *Accounting Principles and Practices Discussed in Reports of Company Failures* (Sydney–Melbourne: ASA General Council, 1966).

Australian Society of Certified Practising Accountants (ASCPA) and The Institute of Chartered Accountants in Australia (ICAA), *A Research Study on Financial Reporting and Auditing – Bridging the Expectations Gap* (Melbourne: ASCPA and ICAA, 1993).

Barchard, D., *Asil Nadir and the Rise and Fall of Polly Peck* (London: Victor Gollancz Ltd, 1992).

Barry, P., *The Rise and Fall of Alan Bond* (Sydney: Bantam Books, 1990).

Barry, P., *Rich Kids* (Auckland: Bantam, 2002).

Baxt, R. and Lane, T., 'Developments in relation to corporate groups and the responsibilities of directors', *Company and Securities Law Journal*, November 1998, pp. 628–51.

Beattie, V., Fearnley, S. and Brandt, R., *Behind Closed Doors: What a company audit is all about* (Wiltshire: Palgrave/The Institute of Chartered Accountants in England and Wales, 2001).

Berle, A.A. and Means, G.C., *The Modern Corporation and Private Property* (New York: Macmillan, 1932).

Blumberg, P., *The Law of Corporate Groups* (Boston: Little, Brown and Co., 1983).

Bosch, H., *The Workings of a Watchdog* (Melbourne: William Heinemann Australia, 1990).

Bosch, H., *Corporate Procedures and Conduct* (Sydney: Institute of Directors, 1991, 1993).

Bower, T., *Maxwell: The Outsider* (London: Mandarin Paperbacks, 1991).

Bresciani-Turroni, C., *The Economics of Inflation* (London: Allen & Unwin, 1937).

Briloff, A.J., *Unaccountable Accounting* (New York: Harper & Row, 1972).

Briloff, A.J., *More Debits Than Credits: The burnt investor's guide to financial statements* (New York: Harper & Row, 1976).

Briloff, A.J., *Truth about Accounting* (New York: Harper & Row, 1982).

Brokensha, P., *Corporate Ethics: A guide for Australian managers* (Adelaide: Social Science Press, 1993).

Brooks, C., *The Royal Mail Case* (Toronto: Law Book Co., 1933).

Cadbury Committee, *Code of Corporate Governance – Interim and Final* (London: HMSO, 1991, 1992).

Cassidy, J. *Dot.con: The greatest story ever told* (London: Allen Lane, The Penguin Press, 2002).

CCH, *Collapse Incorporated* (Sydney: CCH, 2001).

Chambers, R.J., *Securities and Obscurities: A case for reform of the law of company accounts* (Melbourne: Gower Press, 1973a); reproduced as *Accounting in Disarray* (New York: Garland Publishing Inc., 1986).

Chambers, R.J., 'Observation as a Method of Inquiry – The background of Securities and Obscurities', *Abacus*, December 1973.

Clarke, F.L. and Dean, G.W., *Contributions of Limperg and Schmidt to the Replacement Cost Debate in the 1920s* (New York: Garland Publishing Inc., 1990).

Clarke, F.L. and Dean, G.W., *Replacement Cost Accounting and Reform in Post–World War I Germany* (New York: Garland Publishing Inc., 1990).

Clarke, F.L., Dean, G.W. and Oliver, K.G., *Corporate Collapse: Regulatory, accounting and ethical failure* (Melbourne: Cambridge University Press, 1997).

Companies and Securities Advisory Committee, Discussion Paper No. 3: *Civil Liability of Company Auditors* (Sydney: NSW Government Printer, 1985).

Companies and Securities Advisory Committee, *Corporate Groups Final Report* (Sydney: CASAC, May 2000)

Craswell, A.T., *Auditing* (New York: Garland Publishing Inc., 1986).

Cronje, S. *et al.*, *Lonrho: A portrait of a multinational* (London: Penguin, 1976).

Daly, M.T., *Sydney Boom, Sydney Bust: The city and its property market 1850–1981* (Sydney: Allen & Unwin, 1982).

Dean, G.W. and Clarke F.L., 'Anatomy of a Failure: A methodological experiment – the case of ASL', in M. Juttner, and T. Valentine (eds), *The Economics and Management of Financial Institutions* (Sydney: Longman Cheshire, 1987).

Dean, G.W., 'Editorial', *Abacus*, February 2002, pp. i–iv.

Department of Trade and Industry, *Mirror Group Newspapers, plc, Vols One and Two* (London: The Stationery Office, 2001).

Dirks, R.L. and Goss, L., *The Great Wall Street Scandal* (New York: McGraw-Hill, 1974).

Dun and Bradstreet Corporation, *The Business Failure Record*, 1981 (New York: Dun and Bradstreet, 1982).

Fischel, D., *Payback: The Conspiracy to Destroy Michael Milken* (New York: Harper Business, 1995).

Fisse, B. and Braithwaite, J., *Corporations, Crime and Accountability* (Melbourne: Cambridge University Press, 1993).

Ford, H.A.J., *Principles of Company Law*, 5th edn (Sydney: Butterworths, 1990).

Fox, L., *Enron: The rise and fall* (New Jersey: Wiley, 2003).

Fusaro, P. and Miller, Ross, M., *What Went Wrong at Enron* (New Jersey: John Wiley & Sons Inc., 2002).

Gaa, J.A., *The Ethical Foundations of Public Accounting* (Vancouver, B.C: Canadian Certified General Accountants Research Foundation, 1993).

Galbraith, J.R., *The Great Crash 1929* (London: Pelican, 1971).

Garnsey, G., *Holding Companies and Their Published Accounts* (London: Gee & Co., 1923), reproduced as *Holding Companies and Their Published Accounts: Limitations of a Balance Sheet* (New York: Garland Publishing Inc., 1982).

Gower, L.C.B., *Gower's Principles of Modern Company Law*, 3rd edn (London: Law Book Co., 1969).

Gower, L.C.B., *Gower's Principles of Modern Company Law*, 4th edn (London: Stevens and Co., 1979).

Greatorex, D. *et al.*, *Corporate Collapses: Lessons for the future* (Sydney: The Institute of Chartered Accountants in Australia, 1994).

Green, E. and Moss, M., *A Business of National Importance: The Royal Mail Shipping Group, 1902–1937* (London and New York: Methuen, 1982).

Greising, D. and Morse, L., *Brokers, Bagmen and Moles: Fraud and corruption in the Chicago futures markets* (New York: John Wiley & Sons, Inc., 1991).

Griffiths, I., *Creative Accounting: How to make your profits what you want them to be* (London: Allen & Unwin, 1986).

Guttmann, W. and Meehan, P., *The Great Inflation* (London: Saxon House, 1975).

Haigh, G., *The Battle for BHP* (Melbourne: Allen & Unwin Australia Pty Ltd, 1987).

Haldane, A., *With Intent to Deceive* (Edinburgh: William Blackwood, 1970).

Hilmer, F., *Strictly Boardroom* (London: Gollancz, 1993).

Hirsch, E.D., *Cultural Literacy* (Melbourne: Schwartz Publishing, 1989).

Hirst, R.R. and Wallace, R.W., *Studies in the Australian Capital Market* (Melbourne: Cheshire, 1964).

Holmes, S. and Nicholls, D., *Small Business and Accounting: Building a profitable relationship between owner/managers and accountants* (Sydney: Allen & Unwin, 1990).

Hussey, A.E., *Shareholder and General Public Protection in Limited Liability Enterprises from 1856–1969*, Unpublished MEc Thesis (University of Sydney, 1971).

International Federation of Accountants, *Understanding Financial Statements* (Melbourne: Australian Accounting Research Foundation, 1990).

Jameson, M., *The Practical Art of Creative Accounting* (London: Kogan Page, 1988).

Jamieson, B., *The Accounting Jungle* (Sydney: Business Review Weekly Publications, 1995).

Janetzki, D., *The Gollin Years* (Brisbane: Don Janetzki, 1989).

Johnson, R., 'Back-to-back Loans: A fraud in transition', *Australian Accounting Review*, November 2002, p. 66.

Joint Committee on Public Accounts and Audit (JCPAA), *Report 391, Review of Independent Auditing by Registered Company Auditors*, AGPS, August 2002.

Jubb, P. and Howell, S., *Company Accounting* (Melbourne: Nelson, 1993).

Juttner, M. and Valentine, T. (eds), *The Economics and Management of Financial Institutions* (Melbourne: Longman Cheshire, 1987).

Karmel, P.H. and Brunt, M., *The Structure of the Australian Economy* (Melbourne: Cheshire, 1963).

Keats, C.B., *Magnificent Masquerade* (New York: Funk & Wagnalls, 1964).

Kellogg, I. and Kellogg, L.B., *Fraud, Window Dressing and Negligence in Financial Statements* (New York: McGraw-Hill, 1991).

Kharbanda, O.P. and Stallworthy, E.A., *Corporate Failure: Prediction, panacea and prevention* (Whitstable, Kent: McGraw-Hill, 1985).

Krasnoff, S., *Bob Ansett: The Meaning of Success* (Tewantin, Qld: Shala Press, 1999).

Lawson, D., *Frenzied Finance – The Crime of Amalgamated* (New York: The Ridgway-Thayer Company, 1905)

Levi, E.H., *Point of View: Talks on education* (Chicago: University of Chicago Press, 1969).

Loftus, J. and Miller, M., *Reporting on Solvency and Cash Position*, Accounting Theory Monograph No. 11 (Melbourne: AARF, 2000).

McBarnet, D. and Whelan, C., *Creative Accounting and the Cross-Eyed Javelin Thrower* (Chichester: Wiley, 1999).

McDonald, F., *Insull* (Chicago: Chicago University Press, 1962).

McGill, M., *American Business and the Quick Fix* (New York: Henry Holt and Company, 1988).

McManamy, J., *The Dreamtime Casino* (Melbourne: Schwarz and Wilkinson, 1990).

Maher, T., *Bond* (Melbourne: William Heinemann Australia, 1990).

Mantle, J., *For Whom the Bell Tolls: The scandalous inside story of Lloyd's crisis* (London: Mandarin Paperbacks, 1993).

Mattessich, R., *Critique of Accounting* (Westport, CT: Quorum Books, 1995).

Miller, D., *The Icarus Paradox: How exceptional companies bring about their own downfall* (New York: Harper Business, 1990).

Moonitz, M., *Obtaining Agreement on Standards in the Accounting Profession*, Studies in Accounting Research, American Accounting Association, 1974.

Mulford, C.W. and Comiskey, E.E., *The Financial Numbers Game: Detecting creative accounting practices* (New York: John Wiley, 2002).

Naser, K.H.M., *Creative Financial Accounting* (London: Hemel Hempstead, Prentice Hall International, 1993).

Oliver, K.G., *Australian Corporate Failures 1946–88: A random sample of thirty listed industrial companies assessed in the light of Argenti's trajectories*, Honours Thesis, Department of Economic History (University of Sydney, 1990).

Parker, R.H., Wolnizer, P.W. and Nobes, C., *Readings in True and Fair* (New York: Garland Publishing Inc., 1996).

Pecora, F., *Wall Street under Oath: The story of our modern money changers* (New York: Simon & Schuster Inc., 1939).

Pelikan, J., *The Idea of a University: A re-examination* (New Haven: Yale University Press, 1992).

Peters, T.J. and Waterman Jnr, R.H., *In Search of Excellence: Lessons from America's best run companies* (Sydney: Harper and Row, 1982).

Postman, N., *Amusing Ourselves to Death* (London: Methuen, 1987).

Pratten, C., *Company Failure* (London: ICAEW, 1991).

Public Oversight Board, 'Issues in Confronting the Accounting Profession', Report by Public Oversight Board of the SEC Practice section (Stanford, CT: AICPA, 1993).

Ramsay, I. and Stapledon, G., *Corporate Groups*, Melbourne University Centre for Corporate Governance, 1998

Raw, C., *Slater Walker* (London: Andre Deutsch Ltd, 1977).

Raw, C., *The Money Changers: How the Vatican Bank enabled Roberto Calvi to steal $250 million for the heads of the P2 Masonic Lodge* (London: Harvill, 1992).

Reid, M., *The Secondary Banking Crisis, 1973–74: Its causes and course* (London: Macmillan, 1982).

Rezaee, Z., *Financial Statement Fraud: Prevention and detection* (New York: John Wiley, 2002).

Ripley, W., *Main Street and Wall Street* (Lawrence, Kan.: Scholars Book Co., 1927, 1974).

Roslender, R., *Sociological Perspectives on Modern Accountancy* (London: Routledge, 1992).

Ross, B., *The Ariadne Story: The rise and fall of a business empire* (Elwood, Victoria: Greenhouse Publications, 1988).

Ross, J.E. and Kami, M.J., *Corporate Management in Crisis: Why the mighty fall* (Englewood Cliffs, NJ: Prentice-Hall Inc., 1973).

Rothchild, J., *Going for Broke: How Robert Campeau bankrupted the retail industry, jolted the junk bond market and brought the booming eighties to a crashing halt* (New York: Simon & Schuster, 1991).

Russell, B., *The Problems with Philosophy* (London: Oxford University Press, 1912, 1959).

Russell, H.F., *Foozles and Fraud* (Altamone Springs, Fla: Institute of Internal Auditors, 1978).

Salsbury, S., *No Way to Run a Railroad: The untold story of the Penn Central crisis* (New York: McGraw-Hill, 1982).

Salsbury, S. and Sweeney, K., *The Bull, the Bear and the Kangaroo: The history of the Sydney Stock Exchange* (Sydney: Allen & Unwin, 1988).

Schilit, H., *Financial Shenanigans: How to detect accounting gimmicks and fraud in financial reports* (New York: McGraw-Hill, 1993; 2nd edn, 2002).

Shaplen, R., *Kreuger: Genius and Swindler* (1961; reproduced by Garland Publishing, New York, 1990).

Smith, T., *Accounting for Growth: Stripping the camouflage from company accounts* (London: Century Business, 1992).

Smith, W.E. and Smith, A.M., *Minamata* (New York: Alskog Sensorium – Holt, Rinehart and Winston, 1975).

Stamp, E. and Marley, C., *Accounting Principles and the City Code* (London: Butterworths, 1970).

Stevens, M., *The Accounting Wars* (New York: Colliers Books, 1986).

Stewart, J.B., *Den of Thieves* (New York: Simon & Schuster, 1991).

Sugarman, D. and Teubner, G. (eds), *Regulating Corporate Groups in Europe* (Firenze: European University Institute, 1990).

Sykes, T., *The Money Miners: Australia's mining boom 1969–70* (Sydney: Wildcat Press, 1978).

Sykes, T., *Two Centuries of Panic: A history of corporate collapses in Australia* (Sydney: Allen & Unwin, 1988).

Sykes, T., *The Bold Riders* (Sydney: Allen & Unwin, 1994; 2nd edn 1996).

Toffler, A., *Adaptive Corporation* (London: Pan Books, 1984).

Tomasic, R. and Bottomley, S., *Directing the Top 500 – Corporate governance and accountability in Australian companies* (Sydney: Allen & Unwin, 1993).

Truell, P. and Gurwin, L., *BCCI – The Inside Story of the World's Most Corrupt Financial Empire* (London: Bloomsbury Publishing Ltd, 1992).

Twentieth Century Fund, *Abuse on Wall Street: Conflicts of interest in the securities markets* (Westport, CT: Quorum Books, 1937, 1980).

UNITEC, *Responsibilities and Liabilities of Accountants and Auditors: proceedings of a forum* (New York and Geneva: United Nations, 1996).

Valance, A., *A Very Private Enterprise* (London: Thames and Hudson, 1955).

Van Dongen, Y., *Brierley: The man behind the corporate legend* (Auckland: Viking Press, 1990).

Walker, R.G., *Consolidated Statements: A history and analysis* (New York: Arno Press Inc., 1978).

Walker, R.G. and Walker, B.C., *Privatisation – Sell Off or Sell Out?: The Australian experience* (Sydney: ABC Books, 2000).

Weisman, S.L., *Need and Greed: The story of the largest ponzi scheme in American history* (Syracuse: Syracuse University Press, 1999).

Whipple, R.T.M. (ed.), *Accounting for Property Development* (Sydney: Law Book Co., 1986).

Woolf, E., *Auditing Today* (Englewood Cliffs; London: Prentice-Hall, 1982).

Working Party of Ministerial Council for Corporations, *Professional Liability in Relation to Corporations Law Matters* (Canberra: Commonwealth Government Printer, 1993).

Index